Future Practices of Citizenship in Asia and the West

International Institute for Asian Studies

Publications

The International Institute for Asian Studies (IIAS) is a research and exchange platform based in Leiden, the Netherlands. Its objective is to encourage the interdisciplinary and comparative study of Asia and to promote (inter)national cooperation. IIAS focuses on the humanities and social sciences and on their interaction with other sciences. It stimulates scholarship on Asia and is instrumental in forging research networks among Asia Scholars. Its main research interests are reflected in the four book series published with Amsterdam University Press: Global Asia, Asian Cities, Asian Heritages and Humanities Across Borders (HAB) Methodologies.

IIAS acts as an international mediator, bringing together various parties in Asia and other parts of the world. The Institute works as a clearinghouse of knowledge and information. This entails activities such as providing information services, the construction and support of international networks and cooperative projects, and the organization of seminars and conferences. In this way, IIAS functions as a window on Europe for non-European scholars and contributes to the cultural rapprochement between Europe and Asia.

IIAS Publications Officer: Mary Lynn van Dijk

Asian Cities

The Asian Cities Series explores urban cultures, societies and developments from the ancient to the contemporary city, from West Asia and the Near East to East Asia and the Pacifijic. The series focuses on three avenues of inquiry: evolving and competing ideas of the city across time and space; urban residents and their interactions in the production, shaping and contestation of the city; and urban challenges of the future as they relate to human well-being, the environment, heritage and public life.

Future Practices of Citizenship in Asia and the West

Care of the Self
(Volume III)

Edited by
Gregory Bracken,
Paul Rabé,
Nurul Azreen Azlan

Routledge
Taylor & Francis Group
LONDON AND NEW YORK

This publication was generously supported by the Spatial Planning and Strategy section of TU Delft's Faculty of Architecture and the Built Environment and the Urban Knowledge Network Asia of the International Institute for Asian Studies.

First published in 2025 by Amsterdam University Press Ltd.

Published 2025 by Routledge
4 Park Square, Milton Park, Abingdon, Oxon OX14 4RN
605 Third Avenue, New York, NY 10158

Routledge is an imprint of the Taylor & Francis Group, an informa business

ISBN: 9789048562077 (hbk)
ISBN: 9781041179931 (pbk)
ISBN: 9781003696261 (ebk)

NUR 696

Cover illustration: Bersih 4 protest, Kuala Lumpur, August 2015. Photo by Nurul Azreen Azlan.

Cover design: Coördesign, Leiden

DOI 10.5117/9789048562077

Table of Contents

Part III. Future Challenges

Introduction

Gregory Bracken, Paul Rabé, Nurul Azreen Azlan

This book is the final volume in a trilogy dedicated to Citizenship and the Care of the Self. The first volume, *Ancient and Modern Practices of Citizenship in Asia and the West* (2019), examined how citizenship was initially formulated in the ancient East and West. It also looked at issues of sexuality, identity, politics, and literature in ancient China, including concepts such as the *Dao* (道) and *Junzi* (君子, the Confucian concept of 'gentleman'), as well as the Japanese concept of *Ma* (間) and the Javanese concept of home (*omah*, the expression of one's self and outlook on life). The second volume, *Contemporary Practices of Citizenship in Asia and the West* (2020), examined how present-day communities and societies act and interact, sometimes positively, with self-help organisations, and sometimes less so, as when village mores follow migrants to a city.

The papers in the first volume took a more overtly philosophical/theoretical stance, laying the groundwork for our understanding of citizenship. The second volume, however, brought these theories to life, showing their practical application in contemporary citizenship practices. It ended with an afterword titled 'The Right to the City', which continued the discussion of the last chapter, '"Care of the Self" and Discipline in Smart Cities: Sensors in Singapore' by Joost Alleblas and Steven Dorrestijn, in which the roles of human agency and citizenship practices were highlighted against the challenges facing societies increasingly run by algorithms. This practical approach harks back to the concerns of the first chapter in Volume One, 'Citizenship and the Good Life' by Gregory Bracken, which showed how the ancients, in both East and West, understood that to be a proper citizen, one had to be actively engaged in society.

Continuing the narrative from the first two volumes, exploring future citizenship practices in this third and final volume was only logical. This continuity of discussion is particularly important given the increasing challenges to human agency in the twenty-first century. These challenges, from authoritarian regimes and the ever-increasing abdication of human

Gregory Bracken, Paul Rabé, Nurul Azreen Azlan (eds), *Future Practices of Citizenship in Asia and the West: Care of the Self (Volume III)*. Taylor & Francis Group, 2025
DOI: 10.5117/9789048562077_INTR

responsibility in decision-making to social media-driven algorithms, are significant and demand our attention. This third volume continues the exploration of citizenship, from its ancient roots to its modern applications and into its future implications.

In this third volume (as in the previous two in the trilogy), investigations into Asian settings were the focus, although it also contains chapters dealing with Western cases. We, as editors, were particularly interested in investigations that compared Asian and Western settings. However, as many of the chapters, even those dealing with specifically Asian issues, are closely concerned with Western concepts like democracy, it made sense to keep 'the West' in the titles of each of the volumes. What unites the three volumes (apart from their rich scholarship and people-centred approach) is Michel Foucault's concept of the Care of the Self, which was the point of departure for the entire project. Foucault's investigation into how humans govern themselves to act responsibly as citizens proves as relevant today as when he first developed it half a century ago with his seminal *History of Sexuality* series. Particularly Volume Three, *The Care of the Self* (New York, 1988 [1984]), was the point of departure for this series investigating the rights and responsibilities of citizenship in Asia and the West. Given the current challenges to citizens' rights, migrants' rights, and democracy itself, not to mention the ever-present backdrop of the algorithm-driven Digital Age, the concept of the Care of the Self is more important than ever for finding ways of understanding and maintaining human rights.

In keeping with the previous two books in this trilogy, the twelve chapters in Volume Three have been written by various scholars, both Asian and Western. The authors range from young researchers just starting their academic careers to well-established scholars providing their insights and experience. And, just as with the previous two volumes, the contributors to the third come from a wide range of disciplines, including anthropology, archaeology, architecture, art history, environmental studies, gender studies, geography, planning, political science, sociology, and urban studies. A number of these contributors are NGO workers.

A note on citizenship

According to Jon Alexander and Ariane Conrad, citizenship is not about the passport we hold, and it goes far beyond the duty to vote in elections. 'It's a state of engagement, more verb than noun' (Alexander and Conrad 2022, 7). They argue that '[w]e must see ourselves as Citizens – people who actively shape the world around us, who cultivate meaningful connections to their community and institutions, who can imagine a different and better life, who care and take responsibility, and who create opportunities for others to do the same' (11). 'To be a Citizen is to care, to take responsibility [and] cultivate meaningful connection to a web of relationships and institutions'; 'To be a Citizen implies engagement, contribution, and action rather than a passive state of being or receiving' (95).

Alexander and Conrad lament that 'too many of us are not engaging in the world around us. We have—understandably—lost faith in our institutions, especially our governments' (12). Yet, there is hope because they see citizen organisations as 'rooted in a deep and resilient belief in humanity'. They believe human nature wants 'to contribute positively and meaningfully to shape the communities and societies we are part of' (24). They also think 'we are meaningful as individuals only through our interconnection' (28).

James Holston, in *Insurgent Citizenship: Disjunctions of Democracy and Modernity in Brazil* (Princeton 2008), argues that democracies hold 'particular promise for more egalitarian citizenships and thus for greater justice and dignity in the organization of differences' (Holston 2002, 3). Yet most 'experience tremendous conflict among citizens, as principle collides with prejudice over the terms of national membership and the distribution of rights'. He argues that 'citizen conflicts have increased significantly with the extraordinary democratization and urbanization of the twentieth century'. In several chapters of this book, Holston examines the sort of citizen activism that can be seen. His account of the struggles of residents of peripheral Sao Paulo resonates in particular with the chapters in Part One, where citizens' and migrants' rights are investigated, but also with some of the chapters in Part Two, where we see that repressive regimes use their responses to the COVID-19 pandemic to clamp down on opposition. We even see this to a certain extent in Part Three, where governments or big businesses use digital apps and even environmental concerns to expand power at the expense of ordinary citizens.

Two chapters in Part Three also show the *positive* effects that apps and environmentalism can have on people's rights: namely, Chapter Ten, 'Establishing Green Habits: The Role of NGOs in Depoliticising Environmental Governance in Urban China' by Virginie Arantes, and Chapter Twelve, 'Care of the Self as a Spatial Practice: The Digital Tools Supporting Physical Activities of Migrant Domestic Workers' by Caterina Villani, Barui Kurniawan Waruwu, and Kin Wai Michael Siu. These chapters show the possibility of a meaningful future for those who choose to be active citizens.

James Holston's work shows that 'the dominant historical formulations of citizenship both produce and limit possible counter-formulations [and that] the insurgent and the entrenched remain conjoined in dangerous and corrosive entanglements' (Holston 2008, 4). His formulation of citizenship uses 'social differences that are not the basis of national membership—primarily differences of education, property, race, gender, and occupation —to distribute different treatment to different categories of citizens' (7). As a result, it 'generates a gradation of rights among them, in which most rights are available only to particular kinds of citizens and exercised as the privilege of particular social categories'. 'Citizenships do not directly create most of the differences they use. Rather, they are foundational means by which nation-states recognize and manage some differences as systematically salient by legitimating or equalizing them for various purposes'. Holsten sees citizenship as 'a mechanism to distribute inequality', where it 'uses such social qualifications to organize its political, civil, and social dimensions and to regulate its distribution of powers' (7).

Holston's focus on insurgency shows how it 'perpetuates attributes of the historically dominant citizenship': things like property ownership and legalising of illegal or special rights. Yet he also shows that 'rather than merely nourish new versions of the hegemonic, the insurgent disrupts' (13). The disparity he sees in Brazil between the form of government and the substance of citizenship 'suggests that all democracies—emerging and established—are normally disjunctive in their realization of citizenship' (14). This 'indicates not only that the timing and substance of citizenship's development vary in different historical and national contexts but also that this development is never cumulative, linear, or evenly distributed. Rather, citizenship always simultaneously expands and erodes in uneven ways' (14–15). According to Holston, the problem in Brazil is not with 'incomplete modernity, dysfunctional citizenship, ineffective law, deficient nationality, or failed democracy [but with] North Atlantic formulations [that] appear as particulars as well, though ones often presented as universals'. According to Holston, citizenship came to be understood as national (Holston 2008, 21), and national governments came to 'rely on citizenship as a basic means and rationality for organizing their nation-states. Imposing it on populations within their borders through specific programs, policies, plans, and works'.

In our book, we also see what Holston calls 'programs, policies, plans, and works' being applied by authoritarian regimes, which sometimes use them as a means of repression (for example, using responses to COVID-19 as a pretext to clamp down on freedom of expression in South and Southeast Asia, or on citizen participation in Nepal). However, we also see more benign efforts, such as a comparison between the responses of the Netherlands and Vietnam to the pandemic and an in depth look at South Korea's efforts to keep the disease under control. These issues are explored in Part Two.

Part One begins with citizens' rights, specifically citizens whose rights are under threat. Here, we see indigenous peoples carving out spaces for themselves in the cities of Canada and Japan. We also see the effects of market socialism on women's rights in Vietnam. Part One also explores migrant activism in China and youth leadership in Indonesia.

Part Three deals with what we call 'future challenges'. The first two chapters deal with what is probably the most existential crisis facing the world in the twenty-first century: climate change and the degradation of the environment. Here, we see environmental activism in Cambodia and 'green' citizenship of environmental governance in urban China.

The final two chapters examine the effects digital tools are having on society. Here, we see a specific example of how a new travel app in Vietnam affects motorcycle taxi drivers in Hanoi and Ho Chi Minh City. The final chapter shows some of the more positive aspects of digital tool use, this time by female migrants in Hong Kong.

Following these two final chapters, the editors have written an epilogue examining citizens' rights in the digital age. This highlights the growing reliance on algorithms for decision-making, causing greater polarisation of public discourse on social media while also making it increasingly difficult for many people to distinguish fact from fiction.

The chapters

Part One

Chapter One, by Mark K. Watson, is called 'Finding Our Voice: Returning to People's Ordinary Practices of Care in Discussions of Indigenous Citizenship in Tokyo and Montreal'. It is comparative ethnographic research into two indigenous peoples in cities: the Ainu in Tokyo and the Inuit in Montreal, where we see how they manage to 'find their voice' by crafting spaces and creating positions from where they can speak. We also see how this is a vulnerable and contested process, yet it is also a practice of care enabling the establishment of new urban articulations of their Indigenous citizenship.

Chapter Two, 'Ethical Citizenship in the Configuration of Market Socialism: Values and Sacrifices of Women Working in the NGO Sector in Post-Reform Vietnam', is by Binh Thi An Trinh and researches the life history of women working in Vietnam's NGOs. It examines their choices about philanthropy, the consumption of goods, and the remoralising of wealth. It reveals how the symbolic and moral values of their sacrifices for collective welfare show that morality, while accentuating women's prestige, also reproduces their inferiority about the cultural and gender norms approved by the state. This is exacerbated by the pressures of competition from marketisation and privatisation in Vietnam.

The next chapter is 'Practicing Citizenship in Urban China: A Case Study of Migrant Activism in Hangzhou' by Jun Chu. This is an ethnographic study of a migrant organisation in Hangzhou that focuses on the discursive contestations of self-organised migrant workers in the city. Analysing citizenship practices through the lens of migrant activism allows us to see how these practices challenge dominant discourses by repositioning migrant workers as subjects, thereby negotiating citizenship 'from below'. Here, we see the entanglement of migrant activism and technologies of active citizenship within discourses and practices of self-help, thereby raising awareness of the blurring of boundaries between activism and governance.

The final chapter in Part One is 'Youth Leadership and Urban Citizenship in Indonesian Cities' by Lily Song, John Taylor, and Fildzah Husna Amalina. It presents a case study of the Urban Citizenship Academy (UCA), an initiative founded in 2015, by Kota Kita, the Indonesian participatory planning organisation, to equip young people seeking to address social issues across the country's cities with concepts and tools to take action.

Part Two

Part Two begins with Chapter Five, '"Don't say that!" Artistic Freedom: Government and Citizen Responses to COVID-19 in South and Southeast Asia' by Julie Trébault and Manojna Yeluri. It shows how—against a backdrop of governments around the world underreporting virus numbers, spreading misinformation, and failing to respond to the crisis adequately, and also, in some cases, using the pandemic as an excuse to target, harass, and even imprison artists and creative practitioners, accusing them of spreading misinformation or of trying to start civil unrest—these artists and activists dared to use their platforms to criticise government responses to the pandemic.

Chapter Six, by Vishnu Kumari Tandon, is 'The Disproportionate Effect of COVID-19 on Citizen Participation in Nepal'. It shows how citizen participation was affected during the first wave of the disease, when different groups were treated differently, with people from marginalised communities being left worse off.

'Connecting Government COVID-19 Measures and the Exercise of Citizenship: A Comparative Case Study of the Netherlands and Vietnam' by Seohee

Kwak looks at COVID-19 responses in these two countries, where there are quite different levels of citizen freedom. The chapter investigating incidents in 2020–2021 shows how the Dutch and Vietnamese governments restricted citizens' freedoms to control the pandemic. However, the intensity of that control showed marked differences, which the author attributes to differently constructed norms of citizenship and the influence of the existing formal political institutions.

Part Two concludes with Chapter Eight. Suk-Ki Kong and Hyun-Chin Lim's 'Reclaiming Democratic Citizenship While Tackling COVID-19 in South Korea' revisits the 'K-quarantine' model to reflect critically on the effects the country's management of the pandemic has had on democratic citizenship. Initially highly effective in managing the pandemic, the Korean government ran into trouble when confronted with the practices of discrimination, exclusion, and inequality in Korean society, leading, as we also saw happen in Chapter Six, to some unjust social impacts. This chapter calls for reclaiming democratic citizenship to reduce these unjust and unequal social impacts.

Part Three

The first two chapters in Part Three examine issues surrounding what is perhaps the biggest challenge the world is facing today: sustainable development. Here, we see environmental activism in Cambodia and new 'green' citizenship in China.

Chapter Nine is 'Cambodia's New "Ecological Citizens": Looking at Environmental Activism in the Kingdom Today' by Stephanie Benzaquen-Gautier. This examines the Cambodian government's repression of environmental activism by labelling Mother Nature Cambodia's activists as 'traitors' or 'enemies of the state'. This chapter shows how this group, through its use of images, including videos, is enacting a novel form of critical citizenship, which even suggests a potential for opening up radically new politics, particularly for younger generations.

Chapter Ten, 'Establishing Green Habits: The Role of NGOs in Depoliticising Environmental Governance in Urban China' by Virginie Arantes, examines how environmental NGOs have become key players in cultivating new forms of green citizenship in China's urban areas. By focusing on the actions of NGOs at the local level, this chapter offers new opportunities for assessing the heterogeneous relationships through which environmental governance is mobilised and enacted in authoritarian settings. The chapter shows how NGOs are subjugated to the post-political reality of the eco-city and how their actions are curtailed by the choreography of promoting and cultivating a green community consciousness in China and contributes to a better understanding of new technologies, tools, and tactics of state power through non-confrontational, everyday means.

The final two chapters of the book look at apps and social media. Chapter Eleven, 'Reclaiming the Streets from the Apps? Rethinking Future Practices of Urban Citizenship in the Digital Age: Perspectives from Vietnam' by Marie Gibert-Flutre, Guillaume Trân Huu, and Quê Trân Dinh, shows the production of 'platform-mediated public spaces' in Vietnam, where the growing use of digital applications (apps) are helping transform the interactions between citizens and their city. Drawing on Henri Lefebvre's conception of space as an active political production, the authors hypothesise that various modes of collective organisation (including resistance) are emerging in the face-off between workers (in this case, motorcycle taxi drivers) and two forms of power: the authoritarian state and the private international platform that runs the GrabBike app, with ramifications for access to public space where urban and digital space are not merely passive backdrops but active political constructions.

Chapter Twelve shows how dealing with the digital can have a more positive effect. 'Care of the Self as a Spatial Practice: The Digital Tools Supporting Physical Activities of Migrant Domestic Workers' by Caterina Villani, Barui Kurniawan Waruwu, and Kin Wai Michael Siu explores collective mediated fitness practices of low-income migrant women employed as domestic workers in Hong Kong. This chapter explores smartphone technologies' impact on the spatio-temporal structuring of care practices. Using highly visible examples of fitness groups (Zumba, yoga, and martial arts) the authors analyse how digital tools that support these practices, as well as their actual presence in urban space and the relationship between these activities and citizenship, defy the usual structures of power that normally restrict this group.

The book ends with an Epilogue, 'Citizenship in the Digital Age', which draws attention to an increasing reliance on algorithms for decision-making, arguing that social media is making public discourse more polarised, and harder for some people to distinguish fact from fiction. The current business model of seeking profit over public service leads the editors to see the current climate of surveillance capitalism (in which this is taking place) as detrimental to citizens' rights.

Conclusion

Reading these chapters should sharpen our understanding of some issues facing citizens and their rights in the twenty-first century, particularly in situations where those rights are under threat. There are also some positive examples of voices being heard and people working together in large and small communities to ensure their voices *are* heard.

James Holston thinks we need 'a revision of many standard assumptions about democratization' (Holston 2008, 310). He sees 'new democratization [as] overwhelmingly non-North Atlantic' (311). He stresses that 'the extension of democracy to the civil, socioeconomic, legal, and cultural aspects of citizenship is as central to the concept of modern democracy as its extension to the political' (311).

Holston references Aristotle's *Politics* in establishing a distinction in the West between the political and the realm of household affairs, which it excludes. He quotes Giorgio Agamben (1998) as saying that Aristotle distinguishes the political (the *polis*), as existing for the good life (something we saw in Chapter One of Volume One), from the household, or *oikos*, which is related to 'mere life' (Holston 2008, 311). Yet, as Holston points out, 'the political does not exclude this domestic realm by mere omission. The *polis* acts on the *oikos* by confining it to the custody of the head of household, the *paterfamilias*, as its sole authority' (311). This neatly brings the domestic into the political, showing that activities in the home or the everyday realm can indeed impact the political life of a city or state. This is something we see in a number of the papers in this book, especially those that highlight the everyday acts of defiance that shape lives and the societies that frame them.

This also relates to Michel Foucault's reconceptualising of politics into biopolitics in *The History of Sexuality, Volume One: An Introduction* (1990 [1976]). Here, he saw power increasingly revolving around managing the biological life of populations (something we also highlight in our Epilogue when looking at surveillance capitalism). This reconceptualization of politics into biopolitics led Foucault to formulate his famous concept of the Care of the Self (in Volume Three of *The History of Sexuality*). Here, he showed that there could be a response to these impositions because 'where there is power, there is resistance' (Foucault 1988 [1984], 141).

Using Foucault's Care of the Self is a good way to try and ensure that every member of a society has the chance to flourish. Humanity will have a bright future if its societies and cities are places that enable good things to happen to and for their citizens. We, as editors, think that the outlook for the future is optimistic because of the very phenomena highlighted in this book, such as the bottom-up activism that gives people a voice or allows them to have increasing agency in their society. Even chapters that show negative things, like repressive regimes clamping down on citizens' rights, can also have a positive effect simply by drawing attention to these excesses; they could even act as a warning when these patterns of behaviour emerge elsewhere in the future. However, by building on the good examples in these chapters, it should be possible to allow every member of society to flourish, whatever challenges lie ahead.

Bibliography

Agamben, Giorgio. 1998. *Homo Sacer: Sovereign Power and Bare Life* (trans. Daniel Heller-Roazen). Redwood City: Stanford University Press.

Alexander, Jon and Ariane Conrad. 2022. *Citizens*. Kingston upon Thames: Canbury Press.

Bracken, Gregory. 2018. 'Citizenship and the Good Life' in Gregory Bracken (ed.) *Ancient and Modern Practices of Citizenship in Asia and the West: Care of the Self Volume I* (21–46). Amsterdam: Amsterdam University Press.

Foucault, Michel. 1988 [1984]. *The History of Sexuality Volume III: The Care of the Self* (trans. Robert Hurley). New York: Vintage.

Foucault, Michel. 1990 [1976]. *The History of Sexuality Volume I: An Introduction* (trans. Robert Hurley). New York: Vintage.

Foucault, Michel. 1995 [1975]. *Discipline and Punish: The Birth of the Prison* (trans. Alan Sheriden). New York: Vintage.

Holston, James. 2008. *Insurgent Citizenship: Disjunctions of Democracy and Modernity in Brazil*. Princeton: Princeton University Press.

About the authors

Gregory Bracken is Assistant Professor of Spatial Planning and Strategy at the TU Delft and one of the co-founders of Footprint, the journal dedicated to architecture theory. From 2009 to 2015 he was a Research Fellow at the International Institute for Asian Studies (IIAS) Leiden, where he co-founded the Urban Knowledge Network Asia (UKNA). His publications include *The Shanghai Alleyway House: A Vanishing Urban Vernacular* (2013), *Asian Cities: Colonial to Global* (2015), *Contemporary Practices of Citizenship in Asia and the West* (2020), and *Ancient and Modern Practices of Citizenship in Asia and the West* (2019).
G.Bracken@tudelft.nl

Paul Rabé is the Academic Coordinator of the Cities Cluster at the International Institute for Asian Studies (IIAS), Leiden, as well as the overall

coordinator of the Urban Knowledge Network Asia (UKNA) and the River Cities Network: Engaging with Waterways in the Anthropocene (RCN). Paul is also series editor of Amsterdam University Press's Asian Cities Book Series and is the Lead Expert in Urban Land Governance at the Institute for Housing and Urban Development Studies (IHS), Erasmus University Rotterdam, where he is also joint coordinator of the Urban Environment, Sustainability, and Climate Change academic track. A political scientist by training with a doctoral degree (2009) in policy, planning, and development from the University of Southern California's Sol Price School of Public Policy, Paul has over 25 years of experience in advisory work, capacity development, research, and teaching on urban policy topics, focused on urban land governance and the intersection of land (use) and the management of water and water bodies in urban and peri-urban areas.
p.e.rabe@iias.nl

Nurul Azreen Azlan is Lecturer in Architecture and Urbanism at Manchester School of Architecture (MSA). After graduating as a Part II architect from Universiti Teknologi Malaysia and spending some time in practice, she pursued a master's in urban design at the Bartlett, UCL. She completed her PhD at the TU Delft, where she wrote a dissertation on the spaces of protest in post-colonial Kuala Lumpur (2018). Post-PhD, she taught and researched architecture and urban design at Universiti Teknologi Malaysia (2018-2022). Prior to joining MSA, she was an NUS Fellow at the Asia Research Institute (ARI), National University of Singapore, under the NUS Southeast Asia Fellows Programme.
n.azlan@mmu.ac.uk

Part I.

Citizens' Rights

1. Finding Our Voice

Returning to People's Ordinary Practices of Care in Discussions of Indigenous Citizenship in Tokyo and Montreal

Mark K. Watson

Abstract: In this chapter, I draw on comparative ethnographic research with two Indigenous peoples in cities, Ainu in Tokyo and Inuit in Montreal, to illustrate how they have had to create positions from which to speak. Essentially, they have had to 'find their voice'. Far from being freely given, 'voice' is a vulnerable and contested process, yet it is also a practice of care. In two specific acts of caring citizenship—a ceremonial ritual in Tokyo and a radio show in Montreal—I show how key Ainu and Inuit actors have created new words and forms of expression to return people's attention to what is at stake in everyday life. In doing so, they point to the possibility of new *urban* articulations of Indigenous citizenship.

Keywords: Indigenous peoples, voice, urban migration, Tokyo, Montreal

Introduction

The migration of Indigenous peoples to cities is a poorly understood yet pressing issue affecting Indigenous communities globally, especially in Asia (Watson 2014; 2013; 2010). Despite the lack of globally aggregated statistics, an assessment of the available research would put the total percentage of Indigenous peoples living in and around cities between sixty and seventy-five percent. It was Tahara Kaori, an Ainu representative at the first session of the United Nations Permanent Forum on Indigenous Issues (UNPFII) in New York in 2002, who called for the issue of urbanisation to be given greater attention at the international level (Ainu Association of Sapporo 2002). Since then, several high-level UN-sponsored seminars dedicated

Gregory Bracken, Paul Rabé, Nurul Azreen Azlan (eds), *Future Practices of Citizenship in Asia and the West: Care of the Self (Volume III)*. Taylor & Francis Group, 2025
DOI: 10.5117/9789048562077_CH01

to the experiences of urban Indigenous migrants have been organised and important reports have been published (see Yescas Angeles Trujano 2010; UN-HABITAT 2010; Internal Displacement Monitoring Centre 2021). However, despite these efforts, the ordinary fact of migration for Indigenous peoples has yet to garner the kind of international attention that it deserves. This research aims to highlight the need for such attention and to contribute to a better understanding of the challenges faced by urban Indigenous migrants.

By drawing attention to the particular cases of Ainu in Tokyo and Inuit in Montreal, my aim in what follows is to show how specific individuals, not 'leaders' necessarily but principal figures within both urban Indigenous movements, return people, by way of their own actions, to the importance of the ordinary, everyday reality of taking care of one another. Through this ethics of care, I argue that people transform the idea of Indigenous citizenship in cities from an abstract concept of autonomous rights into a practical, caring, and iterative form of social action.

I divide this chapter into three sections. First, I discuss the marginalisation of Indigenous peoples in cities and the struggles of urban-based movements to 'find their voice'. Drawing on the work of Stanley Cavell, I point out that articulating an Indigenous 'voice' in the city is far from self-evident, but a publicly vulnerable activity. Marking out a space to speak from in the city forces individuals to make themselves known to others. While this can inspire people to perceive being Ainu or being Inuit in the city differently and actively, 'having a voice' invariably risks criticism and even repudiation. This reaction is heightened when urban Indigenous voices are seen as attempts to contest and rework not only the language of rights associated with traditional, land-based ideas of Indigenous citizenship but also the representations of Indigenous migration as signifying loss and dislocation perpetuated by 'push-pull' models in academic research. For this reason, I argue that giving voice to people's immediate, ordinary urban realities constitutes a 'plea for realism'. This turns citizenship from an 'ethic of justice' into a practice of care attentive to highlighting how Indigenous life looks and feels close at hand *and* how one should respond to this (Diamond 1991; Laugier 2022).

In the second section, I turn to the case of the Ainu people in Tokyo by discussing the annual performance of an *icharpa*. The Ainu use this ceremony to memorialise the deaths not only of Ainu at a government-run school in Tokyo in the 1870s but of all Ainu who have died outside of their traditional northern homelands of Hokkaido. Through this ceremony and its identification of *kamuy* (deities) in the urban landscape, Ainu call attention to the ordinary yet vital networks of (inter)dependence and mutual care that make urban Ainu life possible. I trace this sense of emplacement back to the early 1970s, to the pioneering actions of an Ainu woman and her efforts to exercise an Ainu voice and speak for others as 'Tokyo Ainu'. Moving through the appearance of different self-organisations and their focus on promoting cultural practice thereafter draws attention to interesting and important ways to practice care as the grounds for a new political discussion amongst Ainu about the changing nature of 'Indigenous citizenship'.

In the third section, I discuss the situation of Inuit in Montreal through Nipivut (meaning 'Our Voice' in Inuktut), an Inuit radio show in Montreal. Radio has been at the heart of Inuit life in communities across northern Canada's four Inuit land claims regions since its introduction in the 1950s. The appearance of an Inuit radio show in Montreal in 2015 reflected the city's status as having the third-largest urban Inuit population in the country. In contrast to the Ainu case study, however, Inuit citizenship in Montreal has always been about their 'right to the city'. I explore the reasons for this and its implications for Inuit living in the city (as opposed to passing through to access its services) and how the Nipivut show reinterprets this right to 'our voice' as the right to be heard.

In conclusion, I return to the value of citizenship as a practice of care, and how these acts of attentiveness for Ainu in Tokyo and Inuit in Montreal make new connections to a common urban identity that helps people find ways of 'going on' together in the city.

Indigenous citizenship in cities: From an 'ethic of justice' to an 'ethics of care'

Any discussion of what Indigenous citizenship looks like in cities must inevitably respond to the fact that the depth and extent of what an Indigenous identity constitutes is already determined in advance (Owen 2006, 151). Simply put, Indigenous peoples' experiences in cities contradict or otherwise challenge the nature of 'Indigeneity' when understood as a political identity specified and fixed by international principles associated with an 'ethic of justice' (Owen 2006, 150; Niezen 2003). This ethic reinforces a moral consensus around justice for Indigenous peoples. Enshrined in the United Nations Declaration on the Rights of Indigenous Peoples (2007), this ethic protects Indigenous peoples' rights to a distinct way of life. It secures a measure of political self-determination delimited by territorial boundaries, usually at the periphery of nation-states.

Bringing abstract legal reasoning to bear on specific, historical claims by Indigenous communities against nation-states has transformed Indigenous issues into universal questions of fairness, individual and collective rights, and the application of the principles laid out in UNDRIP. Based on this, Indigenous citizenship is commonly referred to when discussing Indigenous struggles over the fundamental right to collective self-determination as a 'people'—a right protected in Article 1 of UNDRIP. Recognition of this 'right' leads to the expectation that national governments establish a differentiated citizenship status for Indigenous peoples within their legal or constitutional framework[1].

While Indigenous citizenship is a core pillar of the international Indigenous peoples' movement, from an urban perspective, people recognise that it limits any activity aimed at extending, revising, or transforming Indigenous identities. This has important consequences. Indigenous peoples attempting to 'find their voice' in cities are often caught up in a perplexing dilemma where speaking in the language of the moral consensus—of land use, usufructuary rights, autochthonous lifeways, and so on—means that they are not able to express what is at stake in their ordinary, everyday lives. To this end, the moral consensus denies people in cities the opportunity to find new words and forms of expression to connect others (and themselves) to their experiences, thus excluding them from conversations about Indigenous justice (Owen 2006, 151).

In addition, we recognise the deleterious circulation of ideas about migration within research and its role in suppressing Indigenous voices in cities. Policymakers often diminish the realities of Indigenous migration by reducing it to a side-effect of 'bigger' issues—i.e., forced displacement due to violent conflict or development projects, or the intergenerational impacts of natural disasters and pressures associated with climate change. This increases reliance on the classic 'push-pull' model to explain the causes and impacts of urban Indigenous migration. Admittedly, the application of this model has its benefits. For example, it can help draw public attention to how mobility and people's experiences of it are embedded in local contexts and affected by particular and often traumatic events. However, the model's narrative effects are far more problematic and wide-ranging.

1 The notion of 'Indigenous citizenship' carries essential legal and political weight. On the one hand, these 'powers of (Indigenous) action' remain private in as much as they refer to the capacity of local Indigenous communities to sustain their way of life through state recognition of an array of 'traditional practices'; on the other hand, the attribution of local powers can conflict with 'public' interests because those same practices presuppose unconditional access to, use of, and some measure of sovereignty and protection over, (large) expanses of land, waterways, and other 'national' resources.

First of all, reducing Indigenous mobility to a confluence of 'push factors' not only robs people of their agency but also mobility of its politics. As Tim Cresswell (2010) persuasively argues, the 'push-pull' theory of migration is fundamentally flawed simply because it is not about human movement at all, but about how one 'place' pushes people out and another 'place' pulls people in. Thinking of migration as more about places than people downplays insight into the lived experiences of people who move. It also ignores the motivations and worldviews of the individuals themselves and how they navigate what is at stake in when they move.

Secondly, the 'pull' lever of the model assumes that cities attract migrants by providing opportunities to access amenities and resources unavailable 'at home'. This ignores accounts of the social and political barriers that many Indigenous migrants face when entering the city. It also disregards the moral context of city life in which essentialist and often discriminatory representations of Indigenous people as a 'social problem' circulate. This is, of course, not just the case for Indigenous peoples. Refugees and other marginalised social groups encounter similar situations.

Finally, the 'push-pull' model presupposes out-migration to be transformative for individuals and family groups who are choosing to 'move away from' their Indigenous heritage linked to specific places. Consequently, Indigenous migrants can find themselves stereotyped and discriminated against in cities based on the assumption that, as 'strangers' to the urban environment, they have neither a legitimate claim to belong there nor a legal entitlement to an (authentic) Indigenous identity.

Confronted by this sceptical logic, migrants are responsible for allowing community members to give and weigh reasons about what matters, what counts for them, and why (Norris 2006, 2). This attention to others does not assume new certainties about 'community' but inspires new articulations of a common identity and hope for a collective 'voice'.

'Finding our voice' through an ethics of care

The concept of 'voice' is an all too neglected and under-theorised dynamic of citizenship. This is less surprising, perhaps, if, in line with the philosopher Stanley Cavell, we acknowledge that 'voice' is not a freely given activity but more a question about the fragility and depth of claims we make to the community about who *I* am in relation to *us*. For Cavell, voice is a vulnerable and textured activity, embedded in ordinary human situations and everyday practices. One uses words to reach out to and seek 'attunement' with others, hoping to make sense while continually opening oneself up to the possibility of criticism, rebuke, and repudiation. Whether what one says and does resonates with others is contingent upon the 'range of consent' to one's actions (Hammer 2002, 132): the inclination of others, that is, to choose not to reject but to find ways of 'going on' with one's examples (i.e., words and actions) by imagining and undertaking new actions of their own (Laugier 2020, 14).

To speak, to 'find one's voice' (to use Cavell's idiom), reminds people of what is at stake in making oneself known as a representative speaker: the acknowledgment that not only do others speak for you, but that you also speak for others (Hammer, 132). This brings ethics back to the everyday domain—to realise that questions of voice are indivisible from practices of care. After all, caring activities are grounded in relationships and, in the Tokyo Ainu and Montreal Inuit case studies, at least made sense through exploring and extending new words and forms of expression that—proponents hope—meaningfully (re)connect people with each other and their experiences.

In this way, practical ethics recalls what Sandra Laugier (2022) terms a 'plea for realism'. It makes space for agents to find their own way of responding to particular moral problems and allows people the opportunity to amplify the concerns of others and shed new light on the contexts of people's dependency and vulnerability. Nevertheless, this is not a straightforward exercise of political agency.

For urban Indigenous leaders, taking responsibility for care is always a precarious and risky undertaking because it returns them to 'the rough ground' of trying to make a difference in the world. As I move on to demonstrate in the case studies below, this characterises an important shift in thinking about citizenship as it relates to the reality of Indigenous life. In an ethics of care approach, responsibility is not an abstract concept. Instead, it is about how people experience and express their responsibilities (to themselves and each other) within specific social contexts (Barnes 2007, 67). Thus, rather than being fixed, care practices allow ideas about being Indigenous in the city to remain open to change (Sevenhuijsen 1998, 15). This brings ethics back to the conditions of ordinary life, ordinary language, and the need to care for our words and expressions (Laugier 2022, 4). I now turn to discuss how this relates to the situation of Ainu living in and around Tokyo, Japan.

Making Ainu citizens in Tokyo

Inaugural 'Shinrit Mosir Koicharpa' ceremony – Shiba Park, Tokyo, 2003

Under the shadow of a tree, fleeting protection from the intense blaze of Tokyo's August sun, over twenty Ainu men, women, and children wearing traditional kimonos sit on hand-woven tatami mats on either side of a fifteen-foot-long hearth situated in a park next to Zozoji, a major Buddhist temple and landmark in Japan's capital. Unmoved by the high summer screech of cicadas, people in haphazard rows at least three deep intently watch this first performance of a *shinrit mosir koicharpa*, or 'memorial for the world of ancestors' (hereafter '*icharpa*') by Ainu living in the capital region. Ainu are the Indigenous peoples of Japan. Since at least the 1950s, increasing numbers have moved to Tokyo and other southern cities from the island of Hokkaido, their traditional northern homelands. A number of the friends and supporters of the Tokyo Ainu movement present know about the years of work the principal organisers have invested in making this ritual happen. However, probably only a handful of them fully understand what is at stake in this performance by which Ainu living outside Hokkaido seek to give themselves, and those who have gone before them, a voice in their peoples' history.

The ritual unfolds. The men closest to *fuchi-kamuy* (the deity of fire who, in Ainu belief, is also the mediator between the human world and the world of *kamuy*, or deities) use *ikepasuy* (prayer sticks) in unspoken rhythm to gift her *tonoto* (Ainu saké). The head elders recount incantations they have convincingly memorised in Ainu, asking for *fuchi-kamuy*'s support. They ask her to help animate by contacting five principal *kamuy* in the capital region[2].

An elder (woman) slowly gets up from her seat, holding a bowl of fruit. She moves, accompanied by a child, to the head of the hearth and crouches in front of five tall willow sticks standing in a *nusa* (altar). About four feet high, the sticks have been shaven from the top, causing the bark to curl and fall back down each shaft like locks of hair. These *inau* symbolise (and their craftsmanship is also said to please) the *kamuy* in the landscape and allow the Ainu participants to address and respond to the *kamuy* in person. And yet, as more traditional offerings are laid out in front of the *nusa* and further prayers are spoken, little is being fetishised.

The *inau* have no intrinsic power: all participants recognise that they were only crafted sometime prior to the ritual; in fact, most of the makers are seated around the hearth. Still, the power of the ritual turns on the intrinsic value of the *inau* to the Ainu participants. The *inau* have been made with care for the explicit purpose of forming new associations and moral relations between Ainu and the cityscape.

2 On that day, these were *kotan kor kamuy* (a physical household, which characterised the capital region as a domestic space of everyday Ainu life); *nupuri kamuy* (deity of mountains); *rera cise kamuy* (the name of an Ainu-run restaurant in Tokyo at the time); *wakka us kamuy* (deity of water); and *sir kor kamuy* (deity of the earth).

At the ritual's close, the principal elder invites everyone to a local hall for a celebratory feast. As traditional Ainu foods are served, individuals can stand up and share personal thoughts about what the day has meant to them. Several Ainu take to the stage. They each, in turn, speak for themselves but in similar ways, not only about the collective and cultural value of the *icharpa*, but also, and perhaps more unexpectedly, about seeing people around them, Ainu and Wajin together, sharing what matters for Ainu in the capital region.

'Join hands now'

Care for the expression 'Tokyo Ainu' was epitomised that day Ainu held the first *icharpa* ceremony outside of Hokkaido. I have argued elsewhere that the ritual practice was an act of *re*territorialisation (Watson 2013). Through association with *kamuy*, a new sense of a collective Ainu self was brought into being, extending out into the urban landscape and, if suitably acknowledged, into the bodily experience of Ainu in the city. Bringing the relationship between Ainu and *kamuy* to life identifies the lived experience of Ainu as the locus of ethnic continuity. Indeed, as Chiri Mashiho, the native Ainu linguist, points out, the mutual relationship between Ainu and *kamuy* is constitutive of being 'Ainu', i.e., a human being. Therefore, bringing *kamuy* back was an important moment, a moral expression of a permanent Ainu presence in Tokyo that publicly reimagined the city as a new and legitimate extension of Ainu society.

The *icharpa* was not an isolated event but another response to the long-standing efforts of specific individuals to draw attention to the plight of Ainu in the city. One such change agent was a young woman, Ukaji Shizue. On February 8, 1972, Ukaji placed an advertisement in the Asahi Shimbun, asking for Ainu in the capital to 'Join Hands Now' (ウタリたちよ,手をつなごう). Originally from southern Hokkaido, Ukaji moved to Tokyo at the end of the 1950s and became accustomed to seeing an increasing number of Ainu on the streets in Tokyo. However, she quickly noticed that other Ainu consciously avoided eye contact. This was not unexpected. 'Ainu' is a word with a difficult social history in Japan and one that, for most Ainu during the twentieth century, had become, as Sala describes, 'an unendurable burden in a highly prejudiced society' (1975, 56). Still, Ukaji understood the pressures on Ainu to hide in public by passing as Wajin. Having experienced crippling discrimination as a young person, she wanted to save other Ainu from social suffering by creating opportunities in the city for migrants to express themselves freely and cultivate pride in their shared Indigenous heritage. Over 100 people attended a meeting arranged by Ukaji. Soon after, the *Tokyo Utari Kai* (Tokyo Utari Association), the first Ainu organisation in Tokyo, was founded.

At the association's meetings, individuals shared stories of discrimination in their place of work and their experiences of social hardships[3]. However, many also voiced their aspiration to meet up with other Ainu on a more regular basis. This included the desire to practice woodwork, clothwork, and other cultural practices that most had only scarce knowledge of but nevertheless fondly remembered from time spent as a child with grandparents. Based on these conversations, Ukaji and others decided to lobby the metropolitan government for equal employment opportunities and an Ainu community centre in the city.

Predictably, metropolitan officials rejected the Ainu group's petition out of hand. Within weeks, everyone gave up except Ukaji. For months, she returned to stand outside the government offices in silent protest until a leading official unexpectedly walked out of the central government building one morning and offered Ukaji his hand and, with it, the support of the Tokyo government's ruling party. The support was not for a community centre but for funding basic research. This became the first survey of the living conditions of Ainu in the capital region. The results were published in 1975, and in 1988 the survey was repeated and expanded, again with government funding (Tōkyō to Kikaku Chō Seikyoku Chōsabu 1975; Tōkyō to Kikaku Shingitsu 1989; see also Watson 2014a, 80–83). For the first time, this survey publicly highlighted the breadth of social inequalities Ainu faced compared to the general population: higher unemployment rates, lower educational success, etc. As a direct result, a new employment counsellor position was created within the Department for Social Welfare, dedicated to helping Ainu navigate the urban labour market. This position also proposed to support and act on Ainu complaints of discrimination encountered in the workplace.

Ukaji's intervention in the early 1970s brought about a new understanding of Ainu in the capital region. It represented a 'creative break' from normal ways of thinking and talking about Ainu. In many respects, it characterised what Isin (2008) calls an 'act of citizenship' without which it would be impossible to imagine the transformation of Ainu in Tokyo from subjects to (urban) Indigenous citizens. However, in making her position known, Ukaji received her share of pushback. Unwanted support from activists on the far left of the Japanese political spectrum sat with responses from Ainu who did

3 Based on these conversations, Ukaji and small group of Ainu friends decided to lobby the metropolitan government for equal employment opportunities and for an Ainu community center in the city.

not like having her draw attention to an issue they had purposefully sought to leave behind by moving to the city. Still, in the following decades, the gains secured by Ukaji allowed other Ainu self-organisations to pursue their claims to a political community in the city. In many respects, in standing up for what she believed in, Ukaji personified Cavell's democratic hero: the individual 'offering herself, the expressions of herself and her position, as representing an alternative *self* for [...] others' (Hammer 2002, 133; italics in original). By knowing when and how to trust her experience and then taking responsibility for how she expressed it (Laugier 2022), Ukaji exemplified an ethics of care in exercising an 'Ainu voice' that, for the first time, was speaking *for* Ainu in the capital region as 'Tokyo Ainu'.

Tokyo Ainu: A new sense of common identity

Returning ethics of care to the rough ground of everyday life is to return to our ordinary use of language, words, and expressions and to recognise how questions of voice are indivisible from practices of care. For example, the Tokyo Ainu identifier publicly claimed a new regional identity. Its use reconceptualised the inherited language of citizenship by focusing on the quality of relations between selves and others and the urban world around them as the marker of people's well-being as Ainu citizens (Bowden 1997, 168). Reference to this label also inspired people to establish their own terms, a new moral vocabulary, for talking about 'care' as an activity. What is most important about this is that it presupposed the social and political agency of Ainu in the capital region and their capacity to exercise it in ways that did not rely on a preconceived idea of who Ainu are (as in Hokkaido), but remained open to the complex range of people's needs, relations, and values (Bowden 1997, 166). Indeed, we can think of the symbolic (moral) work of the *icharpa* as a continuing act of citizenship in this sense, representative of all Ainu in the capital.

Yet the performance of the *icharpa* was also doing something else important. Its organising rationale was to memorialise the death in 1872 of four Ainu at a government-run agricultural school located very close to the ceremonial site. However, in the words of a principal elder at the time, the *icharpa* was also a memorial for all Ainu who had left the homeland over time and died without returning (アイヌモシリを離れ帰れず死んだアイヌウタリのことも供養をする). As an example of the kind of 'creative' and 'inventive' work that Ainu had to undertake in order to carry on at the margins of Japanese society (Muecke 2004, 158), the *icharpa* was also an expression of the responsibilities of the Ainu participants towards others. In fact, from the 1980s on, cultural practice became the primary medium used by Ainu in the city to engage with one another and foster and strengthen the sense of urban Ainu collectivity that Ukaji had originally initiated through her activism.

In Tokyo, the actions of the *Tokyo Utari Kai* diffused after its disbandment in 1977 into the founding of four different Ainu self-organisations, which by the mid-1980s were all dedicated to different facets of cultural promotion and preservation. Except for one organisation focused on activities of Ainu-Wajin exchange, the primary role of these organisations was to make 'community' present to people in the city. The cultivation of Ainu networks built on fostering new and caring relations between Ainu in the city, many of whom had likely avoided meeting other local Ainu. Such attentiveness to the circumstances of others gave people new insights into the urban Ainu situation. For community organisers, this further reinforced the social value of 'joining hands' by creating supportive environments in rented office spaces and rooms in community centres where individuals could express—and work through—their personal attachment to Ainu heritage with others through different cultural practices.

The focus of these cultural groups varied. Some prioritised Ainu language learning and sharing Ainu food, others dancing and craftwork. By the early 1990s, a new collective and political sensibility emerged. Previously, individuals in Tokyo from different 'home' regions in Hokkaido identified themselves as Ainu. These activities, however, inspired a new kind of cultural and political voice that expressed people's belonging to the capital region as Ainu. In the practice of 'traditional Ainu dances', for example, individuals found that the need to translate one's observation and feeling of natural phenomena such as trees, wind, or wildlife into physical movement could be done in the city; by the mid-2000s this developed into experiments by different Ainu youth groups, who started to play with urban (music) influences in their performances. The *Rera no Kai* (The Ainu Association of Wind) found a similar sense of place-making possible with Ainu food. One activist, in particular, was keen to take Ainu on day trips around the wider Kanto region to show them the availability of wild plants traditionally used in Ainu dishes. Indeed, the *Rera no Kai* opened a successful Ainu restaurant in Nakano ward to the west of the city in 1995 (Rera no Kai 1997; see also Watson 2007, 2014). The activities of the separate groups continued into the 2000s, but a new contact group (*renrakukai*) was formed. This group acted on behalf of all Ainu groups in the capital region in discussions (and eventual negotiations) with various government and prefectural offices over Ainu legislation and the need to include Tokyo Ainu in such deliberations.

Returning to the ethics of care, we recognise the value of cultural practice in allowing Ainu individuals to situate themselves in the world and relate to others in ways that draw on and work through, without necessarily resolving, struggles for personal and collective meaning. What a realistic ethics provides us with in this case is how the term 'cultural practice' comes to life, so to speak, when set against the background of the social marginalisation of Ainu in cities (Laugier 2022, 6). In this respect, a 'plea for realism' draws attention to care practices as the grounds for a new political discussion about the changing nature of 'Indigenous citizenship'. It opens up new possibilities for Ainu in Tokyo to adopt a political status that does not exist in binary opposition to rural-dwelling and rights-bearing Hokkaido Ainu, but rather in terms and in a language that understands everyday life in the city as a social and historical extension of the Ainu nation.

Montrealmiut and Inuit rights to the city

Montreal 2016

A dark February night. The wind gusting down St. Laurent, one of Montreal's major streets, is bitingly cold. Everyone outside the Native Friendship Centre is getting used to the short, sharp whistle as the wind batters the canvas and swirls snow around the radio equipment under the CKUT90.3FM tent. Those waiting for the Nipivut show to begin are trying their best to stay warm. Annie, a much-loved Inuit social worker in the city, is at the centre of things. Brushing the snow off her headphones, she places them over her thick toque and greets people around her. The Nipivut team, a small crew of three or four people who put together the bi-weekly Inuit radio show, is ready. For several weeks, Annie and the show's producer have been planning this outside broadcast as part of a National Homelessness Radio Marathon. People share a sense of anticipation and excitement. The radio team understands this is the first time the voices of homeless Inuit in the city will be heard nationwide. The producer signals a minute to go. Annie quietly turns to an older Inuk man and younger woman sitting beside her, reminding them of who she'll be coming to first; like many Inuit struggling with homelessness, they know Annie well. A couple of other people have promised to show up later in the hour. The theme tune comes in over the speakers on the sidewalk. Nipivut is on air.

Nipivut means 'Our Voice' in Inuktut. The show went on air in October 2015 on CKUT90.3FM, a campus-community radio station in Montreal, becoming the first Inuit radio show in southern Canada. The need for the Nipivut show reflected the large and still growing population of Inuit in and around Montreal. Recent statistics indicate that over 30 percent of Inuit live outside the Arctic and in southern urban centres. While the city is home to a burgeoning Inuit middle class (e.g., students, artists, company employees), many Inuit struggle with making ends meet. While Inuit make up only 10 percent of the Indigenous population in Montreal, they are estimated to account for 40 percent of the city's Indigenous homeless population. Annie is keen to use this particular Nipivut show to focus public attention on this stark social disparity.

Six people sit and talk with Annie in Inuktut during the show. They openly share difficult and emotionally charged stories of loss, displacement, and suffering. Some speak of the distress they experienced in home communities and how they came to move south. Some mention ongoing or past struggles with alcohol. Several speak of not having any government identification and the difficulty of attaining it in adulthood. Others recall stories of violence they have seen or been caught up in, not just on the streets but also in shelters, impeding the search for somewhere safe to sleep, even in the depth of winter. Despite these personal hardships, everyone ends by wishing those present to care for each other in whatever situation they find themselves in.

The live broadcast goes well[4]. For Annie, the show represents a natural extension of her lifelong commitment to helping Inuit, particularly the needy, make themselves and their situations known to others. Amidst the tears shed on air, the show made public what Annie privately understood to be at stake. Giving homeless Inuit the time and space to describe the difficulty of their reality—a reality that others all too quickly choose to avoid (acknowledging)—inevitably returns people, in one way or another, to the defining question of 'community': Who am 'I' in relation to 'us'?

Our Voice

In distinction from the cultural acts of citizenship that Ainu employ in Tokyo, the Nipivut radio show is characteristic of Inuit efforts to enact their 'right to the city'. The first Nipivut radio show went live to air on October 6, 2015, from a basement studio of CKUT 90.3FM. The show's founding responded to calls for a radio show made over ten years prior by Inuit in the city (see Tungasuvvingat Inuit 2005). The show's ambition was to facilitate dialogue between Inuit to amplify the diversity of Inuit voices and experiences and connect Inuit.

Radio has a long and important history in Inuit communities across the Arctic. As the first Inuit radio show to be broadcast predominantly in Inuktut in and to a southern Canadian city, Nipivut spoke, not uncontroversially, to Montreal and the region of southern Quebec as an extension of, not

4 In fact, a year later it would be cited in the reasoning behind the show being awarded best in Indigenous programming at an annual national radio ceremony.

separate from, Inuit Nunaat (the term for the four Inuit Arctic land claims regions). The show's title was taken from a list that a well-known Inuit elder in Ottawa had willingly provided the team with.

The first-person plural in Nipivut—'Our Voice'—did not represent something already existing. The show's title was 'Our Voice', but as with the show above, Annie, deliberately or otherwise, was drawing attention to the limits of 'voice' as something people would take for granted. Although Inuit had been moving to Montreal since at least the 1960s to either live or access different services, the city lacked the networks of self-organisation Ainu had implemented in Tokyo. If anything, the Nipivut show symbolised a caring response to a vulnerable sense of collectivity and solidarity of Inuit in the city. In referring to Cavell, the show's title was always a claim to community. The responsibility for making an Inuit voice from Montreal present in the world rested with Annie and a small and often changing collective of individuals who, in conversation with each other and with different guests, were (re)iterating the meaning and purpose of their contribution to the 'Voice' of urban Inuit, show by show.

The right to the city as the right to be heard

There is no one story of being Inuit in the city. Some are in situations of homelessness, but some are also short and long-term patients in hospitals (upwards of 30 percent of the population of Nunavik, the land claim region in northern Quebec, pass through the city every year for medical treatment), students attending colleges and universities, a thriving community of artists and musicians as well as a growing middle class, including employees of major Inuit corporations. These experiences reflect two separate claims to an Inuit 'right to the city'.

First coined by the sociologist Henri Lefebvre (1968), the term 'right to the city' has become part of the vernacular of urban organisations around the world, especially for people working with and on behalf of underprivileged groups and individuals to participate in the everyday life and future planning of cities (Attoh 2011). Over the last 60 years or more, this 'right to the city' for Inuit—sometimes formalised in land claims agreements or bilateral agreements with certain service providers—has been about the right to access communal goods not available in northern communities, such as tertiary healthcare, postsecondary education, safe and secure accommodations, wide-ranging employment opportunities, etc. However, another emergent position regarding this 'right' has come to stand for the right of 'montrealmiut' (meaning 'Montreal Inuit' in Inuktut) to access communal goods *in* the city, such as country food, community buildings, or opportunities for social exchange or language use.

One recalls that the right to the city is not an actual right but a fictive claim. On the one hand, speaking of a 'right' to healthcare and education is not symbolic but the precondition for Inuit citizenship within the Canadian social welfare state (a system that guarantees citizens access to all basic social provisions). On the other hand, the growing numbers of Inuit living in and moving through the city underline people's efforts to negotiate their particular circumstances as Inuit in Montreal. This right to the city, and the status of *montrealmiut,* is vulnerable, often contested, and in the 'rough ground' of inter-ethnic relations, is set against discriminatory public attitudes towards Inuit fed by the idea that Inuit do not belong in the city. This came to a dispiriting low in 2010 when an anonymous campaign group in a north Montreal neighbourhood resisted the building of an Inuit out-patient centre in the local area by distributing flyers in local residents' mailboxes associating Inuit with homelessness, drug use, poor hygiene, and declining house prices. As the local mayor did not choose to explicitly distance herself from that position at the time, amidst public consternation the Inuit rescinded their application.

For this reason, I think what is at stake in Nipivut is remarkably similar to the example of the *icharpa*: that is, an expression of collective responsibility responding to the perceived needs of individuals and to the 'necessity of *giving voice* to the perspectives and experiences of those who are often marginalised or stigmatised' (Barnes 2007, 70; my italics). In both examples, responsible (urban Indigenous) citizenship is much less about networking based on the assumption of a given sense of collectivity than about finding each other in community in the city. Strengthening horizontal ties in this way constitutes a meaningful return to an ethics of care. Attending to people's ordinary, everyday lives by giving them a voice also helps define what matters to them. This approach to care also changes, shapes (and challenges) people's identities through their actions and interactions, conversations and disagreements, and exchange of stories and opinions with others (Sevenhuijsen 1998, 15). At the same time, it draws attention to the role of Annie as a central galvanising figure in the community and a committed social worker who knows and feels all too well what Inuit life in the city is like, particularly for those on the margins of society.

Conclusion

Around the world, conventional ideas of Indigenous citizenship reinforce essentialist representations of 'spatial stability' (Gordillo 2010)—i.e., a historical way of life delimited by territorial boundaries. Consequently, urban migration is thought to symbolise the loss of an individual's legitimate claim to a distinct Indigenous identity[5]. Not only does this image ignore the historical realities of Indigenous peoples' resistance to structures of colonialism by engaging with (*not* disengaging from) the modern social order (see Sahlins 1999), but it also serves to naively interpret Indigenous autonomy and agency as geographically determined. Unintentionally or otherwise, this essentialist politics draws attention away from and undermines the vital importance of everyday connections and ordinary extensions to community life that people maintain across vast distances (Clifford 1994). These connections include those diasporic linkages with family members and friends living in cities. They also anticipate the network of relations formed and fostered between people within cities.

From an urban Indigenous perspective, marking out a space from which to speak in the city is often contested. 'Finding a voice' is a publicly textured and vulnerable activity that responds to and is shaped by particular circumstances and social contexts. Cavell says voice is about reconnecting with one's experiences and finding adequate words to express their common significance to others. Furthermore, he maintains that precisely by resisting conditions of voicelessness, certain individuals seek to exercise a political voice, thus finding that they have to discover and define their position in relation to others (Hammer 2002, 132). In this way, voice is as much about responsivity as about self-asserted action. As Ukaji and Annie demonstrate, each in their own way, what counts is a principal agent's 'offering herself, the expressions of herself and her position, as representing an alternative *self* for [...] others' (Hammer 2002, 133; italics in original). These are the stakes of voice understood as an activity encompassing people's care practices.

In practice, care is no less valuable than more conventional concepts of citizenship, such as rights and justice. On the contrary, 'a caring orientation' is the basis for any claim to justice. It is based on 'engaging in caring practices and reflecting and debating the values and virtues necessary for care' (Barnes 2007, 63). In the words of Sandra Laugier, 'caring is seeing' and being attentive to the world; it brings into focus what people are unable to see but which is right before their eyes (Laugier 2020, 58–59; Wittgenstein 1988[1953], 129). Simply put, an ethic of care does not draw inspiration from

5 Recursively, studies also report that home communities can characterise individuals as being 'contaminated' by urban influences and therefore 'less healthy' upon their return (Swanson 2007, 716).

abstract notions of what is 'just' but focuses on what is 'important' and what matters to people (Laugier 2020, 24).

Through these acts of attentiveness Ainu in Tokyo and Inuit in Montreal are making new connections between care and citizenship based on people's everyday experiences. While the performance of the *icharpa* in Tokyo and the production of the Nipivut radio show in Montreal may at first appear to be distinct, even incomparable, social events, an ethics of care approach draws attention to how both constitute local acts of citizenship aimed at helping people find ways of 'going on' together, returning to the rough ground of everyday life and finding creative ways to elucidate their claims to belonging as Indigenous citizens in their metropolitan environments.

Bibliography

Attoh, Kafui A. 2011. 'What Kind of Right is the Right to the City?' *Progress in Human Geography*, 35(5), 669–685.

Barnes, Marian. 2007. 'Participation, Citizenship and a Feminist Ethic of Care', in Susan Balloch and Michael Hill (eds.) *Care, Community and Citizenship: Research and Practice in a Changing Policy Context* (59–74). Bristol: Policy Press.

Bowden, Peter. 1997. *Caring: Gender-sensitive Ethics*. Abingdon: Routledge.

Cavell, Stanley. 1979. *The Claim of Reason: Wittgenstein, Skepticism, Morality and Tragedy*. Oxford: Oxford University Press.

Cavell, Stanley. 2004. *Cities of Words: Pedagogical Letters on a Register of the Moral Life*. Cambridge MA: Belknap.

Clifford, James. 1994. 'Diasporas', *Cultural Anthropology*, 9(3): 302–38.

Cresswell, Tim. 2010. 'Towards a Politics of Mobility', *Environment and Planning D: Society and Space*, 28(1), 17–31.

Diamond, Cora. 1991. *The Realistic Spirit: Wittgenstein, Philosophy, and the Mind*. Cambridge MA: MIT Press.

Gordillo, Gaston. 2011. 'Longing for Elsewhere: Guaraní Reterritorializations', *Comparative Studies in Society and History*, 53(4), 855–81.

Hammer, Espen. 2002. *Stanley Cavell: Skepticism, Subjectivity, and the Ordinary*. Cambridge: Cambridge University Press.

Human Rights Council. 2019. 'Indigenous Peoples' Rights in the Contexts of Borders, Migration and Displacement', A/HRC/EMRIP/2019/2/Rev.1.

Internal Displacement Monitoring Centre. 2021. *When Land, Knowledge, Roots are Lost: Indigenous Peoples and Displacement*, Geneva: IDMC. https://www.internal-displacement.org/publications/when-land-knowledge-and-roots-are-lost-indigenous-peoples-and-displacement.

Isin, Engin F. 2008. 'Theorizing Acts of Citizenship', in Engin F. Isin and Greg M. Nielsen (eds.) *Acts of Citizenship*. London: Zed Books.

Laugier, Sandra. 2020. *Politics of the Ordinary: Care, Ethics, and Forms of Life*. Leuven: Peeters.

Laugier, Sandra. 2022. 'Wittgenstein and Care Ethics as a Plea for Realism', *Philosophies*, 7(4), 86.

Lefebvre, Henri. 1968. *The Sociology of Marx* (trans. N. Guterman). New York: Vintage.

Minority Rights Group International. 2015. *State of the World's Minorities and Indigenous Peoples, 2015: A Focus on Cities*. Minority Rights Group International.

Muecke, Stephen. 2004. *Ancient & Modern: Time, Culture and Indigenous Philosophy*. Randwick: University of New South Wales Press.

Neizen, Ronald. 2003. *The Origins of Indigenism: Human Rights and the Politics of Identity*. Oakland: University of California Press.

Norris, Andrew. 2006. 'Introduction: Stanley Cavell and the Claim to Community' in Andrew Norris (ed.), *The Claim to Community: Essays on Stanley Cavell and Political Philosophy* (1–18). Redwood City: Stanford University Press.

Owen, David. 2006. 'Perfectionism, Parrhesia, and the Care of the Self: Foucault and Cavell on Ethics and Politics', in Andrew Norris (ed.), *The Claim to Community: Essays on Stanley Cavell and Political Philosophy* (128–155). Redwood City: Stanford University Press.

Rera no Kai (ed.). 1997. *Rera Cise e no Michi – Kōshite Tōkyō ni Ainu Ryōriten ga Dekita* [The Road towards the Rera Cise: The Making of an Ainu Restaurant in Tokyo]. Tokyo: Gendai Kikakushitsu.

Sahlins, Marshall. 1999. 'What is Anthropological Enlightenment? Some Lessons of the Twentieth Century', *Annual Review of Anthropology*, 28, i–xxiii.

Sala, Gary Clark. 1975. 'Protest and the Ainu of Hokkaido', *Japan Interpreter*, 10(1), 44–65.

Sevenhuijsen, Selma. 1998. *Citizenship and the Ethics of Care: Feminist Considerations on Justice, Morality and Politics*. Abingdon: Routledge.

Swanson, Kate. 2007. 'Revanchist Urbanism Heads South: The Regulation of Indigenous Beggars and Street Vendors in Ecuador', *Antipode: A Journal of Radical Geography*, 39(4), 708–28.

Tōkyō to Kikaku Shingitsu. 1989. *Tōkyō Zaijyū Utari Jittai Chōsa Hōkokusho* [Report on the Survey of the Socioeconomic Conditions of Ainu Residents in Tokyo]. Tōkyō to Kikaku Shingitsu.

Tōkyō to Kikaku Chō seikyoku Chōsabu. 1975. *Tōkyō Zaijyū Utari Jittai Chōsa Hōkokusho* [Report on the Survey of the Socio-economic Conditions of Ainu Residents in Tokyo]. Tōkyō to Kikaku Chō seikyoku Chōsabu.

Tungasuvvingat Inuit. 2006. *National Urban Inuit One Voice Workshop*, Ottawa, 26–27 October 2005. Tungasuvvingat Inuit.

UN-HABITAT. 2010. *Urban Indigenous Peoples and Migration: A Review of Policies, Programmes and Practices*. Nairobi, Kenya.

Watson, Mark K. 2007. 'Indigenous Food and Foodways: Mapping the Production of Ainu Food in Tokyo' in Sidney C.H. Cheung et al (eds.), *Food and Foodways in Asia: Resource, Tradition and Cooking* (129–142). Abingdon: Routledge.

Watson, Mark K. 2010. 'Diasporic Indigeneity: Place and the Articulation of Ainu Identity in Tokyo, Japan', *Environment and Planning A*, 42(2), 268–284.

Watson, Mark K. 2013. 'Aïnous de Tokyo: une Nouvelle Géographie Politique Autochtone au Japon?' *Diversité Urbaine*, 13(1), 45–64.

Watson, Mark K. 2014a. *Japan's Ainu Minority in Tokyo: Diasporic Indigeneity and Urban Politics*. Abingdon: Routledge.

Watson, Mark K. 2014b. 'Cities: Indigeneity and Belonging' in H. Glenn Penny and Laura Graham (eds.), *Performing Indigeneity: Global Histories and Contemporary Experiences* (390–414). Lincoln: University of Nebraska Press.

Watson, Mark K. 2015. 'Heading South: Bringing Urban Inuit Migration into Northern Policy Debates' in *Quebec Policy on the Arctic: Challenges and Perspectives* (35–38). Seattle: University of Washington Press.

Watson, Mark K., Christopher Fletcher, Donna Patrick, and Sara Breitkreutz. 2021. 'Listening to Nipivut ("Our Voice"): Restorying Inuit in Montreal' in Pamela Stern (ed.) *Inuit Worlds* (70–86). Abingdon: Routledge.

Wittgenstein, Ludwig. 1988 [1953]. *Philosophical Investigations* (trans. G.E.M. Anscombe). Hoboken: Wiley-Blackwell.

Yescas Angeles Trujano, Carlos. 2008. *Indigenous Routes: A Framework for Understanding Indigenous Migration* (83). Geneva: International Organization for Migration.

About the author

Mark K. Watson is Associate Professor in the Department of Sociology and Anthropology at Concordia University, Montreal. Since the early 2000s, he has engaged in various participatory action research projects as part of a long-term commitment to research in Canada and Japan on urban Indigenous migration. Author of *Japan's Ainu Minority in Tokyo: diasporic Indigeneity and urban politics* (Routledge, 2014) and co-editor of the book *Beyond Ainu Studies; changing academic and public perspectives* (University of Hawai'i, 2014), he is currently exploring the theory and practice of action-oriented and collaborative inquiry as well as the ethical intersection of ordinary language philosophy with applied anthropological practice.
mark.watson@concordia.ca

2. Ethical Citizenship in the Configuration of Market Socialism

Values and Sacrifices of Women Working in the NGO Sector in Post-Reform Vietnam

Binh Thi An Trinh

Abstract: Ethical citizenship is an idea central to the economic restructuring process that works in tandem with the sovereign rule, in which citizenship components are reimagined and rearticulated in ways corresponding to the neoliberal logic and morality of self-reliance and self-care. In Vietnam, the socialist state also uses morality to shape the malleable subject not only of the market rule but also of the state's rule. This paper presents a form of citizenship associated with moral and gender norms practised by women working in non-governmental organisations (NGOs) in Vietnam. Women's choices regarding philanthropy, consumption of goods, and acts of remoralising wealth indicate that morality, while accentuating women's prestige, also engenders their inferiority in Vietnam's market society.

Keywords: Ethical citizenship, gender, philanthropy, consumption, market socialism, governmentality

Introduction: Governance with liberalisation in Vietnam's socialist-oriented market economy

In the late 1980s, Vietnam's socialist state initiated a series of economic reforms known as *đổi mới* ('economic renovation'). These reforms included market liberalisation, privatisation of a large part of the state sector, and opening up to the world economy. Vietnam shifted from a closed economy with limited trading relations with members of the former Soviet Bloc to

Gregory Bracken, Paul Rabé, Nurul Azreen Azlan (eds), *Future Practices of Citizenship in Asia and the West: Care of the Self (Volume III)*. Taylor & Francis Group, 2025
DOI: 10.5117/9789048562077_CH02

an open economy, focusing on export-oriented industrialisation to attract foreign capital, thereby contributing to its steady and high-level economic growth. From the outside, Vietnam's economic transformation seemed to replicate the successes of late industrialisation in the East-Asian economies, where state-led reforms accounted for the consolidation of liberal democracy and capitalist development. Nevertheless, market forces and foreign capital seemed to bolster the power of the socialist state, which retained a profound grip on the economy (Beresford 2008; Gainsborough 2010; Bui 2013). Above all, the project of market socialism that has transformed some of the remaining socialist states in Asia (led by the example of China and Vietnam) does not entirely reflect the World Bank's transitional or the East-Asian development models. As noted by one scholar, Vietnam's socialist-oriented market economy is not merely an 'empty' slogan because socialism is manifested through the state's monopolies of strategic economic sectors, joint ventures with foreign investors, or networks with business elites (Hayton 2010: 3). State control is prominent in socialism to preserve the ruling power of the party-state (Kornai 1992: 71).

However, this does not mean that market reforms leave the socialist state intact. To say the least, market liberalisation has changed the mode of control by the socialist state, which must then be kept to a minimum to maximise the efficiency of private-sector choices. Since the collapse of the Soviet Bloc, rapid economic growth has become an alternative source of legitimacy for the socialist states of Vietnam and China. Such growth depends on the competitiveness of individuals, businesses, and national territories across global markets (Ong 1999 2006; Zhang and Ong 2008; Bui 2015). To encourage high-level economic performance, state rules are often blended with those of the marketplace to stimulate the private pursuits of individuals in the market economy. Research into the late socialist transformation in China and Vietnam suggests that the governance is shifting away from state interventions toward a greater reliance on the self-government of individuals within market facilities, a modus operandi comparable to that of neoliberal governments (Harvey 2005; Ong 2006; Nguyen-vo 2008; Zhang and Ong 2008; Nguyen 2018). According to Michel Foucault, neoliberal government is associated with a technology of government, or governmentality, which advances the pragmatic use of liberalism for self-government and self-discipline in line with economic rationality and calculation (Foucault in Rabinow 1997: 73-79). In this mode of governance, the state can govern people from a distance, as malleable subjects of the marketplace (Dillon 1995; Ong 2006).

This paper presents a form of ethical citizenship that has emerged from the process of market liberalisation in post-socialist Vietnam. By mentioning post-socialism, I refer to the period of post-reform economy that followed the eradication of the centrally planned economy. This new era is marked by a robust process of marketisation and privatisation, which allows Vietnamese people to adopt entrepreneurial strategies for private pursuits in the market. By looking at the private pursuits of women working in the NGO sector, I will underline women's choices in the market which, I argue, are still constrained by the idea of the ethical woman. This idea is shaped by a mode of governmentality that allows the socialist state to govern people as subjects of market liberalisation.

Governmentality, sovereignty, and citizenship

With market liberalisation, Vietnam's socialist state withdrew from traditional and direct forms of intervention into the choices made by private individuals, and began to follow the rules of market competition and economic maximisation—although it is noted that it retains mode of surveillance of those free and entrepreneurial activities that came with market motions (Nguyen-vo 2008; Leshkowich 2012; 2014; Bui 2013). According to Ong (2006), authoritarian and socialist states in East and Southeast Asia use techniques of governmentality to create special economic zones in which market rule is enacted for new economic possibilities. In some cases, the effects of this governing strategy go beyond their borders to enable economic competition on a global scale, with the state remaining repressive in the space within its borders.

Governmentality comprises technologies of government that allow a ruler to configure the conditions for self-government. This involves arrangements with human problems and solutions artificially arranged, to provide a set of calculating strategies for people to live according to their desire to improve (Li 2007: 5). According to Ong (2006: 6), the technologies of subjectivities and subjectification of governmentality invoke two optimising strategies: first, to engage the population in practices of self-government and self-animation, adhering to expert advice regarding health, productivity, and capital accumulation, which is politically configured by the state; and second, to make administrative arrangements targeting diverse population groups in ways to realise particular ruling outcomes. The interventions create conditions allowing for neoliberal exceptions whereby private individuals can freely pursue entrepreneurial strategies to accumulate global capital under a regime that represses free rights (Harvey 2005; Ong 2006; Nguyen 2018). Ong points out that, as part of the governing strategies, these interventions interact with elements of ruling and citizenship that produce diverse citizenship outcomes. Citizenship components, such as rights, entitlements, benefits and a nation, become increasingly rearticulated, reimagined, and redefined within the neoliberal logic of self-government that allows people to make citizenship-like claims in diverse locations (Ong 2006: 6-7). At the same time, those who fail on these terms may face exclusion (Ong 2006: 7).

State sovereignty used to be seen as the power to compel subjects to be obedient through a juridical process (as the subject of rights). According to Dillon (1995: 324), state power also works through subjectification involving a power/knowledge mechanism, motivating people to act and discipline their behaviour collectively and responsibly on the tenets of normalisation and empowerment. The purpose of the technology of governmentality is, by arranging things in order, to shape calculable subjects in calculable spaces for optimising strategies desirable for the ruling purposes of the state (Dillon 1995; Li 2007: 5). According to Ong (2006: 7), state sovereignty should not be seen as a politically singular entity but a mix of varied, sometimes contradictory, ruling strategies adhering to particular economic outcomes, spaces, and governing techniques. With the example of 'zones of variegated sovereignty', she points out that a neoliberal exception was created under the rule of authoritarian states in East and Southeast Asia to allow for calculable and entrepreneurial traits to thrive. Interventions with sovereign rule allow the state to subject people to different categories of citizens using a combination of disciplinary, caring, and punitive techniques (Ong 1999: 22). As I will show, the socialist state in Vietnam also employs these techniques to create zones of variegated sovereignty to govern people across overlapping spaces, domestically, publicly, nationally, and internationally. Ruling with sovereign principles is essential for the state to shape malleable subjects for the market socialist project.

The ethical citizenship of market socialism

This paper explores citizenship practices associated with market reforms in Vietnam. Specifically, it focuses on the moral and gender aspects of citizenship involved with the optimising strategies of post-socialist women working in NGOs within the context of marketisation and privatisation. The idea of ethical citizenship explored by this paper is close to the idea of the moral subject, emphasising the moral obligation of self-government and self-care, and the will to act upon calculative and entrepreneurial knowledge to maximise welfare, something that is central to welfare restructuring programs (Inda 2006; Muehlebach 2012; Nguyen 2018). Instead of being enforced through rights, the moral basis of citizenship encourages individuals to willingly adhere to a sense of normalcy and the responsibility to act rationally and responsibly for their own well-being and the well-being of the community (Inda 2006; Nguyen 2018).

Constructing citizenship built on the moral fundamentals of self-government and self-reliance is key for the restructuring process in Vietnam as the state ceases to be the main provider of people's welfare. In this respect, Nguyen (2018) has pointed out a form of ethical citizenship associated with the socialisation policy used by the socialist state to privatise public services. The logic of socialisation, nevertheless, often evokes the socialist genealogy of the collectivisation of the means of production for the welfare of all people. The welfare of the people was traditionally and solely provided by the state but has now become everyone's responsibility. The state still claims overall responsibility for collective welfare but insists that this must be realised through individualised and privatised means (Nguyen and Chu 2016; Nguyen 2018: 634). With marketisation, people are encouraged to adopt entrepreneurial skills and market practices to maximise goods for their welfare. Those who have such skills are idealised by the state as the new socialist persons who care for the collective welfare (Dinh 2003; Leshkowich 2012; Harms 2014; Nguyen 2018).

Although appeals to socialist welfare have lost much of their influence in the face of a rising market, these moral and ideological appeals are still useful for normalising behaviours of accumulation (Bui 2015). This is especially true given the moral and political ambivalence towards private wealth in Vietnam (Jellema 2005: 235-236; Leshkowich 2012: 97). According to Jellema, members of the newly rich in Vietnam are particularly anxious about how they need to 'remoralise wealth'. They fear moral and legal punishments that could hamper their material and spiritual well-being, which is exacerbated by uncertain economic conditions. Their fear is not unfounded, considering the past hostility of the revolutionary government towards proprietors and land-owners during the post-war land reforms (Leshkowich 2014; Malarney 2002). When such a past is not easily forgotten, daily newspapers and TV programs keep running anti-corruption headlines informing people of harsh punishment against those convicted of corruption (Jellema 2005: 235). At the same time, state-sponsored emulation campaigns continue to feed people with messages and instructions to portray themselves with moral appropriateness (Pettus 2003: 103-104). The messages are particularly directed towards the new middle-class populations on properly displaying their new wealth (Leshkowich 2014: 175; Nguyen-Vo 2008: 106-114). In this respect, Leshkowich (2012: 98) was right to suggest that morality is rendered as both the problem of and solution to private wealth and is therefore key to the state's efforts to liberate and constrain people's choices in the context of market liberalisation in Vietnam.

Interventions for privatisation and marketisation also provide a novel notion of citizenship that accentuates one's responsibility of self-government and optimisation idealised by the state's goals of industrialisation and modernisation. Anthropologies of market socialism in Vietnam and China are, in this respect, useful in that they recognise a discursive construct of citizenship that links people's credentials to their possession (or dispossession) of human capital or qualities deemed important for the national project of modernisation. In China, alongside state-led economic reforms, the idea of *suzhi* (quality of people) has emerged as a powerful concept that shapes the contemporary idea of today's Chinese citizens as inseparable from the vision of a modern and industrialised nation. Here, we see the slogan 'Socialism with Chinese characteristics' evolving along with people's everyday practices within the marketplace (Anagnost 2004; Zhang and Ong 2008). In Vietnam, Nguyen (2018) also unpacks the notion of *dân trí*, or intellectual level, which appears in the popular discourse as the driving force behind the national modernisation and industrialisation attempts. This *intellectual level* also indicates the causes and effects of one's living conditions and its relationship with national development (Nguyen 2018: 633–634). *Dân trí*, in this respect, bears a strong resemblance to the idea of *suzhi*. Both instil the idea that one's self-worth corresponds to one's possession of qualities validated by the market, which are idealised and exploited as a source of middle-class distinction by different groups in society (Anagnost 2004; Drummond 2004; Harms 2014; Nguyen 2018). As Nguyen (2018: 633-634) points out, a form of ethical citizenship emerges that is consistent with the notion of *dân trí*: people who possess economic talents are idealised while those who fail to demonstrate these capacities are stigmatised for their moral failings.

Writing about ethical citizenship, Andrea Muehlebach (2012) points to another form associated with voluntary labour of social workers in Italy, many of whom are immigrants, unemployed, and pensioners. By caring for public welfare, these populations appear to be a moral symbol of the Catholic and socialist society in the context of state welfare reduction. For those in jeopardy (because they are often seen as dependent populations), voluntary workers accumulate social relations during their care work to accentuate an indispensable role in a society which is experiencing a decline in solidarity and trust. According to Muehlebach, the values associated with the unpaid and voluntary labour of care for collective welfare had particular appeal for some disadvantaged groups. Instead of aligning with economic values, these individuals actively engaged with the symbolic values of voluntary work and selfless acts of compassion and care, thereby gaining a sense of belonging and significance in society. This form of ethical citizenship was particularly noticeable among those who feared being isolated or excluded. Through care-giving acts, people display a role and power to participate in their communities. As some past research indicates, women tend to align their domestic products and feminist labour with the regime of humanitarianism and voluntarism as a distinct source of value for subjectivities of the upper and middle classes (Bornstein 2012; Malkki 2015; Trinh 2022).

The women working in the NGO sector in post-reform Vietnam also demonstrate a distinctive form of ethical citizenship, with symbolic values accumulated and produced by their work of caring for the vulnerable. With the reduction of public welfare, women's active engagement as professional caregivers in non-governmental and non-profit organisations appears to be a symbol of empowerment. This empowerment is consolidated by the logic of self-government and self-care, which is naturalised in the context of marketisation and privatisation in Vietnam. This idea is also empowering because of the socialist credentials for women's sacrifices and reproductive labour to provide for collective welfare. Furthermore, their strategies to align with the value in terms of morality rather than wealth also reveal a kind of anxiety distinctively associated with political and moral paradoxes inherent to the configuration of Vietnam's market socialism. As I will show, the anxieties encountered by Vietnamese middle-class women are provoked by the uncertainty associated with wealth, not only because of the unpredictable economic situation but also because cultural and socialist norms continue to demonise acts of wealth accumulation. It is ironic that although women in socialism are often celebrated for a liberated role in the formal economy, they continue to be idealised by the socialist state for their reproductive labour and domestic roles. This vision of women continues to normalise women's moral code of modesty and their sacrifices for the family and society (Pettus 2003; Shohet 2017). In the context of marketisation and state welfare reduction, this vision of women has become increasingly interpolated with economic implications. By exploring women's performance in philanthropy and consumption and their attitudes to wealth, this paper will show a distinctive form of ethical citizenship demonstrated by women working in the NGO sector in Vietnam, where they are expected to toil in the name of market liberalisation and empowerment.

The findings presented in this paper are drawn from an analysis of the narratives and life histories of women working in NGOs based on six months of fieldwork in Hanoi between 2016 and 2017. I met and interviewed my informants through a snowball sampling approach that helped me generate qualitative data from narrative interviews, focus group discussions, concept mapping, and participant observation. The informants for this research came from different age groups and different types of organisations, including local and international NGOs and a few state-owned mass organisations. Mass organisations compose a distinct form of social organisation in Vietnam's socialist system. The informants' names are changed to avoid possible disclosure of their identities. All informants were asked for consent to ensure their participation was voluntary and free from coercion.

Women and philanthropy

Muehlebach (2012), when writing about the voluntary sector in Italy, suggests that a form of ethical citizenship emerges alongside the neoliberal restructuring process, aligning with the unpaid labour of voluntary workers and accentuating the neoliberal (and moral) logic of self-government and self-care. The active engagement in the work to care for the welfare of others in a context of intensifying private accumulation brings about social compassion and love in a society which is experiencing a decline in trust and solidarity. Nguyen (2018 2019) also suggests the distinctive appeal of voluntary and philanthropic activities in terms of empowerment, granting people in the waste industry in Vietnam a sense of belonging and a role in society. For women in Vietnam, that role is often seen by the state as a reproductive one (Marr 1981: 250-251). The decline of public welfare has also motivated women to accentuate their supposedly endogenous power in a productive economy. This tradition is ironically empowered by the free market, which enables women to freely choose to work in low- and unpaid voluntary work in NGOs.

During my conversations with the informants, they often talked with pride about their contribution to society. For example, Cuc, who was in her late 50s and used to work as a researcher in a state-owned research institute, spoke of the 'practical' contribution of the NGO work compared to her previous job:

> After moving to this development sector, I found that, 'Ah, there are so many different things in real life'. I felt that I was able to use the knowledge

> I gained from the university, from my previous job in the research institute, and my graduate course abroad in the development area. I enjoyed this more because I was able to contribute to practical areas. That was my feeling when I moved to work in this sector (Cuc, interview).

People working in the NGO sector have relatively high education levels. The women I met have at least a university degree. It is common for individuals in senior or middle management positions to hold a postgraduate degree, with some having completed their education overseas. Like Cuc, several highly educated young women also aspired to work in NGOs to contribute their knowledge and skills to improve the well-being of poor and vulnerable communities rather than individualistically generating wealth. Some informants said that they had refused better-salaried jobs in state and business sectors to work for NGOs to satisfy their need to care for the poor and less privileged. Many young women started to work in NGOs as unpaid interns or volunteers before taking official posts. For example, Hue started to work for a local NGO as an unpaid intern. Though working without pay, she told me about her desire to help poor people with the legal knowledge she had gained from law school:

> I started to know there were projects like that only when coming to work in the NGO. (At that time) I only thought I could help someone, but did not know how to run or manage a project (Hue, interview).

This is a common practice for young people, often students, to start to work in the NGO as volunteers or interns. Some people decided to work for NGOs after working in the state or business sectors. During the interviews, informants often said they chose to work in the NGO sector to use their knowledge and skills to help the vulnerable in local communities. For example, Nhai worked for the state and business sectors before working for a local NGO. After completing a Master's degree in Australia, she quit her job as a civil servant and worked for a state-owned business. She then left this second job to work in a local NGO. According to her, business owners only concentrate on individualistic profits and ignore the collective benefits to the community. She also expressed a keen interest in working in the non-profit sector for the opportunities to contribute to the local community rather than for personal wealth. After three previous applications to work for a local NGO had failed, she was accepted for her current job. However, she was happy with having had to wait, as this was the right opportunity to contribute to the well-being of local communities:

> I am not suitable for businesses. Because Vietnamese businesses only concentrate on short-term benefits. In my view, there are other factors more important. People often think that this is exaggerated, so they do not care about the ethics of doing business or the quality of life of workers, thereby producing too much that causes pressures on the environment or too much competition in the business sector. That [job] was neither suitable for me nor relevant to what I learned at university. When I thought I had gained enough work experience after one year, I went to the non-profit [sector] (Nhai, interview).

It is also a common practice for women who work in NGOs to want to contribute to society. Like Cuc, who spoke of the 'practicality' of her choice to work in NGOs, many highly educated women regard NGOs as the places best suited to realising these aspirations with their professional skills and knowledge of helping the less privileged and the poor. The way the women relate the value of their labour to humanitarian causes seems to resonate with Malkki's (2015: 3-4) proposition regarding the need to help. Women derive a sense of self-worth by using their feminised labour or domestic products to care for those in need and to build imaginary relations with world communities and humanitarian causes. It can also be said that these women are attracted to humanitarian work by the need to demonstrate the value of their labour, knowledge, and skills, which are objectified by the vulnerable or the beneficiaries. The need to help is also driven subjectively by what these women perceive as 'good' and 'kind' and their beliefs in the returns in terms of economic and emotional well-being (Trinh 2022: 109; Leshkowich, 2012: 101-103). My informants explained the importance of acts of kindness to their well-being in this sense. For example, Nhung mentioned how happy it made her to offer kindness and help to others while working in the NGO sector:

> Working in NGOs is beyond making money. There were times I worked not because of money but to help someone. It means when you work, you have done something kind [*việc thiện*]. I mean when I work, I truly feel that I am doing a 'kind' job. Honestly! That is the feeling when I am working. I am helping this community or this province or contributing to [a policy]. Certainly, I did not make the policy alone. However, when I try my best, I will contribute to change the policy. Therefore, I am happy with that (Nhung, interview).

Although earning less than those in for-profit sectors, women working in the non-profit sector often emphasised the values they were producing for society. Many expressed pride regarding their contributions to society. Compared to those working only for wealth, they spoke of the emotional benefits of doing good work for local communities. For example, Ngan said that this job gave her more spiritual relief and greater work satisfaction than that experienced by people she knew who worked for higher salaries. Compared to people working in the for-profit sectors, she particularly highlighted the value of her labour for its contribution to social good rather than to mere individualistic wealth:

> Spiritually, I am more satisfied than people working in other occupations. I have higher occupational satisfaction... Honestly, my income is no lower than the salary in other sectors. However, I am more satisfied with my job. There are more benefits in the sense that I am always satisfied because I think I am useful to society. I am contributing to the benefits of disadvantaged people or society in general (Ngan, interview).

Like Ngan, other women I met also talked about the spiritual returns from working in NGOs because of their contributions to the community. Rather than talking directly about their wealth, they talked about the merits of good deeds done for their communities, which benefited them in other ways, like the good health of their children, harmonious family relations, good education, and other aspects of well-being. For example, Ngoc, also a Buddhist, told me that she had everything she needed in her life, and that she knew when to stop when something was enough. She spoke of the benefits of having enough for herself and then giving away to others, which accounted for the harmony and happiness of her family:

> I think that although I am not rich, I have other things that richer people don't have. For example, because I did not fight for the assets of the husband's family, our family is still surviving. Because I don't compete with the others for the assets of my husband's family, we are still proletariat. We can prove to each other that we live with each other for being proletariat. [Smiles] (Ngoc, interview).

Likewise, Truc told me about the benefits of living ethically. She talked about the proud tradition in her family, most of whose members were professionally successful and had enjoyed good educations from prestigious universities, both domestic and abroad. Truc was a PhD candidate studying mental health at an Australian university after working on many health projects with a local NGO specialising in public health in Vietnam. She mentioned the importance of living ethically for the benefits she could pass on to her offspring, just as she had received them from her ancestors:

> What can I say about ethics [*đức*]? Until now, we are all well-educated. That was the ethics that our ancestors have passed to us... We have to be ethical so that our descendants can benefit from it. Do not only grapple with the short-term benefits (Truc, interview).

Although my informants seldom discussed how they obtained their wealth, many seemed to belong to economically privileged groups. They possessed a range of consumer goods that indicated their high economic status. This brings us to the second aspect of ethical citizenship: consumer goods. As I will explain in the following section, consumer goods have increasingly become symbols of the middle and upper classes in Vietnam's post-socialist society. Consumer goods also symbolise women's virtues in relation to their caring responsibilities. With the expansion of commodity markets, consumption seems to be an essential way for these women to demonstrate their domestic duties, which are increasingly linked to materialistic and market values.

Women and consumption

Research into the middle class in Asia often reports consumer goods as symbolic of the new middle-class status despite their ambiguous political position (Robison and Goodman 1996: 7). According to Leichty (2003), members of the new middle class are engaged in a status competition for 'fashion' to counter the uncertainty of a middle position that is neither high nor low. Research about the new middle class in Vietnam suggests that consumer goods confer a distinctive status upon Vietnamese women who, through consumption, aim to convey the idea that they are not only modern but also proper and moral women (Drummond 2004 2012; Leshkowich 2012; Nguyen-Marshall, Drummond and Bélanger 2012). This idea is contingent on expert advice, emulation campaigns, household competitions, and mass media that inform women daily, as consumer citizens, to make 'correct' choices about their appearance, education, financial management, and skills for caring for the members of their families (Pettus 2003; Drummond 2004; Leshkowich 2012). Clear messages from TV soap operas, expert advice, daily anecdotes in women's magazines, street posters or loudspeakers, and advertisements on mass and social media dictate appropriate looks and behaviour to women.

These messages also guide women's choices by projecting specific expectations of their conduct in the market (Drummond 2004; Leshkowich 2012). I also found that consumer goods symbolise women's compliance with their traditional domestic duties, which are increasingly associated with the quality and quantity of goods they consume in the market.

My research underlined the central role of consumption in women's domestic responsibilities. Like Drummond (2012), who wrote about women's skills in choosing, I found that professional NGO women often demonstrated the necessary skills to select products and services at the right price and of types and quality symbolic of their status. With the vast variety of goods and services mushrooming in the market, these salaried women must become experts not only in their knowledge of hard facts (i.e., quality, prices) but also of symbolic values (i.e., fashion, modernity, appropriateness) to make correct choices within the mass-produced consumer goods market. As mentioned elsewhere, the women working in NGOs who considered themselves intellectuals were especially skilled in selecting consumer goods and products symbolic of their middle-class status (Trinh 2022: 108). During our conversations, my informants often compared themselves with others, often richer people, based on their possession of certain products such as private houses or cars. One informant told me that she was lower middle class because she could only afford certain goods and services that are considered 'lower middle class', compared to wealthier others who could afford private houses or cars:

> You see, people who earn a high income, I mean the income of the middle class, would be able to buy houses and cars. I am not talking about the rich. I can only afford leisure activities, like travelling. I cannot afford to buy a house or a car. I will need to save to death to buy a house or a car. [Finish, right?] Therefore, I consider myself lower middle class (Ngan, interview).

Meanwhile, Dong, who had just recently bought a flat in an apartment building in a newly developed residential area, spoke of it with pleasure:

> I am very happy with my new flat because it is spacious and airy. It is located in a considerably high-end and civilised area with good security. I am happy with everything (Dong, interview).

In the urban landscape with its mix of populations, Vietnamese urbanites are aware of the ranges of consumer goods available to differentiate them from the lower classes (Drummond 2012). And just as Liechty (2003) describes the status competition evidenced by people's possession of products symbolic of the taste or fashion of the middle class, the acquisition of products and services of better quality and higher value also symbolises the upper- and middle classes in Vietnam. Moreover, acts of acquisition demonstrate not only one's identity but also one's responsibilities to collective causes. As Harms (2014) points out, products and services symbolic of modernity and civility are also more expensive, giving Vietnamese urbanites a sense of higher self-esteem as responsible citizens, as they are contributing to the collective cause of developing a modern and civilised municipal community. This idea seemed to ring true with the women working in NGOs in Hanoi, who also strived to acquire items of higher value. For example, Ngan said,

> How do people usually evaluate you? They look at your house to see how nice it looks or look at your car to see what style it is. They look at the 'ABC' things that you have (Ngan, interview).

Our discussions often centred around the use of consumer goods as a way to gauge social status. It is typical for middle-class consumers to take pride in their role in contributing to the modernity and civility of their families or communities. On the other hand, poorer individuals often feel inferior due to their poor appearance or lifestyle. There was an implicit competition for status through the acquisition of goods and services. One informant spoke of the competition for a better house in a neighbourhood:

> The surrounding people were professors or doctorate holders. They look 'smart' ['*oách*']. They had good [salary] occupations, for example, teaching jobs, while my parents were only manual workers. Some people rebuilt or repaired their houses with a beautiful appearance because they earned better. Because our house was shabby, the voice or image of my parents was weaker than the other neighbours, right? (Xuan, interview).

While it is common for people to compete for middle-class status through the symbolic values of consumer goods, I also found a distinctive value, not necessarily associated with the face value of the goods but rather with women's domestic roles. Compared to wealthier people, who gain prestige from wealth alone, these middle-class women claim prestige from selecting the best things for the well-being of their loved ones in their families, such as children or parents. Xuan, as mentioned earlier, told me about her responsibilities for improving the prestige of her family in the local community by acquiring modern housing equipment:

> I bought myself and my brother a motorbike each. I bought my brother a computer to study at university. I paid to repair many things inside our house. I had our house renovated and the kitchen repaired with my own money. I bought many home appliances like a washing machine, a fridge, and other things like that. My parents were poor. I took over that responsibility because I earned a high salary. Because I saved up, I managed to [buy] many things (Xuan, interview).

With a high salary from working in a foreign NGO, Xuan said she was fortunate to be able to help her parents ease their economic burdens. Likewise, many other women working in local NGOs who earned less also spent most of what they earned on their children. Tien, for example, is a mother of two. She said she prioritised buying goods for her children while spending little for herself:

> When I had my children, I prioritised my spending on their needs. If I spend money on myself, I only want to spend it on leisure activities. I have simple needs. I do not like shopping. For example, my husband buys me a mobile phone and a laptop. I only buy a few clothes for myself. I only buy stuff that I need... Our salaries are now prioritised for my children's needs. Our children's needs are prioritised when the parents' needs are minor (Tien, interview).

With the development of the commodity economy, women's love and care are increasingly associated with materialistic and commoditised practices. Through consumption, these women often showed the efficacy of their sacrifice to optimise consumption for the happy family. As they strived to attain higher-valued goods, the quality and quantity of goods often symbolised their sacrifice and dedication to the family's betterment.

According to Pettus (2003: 4-6), the sacrifices made by women in Vietnam indicate their 'true Vietnamese woman' character, an idea which has been reinforced by the socialist state during periods of wars as well as socialist development. The state honours women as Vietnam's heroic mothers, commemorating their sacrifices of sons and their productive labour during wars for the national interest. In the context of marketisation, the state praises women's sacrifices for the sake of happy families. Women are consistently reminded to minimise their own desires in order to maintain harmonious family relationships and to utilise their consumption skills to better care for their families (Pettus 2003; Drummond 2004; Nguyen-vo, 2008; Leshkowich, 2012).

This happy family formula, as several studies reveal, can be found in the state-led campaign for *Gia đình văn hóa* ('cultured families'), led by the Vietnam Women's Union since the 1990s. This campaign emphasises the need to protect and maintain Vietnamese family culture as the basis for developing human qualities to support the national strategy of modernisation and industrialisation (Hayton 2010). Women are reminded to employ their traditional domestic talents to nurture and build happy and progressive families (Pettus 2003; Drummond 2004; Nguyen-vo 2008; Leshkowich 2012). By emphasising culture and morality as the foundation of a happy family, the campaign continues to promote the traditional feminine role of sacrifice, modesty, and attentiveness to elders, husbands, and children for a happy family (Shohet 2017; Pettus 2003). Repetition of these female virtues as rooted within Vietnam's socialist and Confucian traditions, underlines women's sacrifices as symbols of their prestige within the Vietnamese family and society, allowing them to reconcile social tensions that address women in the market economy (Leshkowich 2014; Shohet 2017). Glorification of sacrifice also accounts for the distinctive prestige of NGO middle-class women who care for collective welfare. By contrast, other wealthier groups continue to face criticism and uncertainty, as their private wealth continues to be the target of social scrutiny and state-led anti-corruption campaigns (Jellema 2005: 235). My final section will examine women's perception of corruption and their attempts to remoralise wealth through acts of sacrifice and giving.

Wealth, corruption, and remoralising acts

During my fieldwork in Hanoi, my informants often mentioned the pervasiveness of corruption. According to Gainsborough (2010), the pervasive corruption in Vietnam was considered to be deeply rooted in the social relationships through which people extract wealth. Furthermore, according to MacLean (2012: 595), the word for corruption (*tham nhũng*) in Vietnamese is composed of the words 'greed' (*tham*) and 'harassment' (*nhũng nhiễu*), indicating the nuisance caused by personal greed, often envisaged as the act of eating people's money (*ăn tiền*). An ethnographical study by MacLean (2012) of anti-corruption campaigns suggests that efforts to eradicate corruption in Vietnam focus mainly on tracking and tracing individual compliance or non-compliance with the socialist norms of morality. Moreover, according to Leshkowich (2012: 98), using morality to guide people toward correct conduct resembles the technique of 'rendering moral'. Morality is rendered as both the problem of and solution to private wealth. When wealth is intensively criticised, scrutinised and linked to corruption, people look for alternative forms of wealth disbursement, e.g., through consumption and charitable activities. Such acts are tolerated according to state-approved ethical norms and platforms as being in line with its efforts toward marketisation and privatisation. This situation accurately reflects Jellema's (2005) depiction of 'remoralising' practices that particularly appeal to the newly rich in Vietnam, who feel a strong need to compensate for and restore the moral value of their newfound wealth (Leshkowich 2012; Nguyen 2018).

In this respect, one can consider how women perceive corruption and remoralising practices. My informants mentioned the prevalence of corrupt practices in daily life, with many comparing their salaries to those of richer government employees (in terms of their unofficial income (*lậu*) despite their supposedly lower salary (*lương*)). While *lương* is the official monthly income of employees according to their labour contract, *lậu,* or the fringed income, is often anticipated as one of the main components of their monthly income. In Vietnamese, *lậu* is often besmirched with a suggestion of corrupt or illegal acts. For example, the word *lậu in buôn lậu* means illegal trade. With the rise of corruption in particular, *lậu* in *lương lậu* (salary and benefits) is used less to indicate fringe benefits and is now recognised more as a primary source of income for salaried people, often from bribery. For example, on *Nhân dân hàng tháng*, the news website of the Vietnamese Communist Party, *lậu* was addressed directly as a corrupt source of the wealth of government officials:

> There are multiple forms for *lậu*. There is '*lậu*', which is considered as a 'legitimate' bonus; for example, the amount from the cash envelopes that government people received for several reasons could be larger than their salary. Though their salary was low, they dined every day in luxurious restaurants from the corrupt money [*tiền chùa*], from other people's money (Tran in *Nhân dân hàng tháng* 2018).

My informants also spoke of corruption as a popular way for people to become rich quickly. In an interview with Hop, she said that many of her friends in the state sector had become rich because they were corrupt:

> My friends who are working for the state are rich now. They have to take bribes and gifts to become rich. How can they be rich from their state salary? (Hop, interview).

Moreover, it was common for people to link wealth with corrupt practices. Nhung, who had recently returned to work in an international NGO after having worked in the business sector, also mentioned the profits earned from business as corrupt and unethical:

> When you work in business, you have to be brutal to make money. There is a saying 'blood money' ['*đồng tiền xương máu*']. In my opinion, it is not ethical (Nhung, interview).

Since money is often associated with corruption, people with high salaries are also exposed to rumours of corruption. For example, Dang, who was working in a foreign NGO, complained that people associated her income, and the expensive services she used while working for a foreign organisation, with corruption. According to her, members of her family often assumed that she was rich because of corruption:

> There is a stereotype with the thinking that if you go on a business trip, you will eat at restaurants; there will be cars to pick you up, and you will receive cash envelopes. For every trip I take, I always have to explain it to them. But in their mind, they think that no matter what you say, you will have cash envelopes (Dang, interview).

Because individual gains are often considered corruption, it is understandable that these women are drawn to the cause of NGO work. In contrast to people working for private wealth, my informants often highlighted the value of NGO work as distinctively moral and beneficial for vulnerable communities. For example, Nhung criticised extracting wealth as stealing while highlighting the morality of NGO workers:

> If you are corrupt in NGOs, it is no different from stealing from the poor. If you are not corrupt, you have enough money to buy books or to build schools. Are you not ashamed of that? If you do not have good morality, you cannot work in an NGO. In business, they do it all the time. It is the business culture. Morality is very important in NGOs. Because NGOs are not the place for you to generate wealth (Nhung, interview).

Where means of private accumulation are easily associated with corruption, these women, without speaking directly about private wealth, described their modesty regarding their lifestyles, mediocre salaries, and caregiving services to the vulnerable. For example, Truc said that members of her family used to call her 'Bolshevik' for her aspiration to help other people rather than become rich:

> I do not expect to be rich because, in my point of view, I only need enough food to eat and enough money to pay for my daughter's nursery. I do not hope to be extremely rich. I only need to feel that I am useful in society. That is enough (Truc, interview).

Like Nhung and Truc, other informants often linked their work with its benefits to communities, supposedly insulating them from profit-hungry and corrupt approaches. For example, Ngan said,

> I mean, I am working for the general benefit of society. Secondly, when working in NGOs, there is no corruption. Everything is transparent. I do not have to think a lot about that (Ngan, interview).

The perception of corruption as unethical and its assumed link to personal wealth compel people to seek ways to 'remoralise' their wealth. This is reflected in their deliberate choice to work in non-profit and humanitarian sectors. Women working in NGOs value the opportunity to work to help vulnerable communities, which is perceived as ethical work rather than for merely private wealth, often viewed as unethical. In a society that desires to restore morality to wealth, NGOs provide an ideal platform for charitable endeavours. As organisations dedicated to caring work, NGOs hold particular appeal for women, who are traditionally known for their caring and sacrificial nature. This reflects another dimension of women as ethical citizens: their efforts to help others not only contribute to their self-worth but also, when combined with their reproductive labour, enhance their reputation as moral workers who prioritise collective well-being over personal wealth. However, it is paradoxical that these moral values, while symbolising women's prestige based on norms of sacrifice and modesty, continue to perpetuate women's inferior status quo in Vietnamese patriarchal society.

Conclusion: The idea of ethical women in Vietnam's market socialism

With market liberalisation, women working in the NGO sector in Vietnam have reified the distinctive values taken from care-giving acts and humanitarian work. Rather than dealing in monetised terms, acts of selfless care in non-governmental organisations offer them value in terms of prestige, social relations, and compassion, which are more desirable than monetary value, often stigmatised as unethical and corrupt. The values associated with humanitarian and voluntary industries, also revealed by a growing body of anthropological studies, especially appeal to women and other groups anxious about being marginalised as dependents (Muehlebach 2012), excluded (Malkki 2015), or aspiring to proclaim middle-class status through acts of caring and giving (Borstein 2012). With marketisation and privatisation, the idea of the ethical woman, demonstrated by her fulfilment of domestic duties, has increasingly come to be associated with materialised and commoditised items, with the quantity and quality of consumer goods becoming symbolic of their love and care. It seems clear that women continue to reproduce traditional norms of gender and morality through everyday caregiving practices. The women's pursuit of values in terms of morality reveals the gendered aspects of ethical citizenship enforced by market liberalisation. Ironically, when liberty is considered the basis of market ethics, the market seems to suppress women trying to follow their own pursuits. Deemed free, yet once again they are constrained by the very idea of the ethical woman.

Bibliography

Anagnost, Ann. 2004. 'The Corporeal Politics of Quality (*suzhi*)', *Public Culture*, 16(2), 189–208. Doi:10.1215/08992363-16-2-189.

Beresford, Melanie. 2008. 'Doi Moi in Review: The Challenges of Building Market Socialism in Vietnam', *Journal of Contemporary Asia*, 38(2), 221–243.

Bornstein, Erica. 2012. *Disquieting Gifts: Humanitarianism in New Delhi*. Redwood City: Stanford University Press.

Bui, Hai Thiem. 2015. 'In Search of a Post-socialist Mode of Governmentality: The Double Movement of Accommodating and Resisting Neo-liberalism in Vietnam', *Asian Journal of Social Science*, 43(1–2): 80–102. Doi:10.1163/15685314-04301005.

Bui, Hai Thiem. 2013. 'The Development of Civil Society and Dynamics of Governance in Vietnam's One Party Rule', *Global Change, Peace and Security*, 25(1), 77–93. Doi:10.1080/14781158.2013.758100.

Dillon, Michael. 1995. 'Sovereignty and Governmentality: From the Problematics of the "New World Order" to the Ethical Problematic of the World Order', *Alternatives: Global, Local, Political*, 20(3), 323–368.

Dinh, Van Anh. 2003. *Developing the Socialist-oriented Market Economy in Vietnam: A Reference Book*. Hanoi: (Government Document) Central Institute for Economic Management/Statistical Publisher.

Drummond, Lisa Barbara Welch. 2004. 'The Modern "Vietnamese Woman": Socialization and Women's Magazines', in *Gender Practices in Contemporary Vietnam* (158–178). Singapore: Singapore University Press.

Drummond, Lisa Barbara Welch. 2012. 'Middle Class Landscapes in a Transforming City: Hanoi in the 21st Century', in *The Reinvention of Distinction: Modernity and the Middle Class in Urban Vietnam* (79–93). New York: Springer.

Gainsborough, Martin. 2010. *Vietnam: Rethinking the State*. London: Zed Books.

Harms, Erik. 2014. 'Civility's Footprint: Ethnographic Conversations about Urban Civility and Sustainability in Ho Chi Minh City', *Journal of Social Issues in Southeast Asia*, 29(2): 223. Doi:10.1355/sj29-2a.

Harvey, David. 2005. *A Brief History of Neoliberalism*. Oxford: Oxford University Press.

Hayton, Bill. 2010 *Vietnam: Rising Dragon*. New Haven CT: Yale University Press.

Inda, Jonathan Xavier. 2006. *Targeting Immigrants: Government, Technology, and Ethics*. Oxford: Blackwell Publishing.

Jellema, Kate. 2005. 'Making good on debt: The Remoralisation of Wealth in Post-Revolutionary Vietnam', *Asia Pacific Journal of Anthropology* 6(3), 231–248. Doi:10.1080/14442210500339579.

Kornai, Janos. 1992. *The Socialist System: The Political Economy of Communism*. Oxford: Clarendon Press.

Leshkowich, Ann Marie. 2012. 'Finances, Family, Fashion, Fitness and... Freedom? The Changing Lives of Urban Middle-Class Vietnamese Women', in *The Reinvention of Distinction: Modernity and the Middle Class in Urban Vietnam* (95–113). New York: Springer.

Leshkowich, Ann Marie. 2014. *Essential Trade: Vietnamese Women in a Changing Marketplace*. Honolulu: University of Hawai'i Press.

Li, Tania Murray. 2007. *The Will to Improve: Governmentality, Development, and the Practice of Politics*. Durham NC: Duke University Press.

Liechty, Mark. 2003. *Suitably Modern: Making Middle-class Culture in a New Consumer Society*. Princeton: Princeton University Press.

MacLean, Ken. 2012. 'Enacting Anticorruption: The Reconfiguration of Audit Regimes in Contemporary Vietnam', *Positions* 20(2), 595–625. doi:10.1215/10679847-1538524

Malkki, Liisa. 2015. *The Need to Help: The Domestic Arts of International Humanitarianism*. Durham NC: Duke University Press.

Marr, David G. 1981. *Vietnamese Tradition on Trial, 1920-1945*. Berkeley: University of California Press.

Muehlebach, Andrea. 2012. *The Moral Neoliberal: Welfare and Citizenship in Italy.* Chicago: University of Chicago Press.

Nguyen, Minh. 2018. 'Vietnam's "Socialization" Policy and the Moral Subject in a Privatizing Economy', *Economy and Society*, 47(4), 627–647. doi:10.1080/03085147.2018.1544397.

Nguyen, Minh. 2019. *Waste and Wealth – An Ethnography of Labor, Value, and Morality in a Vietnamese Recycling Economy.* New York: Oxford University Press.

Nguyen, Thi Ngoc Ha, and Thi Thanh Vui Chu. 2016. 'Socializing Education and Healthcare in Vietnam Market Economy', *Vietnam Social Science*, 1(171), 21–26.

Nguyen-Marshall, Van, Lisa Barbara Welch Drummond, and Danièle Bélanger. 2012. *The Reinvention of Distinction: Modernity and the Middle Class in Urban Vietnam*. New York: Springer.

Nguyen-vo, Thu Huong. 2008. *The Ironies of Freedom: Sex, Culture, and Neoliberal Governance in Vietnam*. Seattle: University of Washington Press.

Ong, Aihwa. 1999. *Flexible Citizenship The Cultural Logics of Transnationality.* Durham NC: Duke University Press.

Ong, Aihwa. 2006. *Neoliberalism as Exception: Mutations in Citizenship and Sovereignty.* Durham NC: Duke University Press.

Pettus, Ashley. 2003. *Between Sacrifice and Desire: National Identity and the Governing of Femininity in Vietnam*. Abingdon: Routledge.

Rabinow, Paul (ed.). 1997. *The Essential Works of Michel Foucault, 1954–1984: Vol.1, Ethics: Subjectivity and Truth*. New York: The New Press.

Robison, Richard and David S.G. Goodman (eds.) 1996. *The New Rich in Asia Mobile Phones, McDonald's and Middle-class Revolution*. Oxon: Routledge.

Shohet, Merav. 2017. 'Troubling Love: Gender, Class, and Sideshadowing the "Happy Family" in Vietnam', *Ethos* 45(4): 555–576. doi:10.1111/etho.12177.

Tran, Quang. 2018. 'Lương và lậu', *Nhân dân hàng tháng*. https://www.nhandan.com.vn/hangthang/item/37175402-luong-va-lau.html.

Trinh, Binh. 2022. 'The Moral Middle-class in Market Socialism: An Investigation into the Personhood of Women Working in NGOs in Vietnam', *Asian Journal of Social Science*, 50(2), 104–111. doi.org/10.1016/j.ajss.2021.12.002.

Zhang, Li and Aihwa Ong. 2008. *Privatizing China: Socialism from Afar.* Ithaca: Cornell University Press.

About the author

Dr Binh Thi An Trinh is an independent scholar from Vietnam. She graduated from the University of Leeds in 2020 with a Doctoral degree in Politics and International Studies. Her PhD thesis focuses on narratives and life

histories of women working in NGOs in post-reform Vietnam. Her research specialisation is on ethical citizenship, gender, civil society, the middle class, NGOs, and governance in the context of neoliberal globalisation and on post-socialist and postcolonial economies in East and Southeast Asian regions. Her work lies at the intersection of political economy and anthropology. She specialises in qualitative research and ethnographic methods.
trinhanbinh@gmail.com

3. Practicing Citizenship in Urban China

A Case Study of Migrant Activism in Hangzhou

Jun Chu

Abstract: This chapter focuses on the discursive contestations of self-organised migrant workers in China and analyses their citizenship practices from the angle of migrant activism. Based on my ethnographic study of a migrant organisation in Hangzhou, I examine how these practices challenge the dominant discourse by repositioning migrant workers as subjects and thereby negotiating citizenship 'from below'. The results reveal the entanglement between migrant activism and technologies of active citizenship in the discourses and practices of self-help. This chapter draws attention to the blurring of boundaries between activism and governance in citizenship politics, thereby contributing to the discussion on citizenship beyond the binary division of China and the West.

Keywords: China, citizenship, migrant activism, self-help, subject position

Introduction

Over recent decades, our understanding of the right to the city and citizenship in urban China has been challenged. As a central topic in the issue of citizenship in contemporary China, rural-urban migration draws ongoing scholarly attention from the broader fields of social science and the humanities. The institutional divide between rural and urban— mainly through the Chinese household registration system (*hukou*)[1]—has been the main

1 The hukou system, introduced in China in 1958, served historically as the basis for rationed resource and subsidy allocation within the framework of the socialist planned economy. Since the economic reform of the 1980s, this system has continued to be seen as the main institutional barrier that excludes the rural population, especially migrant workers, from full access to urban citizenship. For more on this, see Solinger (1999).

Gregory Bracken, Paul Rabé, Nurul Azreen Azlan (eds), *Future Practices of Citizenship in Asia and the West: Care of the Self (Volume III)*. Taylor & Francis Group, 2025
DOI: 10.5117/9789048562077_CH03

focus of academic discussion. However, the mechanisms of exclusion and inclusion in the institutions of citizenship are now recognised as differential, localised, and multi-dimensional (Solinger 1999; Zhang and Wang 2010; Wu 2011; Jakimów 2012; Woodman and Guo 2017). Against this background, aspects of citizenship that fall outside formal status and membership are gaining more attention in recent research on rural migrant workers in China: practices, discourses, identity, subjectivities, etc. Along with a broader understanding of citizenship that goes beyond national membership and legal rights, the concept of urban citizenship has become a useful lens to investigate the constantly negotiated relationship between migration and citizenship in the urban context of China. The transformation of citizenship by processes and negotiations involves diverse actors, practices, and discourses in intersecting fields of policy, urban governance, migrant activism, and civil society.

In this chapter, I focus on the citizenship practices of self-organised migrant workers in China and draw particular attention to discursive and representational practices as a digital form of migrant activism. Based on my ethnographic study of migrant self-organisation in Hangzhou, I examine how these practices challenge the dominant discourse by repositioning migrant workers as subjects, thereby negotiating citizenship 'from below'. From both the aspects of 'active citizenship' and 'activist citizenship' (Isin 2009), I demonstrate the intertwined relations between activism and governing technologies in citizenship practices. In the context of rising authoritarianism and shrinking space for labour and citizen activism on the one hand, and the nationwide introduction of urban integration policies towards migrant workers on the other, this chapter suggests a more nuanced understanding of the politics of citizenship within an authoritarian context, which also contains (neo-)liberal governing technologies.

I begin by outlining the approaches of citizenship in relation to migrant activism, particularly concerning theorising citizenship 'after orientalism' (Isin 2012), which goes beyond the binary division of China and the West. Then I briefly introduce this chapter's research background and methods, highlighting some specifics of the methodological thoughts. Subsequently, I present the migrant organisation's discourse production over a decade—linking this with two subject positions of 'grassroots' and 'volunteers'—to show how citizenship practices contest the hitherto subject positions of migrant workers. Finally, I discuss the tension and entanglement between migrant activism and technologies of active citizenship in the discourses and practices of self-help.

Practicing citizenship in urban China: An approach by migrant activism

Although the development of citizenship in China has its historical and cultural particularities, there is a shared opinion that we should take a more integrated view, recognising the articulation of citizenship and the production of modernity in China as connected with global histories, while acknowledging the postcolonial reflections on its conceptual construction in the 'West' (Jakimów 2012; Guo and Guo 2015; Woodman and Guo 2017). That the citizenship approach is being increasingly used as an analytical lens for examining practices in contemporary Chinese society is demonstrated by several authors in the special issue 'Practicing Citizenship in Contemporary China' in the journal *Citizenship Studies* (Guo and Liang 2017; Woodman 2017; Xiong and Li 2017).

Critical studies of citizenship over recent decades have shifted research focus from citizenship as a legal status towards citizenship as practices of making citizens (Isin 2008). Following Thomas H. Marshall's (1950) differentiation between formal citizenship (status) and substantive citizenship (rights), scholars have debated over the concept of citizenship and have extended its understanding, which now includes various political and social struggles of recognition and redistribution as instances of claim-making (Isin and Turner 2002, 2 f.). This new intensity in struggles over citizenship is associated with global movements and flows of capital, labour, and people (Isin and Nielsen 2008). By defining citizenship as 'a social process through which individuals and social groups engage in claiming, expanding or losing rights', the emphasis lies less on legal rules and more on norms, practices, meanings, and identities (Isin and Turner 2002, 4). The practices through which social groups articulate claims to address injustices become essential to understanding citizenship as political subjectivity (Isin 2012, 567).

However, the focus on practices does not necessarily mean neglecting the formal dimensions of citizenship as an institutional framework nor the overarching regime of discourses and representations, which are sites of citizenship where claims-making, struggles, and negotiations occur. On the contrary, status, practice, and discourse are intertwined dimensions that co-produce each other and constitute the contemporary construction of citizenship in China (Jakimów 2015). This construction of Chinese citizenship has been shaped by the 'othering' mechanism towards the rural population— especially the group of migrant workers—and ethnic minorities (Jakimów and Barabantseva 2016).

As a main focus in the literature on citizenship in China, migrant workers' rights and claims of citizenship in the city are also being investigated through the lens of urban citizenship (Zhang 2002; Chen 2005; Zhang and Wang 2010; Ren 2012; Swider 2015). The localised, urbanised, and differentiated character of citizenship in China is interlinked with the trends observed in the global regime of migration and mobility, which render the artificial boundaries in scholarly thinking between internal and transnational migration obsolete (Woodman and Guo 2017; Zhang 2018). For instance, the regulation of residence permits in the city, as well as the adoption of a 'points-based' system as the basis for differentiated access to public services and socioeconomic rights in large cities, resembles techniques and rationalities in the regime of mobility and management of immigration in European and North American countries (Zhang 2018).

The complex system of 'differential inclusion', which currently characterises labour migration regimes with their strategies of filtering that govern labour mobility when travelling beyond national borders, is also being applied to the internal borders of cities, countries, and regions (Mezzadra and Neilson 2013). These fragmentation processes lead to a blurred boundary between inclusion and exclusion in the migration and citizenship regime, thus fostering further diversification of migrants' subject positions (Mezzadra and Neilson 2013, 164). Rather than the binaries of non-citizen/citizen and non-status/status subject positions, policies regulating movement and migration tend to create a 'graduated system' in status and produce variations of 'less than full' statuses of citizenship (Ong 2005; Goldring et al. 2009; Nyers and Rygiel 2012).

This context of transformation enables the emergence of new forms of political activism, citizenship identities, and openings for different concepts of citizenship, highlighting the understanding of migrant activism as a key site for conceptualising migrant citizenship 'from below' (Nyers and Rygiel 2012). Paying more attention to informal forms of citizenship (Sassen 2002) and practices of citizenship by those who were constituted as its 'other' (Isin 2002), scholars investigate how non-citizen migrant groups, through various strategies of claims-making, are involved in ways of engaging in citizenship even when lacking formal citizenship status. This approach is related to the theorisation of 'acts of citizenship' developed by Engin Isin (2008).

Drawing attention to those moments when, regardless of status and substance, subjects constitute themselves as citizens, Isin (2008, 39) defines acts of citizenship as 'those acts that transform forms (orientations, strategies, technologies) and modes (citizens, strangers, outsiders, aliens) of being political by bringing into being new actors as activist citizens (claimants of rights and responsibilities) through creating new sites and scales of struggle'. Using the term 'activist citizenship', Isin (2009) characterises the emergence of new political subjectivities that contrast with the figure of 'active citizenship' based on practices in existing political structures and institutions and tied into governmental practices through which conduct is produced. Understanding the practices by which social groups articulate claims to address injustices becomes essential to understand citizenship as political subjectivity (Isin 2012, 567). He argues,

> Citizenship understood as political subjectivity shifts our attention from fixed categories by which we have come to understand or inherit citizenship to the struggles through which these categories themselves have become stakes. It also shifts our attention from already defined actors to the acts that constitute them. Rather than asking 'who is the citizen?' the question becomes 'what makes the citizen?' (Isin 2009, 383).

Thus, migrant activism, in its diverse forms, opens up the possibility of transforming our thinking about citizenship subjectivities. However, this activist aspect cannot be considered outside the power and domination relations in which struggles for citizenship are situated. As Isin also reminds us, citizenship should be defined as a dynamic institution of domination and empowerment that 'governs *who* citizens (insiders), subjects (strangers, outsiders) and objects (aliens) are and *how* these actors are to govern themselves and each other in a given body politic' (2009, 384, italics in original). Investigating activistic citizenship practices requires focusing on the 'moments of becoming political, when strangers and outsiders question the justice adjured on them by appropriating or overturning those same strategies and technologies of citizenship' (Isin 2002, ix–v).

Concerning the societal contexts where these activistic practices encounter the governing technologies of citizenship regime, arises a crucial question: whether this approach is suitable for explaining the activism, practices, and identities of rural migrant workers in China. In recent reflections on the use of the concept of 'acts of citizenship' in 'non-Western' or 'non-democratic' contexts, Jakimów (2022, 506) draws attention to the importance of non-confrontational acts of citizenship under authoritarianism, and points out that the confrontational quality is not necessarily productive of political subjectivity-formation and citizenship transformation under these circumstances. The authoritarian system of governance requires certain strategies of activist citizenship, which may differ from the definition of 'acts of citizenship' in its original interpretation: questioning, or even breaking the law (Jakimów 2022, 509). Indeed, by theorising acts, Isin (2008) suggests a focus on breaks and ruptures from given orders, practices, and habitus, or in other words, from social-historical patterns. On the other hand, he also calls attention to the emergence of new 'sites', 'scales', and 'acts' through which actors 'enact political subjectivities and transform themselves and others into citizens by articulating ever-changing and expanding rights' (Isin 2009, 368).

Hence, how we identify and interpret the kinds of 'acts' and practices performed by migrants in the constitution of their new political subjectivities of citizenship is not restrained by the legal frame of rights and responsibilities. Practices that challenge the existing frame of inclusion and exclusion within the construction of citizenship, especially those that contest the 'cultural norms that underpin the citizenship orders' (Woodman and Guo 2017, 750), are located in the field of cultural politics, which belongs to crucial sites of citizenship struggles.

In recent years, scholars have drawn more attention to the discursive practices and strategies of migrant NGOs, which challenge the representations of migrant workers in mainstream discourse (Sun 2014; Jakimów 2017; Gleiss et al. 2019). By negotiating the positions of migrant workers in the construction of citizenship, these discursive struggles can potentially transform citizenship discourse in China, which draws on discourses of modernity, post-colonialism, and linear progress through the 'othering' mechanism (Jakimów 2015). For this reason, Jakimów interprets the attempt at promoting new identities of migrant workers to oppose their image as unfit, second-class citizens in the mainstream representations as 'acts of citizenship' in the Chinese context, which does not necessarily take a confrontational form.

However, to what extent do these practices achieve the goal of challenging or even transforming mainstream discourse? How successfully do the organisations as actors engage with the citizenship regime and negotiate the subject positions of migrant workers in the discursive struggles? These questions still require more thorough exploration. To consider the long-term effects and outcomes of activistic practices for transforming citizenship, I argue that Isin's contradistinction between 'activist citizenship' and 'active citizenship' (2009) is very useful for exploring the tension within the discursive practices of migrant activism, which I discovered in my ethnographic study on migrant self-organisation in China. Before proceeding, I will introduce my research background and explain my fieldwork and methods.

Researching migrant activism in Hangzhou: Fieldwork and methods

The research data used in this chapter is based on an ethnographic study conducted in the Chinese metropolis of Hangzhou between 2014 and 2016.

The focus of the research was the twelve-year development of a migrant self-help organisation located in Hangzhou, particularly how it challenged the existing subject positions of the mainstream discourse through its discourses and programs, thereby negotiating an urban policy 'from below'. In addition to the fieldwork phase, another important data source was the extensive collection of digital material I created between 2015 and 2019: media reports, policy papers at city and state levels, online chats, blog texts, self-published magazines, photos and videos, web archives, etc.

For this chapter, I chose the most famous long-term example of migrant self-organisation in Hangzhou. This example represents the characteristics of a migrant NGO that decided to cooperate with governments and trade unions. Because of its influence and impact beyond the local communities, my analysis is more concerned with migrant workers in Hangzhou in general, rather than with a specific group.

This migrant organisation experienced several changes in its development since 2006 when the first online activism appeared with a simple self-made homepage called 'Grassroots'. The small group of migrant workers who maintained its homepage and internal forum became the founders of the NGO initiated in 2008, which had the same name: 'Grassroots'. Located in a migrant community in a suburban area of Hangzhou, the Grassroots NGO was regarded as an extension of the mobilisation within the virtual community to a localised offline form. Many of the migrant workers involved in Grassroots activities, including the founder himself, worked in the garment industry because of its dominant presence in the region at the time. Another important aspect of the membership, especially for core members, was that they were rural migrants, self-employed or small business owners, with more control over their time. In 2010, after its successful self-representation as a solidarity network for migrant workers, Grassroots faced the pressure of institutionalisation. They agreed to launch a parallel organisation, the 'Worker Volunteer Station' (WVS) under the lead of the state-led trade union system. Both organisations still retained their self-organised form. Self-organisation has always been key in both the Grassroots and WVS periods. To bring the migrant workers together, they offered a range of activities, from daily evening events and weekend gatherings to interest group activities, skills training, and cultural holiday events.

Over a decade, the online space for migrant activism was extended and transformed from a self-made website with a forum and blogs to new social media microblogs and WeChat. When I started my field research at the end of 2014, the original Grassroots NGO had closed down the previous year, and only WVS remained. At that time, all digital communication within the organisation and its public self-representation ran mainly on WeChat and partly on the microblog platforms (Tencent, Weibo). The old homepage, 'Grassroots', was closed after my first long field stay in 2015, and the domain was permanently deleted in 2016. For data collection from this homepage, I accessed the historical database of the non-profit project *Internet Archive*, the 'Wayback Machine', where some of the oldest web captures are still stored. The time map of these captures also allowed me to track the change in the organisational self-representation chronologically.

The web archives became relevant in the later phase of my research when I had completed my whole fieldwork phase and started the systematic collection of data on previous discursive activities of the organisation. At this moment, I encountered the problem of data disappearance for political reasons. After the permanent deletion of the homepage, only a few unsorted articles could be found in the old blogs, which belong to the founders of 'Grassroots'. During my research phase, the publicly accessible information about the organisation Grassroots decreased visibly, and many resources were no longer available: from newspaper articles to personal blog texts, from the official news on the websites of the government and the trade unions to the web or blog portals for NGO networks in China, including Grassroots' previous Chinese wiki page (Baidu Wiki).

This ongoing disappearance of data also belongs to strategies of invisibilisation, whereby certain aspects or sections of discourses and representations are 'forgotten' and removed from collective memory in times of social transformation. On this point, William Walters' (2012, 112) observation about genealogy as 'the retrieval of forgotten struggles and subjugated knowledge' is illuminating. In his opinion, practicing genealogy as a struggle means 'to set aside prior conceptions of the "who" of history and look carefully for the unique ways in which groups are made, and make themselves' (Walters 2012, 138). This style of investigation makes the presence of these groups or collectivities visible in political processes and emphasises the importance of politics to the study of governance. Therefore, recovering the lost or forgotten struggles is a way of encountering governmentality and engaging in politics, reflecting this research's topic: practicing citizenship.

Contested subject positions of migrant workers in discursive struggles

In this section, I analyse the discursive practices of migrant self-organisation that call into question the mainstream discourse about migrant workers and constitute new political subjectivities. My analysis extends to include the examination of negotiating or contesting discourses related to citizenship, not merely discourses on the subject figure of 'citizen' or 'urban citizen' but also of relevant subject figures that play a decisive role in the discourses as forms of 'cultural politics' or, more especially, the 'politics of representation' (Hall 2012).

Stuart Hall relates the term 'politics of representation' with the effects and consequences of representation, which is the concern of the discursive approach to the production of meanings: 'how the knowledge which a particular discourse produces connects with power, regulates conduct, makes up or constructs identities and subjectivities, and defines the way certain things are represented, thought about, practised and studied' (2012, 6). In comparison to the well-known term 'politics of recognition', Hall's concept of 'politics of representation' has barely been adopted for analysing migrant workers' struggles over discourses and representations. However, I argue that these struggles demonstrate characteristics of contestation that go beyond the demand for social recognition. By getting access to rights to representation, contesting the marginality and stereotypical quality of the existing images, and creating the counter-position of an alternative, positive imagery, they challenge the dominant regime of representation (Hall 2021[1988], 247). Moreover, the contestation moves forward to a 'struggle around positionalities' (249): how the migrant subject is positioned in the discourse on citizenship and integration in urban China.

During my investigation into the discourse production of both Grassroots and WVS between 2006 and 2016, I identified two essential subject figures at the centre of these discursive struggles: 'grassroots' (*caogen*) and 'volunteer' (*zhiyuanzhe*). Their importance is not only demonstrated by the presence of the former in the organisation's original name but also derives from longstanding contestations over their positioning in the relations of representation. The next two sections illustrate the crucial processes of identification and subject-making within the context of migrant self-organisation in two periods: 'Being grassroots' and 'Becoming worker-volunteer'.

'Being grassroots': Reinterpretation and repositioning

> 'Grassroots' (*caogen*), a despicable name that the urban rich, especially the media, have given to low-income populations, mainly including migrant workers. When I first learned from a newspaper that we migrant workers were called grassroots, my heart was deeply hurt! 'Aimless flowing mob'

> (*mangliu*), 'peasant-worker' (*nongmingong*), grassroots etc. How many such terms can the superior intellectuals in the city create to despise us?' (Xu 2006).

This quote is taken from a blog article written in 2006 by Mr. Xu, the founder of the website 'Grassroots' and, later, of the organisation with the same name. In this blog, titled 'Grassroots', Xu recounted his outrage at being first confronted with the term 'grassroots' and explained his reasons for adopting the term. Considering this naming as a continuation of the previous discriminatory terms such as 'aimless flowing mob' and 'peasant-worker'[2], the author's indignation is triggered by the fact that the social group in cultural dominance (urban elites and intellectuals) could easily create discriminatory terms to define migrant workers. This remarkable sensibility of discursive power and cultural hegemony led him to his clear claim-making: consciously adopting 'grassroots' as a category of identification to detach it from its existing negative context and to re-associate it with a new positive image.

> That was a painful memory. From that day on, I have named myself 'grassroots' because I want to give this name new meanings. [...] Soon, 'grassroots' will gain totally different meanings: solidarity, ambition, perseverance, and aspiration! Grassroots are ordinary but great people who deserve respect! (Xu 2006).

This blog had been written shortly after Xu activated the homepage of 'Grassroots'. As one of the steps for attributing positive meanings to the grassroots subject, ideas of a new 'grassroots spirit' were collected via this homepage. That same year, the first formulation was presented online and contained two core phrases: 'self-help and mutual aid (*zizhuhuzhu*), striving for self-improvement (*ziqiangbuxi*)'. To oppose the marginal subject position to which migrant workers are ascribed, the first online activists mobilised by this homepage sought a united front as counter-positioning. They developed their grassroots discourse in four dimensions: grassroots spirit, grassroots culture, grassroots entrepreneurship, and grassroots dream (Grassroots 2006). Under each concept, different experimental ideas and

2 Both terms had been used in the past in official policy documents and in the media to refer to migrant workers. While the term 'aimless flowing mob' disappeared from public discourse by the 1990s, 'peasant-worker' is still in everyday and official use. For a further analysis of the identity construction 'peasant-worker' see Chen (2005).

plans for a collective approach to the social problems faced by migrant workers were explored and discussed in the virtual community provided by 'Grassroots'. While ambitious future plans were listed on the homepage, the growing group of active members debated the concrete realisation and implementation of their plans.

The activists were fully aware of the idealistic and utopian character of the whole process. In 2008 they reorientated to more realisable plans as Grassroots was finally founded as a local-based unofficial NGO in a migrant community in suburban Hangzhou[3]. In the online document 'Strategic Planning' for the future NGO, dated 8 May 2008, the founding team members formulated the local organisation's aim, mission, and area of activities. In comparison to the expression of previous years, the organising mission sounded less ambitious: 'to build a platform for migrant workers to help each other and improve themselves together, to gather their wisdom, to demonstrate their strength, to enrich their lives and to realise their dreams' (Grassroots 2008).

Here we recognise the shift that occurred during Grassroots' development. Some crucial concepts emerged while others faded away: 'self-help' and 'self-improvement' became the core concepts of the newly established organisation. This is related to the organisational repositioning of Grassroots: it located itself in the field of self-help organisations, while eventually abandoning the early explorations of entrepreneurship and social enterprise for the common good.

Since the early stages of self-representation, the concept 'self-improvement' was often accompanied by *suzhi* (quality)[4] improvement and urban integration for migrant workers. In June 2007, on the 'About us' page of the

3 The migrant workers' NGOs in China often exist in an unofficial way without registration by the Chinese Ministry of Civil Affairs (MCA). In order to acquire legal status as a 'social organisation' (*shehui zuzhi*), all organisations in China must apply to a government-linked 'Professional Supervisory Unit' (*yewu zhuguan danwei*) for review and approval before they can register with the MCA, according to the government's Regulations on the Registration and Management of Social Organizations (1998). This requirement makes the proper registration extremely difficult for most organisations dealing with migrant labour issues.

4 The Chinese term '*suzhi*' literally means 'quality' (for humans) and is still widely used. In the 2000s it has been extensively researched in social science and cultural studies. A genealogical analysis of the emergence of the *suzhi* discourse in China is provided by British anthropologist Andrew Kipnis in his article '*Suzhi*: A Keyword Approach' (2006). According to him, the rise of this discourse in the post-Mao era is linked to a series of political, economic, social, cultural, and linguistic events, including the implementation of birth control policies, the return of competition in the education system and labour markets, and the centrality of nationalism to the Communist Party's self-legitimisation.

Grassroots website, 'self-improvement' was listed as a category of activities under the topic 'What we are doing' and deliberated as follows: 'By organising a series of public service activities such as cultural and sport events, and voluntary actions, as well as by providing various opportunities of learning and training, we continue to improve our *suzhi* as migrant workers, for a better integration into the city' (Grassroots 2007). From the organisation's point of view, promoting 'improving the *suzhi* of migrant workers in all aspects' does not mean accepting the 'low-*suzhi*' image ascribed to migrant workers as a social group. However, it would be an effective way to fight against the prejudiced opinion and represent migrant workers as 'high-*suzhi*' subjects (Grassroots 2006).

The way Grassroots addresses '*suzhi*' and 'self-improvement' is concerned with the marginal position of migrant workers in mainstream discourse, especially in relation to the formation of citizen subjects. In several anthropological works on the discourse of *suzhi* and self-development in China in the early 2000s, scholars focused on the relevance of these discourses to the process of subject formation in Chinese society. They paid attention to the differentiation between 'low-*suzhi*' and 'high-*suzhi*' subjects in the population, especially between migrant workers and middle-class residents in the urban context (Yan 2003, 2008; Anagnost 2004; Pun 2006; Jacka 2009; Tomba 2009; Sun 2009).

Regarding politics of differentiation, migrant workers have been branded 'low-*suzhi*' subjects and are contrasted with the 'high-*suzhi*' citizen-subjects of the urban middle class (Sun 2009, 637 f.). The latter are being promoted in the context of urban 'community building' (*shequ jianshe*) and 'community governance' (*shequ zhili*) in order to cultivate responsible and self-governing subjects who then function as good examples of 'self-improvement' (Tomba 2009, 592 f.). Therefore, the *suzhi* discourse also contributes to the contemporary regime of citizenship by relating it to the processes and institutions that produce and reproduce boundaries and gradations between different types of citizenship and citizen, including those of producing the 'ideal' citizen as well as those that are 'less-than-ideal' (Jacka 2009, 524).

Under these circumstances, the discursive practices of Grassroots gain activistic relevance by seeking to break the stabilised boundary between categories of 'low-*suzhi*' migrants and 'high-*suzhi*' urban citizens, and reposition the migrant subject in the hegemonic regime of representation. Moreover, by running their own homepage, and the self-published magazine 'Grassroots' and the self-organised 'Grassroots Art Group', the organisation was engaging cultural politics with its own discursive and representational production. Although their alternative discourses and representation are not completely detached from the influential, dominant discourse of self-development and *suzhi*, the approach in the logic of self help and mutual aid does not follow an individualistic way of self-development and self-empowerment, but rather a collective one: these practices are based on the goal of improving the living conditions and changing the marginal social positions of migrant workers as a group. Through these practices, the self-organised migrant workers articulate claims to address injustice and hegemonic order in the citizenship regime. These were moments in which migrant subjects, regardless of the status attributed to them, claimed the right to the city and constitute themselves as political subjects of 'activist citizens'.

'Becoming worker volunteers': Negotiating migrant workers' subject position in the discourse of volunteerism

Engaging in the politics of representation did not change after WVS was established as a new organisation in 2010. WVS took over most of the event planning directly from the existing organisation. At the same time, the new 'volunteer network' replaced the previous membership of Grassroots. In adapting to the new emphasis on the status of 'volunteer' within the new organisational context, as well as responding to the emergence of the urban integration policy towards migrant workers in China, core members of Grassroots focused on creating a new discourse and programs for WVS. This section illustrates how these migrant activists conceptually reinterpreted existing self-help principles of grassroots activism into the frame of volunteering and how this constituted the new subject position of 'worker-volunteer'.

By WVS' definition, 'worker volunteer' refers only to volunteers who are themselves migrant workers and, therefore, distinguishes them from volunteers from other backgrounds, especially students and urban residents. The essence of this lies in the so-called 'role change', namely leaving behind the old status of being a person in need to become a helper. To achieve this goal, migrant workers should help and support each other in networks through their volunteering commitment, acquiring of knowledge, skills, and competencies, and improving themselves. This interpretation was based on the core concept of self-help from the time of previous Grassroots. In doing so, the organisation continued its agency in the discursive struggles for migrant workers by challenging state-dominated volunteer discourse and seeking a repositioning for migrant workers.

Since 2014, WVS has constantly tried to interpret the essential characteristic of volunteering in its organisational context: i.e., the principle of self-help and mutual aid among migrant workers. To emphasise this, WVS defined their volunteers as 'self-help volunteers' (*zizhushi zhiyuanzhe*), distinguishing them from volunteers 'in the conventional sense' (WVS 2014a). The necessity of this distinction was explained as follows:

> What do volunteers in the conventional sense do? They help the disabled, the elderly, school children, they work in the field of youth problems and environmental protection or support other disadvantaged groups. These 'other disadvantaged groups' include us migrant workers. According to the mainstream opinions, we deserve pity and need help (WVS 2014a).

Confronted with this dominant image of volunteers in Chinese cities who participate in activities of helping people in need, the discourse development around the terms 'worker volunteer' and 'self-help volunteers' was not easy for WVS. Arguments for the meaning of 'self-help volunteering' referred mainly to the promotion of 'role change of disadvantaged groups' on a collective level: 'We transform ourselves from a "problem group" to a problem-solving group'; 'We are not just helping individuals, but the whole group!' (WVS 2012).

However, efforts to produce an alternative discourse of volunteering specifically for migrant workers were unsuccessful. Rather than concrete practices, the crucial problem was the question of framing and self-positioning. Similar activities of self-organising and self-help had also been associated with grassroots solidarity and received high acceptance by migrant workers in an earlier period. By changing the framing of these activities to volunteerism and redefining mutual help as volunteering, the organisation encountered obstacles to understanding among the participating migrant workers.

To demonstrate this lack of understanding, I cite a passage from an article circulated by the WVS via their public account on Chinese social media WeChat toward the end of 2014. This article aimed to explain and interpret the meaning of the so-called 'self-help volunteering' at WVS.

> Let's give an example: the leader of our dance team, Fan, brought the migrant women together for dance practice. Is that volunteering? Since she is one of us and is present here every day, many people do not think so. But if she changed her status and became a citizen of Hangzhou or a cultural worker from a certain volunteer association and then came to teach our workers to dance, would anyone doubt that she is a volunteer? (WVS 2014b).

This hypothetical question about switching positions goes to the heart of repositioning migrant workers in the dualistic imagination. It also reveals the leading cause of this difficulty: the idea that volunteers should help others is so deeply rooted in the mainstream understanding of this topic that a different interpretation could easily be called into question by the migrants themselves.

This difficulty reflects the broader context of the mainstream discourse on volunteerism in China. Because of this form of participation, migrant workers are hardly represented in the dominant volunteer discourse in China, which makes it difficult for them to understand the activities of self-organisation as volunteering.

I proceed to provide reflective insights into how the dominant discourse defines the subject position of migrant workers and how this definition is being negotiated from below in the context of self-organisation.

Ethnographic studies on the subject of volunteerism in China since the beginning of the twenty-first century often seek to answer the question of how official discourses have constituted the volunteer as a new citizen-subject using strategies and technologies of governing, and to what extent the practices of individual volunteers correspond with this (Rolandsen 2008; Chong 2011; Fleischer 2011; Hoffman 2014). Two earlier studies, by Tony Saich (2000) and David Bray (2006), argue that the state's top-down promotion of volunteering in China goes hand in hand with the shift of state responsibility for social services—increasingly taken over by social organisations (*shehui zuzhi*) and community-based actors. Against this background, both students—as the main target group of the Chinese Youth Volunteer Association—and urban residents of the community (*shequ*) are mobilised for volunteering.

The chosen research object of these ethnographic studies, assuming a 'volunteer' to be a subject with a middle-class character, corresponds with the commonly recognised status of migrant workers as 'disadvantaged groups', reduced almost exclusively to the receiving end of volunteer services. 'Those situated in a "middle-class" category, with consumption power and leisure pursuits, have been urged to "donate" time and money as volunteers and philanthropists to support those excluded from the urban system (e.g., rural migrants)' (Hoffman 2014, 1580).

While 'helping others' and 'self-development' constitute the dominant modes of volunteering for urban youth and the middle class, these self-help aspects are also highly relevant for disadvantaged communities. In a typology of the analytical frameworks for volunteering in a global context, developed by Davis Smith (2000), self-help and mutual aid are described as 'probably the oldest form of voluntary action in which people with shared problems, challenges and conditions work together to address or ameliorate them' in terms of socio-economic support, which therefore plays a significant role in the Global South (Rochester et al. 2010, 24–25). However, this paradigm of volunteering related to activism and civil society has often been underestimated compared to the dominance of the 'non-profit paradigm' characterised by service, professionality, formal structure, and unpaid labour (Rochester et al. 2010, 10–11).

Even in the Chinese context, 'mutual aid' forms one of four core principles that have characterised the country's 'volunteer spirit' (*zhiyuanzhe jingshen*) since the 1990s. These can be seen in the keywords: contribution (*fengxian*), kindness (*youai*), mutual aid (*huzhu*), and improvement (*jinbu*). In addition, one of the earliest and most influential volunteer handbooks in China, the *Manual for Beijing Olympic Volunteers* (2006), also listed 'self-help and mutual aid' as a type of volunteering, along with charity and public campaigning (BOCGO 2006, 5). In its implementation, this type of volunteering is associated mainly with urban communities and is based on mutual help among neighbourhoods organised within the framework of Residents' Committees. The 'China Community Volunteer' system, which has allowed nationwide registration since 2005, barely acknowledges the large populations of migrant workers because they are seen as informal dwellers in the city.

Regarding the case of WVS, I observe an ironic contrast: although the principles of self-help and mutual aid are well accepted in 'community volunteerism' in urban neighbourhoods, migrant workers have difficulty associating them with their own activities. Confronted with the power of discursive dominance, any attempt to reposition themselves within the volunteer discourse leads to a discursive struggle that may take a long time to resolve.

Between 'activist' and 'active' citizenship: A reflection on the self-help concept

While efforts to negotiate at a collective level did not achieve their goal, a paradigm shift was recognisable in volunteer discourse within the organisation between 2014 and 2016. In the summer of 2015, during my daily field stay at WVS, I witnessed various debates and scenes of contradictions, either online in the volunteer chat group or face-to-face in the weekly volunteer meetings and in private conversations. During these everyday discourses and practices, the meanings, legitimations, and expectations of volunteering were frequently contested within the organisational context. Consequently, organisational goals concerning the whole group of migrant workers were visibly marginalised in the discussion on motivations for volunteering. In contrast, however, individual volunteers' personal experiences and perceptions gained a higher priority and had a stronger influence on the orientation of volunteer activities. The following year, these changes at the level of self-interpretation and self-understanding were established in the annual plan of WVS's volunteer program. Despite all the organisation's efforts, the core concept of solidarity-based self-help and mutual aid was weakened and eventually marginalised by the new perspective of individualistic self-development.

The experiences of WVS in shaping its discourse on the 'worker volunteer' reveal the contradictory character of self-organised volunteering as a citizenship practice: they demonstrate both the emergence of political subjectivities and some adoption of technologies of the self. More precisely, these practices concern two different, even opposite, subject positions concerning citizenship: 'activistic citizen' and 'active citizen' (Isin 2009). While the political subjectivities of 'activistic citizens' are constituted during the discursive contestations practised by the migrant self-organisation, their self-help logic is somewhat intertwined with the techniques of empowering and cultivating 'active citizens'.

As the analysis in the last section shows, the self-organised migrant workers were already aware of the process of subjection in the dominant discourse. They decided to contest this with their alternative vision of their societal roles and positions. Comparing the self-organised activities of Grassroots and WVS, migrant activists have maintained these collective goals over the years: i.e., to build a network of mutual support, to gain a better image of migrant workers and a voice of their own, and most importantly, to challenge the position of migrant workers in mainstream discourse. By continuing these practices, they formed new political subjectivities and became political subjects of activist citizenship. However, as Cris Shore and Susan Wright (2011, 18) point out, subjects are not always able to engage successfully with the authoritative and hegemonic power of a policy to define a category of people or a problem, because the process of 'puncturing the aura of government policy' contains three stages. The first two stages have been achieved in the case of WVS. As the intended subjects, a group of migrant workers 'realise the processes of subjection involved', and subsequently 'refuse to accept this image of their subject position or take on its norms and priorities as their own'. But the most decisive stage is the last: will they 'become aware that their critiques and aspirations are shared, and mobilise to contest it collectively'? (Shore and Wright 2011).

For this stage, I observed different outcomes from both periods of discourses and programmes linked with 'grassroots' and 'volunteer'. The grassroots discourse was circulated beyond the original group and successfully mobilised migrant workers across the country, reaching a transregional level. By comparison, the poor acceptance of the subject figure 'self-help volunteer' among their migrant volunteers indicates that a collective mobilisation of contesting and negotiating their subject position is not yet a reality.

Besides the changing organisational and political circumstances faced by the organisation, the relevant subject positions themselves made an essential difference. 'Grassroots' can be understood as a marginal subject position opposite the formal citizen subject. Thus, self-positioning as 'grassroots' contains a significantly higher potential for new political subjectivities among migrants from the perspective of 'activist citizens'. 'Volunteer', on the other hand, already establishes itself as the ideal subject position of the 'active citizen' firmly embedded in the existing structures and institutions of modern liberal citizenship politics. Attempts to adopt this concept and negotiate an alternative position as an actor by engaging in such citizenship politics inevitably encounter existing technologies for governing citizens or even (possibly) becoming collaborators in this governance themselves.

This ambivalent position between 'active' and 'activistic' citizenship partly originates in the core concept of migrant self-organisation: 'self-help'. In other historical-societal contexts, the use of self-help schemes for empowering disadvantaged groups implies a link with governing technologies of citizenship, as American anthropologist Barbara Cruikshank proved in her remarkable work on the creation of citizen subject in US welfare policy, *The Will to Empower* (1999). Cruikshank's concept of 'technologies of citizenship' derives from her analysis of the logic of empowerment shared between neoconservative rationalities and left-wing movements in US society. Using this term, she describes the discourses, programmes, and other tactics aimed at governing people in ways that promote their autonomy, self-sufficiency, and political engagement, transforming individual subjects into citizens (Cruikshank 1999, 4). Within this mode of governance, which is voluntary and coercive at the same time, self-help serves as a technique of governing the poor by 'instrumentalizing and maximizing [their] self-interest' (54).

Although her concept was developed in the 'liberal democratic' context of governments and societies, the logic of empowerment and the principle of self-help still cross the boundary of political definitions of governmentality. As Cruikshank points out, despite using the same term or even applying the same strategy, there could be totally divergent intentions behind the schemes and programmes: e.g., whether to organise and mobilise the group for activism and resistance, or to refashion the individuals into active citizens. In this sense, the technologies of citizenship are the links between subjectivity of citizens and their subjection; between activism and discipline (67).

From this angle, the discursive and organisational change in Grassroots and WVS should be understood within the ambiguous relationship between 'acts of citizenship' and 'technologies of citizenship'. In this case study, the logic of self-help applied in migrant self-organisation has been relocated from grassroots solidarity to urban volunteerism. Not only has this category of self-help activity been redefined and reinterpreted, but the linkage to self-improvement and, further, to the mobilisation logic of self-organisation has been reassembled. The group network remains, while the logic of mobilisation was no longer directed against the injustice of social structures but was absorbed by an individualistic logic of integration through self-improvement. This change ultimately led to a weakening or even falling apart of solidarity among migrant workers who had initially struggled against discrimination and disadvantaged social positions. In the end, 'self-help' could neither mobilise the migrant workers for activist engagements nor active participation in volunteering.

These results show parallels with what Daniel Nehring et al. (2016, 59) call the 'politics of self-help', which is located in the political processes of 'social reprogramming and self-reinvention' where broader political mobilisation and social change on a larger community level become secondary to improving one's own self and personal brand. In the broader context, this tendency echoes the dynamics in politics of citizenship where the technologies and 'acts' of citizenship are more often entangled with each other and where collective mobilisation and individual self-development are no longer separate processes.

Conclusion

This chapter analysed citizenship practices in urban China from the angle of activism, in this case, migrant self-organisation. Discursive contestations over the subject positions of migrant workers constitute the political subjectivities of activist citizens, which represent the aspect of migrant citizenship from below. On the other hand, the shift of subject position from 'grassroots' to 'volunteer' within organisational discourse production points to the blurring of the boundaries between activism and governance in citizenship politics.

The findings of this chapter reveal the ambivalent character of citizenship practices, particularly when informal forms of citizenship and the practices of those constituted as 'others' have become more recognised and established forms. Beyond the context of Chinese society, my conclusion draws attention to the importance of examining outcomes and effects of citizenship practices from a long-term transformative perspective. Contestations over citizenship range from breaking the dichotomous boundary between 'citizen' and 'non-citizen' to dealing with the so called 'less than full' status in fragmented and graduated systems of citizenship. Facing the differences and specifics of political regimes, this investigation and its theorisation of citizenship could benefit from comparative perspectives between societies regarding the connectedness of policy worlds and social movements.

Bibliography

Anagnost, Ann, 2004. 'The Corporeal Politics of Quality (Suzhi)'. *Public Culture*, 16(2): 189-208. doi: 10.1215/08992363-16-2-189.

Beijing Organizing Committee for the Games of the XXIX Olympiad, 2006. *Manual for Beijing Olympic Volunteers*. Zhongguo ren min da xue chu ban she.

Bhambra, Gurminder K. 2014. *Connected Sociologies*. London: Bloomsbury.

Bray, David, 2006. 'Building 'Community': New Strategies of Governance in Urban China'. *Economy and Society*, 35(4), 530–549. doi: 10.1080/03085140600960799.

Bray, David, and Elaine Jeffreys (eds.). 2016. *New Mentalities of Government in China*. Abingdon: Routledge.

Chaudhuri, Bidisha, and Lion Koenig (eds.). 2016. *Politics of the 'Other' in India and China: Western Concepts in Non-Western Contexts*. Abingdon: Routledge.

Chen, Yingfang, 2005. '"Peasant-labor": System and identity' (Chinese version). *Sociological Research (shehuixue yanjiu)*, (3), 119–132.

Chong, Pak Lei G. 2011. 'Volunteers as the "New" Model Citizens: Governing Citizens through Soft Power'. *China Information*, 25(1), 33–59. doi: 10.1177/0920203X10393212.

Cruikshank, Barbara, 1999. *The Will to Empower: Democratic Citizens and Other Subjects*. Ithaca: Cornell University Press.

Fleischer, Friederike. 2011. 'Technology of Self, Technology of Power. Volunteering as Encounter in Guangzhou, China'. *Ethnos*, 76(3), 300–325. doi: 10.1080/00141844.2011.565126.

Gilroy, Paul, Ruth Wilson Gilmore, and Stuart Hall (eds.). 2021. *Selected Writings on Race and Difference*. Durham NC: Duke University Press.

Gleiss, Marielle Stigum, Elin Sæther, and Kathinka Fürst. 2019. 'Re-theorizing Civil Society in China: Agency and the discursive politics of civil society engagement'. *China Information*, 33(1), 3–22. doi: 10.1177/0920203X18790395.

Goldring, Luin, Carolina Berinstein, and Judith K. Bernhard. 2009. 'Institutionalizing Precarious Migratory Status in Canada'. *Citizenship Studies*, 13(3), 239–265. doi: 10.1080/13621020902850643.

Grassroots. 2006. 'The Three Steps of Grassroots Dream' (28 November). https://web.archive.org/web/20070113112243/http://www.hzcgzj.com:80/b6.sbo.2.htm.

Grassroots. 2007. 'About Us' (7 May). https://web.archive.org/web/20070625072111/http://www.hzcgzj.com:80/b5.htm.

Grassroots. 2008. 'The Strategic Planning of Grassroots' (8 May). https://web.archive.org/web/20090106234717/http://www.hzcgzj.com/b5zlgh.htm

Guo, Zhonghua, and Sujian Guo (eds.). 2015. *Theorizing Chinese Citizenship*. Lanham MA: Lexington Books.

Hall, Stuart (ed.). 2012. *Representation: Cultural Representations and Signifying Practices*. Thousand Oaks CA: SAGE.

Hall, Stuart. 2021. 'New Ethnicities' in Paul Gilroy, Ruth Wilson Gilmore, and Stuart Hall (eds.), *Selected Writings on Race and Difference* (246–256). Durham NC: Duke University Press.

Hoffman, Lisa M. 2014. 'The Urban, Politics and Subject Formation', *International Journal of Urban and Regional Research*, 38(5): 1576-1588. Doi: 10.1111/1468–2427.12145.

Isin, Engin F. 2002a. *Being Political: Genealogies of Citizenship*. Minneapolis: University of Minnesota Press.

Isin, Engin F. 2002b. 'City, Democracy and Citizenship: Historical Images, Contemporary Practices' in Engin F. Isin and Bryan S. Turner (eds.), *Handbook of Citizenship Studies* (305–316). Thousand Oaks CA: SAGE.

Isin, Engin F. 2008. 'Theorizing Acts of Citizenship' in Engin F. Isin and Greg Marc Nielsen (eds.), *Acts of Citizenship* (15–43). London: Zed Books.

Isin, Engin F. 2009. 'Citizenship in Flux: The Figure of the Activist Citizen', *Subjectivity*, 29(1): 367–388. Doi: 10.1057/sub.2009.25.

Isin, Engin F. 2012. 'Citizenship after Orientalism: An Unfinished Project'. *Citizenship Studies*, 16(5–6), 563-572. Doi: 10.1080/13621025.2012.698480.

Isin, Engin F. and Greg Marc Nielsen (eds.). 2008. *Acts of Citizenship*. London: Zed Books.

Isin, Engin F. and Bryan S. Turner (eds.). 2002. *Handbook of Citizenship Studies*. Thousand Oaks CA: SAGE.

Jacka, Tamara. 2009. 'Cultivating Citizens: *Suzhi* (Quality) Discourse in the PRC', *Positions: East Asia Cultures Critique*, 17(3), 523–535. Doi: 10.1215/10679847-2009-013.

Jakimów, Małgorzata. 2012. 'Chinese Citizenship 'After Orientalism': Academic Narratives on Internal Migrants in China', *Citizenship Studies*, 16(5–6), 657–671. Doi: 10.1080/13621025.2012.698488.

Jakimów, Małgorzata. 2015. 'Understanding Citizenship beyond the Hukou System: The Role of Migrant Worker NGOs in Transformation of Citizenship in China' in Zhonghua Guo and Sujian Guo (eds.), *Theorizing Chinese Citizenship* (111–132). Lanham MA: Lexington Books.

Jakimów, Małgorzata. 2017. 'Resistance through Accommodation: A Citizenship Approach to Migrant Worker NGOs in China', *Journal of Contemporary China*, 26(108): 915–930. Doi: 10.1080/10670564.2017.1337316.

Jakimów, Małgorzata. 2022. 'Activist Citizenship in Non-Western and Non-democratic Contexts: How to Define "Acts of Citizenship"', *Citizenship Studies*, 26(4-5), 505–511. Doi: 10.1080/13621025.2022.2091232.

Jakimów, Małgorzata and Elena Barabantseva. 2016. '"Othering" in the Construction of Chinese Citizenship' in Bidisha Chaudhuri and Lion Koenig (eds.) *Politics of the 'Other' in India and China: Western Concepts in Non-Western Context* (195–206). Abingdon: Routledge.

Kipnis, Andrew. 2006. 'Suzhi: A Keyword Approach', *The China Quarterly*, 186, 295–313. Doi: 10.1017/S0305741006000166.

Marshall, Thomas Humphrey. 1950. *Citizenship and Social Class and Other Essays*. Cambridge: Cambridge University Press.

Mezzadra, Sandro and Brett Neilson. 2013. *Border as Method or the Multiplication of Labor*. Durham NC: Duke University Press.

Nehring, Daniel, Emmanuel Alvarado, Eric C. Hendriks, and Dylan Kerrigan (eds.). 2016. *Transnational Popular Psychology and the Global Self-Help Industry: The Politics of Contemporary Social Change*. London: Palgrave Macmillan.

Nyers, Peter and Rygiel Kim. 2012. *Citizenship, Migrant Activism and the Politics of Movement*. Abingdon: Routledge.

Ong, Aihwa. 2005. 'Ecologies of Expertise: Assembling Flows, Managing Citizenship' in Aihwa Ong and Stephen J. Collier (eds.), *Global Assemblages: Technology, politics, and ethics as anthropological problems* (337–353). Oxford: Blackwell.

Ong, Aihwa and Stephen J. Collier (eds.). 2005. *Global Assemblages: Technology, Politics, and Ethics as Anthropological Problems*. Oxford: Blackwell.

Pun, Ngai. 2006. *Made in China: Women Factory Workers in a Global Workplace*. Durham NC: Duke University Press.

Ren, Xuefei. 2012. 'Dancing with the State. Migrant Workers, NGOs, and the Remaking of Urban Citizenship in China' in Michael P. Smith and Michael McQuarrie (eds.), *Remaking Urban Citizenship: Organizations, Institutions, and the Right to the City* (99–108). Piscataway: Transaction.

Rochester, Colin, Angela Ellis Paine, Steven Howlett, and Meta Zimmeck. 2010. *Volunteering and Society in the 21st Century*. London: Palgrave Macmillan.

Rolandsen, Unn Målfrid. 2008. 'A Collective of Their Own: Young Volunteers at the Fringes of the Party Realm', *European Journal of East Asian Studies*, 7(1), 101–129. Doi: 10.1163/156805808X333938.

Saich, Tony. 2000. 'Negotiating the State: The Development of Social Organizations in China', *The China Quarterly*, 161, 124-141. Doi: 10.1017/S0305741000003969.

Sassen, Saskia. 2002. 'Towards Post-National and Denationalized Citizenship' in Engin F. Isin and Bryan S. Turner (eds.), *Handbook of Citizenship Studies* (277–291). Thousand Oaks CA: SAGE.

Shore, Cris, Davide Però, and Susan Wright (eds.). 2011. *Policy Worlds: Anthropology and the Analysis of Contemporary Power*. Oxford NY: Berghahn Books.

Smith, David Horton. 1997. 'The Rest of the Nonprofit Sector: Grassroots Associations as the Dark Matter Ignored in Prevailing "Flat Earth" Maps of the Sector', *Nonprofit and Voluntary Sector Quarterly*, 26(2), 114-131. doi: 10.1177/0899764097262002.

Smith, Michael P. and Michael McQuarrie (eds.). 2012. *Remaking Urban Citizenship: Organizations, Institutions, and the Right to the City*. Piscataway: Transaction.

State Council of China. 1998. *Regulations on the Registration and Management of Social Organizations*.

Sun, Wanning. 2009. '*Suzhi* on the Move: Body, Place, and Power', *Positions: East Asia Cultures Critique*, 17(3), 617–642. doi: 10.1215/10679847-2009-017.

Swider, Sarah. 2015. 'Reshaping China's Urban Citizenship: Street Vendors, Chengguan and Struggles over the Right to the City', *Critical Sociology*, 41(4–5), 701–716. doi: 10.1177/0896920514529676.

Tomba, Luigi. 2009. 'Of Quality, Harmony, and Community: Civilization and the Middle Class in Urban China', *Positions: East Asia Cultures Critique*, 17(3), 591–616. doi: 10.1215/10679847-2009-016.

Walters, William. 2012. *Governmentality: Critical Encounters*. Abingdon: Routledge.

Woodman, Sophia. 2017. 'Legitimating Exclusion and Inclusion: "Culture", education and entitlement to local urban citizenship in Tianjin and Lanzhou', *Citizenship Studies*, 21(7), 755–772. doi: 10.1080/13621025.2017.1353739.

Woodman, Sophia and Zhonghua Guo. 2017. 'Introduction: Practicing Citizenship in Contemporary China', *Citizenship Studies*, 21(7), 737–754. doi: 10.1080/13621025.2017.1353740.

WVS. 2012. 'Worker Volunteer: A Change in the Role of Disadvantaged Groups', *Grassroots Magazine*, (13), Prologue.

WVS. 2014a. 'Historical Mission of Worker Volunteers'. https://mp.weixin.qq.com/s/pC2vwwKVqIeXeOcf25Bstw.

WVS. 2014b. 'WVS has a Unique Team of Worker Volunteers'. https://mp.weixin.qq.com/s/FMMoKWubB5gs5FjXTCD1hw.

Xiong, Yihan and Miao Li. 2017. 'Citizenship Education as NGO Intervention: Turning Migrant Children in Shanghai into "New Citizens"', *Citizenship Studies*, 21(7), 792–808. doi: 10.1080/13621025.2017.1353741.

Xu, W. 2006. 'Grassroots' (6 August). http://blog.sina.com.cn/s/blog_95a66896010165oq.html.

Yan, Hairong. 2003. 'Neoliberal Governmentality and Neohumanism: Organizing Suzhi/Value Flow through Labor Recruitment Networks', *Cultural Anthropology*, 18(4), 493–523. doi: 10.1525/can.2003.18.4.493.

Yan, Hairong. 2008. *New Masters, New Servants: Migration, Development, and Women Workers in China*. Durham NC: Duke University Press.

Zhang, Chenchen. 2018. 'Governing Neoliberal Authoritarian Citizenship: Theorizing *Hukou* and the Changing Mobility Regime in China', *Citizenship Studies*, 22(8), 855–881. doi: 10.1080/13621025.2018.1531824.

Zhang, Li. 2002. 'Spatiality and Urban Citizenship in Late Socialist China', *Public Culture*, 14(2), 311–334. doi: 10.1215/08992363-14-2-311.

Zhang, Li and Gui-xin Wang. 2010. 'Urban Citizenship of Rural Migrants in Reform-era China', *Citizenship Studies*, 14(2), 145–166. doi: 10.1080/13621021003594809.

About the author

Jun Chu studied Sociology and completed her PhD in Cultural Anthropology and European Ethnology at the University of Göttingen in the summer of 2022. Her research focused on the negotiation and contestation of urban citizenship in the field of self-organisation and activism, with the case of migrant workers in urban China. Civil society, policy, urban governance and social transformation are among her broader research interests. She is currently a researcher at the Institute for Social Innovation (ISInova) in Berlin.
jun.chu.goe@gmail.com

4. Youth Leadership and Urban Citizenship in Indonesian Cities

Lily Song, John Taylor, and Fildzah Husna Amalina

Abstract: In Indonesia, youth and democracy have been intertwined in several politically-charged and value-laden ways that have partly fuelled a sense of ambivalence and scepticism among young people. Applying the 'right to the city' concept in the Indonesian context to explore youth engagement in urban and environmental dilemmas at localised scales helps open up new conceptions and practices of citizenship and consider related opportunities, tensions, and strategies. This chapter examines the Urban Citizenship Academy (UCA), which enables young people across Indonesian cities to take action on urban social issues. Our analysis and findings address the role of youth leadership and activism, education and training, and intergenerational movement-building in promoting future practices of active and transformative urban citizenship.

Keywords: Youth, democracy, urban citizenship, right to the city, Indonesia

Introduction

Within Indonesia's relatively young democracy, youth and democracy have been intertwined in several important ways. In 1998, President Suharto's resignation ended a 31-year authoritarian regime marked by widespread corruption. Led by student activists, the *Reformasi* movement not only toppled the New Order military dictatorship but further ushered in a series of democratic reforms. Since the colonial era, *pemuda*, ('youth', statistically defined as ages sixteen to thirty by Indonesian Law No. 40/2009) played an integral role in nation-building. Key events include the founding of the first Indonesian national organisation *Budi Utomo* in 1908, the declaration of the *Sumpah Pemuda* ('youth pledge' by young Indonesian nationalists)

Gregory Bracken, Paul Rabé, Nurul Azreen Azlan (eds), *Future Practices of Citizenship in Asia and the West: Care of the Self* (*Volume III*). Taylor & Francis Group, 2025
DOI: 10.5117/9789048562077_CH04

in 1928, the 1945 struggle for independence from the Dutch, Generation 66's overthrow of Soekarno's Old Order, and mass student protests of 1974 and 1978 against Suharto's repressive New Order (Lee 2016, 7). Continuing the historical fervour of 'pemuda nationalism', Generation 98, or the '*Reformasi* generation', executed Indonesia's transition to democracy. Among the tensions and contradictions around institutionalising democracy after 1998 were the symbolic power accorded to *pemuda*, subsequent co-optation of youth organising and activism by political party machines intent on maintaining elite domination, and popularised associations of youth with violence (Lee 2016).

Besides reinstating free elections and restructuring the central government, including its judiciary, legislature, and executive divisions, the *Reformasi* movement spurred politico-institutional and territorial decentralisation of governance (Phelps et al. 2014; Bunnell et al. 2013). New laws provided provincial governments, regencies (administrative units directly under provinces, similar to municipalities), and cities with more autonomy to regulate and manage the aspirations of local communities, hold local elections, and create their own policies and initiatives. Decentralisation also meant that cities would not receive as many fiscal transfers from the central government but would have to raise their own taxes and other public revenues. Hence, the period beginning in the early 2000s brought unprecedented opportunities and challenges to cities, with mayors having to appeal to local voters on their ability to understand and respond to local needs, while also having to seek new local sources to finance these initiatives (Holtzappel and Ramstedt 2009). Moreover, the effects of decentralisation on the cities and their development pathways were by no means even; many struggled to find resources to respond to and address gaps in basic infrastructure and social services (Widianingsih and Morrell 2007).

The post-*Reformasi* era further brought significant changes to Indonesian civil society. The 2000s saw the expansion of an Indonesian civil society that was newly attentive to filling emerging spaces of democratic governance, particularly at local levels (Das 2015). Where young people led oppositional, anti-government protests during Suharto's rule, many now joined the ranks of non-governmental and civil society organisations. In contrast to their highly visible roles in previous political formation and nation-building episodes, young Indonesians generally exhibited a more ambivalent relationship with politics—in some cases, finding a place within party politics and, in other cases, avoiding politics entirely. At the same time, youth comprised a large proportion of the population. By 2010, almost 20 percent of the Indonesian population was below ten years old, around 37 percent was below 20 years old, and around half of the population was below 30 years old. Despite declining fertility rates, the Indonesian median age remained relatively low at 28.7 years in 2020, compared to 38 years in both China and the United States. The country's youth population increasingly concentrated in cities. By 2010, 53.5 percent of Indonesian youth resided in urban areas compared to 46.5 in rural areas (UNFPA Indonesia 2014). Today, young people stand at the forefront of technological adoption in Indonesia, a country with the fourth-highest number of internet users as of 2022—coming just behind the United States.

It was in this context of Indonesian democratisation, decentralisation, and urbanisation that Kota Kita was founded as a non-profit participatory planning organisation in 2009. When the Indonesian government established *Musrenbang* ('participatory planning and budgeting') in 2004, the reform process did not necessarily result in many residents engaging with local governments to highlight community aspirations and set public priorities (Rifai et al. 2016). In many cases, local economic and political elites continued to dominate planning and policy discussions about development. Kota Kita initially focused on the budgetary process in Surakarta (colloquially referred to as Solo), collaborating with neighbourhood-elected leaders and resident volunteers to gather and map data on critical urban issues (e.g., sanitation, water, education, poverty, health care) across 51 neighbourhood districts and to inform the budgeting process. The NGO has since worked in more than 20 Indonesian cities, providing civic education, encouraging open access to information, and facilitating citizen participation and collaboration. In 2013, it organised the Urban Social Forum, a civil society-led forum in Indonesia that brings together civil societies, civil servants, practitioners, and students to work towards improving cities. In 2015, Kota Kita initiated the Urban Citizenship Academy to support young people in cities across Indonesia who expressed a desire to address social issues within their urban environments with training and mentorship.

This chapter presents a case study of the Urban Citizenship Academy (UCA), which since 2015 has trained multiple cohorts of youth activists across different Indonesian cities to identify and analyse urban problems using community engagement and participatory mapping techniques and formulate and implement intervention plans. We examine the UCA programme, resulting youth-led infrastructure-related projects, and impacts on youth leaders. We begin by reviewing the literature on the 'right to the city', focusing closely on implications for Indonesian urban contexts, young people, and participatory governance. We next present the research design and methodology for the case study, followed by an overview of Kota Kita and the Urban Citizenship Academy, including its goals, programme design, and curriculum. The main section presents embedded studies of four UCA groups, including their achievements and outcomes. Our findings and analysis focus on how the UCA programme shaped urban citizenship and activism among youth participants and UCA's strengths and challenges as a programme. The concluding section discusses the implications of our research findings and analysis for youth leadership and activism, education and training, and intergenerational movement-building in promoting future practices of active and transformative urban citizenship.

Literature review

Traditional notions of citizenship, which burgeoned under the Westphalian system that established state sovereignty as the lynchpin of global governing principles, have centred on the nation-state (Linklater 1998), and Indonesian citizenship is no exception. From the late 17th century, Dutch colonists brought the archipelago of over a thousand ethnicities and tribes under imperialist rule. With Indonesian independence in 1949, a newly established Indonesian government unified over 74 million people of differing ethnicities, languages, and religions (Vickers 2003). Following the violent transition from Soekarno's Old Order to the New Order under General Suharto, complete with anti-communist purges, the Indonesian state defined and enshrined citizenship through the theory and practice of Pancasila (Ricklefs 2008). The Suharto regime promoted the five general principles—belief in one God, civilised humanity, national unity, representative and deliberative democracy, and social justice—as a national ideology in ways that reinforced patriarchy and state paternalism. Every Indonesian student and citizen was indoctrinated to uphold Pancasila principles, with youth playing a central and visible role in annual ceremonies and other political rituals (Lee 2016).

The end of the New Order in 1999 and a wave of democratic reforms sparked by the *Reformasi* movement in the 2000s coincided with burgeoning global urban discourses and social mobilizations around the 'right to the city' (Harvey 2008). Neoliberal global restructuring intensified the power of capital in shaping material life and social relations across locales while devolving government authority from national to local and regional scales and reorienting policies from redistribution to competitiveness. Critical urban researchers and scholars revived Henri Lefebvre's concept of the 'right to the city' (Lefebvre 1968; 1973; 1996) to explore alternative forms of citizenship beyond national, liberal-democratic forms related to shared geography and environment (McCann 2002; Purcell 2003). The right to the city concept emphasised the active and transformative citizenship of urban inhabitants exercising their rights to appropriate urban space and participating in the production of urban space, in opposition to capitalistic logic and power interests. Along with flourishing social movements focused on urban questions, global convenings among human rights activists, environmentalists, NGOs, urban poor social movements, local governments, and international bodies such as the United Nations in the 1990s helped internationalise the right to the city, connect it with human rights frameworks, and launch the Global Platform for the Right to the City in 2014[1].

The right to the city found particular meaning and salience in Indonesia, where democratisation reforms had decentralised government authority to give rise to regional and local autonomy, participatory budgeting and planning, and non-governmental organisations such as Kota Kita. It was relevant to the efforts of democracy activists to cultivate a strong civil society movement and responsive government that could mutually counteract the socio-spatial inequalities and environmental destruction resulting from capitalist urban development. The collectivist approach of the right to the city concept also resonated with Indonesian cultural values compared to dominant liberal interpretations of human rights frameworks focused on individual rights and liberties (Bahtiar et al. 2019). In 2015, Kota Kita joined the Global Platform for the Right to the City (GPR2C), leading right-to-the-city campaigns in Indonesia (Rifai 2017). In addition to helping build the GPR2C network in the Asia Pacific region, Kota Kita organised the annual Urban Social Forum around various themes and topics related to the right to the city, and offered civil society capacity-building programmes such as the Urban Citizenship Academy and Women on Wheels. Such programmes introduced participants to the right to the city concept. They helped civil society groups, such as youth or women, to implement practical strategies for spatial intervention and change with decision-makers and resource holders in government and transnational organisations.

Recalling the political and value-laden roles that young Indonesians have historically played in nation-building and their growing ambivalence towards politics, the Urban Citizenship Academy presents an intriguing case

1 The Global Platform for the Right to the City is an open, flexible, diverse network of civil society and local government organisations committed to political action and social change through the promotion, defence and fulfilment of the Right to the City at all levels, paying special attention to people and communities affected by exclusion and marginalisation.

in cultivating youth engagement in political and social action through the promotion, defence, and fulfilment of the right to the city. In fact, previous studies of community governance processes in *kampungs* ('low-income urban villages') in Java have found that younger Indonesians play weaker roles in neighbourhood-level settings. Explanatory sociocultural factors include traditional age-based hierarchies, youth avoidance of the social surveillance and control dimensions of neighbourhood administration and community governance procedures dating back to the Japanese colonial and New Order eras, and the outsider status of some young people who are temporarily residing in kampungs while attending school in a new city (Jellinek 2003; Guinness 1997; Sullivan 1986). To what extent and how does the Urban Citizenship Academy's approach of training youth to engage in urban and environmental dilemmas at localised scales help open up new conceptions and practices of citizenship? The programme further provokes questions about the role of youth in building future practices of active and transformative urban citizenship along with related opportunities, tensions, and strategies. Both sets of questions are at the core of this research and are further addressed in the case analysis and discussion.

Research design and methodology

This chapter includes an embedded case study of Kota Kita's Urban Citizenship Academy that presents findings and analysis of the programme and its impacts. The research was designed as a multi-method study combining secondary research, semi-structured interviews, focus-group interviews, reflective discussions, and participant observation between November 2021 and April 2022. In purpose and design, the UCA case study was an applied research project. Members of the research team include a founder of Kota Kita and the Urban Citizenship Academy, UCA programme trainer, and a university-based researcher with previous research experience with the organisation. The project grew out of their shared commitment to promote Kota Kita's organisational learning with respect to the aims, programme, curriculum, training, outcomes, and impacts of the UCA, including on the leadership, activism, and overall development of youth participants. We were also interested in exploring how the UCA programme relates to intergenerational movement building in advancing future active and transformative urban citizenship practices in Indonesia. Hence our units of analysis included Kota Kita as an organisation, the Urban Citizenship Academy as a programme, groups and individuals that completed the UCA training, and the current generation of young people as a part of the larger democracy movement.

The research began with creating a database of groups that completed the UCA training. Among the descriptive data we compiled and input for each group were their locations, project proposal, and team members. As the UCA database did not include information on project outcomes, we inquired with Kota Kita staff, UCA instructors who contacted UCA participants about various project outcomes. We then selected four UCA groups for 'embedded case studies'—seeking a representative sample of urban contexts and issues that youth groups have chosen to take on through the Urban Citizenship Academy. We also prioritised UCA groups that extended their activities beyond the training programme, whether implementing their campaign over a longer period or converting their initiative into a local organisation that would take on additional activities. The four selected teams were Pahlawan Hijau from Solo (2015), Urban Lotus from Banjarmasin (2020), Omah Biopori from Yogyakarta (2016), and Subcyclist from Surabaya (2016). Each addressed a persistent and widespread urban challenge in Indonesia (e.g., land tenure, environmental hazards, water shortages, mobility injustices). We sent invitation emails asking group members to conduct interviews and received a 100 percent response rate. Semi-structured interviews were conducted on Zoom by research team members using a pre-formulated questionnaire. Each interview lasted around one to one and a half hours. The interview solicitations and conversations took place sequentially (one-by-one) from November 2021 to March 2022. In January 2022, we also conducted a focus group interview and reflective discussion on Zoom with UCA founders and staff from Kota Kita, again using a pre-formulated questionnaire. We then followed up with emailed questions and exchanges as needed. Finally, the team regularly scheduled meetings to collaborate on coding and analysis.

Urban Citizenship Academy (UCA) overview

Goals and programme design

Kota Kita created the Urban Citizenship Academy (UCA) programme in 2015 to prepare a younger generation of activists to replicate and scale-up community- and city-level practices addressing urban dilemmas in ways that promote inclusivity, participation, and good governance. While UCA concepts and tools have evolved over the years, the underlying values have remained consistent: empowering marginalised voices in community development, raising citizen awareness around pressing urban problems, promoting informed and evidence-based decision-making, and organising citizens to engage constructively with local governments. Beginning with a pilot training programme with youth groups in Malang (2015), subsequent series of training have taken place in Solo (2015), Yogyakarta (2015, 2016, 2017), Surabaya (2016), Bandung (2017), and other cities. In total, 312 youth (with an upper age limit of 30 years) comprising 64 groups have undergone the twelve-module training.

Kota Kita has disseminated information about the UCA through materials like posters, sharing them with students and youth networks in the city, and posting them on social media to reach potential participants. Participants must form small groups—usually between four and seven people—and apply to the programme with a proposal outlining their motivations, group profile, and proposed project. There is no cost to apply or participate. The groups are selected based on their profiles as community-minded and active change makers, their ability to articulate a clear vision for their communities, and a convincing, transformative proposal for addressing an issue through the UCA programme. The selection process results in an overrepresentation of university students and graduates, a relatively educationally privileged group within Indonesia, and an underrepresentation of low-income workers (we will return to this later in the chapter). While participants largely come from middle-income households, many have resided as students or young professionals in urban poor communities. They are committed to solving specific social problems in their urban locales and environments. They demonstrate the potential to help bridge kampung residents and other marginalised groups with government agencies and decision-makers.

UCA curriculum

The UCA programme comprises twelve training modules, divided into three distinct phases of four modules each. The training component takes place on three weekends, each taking two full days. The entire programme can take up to two months to complete, including the capstone project, which each team develops as part of the UCA.

The first phase, 'Community Mapping', provides participants with a conceptual understanding of citizenship and the city, the potential role of proactive citizens in shaping their urban environment, and the importance of leadership and teamwork. The modules take participants on a walking site visit to observe urban surroundings up close, helping them to gather observational information about the local context while also giving them techniques to engage effectively with local residents and other stakeholders (e.g., facilitating focus group discussions and interviews). In addition to gaining mapping tools, creating a data collection plan, and designing questionnaires, they learn to build trust and good relations as a pivotal basis for community engagement that leads to new ideas and mobilisation around change processes.

During the second phase, 'Data Analysis', the groups are invited to examine and critically reflect upon their collected data and draw conclusions that may inform their actions. The modules introduce spatial analytical tools, problem trees for exploring root causes of issues and potential solutions, and stakeholder analysis for considering who might be affected and involved in urban problems. They emphasise the presence and interests of different stakeholders (e.g., local residents, government officials, businesses, and vulnerable groups), along with the importance of consulting and working closely with them. Through data analysis and discussion of findings and evidence, the groups develop targeted and practicable solutions, finally selecting one for further design and implementation.

In the third and final stage, 'Building an Advocacy Agenda', groups turn their findings, analysis, and proposed solutions into an advocacy campaign strategy. They focus on a specific policy goal and engage strategic stakeholders, like the local government, to achieve their objective. The modules teach them how to articulate and communicate ideas, for example, using posters, social media, short videos, and targeted messages. Participants also develop strategies to raise awareness and mobilise support among new audiences, often focusing on different interest groups. The programme then organises a public exhibition where groups share their work and advocacy campaign strategy. The UCA groups are also invited to give city officials and other stakeholders a final presentation that could lead to further collaboration.

Embedded case studies of four UCA groups

Pahlawan Hijau, Solo (2015)

Among the earliest UCA groups was Pahlawan Hijau, or 'Green Heroes', made up of three women students, who participated in the 2015 UCA training in Solo, a city in Central Java with a population of over 500,000. One of the members, Evi (now aged 27), was a newcomer to Solo at the time—a student of history who wanted to find ways to contribute to the neighbourhood she lived in and the city as a whole. Evi and the others already had experience volunteering with the local charity organisation Rumah Hebat Indonesia and working with unhoused children and other vulnerable youth. Their proposed project was to design a hands-on educational curriculum for unhoused children in the neighbourhood of Gilingan to teach them about the environmental and health risks of the river where they played. As relatively young UCA participants, the women had some experience in community work but had yet to engage with local government or have an informed understanding of city policies.

According to Evi, the UCA training equipped her team with practical skills to develop a better sense of the problem and a set of educational materials for children. Some of the most instrumental modules were the site visit and mapping exercise, which helped them to understand the land use and spatial context surrounding the river and relate the environmental hazards to where the children played. Learning concepts and tools of community engagement allowed them to approach different community groups and bring previously marginalised voices into larger conversations. The problem tree helped them to identify, tease out, and scrutinise the root causes of water pollution. Finally, the advocacy campaign was critical in turning their analysis into a policy-based strategy. Evi shared that before this module, she was unaware of what advocacy meant or of the need to engage government officials towards whom Pahlawan Hijau members had previously been sceptical. The UCA course, however, convinced them of the need to engage with key decision-makers to address complex issues related to the environment and at-risk youth, leading them to work collaboratively with the *Lurah*, or neighbourhood chief.

Thanks to the group's resourcefulness, Pahlawan Hijau succeeded in raising money to implement their proposal and replicated the curriculum with a community on the island of Maluku. Through their university's Student Study-Service programme, they introduced an environmental education curriculum for young people in rural Maluku. There, the initiative continued under the name 'Rumah Hebat Indonesia' for nearly three years before folding for reasons beyond the group's control. Evi thereafter entered a career in development, applying skills gained through the UCA in other parts of Indonesia. Central to Evi's trajectory has been the use of mapping to work with local communities, particularly as an analytical and communication tool.

***Urban Lotus, Banjarmasin* (2020)**

Among the most recent UCA groups is Urban Lotus, comprising four university graduates who participated in the 2020 training in Banjarmasin, a city in South Kalimantan with a population of over 700,000. One Urban Lotus member, Yanti (aged 26 at the time), related that she and other group members had been volunteers at a local chapter of the national Turun Tangan charity. Still, they wanted to deepen and sustain their involvement with local communities in their city. Urban Lotus proposed raising public awareness of the conditions of Banjarmasin's impoverished riverbank communities, many of whom were threatened by tenure insecurity. They wanted the local government and other groups to have more regard for riverbank communities' heritage and social value.

Group members expressed enthusiasm for training modules in which they learned how to do transect walks, map local conditions and community assets, and engage with local community leaders and residents through focus-group discussions and data collection. During the community visit and data collection exercise, the group began to perceive the complexity of issues faced by riverbank communities and the extent to which they were marginalised and neglected by local authorities. Yanti noted the valuable lesson of learning to share collected data with the communities they visited—to validate and expand on findings. She also found digital video-making skills useful in enabling visual articulation of resident perspectives through short but communicative accounts that could have more reach and influence than raw data.

By the end of the UCA course, Urban Lotus had produced a video that narrates the history, current challenges, and community aspirations of Sungai Jingah residents, based on shared discussions. The video was widely circulated on YouTube and other social media platforms as part of an advocacy campaign proposing an upgrading policy for riverbank communities. Although the team did not continue working together after the UCA training, Yanti used the experience to begin her career as an activist and development worker in Banjarmasin. Previously reluctant to work with local government and push for policy change due to her belief that she would not be respected because of her age and lack of experience, Yanti gained experience, data and analysis skills, and confidence through UCA. As a demonstrably skilled, passionate, and committed professional, she now regularly collaborates with a variety of different groups in the city, including other activists, NGOs, government officials, and the Mayor of Banjarmasin regarding various issues like urban inclusivity and the right to the city.

Omah Biopori, Yogyakarta (2016)

Two UCA trainings took place in 2016. Omah Biopori, a group of five urban planning students, participated in the training in Yogyakarta, the Javanese capital city and cultural hub with a population of over 400,000. Brought to the city from different parts of the country, the students lived in boarding houses in low-income urban villages, known as *kampungs*, on the banks of the Code River. This experience exposed them to poor communities' environmental challenges, such as water scarcity. While the group lacked prior experience working on social issues, they wanted to develop a closer relationship with their host communities and to help in some way. Their project proposal promoted biopores ('biopore infiltration holes') as a sustainable and low-tech solution to the community's interlinked and compounding problems, including water shortages, land subsidence, flooding, and soil erosion[2].

Reflecting on his experiences and takeaways related to the UCA programme, Muhammad Irfan (now 26), shared that the UCA modules on community engagement were particularly useful to Omah Biopori. Their university studies had not prepared them to engage with local communities as a way to understand the local context better. However, the site visit taught them to engage effectively with local leaders and communicate in non-technical, accessible language. From the UCA programme, the team also learned the importance of dedicating time to build trust and understanding with residents about one's intentions and interpretation of the issues. Effective communication and trust-building were essential for installing and maintaining biopores, which would require deep involvement from community members. The problem tree exercise helped the group to better understand the multiple dimensions of water scarcity as a complex urban issue.

The group ultimately could not raise adequate resources to hire the equipment necessary to dig and install biopore infiltration holes in the community. However, the campaign successfully engaged residents and raised awareness about water-related issues and the contributing factors, partly by creating educational posters. As students, the group rarely participated in *gotong royong* ('community works projects') within the kampung communities where they temporarily resided. However, outside the institutionalised venues and procedures of community governance, its members were eager to share their knowledge and help raise awareness about environmental problems that they themselves felt they contributed to. On a personal and professional level, Irfan has taken these lessons into his own life as an urban planner in the private sector, placing great importance on outreach and listening to local populations when implementing urban infrastructure projects.

2 Biopore infiltration holes apply principles of water infiltration to increase the capacity of soil to absorb rain water as a means of flood prevention. Cylindrical holes (diameter 10–30cm) are made into the ground at depths shallower than the water table and filled with organic waste. Through the activities of soil organisms such as worms, plant roots, termites, and other fauna, the holes fill with air and water, serving as flow paths that prevent rainwater from going directly into the sewer.

Subcyclist, Surabaya (2016)

Subcyclist, a portmanteau term combining the words 'Surabaya' and 'cyclist', completed the 2016 UCA training in Surabaya, Indonesia's second-largest city with a population of over 2.8 million. At the time, the three members were young graduates and professionals living in Surabaya, who wanted to share with others their twofold loves: cycling and the local football team, *Persebaya Surabaya*. Their idea was to involve the existing community of football fans (locally known as *Bonek*) to promote bicycling and reduce traffic, congestion, and pollution in the city. Subcyclist also sought to use bicycling to raise awareness about social inequality. While during the colonial era working-class Indonesians of every age and gender widely commuted by bicycle, current recreational cycling tends to be more popular among young men and middle-income groups, some of whom are less cognisant of class segregation and injustices.

The leader and co-founder of the Subcyclist group, Inanta (now aged 35), recalled a moment of awakening during the UCA training field trip while visiting a Surabaya *kampung*. He suddenly saw the extent to which so many of the city's problems, which especially plagued low-income communities, were invisible to the more privileged. Notwithstanding the spatial proximity between the rich and poor, the social and economic contrasts were jarring. Inanta resolved to use bicycling to raise popular awareness about the living conditions and needs of different groups across Surabaya neighbourhoods, as well as to develop innovative solutions. The problem tree helped Subcyclist identify problems and explore solutions, including a citywide campaign to turn at least 1 percent of Surabaya citizens into cyclists. Stakeholder analysis further indicated the necessity of working with local government agencies to change public space and transportation policies to promote bicycling, an option they had never before considered.

After its members had undergone the UCA training, Subcyclist became a popular movement in Surabaya. Between 2016 and 2020 (until the pandemic curtailed outdoor activities), they organised weekly bicycle excursions for fellow football fans of all ages to explore new city areas. During these excursions, they regularly visited *kampungs* and engaged community leaders to identify key challenges and brainstorm interventions the Subcyclist group could help undertake– for example, by promoting cultural events or creating bicycle paths through kampungs and inviting the public to use them. Many of the ideas they put forward and implemented related to walking and bicycling help to promote internal tourism and greater accessibility and trigger long-term public investments and economic development opportunities. Using social media, Subcyclist members have also propagated their campaign beyond Surabaya in other cities, such as Bandung, the capital city of West Java with a population of over 2.4 million.

Table 4.1. Summary of four UCA case studies.

UCA Group	City (date)	Key features	Lessons
Pahlawan Hijau	Solo (2015)	– Educational curriculum raised awareness about environmental and health risks of rivers. – Engaged neighbourhood-level government.	– Mapping and stakeholder analysis developed insightful understanding of problem. – Advocacy campaign turned analysis into policy ideas. – Educational tools can be replicated across other cities.
Subcyclist	Surabaya (2016)	– Working with established football fan community enabled extensive outreach. – Promoted cycling while driving civic activism and community advocacy.	– Stakeholder mapping surfaced importance of advocating to local government to promote bicycling. – Problem tree exercise and target setting helped focus the activity. – Consistent social media presence promotes longer-term success.
Omah Biopori	Yogyakarta (2016)	– Accessible communication material engaged diverse community residents. – Explored low-tech solution for community interventions.	– Community residents are happy to learn from students. – Funding of infrastructure investments continues to be a challenge.
Urban Lotus	Banjarmasin (2020)	– Video campaign about impoverished riverbank communities widely circulated through social media networks.	– Site-based, interactive learning crystalised focus on advocacy campaign proposing upgrading policy for riverbank communities.

Findings and analysis: How did the UCA shape urban citizenship and activism among young participants?

Cultivating place-based identity and belonging

Several interviewees touched on how the Urban Citizenship Academy affirmed and shaped their sense of place-based identity and belonging. Members of the Omah Biopori group shared how they, as students, had felt like outsiders leading parallel lives to those of their host communities and struggled to engage with their neighbours. At the same time, the members developed a strong sense of responsibility for the problems they saw and wanted to understand them better, create a dialogue, and build relationships with neighbours and community leaders. Others echoed the desire to redefine their identity, not to be a transitory student, outsider, young person, or otherwise peripheral actor but to contribute to the local community. For example, Evi from Pahlawan Hijau in Solo underscored that anyone could become 'more of a citizen of the city', even if one is an outsider, by contributing to the urban community. In her words, 'I have this principle, that wherever I live… I need to make a contribution to the community… as a citizen, as a woman, as a student, as an academic, as a researcher, as an activist… as a human'. Where these young people sought to be more locally embedded, the UCA provided them with the concepts and tools to take action.

Forging collective notions of urban citizenship

Interestingly, most UCA participants deemphasized their identities as youth leaders and activists and focused on other urban inhabitants when reflecting on their experiences of the UCA and discussing implications for urban citizenship. Yanti from Urban Lotus said, 'Citizenship means to make the people feel that they have rights to the city, [so] they can speak out about their aspirations… [It means making] everyone feel like they are part of the city itself'. This informed her mission to empower communities to use their voices to speak up and push for positive change. She said, 'We want the aspirations to come directly from the community'. Her group had come together after members were dissatisfied by the arms-length and hierarchical nature of charity work and sought a closer connection with riverbank communities in Banjarmasin. A Subcyclist member likewise highlighted interpersonal and relational dimensions of urban citizenship, 'Being a citizen is, first, not to disturb [the rights of] other citizens. Secondly, it is even better if you can be useful to others'. Such examples of leadership and activism do not focus so much on youth as on fellow urban inhabitants and their right to the city.

Bridging gaps and divides in the city

UCA participants tapped into their position as students and young people to access knowledge, skills, and tools to bridge informational gaps and contribute to urban problem-solving. Pahlawan Hijau and Omah Biopori connected people in low-income riverbank communities with crucial information by developing material in concise and straightforward language. The former taught young children in Gilingan about the environmental and health risks posed by the river where they played. At the same time, the latter engaged residents and raised awareness about water-related issues and the contributing factors along the Gajahwong River. Though unable to address the drivers of the environmental conditions without government intervention, they could, in the interim, raise community awareness. Pahlawan Hijau's Evi emphasised that citizens need to push their government to see and address community problems and include marginalised voices. In the case of Surabaya's Subcyclist, they directly connected kampung communities with other Surabayans through new cycling routes and activities, as well as social media campaigns and cultural events.

Reiterating youth leadership and activism through urban citizenship

UCA participants widely expressed scepticism about *pemuda* ('youth') identity and politics, some citing instances of youth co-optation by powerful interests. This degree of self-consciousness and apprehension led some groups to be wary of reaching out to and working with government agencies, and instead to seek alternative channels. All UCA groups designed their advocacy campaigns using digital technology (e.g., smartphones for filming and video editing) and social media (e.g., Facebook for disseminating information and mobilising people). Groups like Subcyclist and Urban Lotus harnessed technologies to raise awareness and connect people at very little cost, and to do so far and wide amongst new social groups that could help to advocate for urban policy, planning, and development changes. At the same time, the UCA helped many youth realise the importance of engaging decision-makers in addressing complex urban issues. At least some interviewees appear to have overcome their reservations about government and work with public agencies and officials in their subsequent professional capacities.

Programmatic strengths and challenges of UCA

Urban issues are complex by their very nature, and the ones that the UCA groups chose to contend with included some of the most deep-rooted problems faced by Indonesian cities today. Land tenure, water shortages, lack of mobility, and environmental hazards are complex, challenging issues with few easy, short-term remedies. The UCA's structured curriculum and training process equipped young people with otherwise limited resources and experience to begin to understand the local context with input from community residents and leaders, to develop a strategy focused on target groups and key messages within a specific geography, and to intervene in ways that could bring about some positive impact at the local scale. UCA modules and tools considered particularly helpful among interviewed participants included: 1) community mapping activities, which cultivated spatial awareness of social conditions on a local scale; 2) the problem tree, which helped to distinguish multiple sources of problems along with their different impacts; 3) the stakeholder analysis, which helped identify various stakeholders and decision-makers; and 4) the advocacy campaign strategy, which allowed for synthesis of findings and analysis into a focused and practicable solution.

One of the challenges faced by the UCA programme is to sustain youth initiatives beyond the duration of the training. This is not to understate the impact of the longer-term programme on UCA participants who continue to apply UCA lessons as changemakers to other issues and in other localities. Factors such as group composition and cohesion, project focus, timing, and other contextual factors can impact project outcomes. Of the four UCA groups examined, Subcyclist appears the most successful in continuing and expanding their advocacy campaign since the UCA training. This may result from the relative self-sufficiency of the initiative, which relied on their membership of football fans and cyclists rather than technological solutions or external decision-making and funding. For Omah Biopori, the inability to technically demonstrate the biopore infiltration holes, partly because of the cost of acquisition and implementation, constrained growth potential. While UCA is free-of-charge for participants, Kota Kita must cover the cost, and the lack of funds to support project implementation beyond the training can curtail programme outcomes and impact. In the future, fiscal partnership and sponsorship may help extend some UCA projects, and aligning values and objectives with partners and sponsors can help promote consistency and complementarity across Kota Kita's different right-to-the-city initiatives.

Another tension confronting UCA is the selection bias related to the group vision and proposal criteria in its application. It potentially benefits more educationally privileged participants, who have the time and capacity to complete the application process. Kota Kita could conduct community-based outreach to increase the representation of young people from lower-income backgrounds who do not attend university or are otherwise educationally underprivileged. This may help them more directly to advance the right to the city of people and communities most affected by exclusion and marginalisation. It may also help to build long-term capacity within communities, as university-educated students and professionals are more likely to relocate after completing their studies and professional training. That said, many working people from low-income areas have time and capacity limitations, preventing participation in programmes such as UCA. On the other hand, the self-selected youth participants of UCA already bring interest and commitment, and the potential to bridge fellow urban inhabitants with government agencies and processes of public decision-making and resource allocation.

Conclusion

What are the implications of the UCA case study for youth, education, training, and intergenerational movement building in promoting future practices of active and transformative urban citizenship? Young people who have come out of UCA offer an evolving notion and practice of citizenship that is both pragmatic and hopeful. Many are not content to play passive, transient, or disinterested roles in urban environments. UCA offers an alternative vehicle and template for making community, civic, and societal contributions outside the parameters of '*pemuda* nationalism'. Members of Pahlawan Hijau, Urban Lotus, Omah Biopuri, and Subcyclist each dedicated significant time to understanding their local context, learning the needs of the communities they worked with, building relationships and trust, and making concrete interventions, however small. Rather than bold, patriotic acts that might not resonate with local needs, they co-created practical and place-based solutions with others. Claiming and practising the 'right to the city', they actively engaged in urban citizenship and urban transformation as co-constitutive processes that strengthened their sense of belonging and inclusion.

As an education and training programme that targets young activists, the Urban Citizenship Academy is distinct in several ways. The UCA contrasts mainstream educational settings and approaches based on individual merit and achievement. The group and proposal-based application process simultaneously puts forth a conception of relational, collective, place-based, and action-oriented youth leadership and activism. The hands-on approach ameliorates the sense of abstraction, rootlessness, and alienation, which are only exacerbated by digital life and social media culture in traditional higher education settings. By preparing young people to become more socially aware, communicate with diverse publics, and harness their technological skills to expand public awareness around important urban issues, the UCA further strengthens the public sphere at local levels. It helps cultivate new generations of public activists and intellectuals, connects their training with actions involving other urban inhabitants in the public realm, and exerts pressure on public agencies and decision-makers to be more responsive.

Finally, UCA is helping to build an intergenerational movement that can further future active and transformative urban citizenship practices. Youth-led social movements in the pre-*Reformasi* era led to democracy at the national level with the results of regional autonomy, participatory budgeting and planning, and the enforcement of human rights. The post-*Reformasi* context required new skills and capacities among young people and progressive actors, beyond advocating fundamental socio-political issues, to fill the space that had been won—to shape the city's future. UCA pedagogy equips young people to reclaim their identity and power as active citizens within urban spaces at the local scale, thereby furthering the democratic movement. Indeed, youth activists today appear more concerned with problems of waste removal, traffic mitigation, and climate risks than the topic of democracy per se because the communities they live in directly face such issues. The UCA cultivates awareness of their shared responsibility to build cities—that people cannot depend only on the state or the market to meet their needs and that contributing with each other is the most essential 'right to the city'.

Bibliography

Bahtier, Rial Ashari, Aswin Baharuddin, and Seniwati Seniwati. 2019. 'The Strategies of Transnational Social Movement About Right to the City in Indonesia', *Journal of Humanity & Social Justice*, 1(1), 72–94.

Bunnell, Tim, Michelle Miller, Nicholas Phelps, and John Taylor. 2013. 'Urban Development in a Decentralized Indonesia: Two success stories?' *Pacific Affairs*, 86(4), 857–876.

Das, Ashok. 2015. 'Autonomous But Constrained: CBOs and Urban Upgrading in Indonesia', *Cities*, 48, 8–20.

Guinness, Patrick. 1997. 'Constructing and Contesting the Kampung', *Canberra Anthropology*, 20 (1–2), 109–124.

Harvey, David. 2008. 'The Right to the City', *New Left Review*. https://newleftreview.org/issues/ii53/articles/david-harvey-the-right-to-the-city

Holtzappel, Coen J.G. and Martin Ramstedt (eds.). 2009. *Decentralisation and Regional Autonomy in Indonesia: Implementation and Challenges*. Singapore: Institute of Southeast Asian Studies.

Jellinek, Lea. 2003. 'Collapsing Under the Weight of Success: an NGO in Jakarta', *Environment and Urbanization*, 15(1), 171–180.

Lee, Doreen. 2016. *Activist Archives: Youth Culture and the Political Past in Indonesia*. Durham NC: Duke University Press.

Lefebvre, Henri. 1968. *Le Droit à la Ville* [The Right to the City]. Baden-Baden: Anthopos.

Lefebvre, Henri. 1973: *Espace et Politique* [Space and Politics]. Baden-Baden: Anthopos.

Lefebvre, Henri. 1996: *Writings on Cities*. Oxford: Blackwell.

Linklater, Andrew. 1998. *The Transformation of Political Community: Ethical Foundations of the Post-Westphalian Era*. Columbia SC: University of South Carolina Press.

McCann, Eugene J. 2002. 'Space, Citizenship, and the Right to the City: A brief Overview', *GeoJournal*, 58(2/3), 77–79.

Phelps, Nicholas, Tim Bunnell, Michelle Miller, and John Taylor. 2014. 'Urban Inter-referencing within and beyond a Decentralised Indonesia', *Cities*, 39, 37–49.

Purcell, Mark. 2002. 'Excavating Lefebvre: The Right to the City and its Urban Politics of the Inhabitant', *GeoJournal*, 58(2), 99–108.

Purcell, Mark. 2003. 'Citizenship and the Right to the Global City: Reimagining the Capitalist World Order', *International Journal of Urban and Regional Research*, 27(3), 564–590.

Ricklefs, Merle. 2008. *A History of Modern Indonesia Since c. 1200*. Melbourne: Macmillan International Higher Education.

Rifai, Ahmad, Nina Asterina, and Rizqa Hidayani. 2016. *Making all Voices Count: Improving the Transparency, Inclusivity, and Impact of Participatory Budgeting in Indonesian Cities*. https://www.researchgate.net/publication/321049356_Improving_the_transparency_inclusivity_and_impact_of_participatory_budgeting_in_Indonesian_cities.

Sullivan, John. 1986. 'Kampung and State: The Role of Government in the Development of Urban Community in Yogyakarta', *Indonesia*, 41, 63–88.

United Nations Population Fund (UNFPA) Indonesia. 2014. *Annual Report 2014: Delivering Results*.

Vickers, Adrian. 2013. *A History of Modern Indonesia*. Cambridge: Cambridge University Press.

Widianingsih, Ida and Elizabeth Morrell. 2007. 'Participatory Planning in Indonesia: Seeking a New Path to Democracy', *Policy Studies*, 28(1), 1–15.

About the authors

Lily Song is Assistant Professor of Race, Social Justice, and the Built Environment at Northeastern University. As an urban planner, her work focuses on reformulating planning and design to accomplish movement organizers and frontline communities seeking spatial and climate justice. She serves on the advisory board of Yayasan Kota Kita.
l.song@northeastern.edu

John Taylor is an urban planner and the co-founder, and previous director, of Yayasan Kota Kita. He currently chairs the advisory board and has worked on a range of urban development, governance, and planning issues in Latin America, Africa, and Asia.
indojota@gmail.com

Fildzah Husna Amalina is Communications Officer at Yayasan Kota Kita, where she focuses on co-developing, implementing, and evaluating the organisation's communication strategy as part of its urban reform agenda. She is interested in knowledge co-production and coalition building of action-oriented youth-led initiatives.
husna@kotakita.org

Part II.

COVID-19 and Its Responses

5. 'Don't say that!'

Artistic Freedom: Government and Citizen Responses to COVID-19 in South and Southeast Asia

Julie Trébault and Manojna Yeluri

Abstract: Over the course of the COVID-19 pandemic, governments around the world have underreported virus numbers, spread misinformation, or failed to respond adequately to the crisis. Many artists and creative practitioners have used their platform as activists, expressing their criticism, and in return have been aggressively targeted, harassed, and even imprisoned, accused of spreading fake news or misinformation or trying to start civil unrest. The paper examines the implications of this trend for creative expression in the region and explores how governments have manipulated the pandemic to target artists and crush dissidents. It documents specific artist cases to examine the underlying causes and implications of this trend of persecution.

Keywords: Artistic freedom, censorship, COVID-19, South Asia, Southeast Asia

Introduction

The COVID-19 pandemic brought the world to a standstill. It impacted the lives and livelihoods of millions of people in unprecedented ways, particularly members of vulnerable and marginalised groups as well as those with atypical working and living conditions. For the creative sector, the pandemic served a dual role. On the one hand, at a time when much of the world was in disarray, it offered artists and creators a powerful purpose, calling on them to create and share their creations to entertain and inspire people during such dark times. On the other hand, artistic practices and cultural life more broadly were severely curtailed due to the imposition of

Gregory Bracken, Paul Rabé, Nurul Azreen Azlan (eds), *Future Practices of Citizenship in Asia and the West: Care of the Self (Volume III)*. Taylor & Francis Group, 2025
DOI: 10.5117/9789048562077_CH05

curfews and social distancing norms, as well as a lack of financial resources made available to the creative community. As many artists grappled with the loss of community and financial stability, they also found themselves vulnerable to criticism and attacks from those who found their work non-essential or disruptive.

During the course of the COVID-19 pandemic, governments around the world underreported virus numbers, spread misinformation, or failed to respond adequately to the crisis. Many artists and creative practitioners used their platforms to express criticism of how their governments had mismanaged the pandemic. These artists found themselves being aggressively targeted, harassed, and persecuted, accused of spreading fake news or misinformation, or trying to start civil unrest.

In Asia, countries that had already been mired in socio-political upheaval witnessed an aggravating increase in covert and overt instances of censorship and threats to free expression against the backdrop of the pandemic (Yeluri et al. 2021, 43). The numbers were startling, with nearly half of all instances of recorded artist persecution being related to COVID-19 (Freemuse 2021, 15), and the bulk of these instances occurring in the global south—with nearly 14% of violations in the Asia and Pacific region (Freemuse 2021, 20). While not all instances of threats can be attributed to COVID-19-related content, it is nevertheless important to note that the pandemic has had a chilling effect on the state of artistic freedom by restricting opportunities for gathering and free expression through measures such as national security and anti-assembly laws. Additionally, many countries in Asia saw a proliferation of laws designed to control the spread of misinformation about COVID-19. These so-called 'fake news' laws brought with them a number of concerns over privacy, digital security, and censorship. Artists in countries like Bangladesh (Human Rights Watch 2021) were charged under the country's draconian Digital Security Act, for sharing cartoons critical of the country's medical systems. In Malaysia, artist Fahmi Reza (*The Straits Times* 2021) was detained under the country's sedition and communication laws for publishing a Spotify playlist that seemingly insulted the queen over remarks on the availability of vaccines for COVID-19. In certain instances, like that of Filipino artist Bambi Beltran (Rappler 2020), the mere publication of a Facebook post criticising the local government's mismanagement of the pandemic was enough to lead to arrest and detention.

Whether it be through their artwork or their influence, artists played a pivotal role in shaping several pro-democracy movements (*The Conversation* 2020, 25 September) during the pandemic. This role became a cause for concern to many governments and authoritarian regimes that deliberately targeted these artists through a number of measures. This paper aims to present the influence of artists during these tumultuous times, as well as explore the various ways in which governments manipulated the pandemic to target artists and crush dissidents, with an emphasis on South and Southeast Asia.

Owing to the novelty of the subject, the impact of COVID-19 on artistic freedom in South and Southeast Asia has not yet been the subject of extensive scholarly research. However, this paper draws on insights from several scholarly sources that have touched on the subject globally or have sought to better understand the state of artists and the creative economy in Asia, in the aftermath of the COVID-19 pandemic. As the pandemic set in, it exposed many flaws existing in the creative and cultural industries, highlighting the problems of irregular working conditions, exclusionary frameworks, and poor social security infrastructure (Çakır et al. 2022). Many countries used the pandemic as an excuse either to regard artists as non-essential workers or to further inhibit artistic freedom. Interestingly, the existence of gaps in the creative ecosystem, with respect to both socio-economic security and legal safeguards for artistic freedom, existed prior to the onset of the COVID-19 crisis but were found to be greatly exacerbated by it (Cuny 2021). The growing awareness of these pitfalls in the system was a cause for concern, and an urgent call for action to brainstorm solutions to remedy the plight of artists everywhere.

In Asia, more specifically Southeast Asia, these global challenges translated into region-specific difficulties for artists, including a lack of strong policies for the creative and cultural industries. Although the creative industries were considered an important part of the Southeast Asian economy, many artists and initiatives struggled with a lack of consistent funding and cross-sectoral solidarity—problems that were aggravated by the pandemic. Many Southeast Asian countries lacked a shared definition of artistic freedom (Janamohanan et al. 2021). This led to many artists experiencing censorship and backlash from both state and non-state actors in their countries. On a positive note, many artists sought the support of the community to stay afloat during the pandemic, as well as to stay connected with each other during times of social and economic upheaval. During the pandemic, socio-economic and socio-political volatility in Asia grew, resulting in violations of basic fundamental freedoms and human rights. This trend was noted in South Asia, where civic space and freedoms were severely curtailed in countries like Afghanistan, Bangladesh, India, Maldives, Nepal, Pakistan, and Sri Lanka (Blomqvist 2021). These countries witnessed a rise in legislation curtailing digital security and artistic freedom, as well as fake news laws, all of which had evolved as a result of the pandemic.

From the abovementioned insights, it is clear that much of Southeast and South Asia struggled with the pandemic, particularly the creative community. While socio-economic challenges left artists in the regions pondering over the future of their livelihoods and practices, growing tensions with political forces paved the way for critical anxieties surrounding the right to freely express themselves. Stakeholders from the creative, human rights, and legal worlds identified and discussed new and concerning patterns of persecution for artists in Southeast and South Asia as early as December 2020. For instance, discussions in a closed virtual workshop on artistic freedom in Asia, convened by Artists at Risk Connection (ARC), foreshadowed the coup in Myanmar as well as several other instances of persecution later witnessed in Thailand, Malaysia, and Bangladesh (Yeluri et al. 2021). During the pandemic, artists in South and Southeast Asia found themselves grappling with censorship, restricted mobility, and surveillance. Most notably, artists who created and shared their opinions with a view to educate others about COVID-19 or constructively criticise the mismanagement of the pandemic by their governments were faced with rising threats of detention, fines, and imprisonment (Freemuse 2021, 15). Thus, the pandemic facilitated the creation of a landscape of anxiety and fear for artists in the region.

Research design

This paper draws on findings from our work with Artists at Risk Connection Program. PEN America[1] created the Artists at Risk Connection (ARC), an international network to protect persecuted artists around the world and defend their freedom to create. PEN America has fought for freedom of expression and the right to write in peace for nearly one hundred years. Just as writers often become targets of violence, censorship, and other forms of persecution, so too do artists of other disciplines, often without the networks of support that are available to writers and journalists. The Artists at Risk Connection (ARC) expands the organisation's mission to include artists of all disciplines. ARC aims to safeguard the right to artistic freedom of expression and ensure that artists and cultural practitioners everywhere can live and work without fear. ARC achieves this mission by connecting

1 For more information see https://pen.org and https://artistsatriskconnection.org

persecuted artists to our growing global network of resources, facilitating cooperation between human rights and art organisations, amplifying the stories and work of artists at risk, and enhancing the visibility of the field of artistic freedom. Since its creation, ARC has connected more than 500 threatened artists, including visual artists, writers, filmmakers, musicians, cartoonists, and more, living in seventy-one different countries, to organisations that can provide them with urgent relocation funds, legal aid, immigration counsel, public advocacy, emergency grants, fellowship and residency referrals, and/or housing.

The past two years have seen a staggering number of cases in which state authorities and governments have used the COVID-19 pandemic to disguise efforts to restrict free expression and threaten government critics. This global trend of persecution has been prevalent in Asia as well, with a number of disquieting instances arising in countries like Bangladesh, India, Thailand, Myanmar, Malaysia, and the Philippines. To better understand and address these human rights and artistic freedom challenges in Asia, ARC partnered with FORUM-ASIA and the Mekong Cultural Hub to organise two closed-door virtual discussions, one in late 2020 and the other in late 2021. Both of these centred on sharing and consolidating the strategies of various artists and cultural rights defenders in Asia. The closed-door virtual workshops brought together experienced stakeholders from across South, Southeast, East, and Central Asia from diverse professional backgrounds, such as artists, activists, cultural practitioners, lawyers, scholars, and representatives from art and human rights organisations. The objective of these gatherings was to create a safe space and facilitate dialogue on critical issues related to upholding artistic freedom in Asia. They resulted in a stronger network of artists, human rights organisations, and other stakeholders who can share information and resources that are valuable to artists at risk. Additionally, more artists have begun to share their experiences openly, coordinating cross-border solidarity campaigns while offering suggestions on how human rights organisations, lawyers, and policy makers can better assist artists.

The pandemic has also resulted in challenges to relocation efforts and artist mobility, preventing immediate assistance to artists at risk and providing government authorities in various countries with a smoke screen to hide their nefarious efforts to maintain control. This paper aims to better understand this disturbing trend of persecution and is structured into four sections. The first section provides an overview of the relationship between creative expression and COVID-19 in Asia, exploring the role played by artists and art during the pandemic. It lays particular emphasis on the various ways in which artists have helped people stay connected, inspired, and informed during such a tumultuous time. This section also highlights the role of artists as activists and advocates for change, later touching on the state of artistic freedom in Asia and the crackdown on free expression due to COVID-19. The second part of this paper presents case studies of artists who endured threats and censorship in retaliation for their criticism of the poor handling of the COVID-19 crisis. These case studies illustrate the hardships faced by artists from different parts of Asia and highlight the ways in which various legislative measures were implemented during the pandemic in an effort to stifle artists and free expression. The third part explores the various tools and legal measures used by governments to restrict freedom of expression. It includes an overview of disinformation or fake news laws, anti-assembly laws, and similar laws that owed their existence to the pandemic or became more stringent against the backdrop of the global health crisis. Finally, the fourth section of this paper consolidates the findings and recommendations gleaned from discussions on the subject from the aforementioned workshops, as well as from our work with artists at risk.

This paper has been developed based on research obtained from the experiences of the authors (Julie Trébault and Manojna Yeluri) while working for Artists at Risk Connection. Trébault is the director of the programme, overseeing the functioning of the project, and Yeluri is the Asia Regional Representative, strengthening the ARC network in Asia. Through referrals and case work, independent research, as well as by participating in several working groups and networks, ARC has been able to aggregate case studies and anecdotal and quantitative data to allow for further study and analysis of the subject of this paper. The artist case studies mentioned in this paper have been studied and described based either on personal interactions with the artist or on information widely available in the public domain. Owing to the nature of the subject matter, the security and confidentiality of artists who may find themselves in vulnerable situations due to their work, and the novelty of the research, particularly undertaken in the regions of South and Southeast Asia, we acknowledge that the research of this paper cannot be assumed to reflect all situations across the region.

Furthermore, our research and case studies have largely focused on South and Southeast Asian artists. This emphasis is due to our familiarity with a higher number of cases reported from this specific region, alongside relatively greater media coverage of such incidents in comparison to other parts of Asia. Our artist networks in South and Southeast Asia have also been more willing to share their experiences of engaging with COVID-19 through their artwork, and the resulting responses from the governments in their respective countries, thus providing us with a deeper and more dynamic understanding of the state of artistic freedom in this part of Asia, especially against the backdrop of the pandemic. Our paper, while occasionally referring to Central and East Asia, does not delve deeply into the experiences of artists and artistic freedom in these regions. It is intended to serve as a springboard for further research and exploration of the subject that would also include Central and East Asia, as well as to gather enough quantitative and qualitative data to better understand and trace trends of persecution and the impact of COVID-19 on artistic freedom in other countries of Asia.

Creative expression and COVID-19 in South and Southeast Asia

Connecting people through creativity

As the pandemic evolved, so did our collective understanding of the urgent need to explore alternative ways of living, working, and connecting. Beginning in March 2020, governments around the world were advised to call for social distancing and the closure of public spaces (World Health Organisation 2020). The onset of closures and curfews was accompanied by a growing realisation that COVID-19 would not only have a serious impact on healthcare systems and medical access but also on our participation in community and cultural life. In response to a growing sense of anxiety and despair, many artists and cultural practitioners offered creative outlets to help people stay connected, calm, and entertained. These outlets ranged from contributions to audio-visual streaming platforms, social media-enabled workshops, and unconventional artistic presentations like balcony concerts and virtual exhibitions (*The Art Newspaper* 2020).

Despite critical opinions shared by the press on the nonessential nature of artists and their work (*The Strait Times* 2020), creative work proved to be essential in helping the world survive the pandemic. Artists assisted in the pivot of school and education programmes to digital platforms—in Bucheon, South Korea, theatre artists created and facilitated the 'Online Culture Delivery' initiative, a programme that consisted of online book-reading sessions primarily aimed at children (UNESCO no date, 20). Artists collaborated with creative institutions to help digitise and distribute their performances as online shows. An example was the National Centre for Performing Arts (NCPA) in Mumbai, India, which launched the digital 'NCPA@home' series, which showcased performances from their archives (*The Hindu* 2021). In addition to helping people stay connected, artists also worked hard to find alternative ways to keep art forms alive. Cambodia's

Phare Performing Social Enterprise (PPSE) is a powerful example of this. Based in Siem Reap, PPSE typically supports employment for artists working in theatre and the circus arts. With the onset of COVID-19, PPSE pivoted to the creation of programmes that were better suited to local rather than global audiences, as well as providing artists employment opportunities during the pandemic (UNESCO 2021, 50–51). Other artists, like Filipino illustrator Robert Alejandro, announced free drawing classes to be streamed via Facebook. This initiative attracted students of all ages, helping people stay connected to their creativity during tumultuous and uncertain times (*Adobo Magazine* 2020).

Artists as activists and advocates for change

In addition to connecting people, artists and art proved to be instrumental in educating communities during the pandemic. Artists were encouraged to use their work and mediums to communicate information regarding the spread of COVID-19 and the importance of social distancing norms. They also helped to promote vaccination drives (Nikkei Asia 2020). In Vietnam, graphic posters like that of Le Duc Hiep featuring masked health workers were among numerous artworks aimed at instilling a sense of awareness about the COVID-19 virus (*The Guardian* 2020). Singaporean artist Weiman Kow created her unique 'Infocomics' series—a blend of infographics and comic panels — to help share information and tips on how to maintain good hygiene and stay safe during the pandemic (*The Hindu* 2020). In March 2021, the World Health Organisation partnered with stakeholders in the arts world to spearhead a campaign addressing the mental health toll of the pandemic (*The Art Newspaper* 2021).

The creative community also played a powerful role in raising funds for COVID-19 relief efforts. For instance, in India, several arts organisations and institutions worked towards collecting funds for relief efforts (*Business Line* 2021). Against the backdrop of a devastating second wave of coronavirus cases in March 2021, illustrators, musicians, poets, and even bakers in India found themselves raising funds for frontline workers and organisations in an effort to help impacted communities to procure basic supplies like oximeters, thermometers, basic medicines, and masks (Hyperallergic 2021).

On a larger scale, the COVID-19 pandemic highlighted gaps in the existing socio-economic and political framework—gaps that hinted at unequal distribution of financial resources, access to healthcare, and skewed functioning of governments (*The Conversation* 2020, 25 September). Whether it was the slow and sporadic distribution of vaccines, the crumbling medical infrastructure, the lack of safeguards for public hygiene, or the unpreparedness of state authorities in the face of such a crisis, governments in many Asian countries like India, Bangladesh, and Malaysia were under fire for their mismanagement of the pandemic. Leveraging their skill and influence, many artists used their work to express their criticism of their governments, producing artwork that was accessible both in person and digitally. Their artworks reflected the challenges faced by regular citizens, and captured the essence of their daily experiences of navigating the pandemic. Across Asia, a body of work began to emerge, created and shared with the intention of showcasing the plight and responses of ordinary people in the face of disparities and hurdles posed by their governments. These works took the form of visual art, comics, songs, poetry, graphic design, and much more. As artists increasingly turned to their creative disciplines and social media platforms to express their discontentment, they found themselves deliberately targeted by state authorities. It gradually became apparent that governments were using the COVID-19 pandemic as a means to silence artists and citizen responses that were critical of their functioning (*The Art Newspaper* 2021).

Cases of artist persecution and harassment

An understanding of the reactions of governments to artist-led initiatives and responses centred around the crisis of COVID-19 can be obtained through a closer examination of cases of artist persecution in the region. In South and Southeast Asia, artists and creative practitioners found themselves deliberately targeted for their work or statements that were critical of their government's management of the pandemic. This paper discusses four such cases, with the intention of sharing the experiences of the artists while also highlighting the usage of tools such as digital security laws, fake news laws, and social media as a means to curb freedom of expression. Each case belongs to a different country —Malaysia, Bangladesh, the Philippines, and Thailand. These cases have been selected for inclusion in this paper for their widespread coverage in regional media, as well as their ability to demonstrate the far-reaching impacts of government restrictions on artistic freedom in South and Southeast Asia.

Fahmi Reza (Malaysia)

In April 2021, Malaysian graphic artist and filmmaker Fahmi Reza was arrested for allegedly insulting the country's Queen by creating a Spotify playlist using the Queen's image and including the title 'Dengi Ke?' or 'Are you jealous?' The title was a direct reference to a response by the Queen to a query about the status of vaccinations for those interacting with her (*Republic World* 2021). Reza was arrested on grounds of sedition and for violating the Communications and Multimedia Act of 1998.

In June 2021, Reza was arrested and called in for questioning nearly six times for his work criticising and questioning the government (Podcast interview, Fahmi Reza 2021). Reza shared that the people of Malaysia were frustrated with the poor handling of the COVID-19 crisis and took to digital protests in light of social distancing norms and assembly restrictions. The hashtag 'Kerajaan Gagal', meaning 'Failed Government', was regularly trending.

Ultimately, the charges against Reza were dropped in August 2021 without Reza having to appear in court (*FMT* 2021). His arrest received worldwide criticism for being arbitrary and a violation of his right to free speech and expression. The arrest also brought into question the accountability of streaming and social media platforms with respect to the upholding of citizen rights (*Vice* 2021).

***Ahmed Kabir Kishore* (*Bangladesh*)**

Cartoonist Ahmed Kabir Kishore was arrested in May 2020 in Dhaka, under Bangladesh's Digital Security Act, for allegedly 'spreading rumours and misinformation on Facebook about the coronavirus situation'. The cause for his detention was publishing Facebook posts of satirical cartoons and comments critical of the Bangladeshi government's response to the COVID-19 pandemic. Ironically, Kishore was one of the ten people named in the complaint filed against him.

One of the cartoons in question, 'Life in the Time of Corona', depicted caricatures of ruling party leaders, claims of corruption in the health sector, and criticism of the government's mismanagement of the coronavirus pandemic (Committee to Protect Journalists 2020). According to research published by the Committee to Protect Journalists (CPJ), authorities claimed that Kishore had violated Sections 21, 25b(ii), 31, and 35 of the Digital Security Act, related, respectively, to publishing propaganda, false or offensive information, and information that can destroy communal harmony and create unrest.

Kishore was released after ten months of detention, during which he suffered brutal torture at the hands of jail authorities. His injuries included a burst eardrum (CPJ 2021). Following his release, Kishore also reported that he had endured unhygienic living conditions during detention despite the surge in COVID-19 cases at the time. He had been denied bail six times and was only released in the aftermath of the backlash of the death of his fellow accused and cellmate, writer-activist Mushtaq Ahmed, who succumbed to injuries endured during his detention.

'Bambi' Beltran (Philippines)

Filmmaker Maria 'Bambi' Beltran, a recipient of DW's Freedom of Speech Award, was detained on April 19, 2020, for a satirical Facebook post (Rappler 2020). On that day, three men showed up at Beltran's house to arrest her. She asked them to show her the arrest warrant. A few days prior to the incident, Edgardo Labella, the mayor of Cebu City in Central Philippines, had publicly vowed to arrest Beltran for sharing a Facebook post describing her city as the epicentre of coronavirus infections 'in the entire solar system'.

Beltran was arrested on charges of violating the Bayanihan Heal As One Act (Congress of the Philippines 2020), a newly implemented law to tackle the pandemic. This gave President Rodrigo Duterte's administration emergency powers to target people using social media and other platforms to spread 'false information' about COVID-19. Beltran spent three days in police custody and was forced to pay a fine of $800 for violating the aforementioned law (DW 2020).

Beltran's unlawful arrest and disproportionate penalty stirred much debate regarding the right to free expression in the Philippines. Beltran's charges were dismissed by a Cebu City Court—a dismissal welcomed by Beltran as a move towards the upholding of freedom of expression in the country, as well as the protection of constitutionally guaranteed rights to ordinary citizens (CDN Digital 2020).

Danai Ussama (Thailand)

Graffiti artist Danai Ussama was charged on March 23, 2020, for his Facebook post sharing that he had not encountered any COVID-19 screening measures at the Suvarnabhumi Airport on his return from Spain on March 16, 2020. Specifically, Ussama was charged under Section 14(2) of the Computer Crimes Act 2017, which punishes 'putting into a computer system false computer data in a manner that is likely to cause panic in the public'. The Technology Crime Suppression Division (TCSD) claimed that Ussama's posting on Facebook qualified under this section and confiscated his phone, which had been used to make the post (Prachatai 2020).

Charges against Ussama were finally dismissed by the Criminal Court in November 2021 on the grounds that Ussama had not intended for his post to create public panic or disruption (Prachatai 2021). Ussama had been told by his peers that the possibility of his winning the case was very low. According to his legal representatives, Thai Lawyers for Human Rights, the

Computer Crimes Act was often used in tandem with the Emergency Decree on Public Administration in Emergency Situation B.E. 2548 (2005), which was used to declare a state of emergency in Thailand from 26 March 2020 (Thai Lawyers for Human Rights 2564 [2021]). This decree lacks measures to ensure checks and balances. It has been misused to curtail citizen rights and civil liberties across Thailand—a move of particular significance in the wake of nationwide student protests that took the country by storm in March 2020. As of September 2022, the Thai government has extended the state of emergency to the end of September, marking the 19th extension since the onset of the pandemic (*Bangkok Post* 2022).

Pushing back on artist rights and artistic freedom

While threats to free expression had occurred at an alarming rate even before COVID-19, the pandemic exacerbated the problem, notably putting artists' lives and livelihoods at risk (Yeluri et al. 2021, 10–11). Thai rapper Danupha Kanatheerakul, who goes by the name Milli, was reported to the police for defamation for tweets that were critical of the Thai government's handling of the COVID-19 crisis (*Union of Catholic Asian News* 2021). Milli, who was ordered to pay a fine, was one of many artists in Thailand who took to social media to share their discontentment with the government. Burmese street artists Zayar Hnaung, Ja Sai, and Naw Htun Aung were arrested for offending religious sentiments by a public mural urging people to stay home and abide by social distancing norms (*Art Review* 2020). The mural in question depicted the grim reaper spreading the coronavirus and dressed in a manner allegedly bearing strong similarities to the garb worn by Buddhist monks.

Through a blend of strategies, several Asian governments have sought to curb artistic freedom and expression. Prominent among them are legislations seeking to control the spread of misinformation about the COVID-19 virus. These 'fake news' laws have either been standalone legislations or read under the scope of digital communication and security laws[2]. Versions of these legislations have emerged all over Asia, with varying degrees of strictness

2 Fake-news laws like Malaysia's The Emergency (Essential Powers) (No. 2) Ordinance 2021 that came into force on March 12, 2021 made the publication or reproduction of any wholly or partly false information related to COVID-19 a punishable offence. The law imposes penalties of up to three years imprisonment and allows authorities to take 'necessary measures' to remove any false information from public access. Furthermore, laws such as Bangladesh's Digital Security Act 2018 came into force prior to the onset of the pandemic to criminalise the publication of false information related to the COVID-19 virus on the grounds that such dissemination disrupts communal harmony, causing civil unrest.

and penalties. What seems to remain true is that these legislations are often responsible for restricting expression that could otherwise be deemed satirical or critical in nature. In Bangladesh and India, cartoonists like Ahmed Kabir Kishore (Cartooning for Peace 2021, 4 March) and Rachita Taneja (Cartooning for Peace 2021, 29 January) have been threatened with varying degrees of punishment, ranging from threats of legal prosecution to incarceration and unlawful detention.

Anti-assembly laws and restrictive policies forbidding in-person interaction in line with social distancing have also been a cause for concern, resulting in the shrinkage of safe spaces for cultural and creative activities (Artists at Risk Connection 2021). The lack of financial support, coupled with the anxiety of arrest, has led to the closure of several public spaces and venues that previously hosted artistic productions. As we recover from the pandemic, it remains to be seen whether these spaces will reopen to the public.

Key findings and analysis

Digital security and fake news laws

The artists' experiences illuminated in the aforementioned case studies indicate that artists throughout the region have been targeted by their governments through a mix of legislative measures, mostly implemented against the backdrop of the pandemic. In 2020, over 50 cases worldwide were recorded of artists being detained, prosecuted, or imprisoned for vocalizing how the pandemic had been mismanaged in their countries (Freemuse 2021, 31).

Although laws related to digital security and the regulation of internet-based communication existed prior to the pandemic, its onset provided governments with a new opportunity to introduce 'emergency measures'—mechanisms that granted unchecked powers to state authorities while transforming the aforementioned laws into more restrictive and aggressive legislative tools (Chatham House 2021). According to Chatham House, new information and cybersecurity laws were introduced in Bangladesh, India, Indonesia, Malaysia, Myanmar, Nepal, Pakistan, the Philippines, Sri Lanka, Thailand, and Vietnam in response to the pandemic. Many of these countries also boast a large number of social media users, the highest number of them distributed across East, South, and Southeast Asia (*Statista* 2022). This raises powerful concerns concerning the role played by social media companies in shaping free speech and expression in Asia and the degree of their complicity or resistance to governments. Questions worth asking include how important it is that social media platforms like Facebook come preloaded into mobile devices and are often used as search tools, often becoming the primary source of news for many (O'Brian 2014).

The pandemic exacerbated the rise in misinformation and the emergence of the infodemic, with people intentionally and unintentionally spreading incorrect information about COVID-19[3]. Thus, in addition to the abovementioned digital security and internet communication regulation laws, governments also began to introduce laws to curb the spread of misinformation. Often called 'fake news' laws, these legislative instruments were enacted extensively in South and Southeast Asia. However, rather than merely focusing on controlling wrongful information, fake news laws have increasingly targeted ordinary citizens critical of their government's actions. This is in line with the case studies of Bambi Beltran and Danai Ussama, both of whom were arrested for expressing via social media opinions that were critical of the government's mishandling of the pandemic in their specific cities and countries.

These legislations (digital security laws and fake news laws) share several common themes, including a) a restriction on certain forms of expression that are deemed to harm public interest and represent a threat to national sovereignty, b) an ambiguous understanding of what constitutes national sovereignty, leading to an undefined and far-reaching scope of acts that might be antagonistic to national security and sovereignty, and c) the granting of excessive or emergency powers to state authorities who may use these powers to do whatever is necessary to remove the alleged misinformation. This includes everything from ordering the social media to take down a post to detaining the citizen who has published an allegedly offensive artwork or post or seizing the artwork and the device(s) from which the publication or dissemination was made.

Laws like Bangladesh's Digital Security Act, 2018 (DSA), the Philippines' Republic Act No. 11469 or the Bayanihan to Heal as One Act 2020, Malaysia's Communication and Multimedia Act 1998, or the more recently proposed Cybersecurity Bill from Myanmar, which effectively forbids the usage of virtual private networks (VPNs) and other digital measures, are all indicative of the growing trend of governments using digital surveillance tools, and

3 The World Health Organisation referred to the spread of misinformation about the COVID-19 virus as an infodemic that resulted in the hospitalisation of nearly 6,000 people in the early months of 2020. It released statements in support of working with trusted media sources to diminish the infodemic in anticipation of vaccine roll outs. See World Health Organisation 2021.

security and communication laws as a means to stifle free speech and target human rights defenders, including artists. Various sections of the DSA have been used to silence the voices of artists, lawyers, bloggers, journalists, and activists (Freemuse 2021, 89).

Another set of COVID-19-related laws was also used to restrict the assembly and movement of human rights defenders, artists, and other citizens during mass protests. Emergency powers granted to local police during the COVID-19 health crisis allowed them to disrupt the activities and mobility of citizens (Citizenship law 2020). As per the 1980 Recommendation Concerning the Status of the Artist, Member States are required 'to provide those engaged in artistic activities with all the means and, in particular, travel and study grants, likely to enable them to establish lively and far-reaching contacts with other cultures' and 'to take all appropriate steps to promote the free international movement of artists' (UNESCO 1980)

Additional grounds: sedition, blasphemy, and mobility laws

While digital security laws and fake news laws have been widely used tools in curbing artistic freedom in Asia under the specific context of the pandemic, these tactics also predate the pandemic. For instance, in Bangladesh, the DSA has been regularly used to curb the performance and dissemination of Baul music—a musical tradition originating with the Baul community native to Bangladesh and West Bengal, India. Over a thousand years old, this music is passed down via oral history from one generation to the next. Baul music is often condemned by Bangladeshi authorities as undesirable and hurtful of religious sentiments—grounds that have been used to charge singers such as Shariat Boyati and Rita Dewan under the DSA, as well as to turn a blind eye to community attacks on musicians of the Baul tradition (Freemuse 2021, 90). Coupled with the lack of access to legal resources, as well as the slow judicial process aggravated by the pandemic, this tactic has contributed to a climate of anxiety for artists in the country.

As can be seen in the case of Malaysian graphic artist, Fahmi Reza, charges of sedition are often used to target artists who are critical of the government or the country's monarchy and their mishandling of the COVID-19 health crisis. These charges have also been used to prosecute critics of other aspects of the government. For example, in India, sedition charges were levied on artists who used their artwork to criticise the government's policies with respect to the Citizenship Amendment Act protests of 2020 as well as the farmer's protests of 2021.

Another set of COVID-19-related laws was also used to restrict the assembly and movement of human rights defenders, artists, and other citizens during mass protests. The emergency powers granted to local police during the COVID-19 health crisis allowed them to disrupt the activities and mobility of citizens (Citizenship Law 2020). As per the 1980 Recommendation Concerning the Status of the Artist, Member States are required 'to provide those engaged in artistic activities with all the means and, in particular, travel and study grants, likely to enable them to establish lively and far-reaching contacts with other cultures' and 'to take all appropriate steps to promote the free international movement of artists' (UNESCO 1980). As such, many argue that such anti-mobility laws violate basic human rights. In India, for instance, artists and communities led peaceful protests against the controversial Citizenship Amendment Act (CAA) at Shaheen Bagh, New Delhi, protests which abruptly ended when local police used anti-gathering restrictions and social distancing norms to effectively clear the protest site (BBC News 2020).

The way forward

There is an urgent need to build sustainable and secure networks that connect artists at risk, cultural institutions, and human rights organisations to facilitate their exchange of important information and resources. These networks can offer artists powerful tools to help them identify solutions, access legal aid, or facilitate relocation measures in the event of severe threats. The networks can also allow artists to connect as citizens in order to better organise themselves as a collective.

Digital security and fake news laws do not offer effective long-term solutions for tackling the infodemic, and there is a need to explore alternative approaches to the problem. Instead, a longer-term, multi-stakeholder approach aimed at tackling the problem of misinformation by increasing media literacy and media transparency is recommended (*The Diplomat* 2021). This approach can also be elevated through the efforts of the creative community, in which artists can play a powerful role in shaping communications of critical issues in ways that are accessible and easy to understand.

It is also recommended to develop and deliver training in areas like digital rights, data security, financial security, and physical and mental well-being to make artists more aware of their rights and available resources. This can be done by way of collaborative workshops organised by international stakeholders, as well as by relying on resources and publications like ARC's Safety Guide for Artists—a manual that explores topics such as defining and understanding risk, preparing for threats, fortifying digital safety, documenting persecution, finding assistance, and recovering from trauma (Fine et al. 2021).

Conclusion

The COVID-19 pandemic dealt a massive and devastating blow to the creative economy. It precipitated an alarming shrinkage of civic spaces available for artists and cultural life (Yeluri et al. 2021, 42). Through a combination of social distancing regulations and anti-assembly laws, governments in South, Southeast, and East Asia have used the pandemic to justify curtailing the mobility of artists. This has impacted the livelihoods and safety of artists in unprecedented ways, leaving them isolated and without the support of their peers. It has also led to targeted stifling of expression that is deemed critical of government action or supposedly in violation of government policies. According to Hong Kong artist and activist Kacey Wong, ordinary laws have also become a means to restrict the activities of cultural institutions (Podcast interview, Kacey Wong 2021), as in the case of the June Fourth Museum in Hong Kong, which was called for closure following its non-compliance with an entertainment licensing requirement from the Food and Environmental Hygiene Department (FEHD) (Reuters 2021).

The growing rise of digital security laws and fake news legislations is deeply concerning. These laws normalise internet-based censorship and unlawful detention under the guise of protecting national security and sovereignty. They are not an effective solution to the problem of misinformation, but instead provide government authorities with sweeping powers to restrict and remove information with scarce justification. Many of these laws violate international human rights principles—Bangladesh's DSA, for instance, is widely known to be violative of international treaties to which Bangladesh is a signatory, including the International Covenant on Civil and Political Rights (ICCPR) (*The Leaflet* 2022). There is thus an urgent need to re-evaluate and understand the relevance of these laws.

Community-based censorship and ostracism, along with state action, are fast becoming commonplace, both online and offline, leaving artists vulnerable and trapped in a climate of fear. Often unable to seek help and thus enduring a sense of isolation, many artists have also begun practising self-censorship.

Having observed the above, it is also important to note that an increasing number of artists are becoming aware of the plight of their counterparts in other countries and are willing to stand in solidarity with them. For instance, in response to the coup in Myanmar, artists from across the world have been contributing to movements such as the Milk Tea Alliance in an effort to rally support for those in Myanmar. The movement also extends to supporting pro-democracy protests in other countries like Thailand and Hong Kong.

In conclusion, this paper illustrates the impact of artists on various citizen-led initiatives and movements against the backdrop of the pandemic, as well as the laws that governments have used during the pandemic to prosecute artists. Owing to the nature of their mediums and content, artistic work has the potential to amplify information and bring people together in ways both unprecedented and invaluable. However, with increasing state and non-state powers in South and Southeast Asia viewing these artistic responses as powerful threats to their own authority, artists and artistic practices are being deliberately targeted and stifled. To overcome these challenges, as well as strive towards building and upholding healthy democracies in the region, it is imperative that the international community takes pains to safeguard artists as activists, celebrating their ability to spark change while also acknowledging their rights as citizens—citizens who are guaranteed fundamental freedoms and are deserving of basic human rights.

Bibliography

Acharekar, Janhavi. 2021. 'Surviving the Pandemic has Forced Artists to Make a Virtue of Being Online', *The Hindu* (8 October). https://www.thehindu.com/entertainment/art/surviving-the-pandemic-has-forced-artists-to-make-a-virtue-of-being-online/article36893422.ece

Adobo Magazine. 2020. 'Quarantine with Free Online Classes', *Adobo Magazine* (17 March).

Ang, Prisca and Chelsea Kiew. 2020. 'Artists Defend Value of Creative Work to Society after Survey Sparks Debate', *The Strait Times* (16 June). https://www.straitstimes.com/lifestyle/arts/artists-defend-value-of-creative-work-to-society-after-survey-sparks-debate

Art Review. 2020. 'Burmese Street Artists Arrested over COVID-19 Mural', *Art Review* (21 April).

Artists At Risk Connection. 2021. 'Arresting Art: Repression, Censorship, and Artistic Freedom in Asia', (PEN America). https://artistsatriskconnection.org/story/arresting-art-repression-censorship-and-artistic-freedom-in-asia

Artists At Risk Connection. 2021. 'A Safety Guide for Artists' (PEN America). https://artistsatriskconnection.org/guide

Artists at Risk Connection. 2021. 'Arresting Art: Repression, Censorship, and Artistic Freedom in Asia' (9 June). repression-censorship-and-artistic-freedom-in-asia

Bangkok Post. 2022. 'State of Emergency extended for two months', *Bangkok Post* (8 July). https://www.bangkokpost.com/thailand/general/2342432/state-of-emergency-extended-for-2-months

Bayanihan To Heal as One Act. 2020. http://legacy.senate.gov.ph/Bayanihan-to-Heal-as-One-Act-RA-11469.pdf

BBC News. 2020. 'Shaheen Bagh: Coronavirus Clears Long-Running India Citizenship protest', *BBC News* (24 March). https://www.bbc.com/news/world-asia-india-52015464

Bhavya Sukeja. 2021. 'Malaysian Artist Fahmi Reza Arrested For "Insulting" Queen With Spotify Playlist', *Republic World* (26 April). https://www.republicworld.com/world-news/rest-of-the-world-news/malaysian-artist-fahmi-reza-arrested-for-insulting-queen-with-spotify-playlist.html

Blomqvist, Olof Robert. 2022. '2021: Fundamental Freedoms in South Asia' (FORUM-ASIA). https://www.forum-asia.org/uploads/wp/2022/04/SoutheastFreedom-FINAL.pdf

Business Line. 2021. 'Artists Join Hands to Raise Money for Covid-19 Relief' (17 May). fundraiser/article34577439.ece

Çakır, Pelin. 2022. 'Learning from the Pandemic: Artistic Freedom & Mobility Beyond the Covid-19 Crisis' (Martin Roth Initiative). https://www.ssoar.info/ssoar/bitstream/handle/document/77261/ssoar-2022-cakr-Learning_from_the_Pandemic_Artistic.pdf?sequence=1&isAllowed=y&lnkname=ssoar-2022-cakr-Learning_from_the_Pandemic_Artistic.pdf

Cartooning for Peace. 2021. 'Alert Bangladesh–Ahmed Kabir Kishore' (4 March). https://www.cartooningforpeace.org/en/soutiens/alerte-bangladesh-ahmed-kabir-kishore/

Cartooning for Peace. 2021. 'Alert India–Rachita Taneja' (29 January). https://www.cartooningforpeace.org/en/soutiens/info-india-rachita-taneja/

CDN Digital, Delta Dyrecka Letigio. 2020. 'Cebu City Court Dismisses Charges against Bambi Beltran' *CDN Digital* (15 September). https://cebudailynews.inquirer.net/340002/cebu-city-court-dismisses-charges-against-bambi-beltran#ixzz7cHG4ktMo

Chatham House. 2021. 'Battle Lines Being Drawn over Online Freedoms in Asia' (22 March). https://www.chathamhouse.org/2021/03/battle-lines-being-drawn-over-online-freedoms-asia

Chen, Heather. 2021. '"Censored" by Spotify and Arrested, a Malaysian Graphic Artist Speaks Out', *Vice* (27 April). https://www.vice.com/en/article/epndzw/malaysia-fahmi-reza-spotify-queen

Citizenship law. 2020. 'Is India Using COVID-19 Emergency to Arrest Protesters?' (28 May). emergency-to-arrest-protesters/a-53603260.

Committee to Protect Journalists. 2020. 'Kabir Kishore', *Committee to Protect Journalists* (5 May). https://cpj.org/data/people/kabir-kishore/

Congress of the Philippines. 2020. Covid-19 National Emergency Act (23 March). http://legacy.senate.gov.ph/Bayanihan-to-Heal-as-One-Act-RA-11469.pdf

CPJ. 2021. 'Jailed under Digital Security Act, Bangladeshi Cartoonist Kabir Kishore Says he was Tortured' (30 March). https://cpj.org/2021/03/jailed-digital-security-act-bangladeshi-cartoonist-kabir-kishore-tortured/

Cuny, Laurence. 2021. 'Freedom and Creativity: Defending Art, Defending Diversity', Special edition 2005 Convention Global Report series (UNESCO-Aschberg Programme for Artists and Cultural Professionals). http://www.globalculturalrelations.org/wp-content/uploads/2022/04/373357eng.pdf

Das, Soumitra. 2021. 'Artists Join Hands to Raise Money for Covid-19 Relief', *Business Line* (17 May).

DW. 2020. 'Maria Victoria Beltran: Filipino Artist Confronts Duterte on COVID-19 Response', *DW* (21 May).

Ecarma, Lorraine. 2020. 'Court Dismisses Cases against Cebu Artist Bambi Beltran', *Rappler* (15 September). https://www.rappler.com/nation/court-dismisses-cases-against-cebu-artist-bambi-beltran/

Freemuse. 2021. 'The State of Artistic Freedom 2021'. https://freemuse.org/media/ck5fvaze/the-state-of-artistic-freedom-2021.pdf

Freeman, Benjamin. 2021. 'Thai Regime Ramps Up Efforts to Silence Critics', *Union of Catholic Asian News* (23 July). https://www.ucanews.com/news/thai-regime-ramps-up-efforts-to-silence-critics/93406

FMT. 2021. 'Fahmi Reza's "Dengki ke" Sedition Case Dropped', *FMT* (24 August). https://www.freemalaysiatoday.com/category/nation/2021/08/24/fahmi-rezas-dengki-ke-sedition-case-dropped/

Harris, Gareth. 2020. 'Inspired by Italy's Spontaneous Singing, Museums Commission Artists to Make "Balcony Art" during Coronavirus Crisis', *The Art Newspaper* (8 April). https://www.theartnewspaper.com/2020/04/08/inspired-by-italys-spontaneous-singing-museums-commission-artists-to-make-balcony-art-during-coronavirus-crisis

Harris, Gareth. 2021. 'Governments are "Weaponising" Covid-19 to Silence Dissident Artist Voices, Report Says', *The Art Newspaper* (1 March).

Human Rights Watch. 2021. *Country Report: Bangladesh, Events of 2020* (Human Rights Watch). https://www.hrw.org/world-report/2021/country-chapters/bangladesh

Humphrey, Chris. 2020. '"In a War, We Draw": Vietnam's Artis Join Fight against Covid-19', *The Guardian* (9 April).

Hyperallergic. 2021. 'How India's Creative Community Became a Beacon of Hope During COVID-19' (3 August). creative-community-became-a-beacon-of-hope-during-covid-19/

Iftikhar, Aliya. 2021. 'Jailed under Digital Security Act, Bangladeshi Cartoonist Kabir Kishore Says He Was Tortured', *CPJ* (30 March). https://cpj.org/2021/03/jailed-digital-security-act-bangladeshi-cartoonist-kabir-kishore-tortured/

Kejriwal, Rohini. 2021. 'How India's Creative Community Became a Beacon of Hope During COVID-19', *Hyperallergic* (3 August). https://hyperallergic.com/660435/how-indias-creative-community-became-a-beacon-of-hope-during-covid-19/

Krishnan, Murali. 2021. 'Citizenship Law: Is India Using COVID-19 Emergency to Arrest Protesters?' *DW* (28 May). https://www.dw.com/en/citizenship-law-is-india-using-covid-19-emergency-to-arrest-protesters/a-53603260

Kumar, Yogesh. 2022. 'Shrinking Space for Liberty in South Asia: Analysing the Digital Security Act, 2018 of Bangladesh', *The Leaflet* (11 July). https://theleaflet.in/shrinking-space-for-liberty-in-south-asia-analysing-the-digital-security-act-2018-of-bangladesh/

Nacar, Pauline. 2020. 'Digital: Robert Alejandro Brings Creativity into the COVID-19 Quarantine with Free Online Classes' (17 March). https://www.adobomagazine.com/digital-news/digital-robert-alejandro-brings-creativity-into-the-covid-19-quarantine-with-free-online-classes/

McGivern, Hannah. 2021. 'World Health Organisation Joins Art World to Launch Global Campaign Confronting Mental Health Toll of Pandemic', *The Art Newspaper* (17 March). https://www.theartnewspaper.com/2021/03/17/world-health-organisation-joins-art-world-to-launch-global-campaign-confronting-mental-health-toll-of-pandemic

Moynihan, Harriet. 2021. 'Battle Lines Being Drawn over Online Freedoms in Asia', *Chatham House* (22 March). https://www.chathamhouse.org/2021/03/battle-lines-being-drawn-over-online-freedoms-asia

O'Brian, Rachel. 2014. 'Mobile Asia Holds Key to Facebook's future growth', Live Mint (3 February). https://www.livemint.com/Industry/L88a0B9aIqwNecMvS1thVO/Mobile-Asia-holds-key-to-Facebooks-future-growth.html

Paine, Jeff. 2021. 'The Future of Asia's Battle Against Online Misinformation', *The Diplomat* (25 June). https://thediplomat.com/2021/06/the-future-of-asias-battle-against-online-misinformation/

Prachatai. 2020. 'Artist Arrested for Posting 'Suvarnabhumi Airport Has No Screening for Covid-19' while in 14-day self-quarantine after his return from Spain', *Prachatai* (27 March). https://prachatai.com/english/node/8432

Prachatai. 2021. 'Charge over Claim Suvarnabhumi Airport Had No Covid-19 Screening Dismissed', *Prachatai* (26 November). https://prachatai.com/english/node/9578

Rappler. 2020. 'Court Dismisses Cases against Cebu Artist Bambi Beltran' (15 September). https://www.rappler.com/nation/court-dismisses-cases-against-cebu-artist-bambi-beltran/

Republic World. 2021. 'Malaysian Artist Fahmi Reza Arrested For 'insulting' Queen With Spotify Playlist' (26 April). https://www.republicworld.com/world-news/rest-of-the-world-news/malaysian-artist-fahmi-reza-arrested-for-insulting-queen-with-spotify-playlist.html

Reuters. 2021. 'HK's June 4th Museum Temporarily Closes over Licensing Probe', *Reuters* (2 June). https://www.reuters.com/world/asia-pacific/hks-june-4th-museum-temporarily-closes-over-licensing-probe-2021-06-02/

Son, Johanna. 2020. 'Asian Artists Hone Weapons in Fight against COVID-19', *Nikkei Asia* (21 April). https://asia.nikkei.com/Life-Arts/Arts/Asian-artists-hone-weapons-in-fight-against-COVID-19

Statista. 2022. 'Distribution of Worldwide Social Media Users in 2022, by Region', *Statista*. https://www.statista.com/statistics/295619/regional-distribution-of-social-media-users-worldwide/

Thai Lawyers for Human Rights. 2021[2564]. *'2020: The Year of Protests, Ceiling Breaking and Political Lawsuits'* (1 December). https://tlhr2014.com/en/archives/24956

The Art Newspaper. 2020. 'Inspired by Italy's Spontaneous Singing, Museums Commission Artists to Make "Balcony Art" during Coronavirus Crisis' (8 April). https://www.theartnewspaper.com/2020/04/08/inspired-by-italys-spontaneous-singing-museums-commission-artists-to-make-balcony-art-during-coronavirus-crisis

The Art Newspaper. 2021. 'Governments are "Weaponising" Covid-19 to Silence Dissident Artist Voices, Report Says' (1 March). https://www.theartnewspaper.com/2021/03/01/governments-are-weaponising-covid-19-to-silence-dissident-artist-voices-report-says

The Art Newspaper. 2021. 'World Health Organisation Joins Art World to Launch Global Campaign Confronting Mental Health Toll of Pandemic' (17 March). https://www.theartnewspaper.com/2021/03/17/world-health-organisation-joins-art-world-to-launch-global-campaign-confronting-mental-health-toll-of-pandemic

The Conversation. 2020. 'Art and Online Activism amid the Pandemic: Lessons from around the World', *The Conversation* (25 September). https://theconversation.com/art-and-online-activism-amid-the-pandemic-lessons-from-around-the-world-140161

The Conversation. 2020. 'The Coronavirus Pandemic has Revealed How Fragile Everyday life is', *The Conversation* (26 April). https://theconversation.com/the-coronavirus-pandemic-has-revealed-how-fragile-everyday-life-is-134637

The Diplomat. 2021. 'The Future of Asia's Battle Against Online Misinformation' (25 June). https://thediplomat.com/2021/06/the-future-of-asias-battle-against-online-misinformation/

The Hindu. 2020. Gautam Sunder, 'Coronavirus: How this Singapore Illustrator's Comics Fight Misinformation in the Age of COVID-19', *The Hindu* (10 March). https://

www.thehindu.com/entertainment/coronavirus-how-this-singapore-illustrators-comics-fight-misinformation-in-the-age-of-covid-19/article31031982.ece
The Leaflet. 2022. 'Shrinking Space for Liberty in South Asia: Analysing the Digital Security Act, 2018 of Bangladesh' (11 July). https://theleaflet.in/shrinking-space-for-liberty-in-south-asia-analysing-the-digital-security-act-2018-of-bangladesh/
The Straits Times. 2021. 'Malaysian Police Arrest Artist for Allegedly Insulting Queen with Spotify Playlist', *The Straits Times* (24 April). https://www.straitstimes.com/asia/se-asia/malaysian-police-arrest-artist-for-allegedly-insulting-queen-with-spotify-playlist
UNESCO. N.d. Creative Cities' Response to COVID-19. https://unesdoc.unesco.org/in/documentViewer.xhtml?v=2.1.196&id=p::usmarcdef_0000374264&file=/in/rest/annotationSVC/DownloadWatermarkedAttachment/attach_import_6121b313-699c-4096-b8a2-17bba28445ed%3F_%3D374264eng.pdf&locale=fr&multi=true&ark=/ark:/48223/pf0000374264/PDF/374264eng.pdf#EN%20type%20set%20with%20ISBN%20FINAL.indd%3A.28541%3A1296
UNESCO. 1980. Recommendation Concerning the Status of the Artist Part IV, (j) and (k). https://en.unesco.org/creativity/sites/creativity/files/passeport-reco1980-en.pdf
UNESCO Creative Cities Network. 2020. 'UNESCO Creative Cities' Response to COVID-19' (UNESCO Creative Cities Network). https://unesdoc.unesco.org/in/documentViewer.xhtml?v=2.1.196&id=p::usmarcdef_0000374264&file=/in/rest/annotationSVC/DownloadWatermarkedAttachment/attach_import_6121b313-699c-4096-b8a2-17bba28445ed%3F_%3D374264eng.pdf&locale=fr&multi=true&ark=/ark:/48223/pf0000374264/PDF/374264eng.pdf#EN%20type%20set%20with%20ISBN%20FINAL.indd%3A.28541%3A1296
UNESCO. 2021. Backstage: Managing Creativity and the Arts in South-East Asia. https://unesdoc.unesco.org/ark:/48223/pf0000375664
UNESCO. 2021. 'Backstage: Managing Creativity and the Arts in South-East Asia', (UNESCO and UNESCO Bangkok). https://unesdoc.unesco.org/in/documentViewer.xhtml?v=2.1.196&id=p::usmarcdef_0000375664&file=/in/rest/annotationSVC/DownloadWatermarkedAttachment/attach_import_02c2980d-e690-4e06-8140-b28d5fd2f87e%3F_%3D375664eng.pdf&locale=en&multi=true&ark=/ark:/48223/pf0000375664/PDF/375664eng.pdf#%5B%7B%22num%22%3A32%2C%22gen%22%3A0%7D%2C%7B%22name%22%3A%22XYZ%22%7D%2C0%2C842%2C0%5D
Union of Catholic Asian News. 2021. 'Thai Regime Ramps Up Efforts to Silence Critics' (23 July). https://www.ucanews.com/news/thai-regime-ramps-up-efforts-to-silence-critics/93406
Vice. 2021. '"Censored" by Spotify and Arrested, a Malaysian Graphic Artist Speaks Out' (27 April). https://www.vice.com/en/article/epndzw/malaysia-fahmi-reza-spotify-queen

World Health Organisation. 2020. 'WHO Director-General's Opening Remarks at the Media Briefing on COVID-19', *World Health Organisation* (11 March). https://www.who.int/director-general/speeches/detail/who-director-general-s-opening-remarks-at-the-media-briefing-on-covid-19---11-march-2020

World Health Organisation. 2021. 'Fighting Misinformation in the Time of COVID-19, One Click at a Time', *World Health Organisation* (27 April). https://www.who.int/news-room/feature-stories/detail/fighting-misinformation-in-the-time-of-covid-19-one-click-at-a-time

Podcasts

Podcast interview with Fahmi Reza. 2021. 'Fahmi Reza On Visual Disobedience' for 'Creating Artistic Resilience', Artists at Risk Connection, Mekong Cultural Hub and FORUM-ASIA (10 September). https://artistsatriskconnection.org/story/fahmi-reza-on-visual-disobedience

Podcast interview with Kacey Wong. 2021. 'Kaey Wong on Art as Resistance' for 'Creating Artistic Resilience', Artists at Risk Connection, Mekong Cultural Hub and FORUM-ASIA (10 September). https://artistsatriskconnection.org/story/kacey-wong-on-art-as-resistance

About the authors

Julie Trébault is the director of Artists at Risk Connection (ARC). This project aims to safeguard the right to artistic freedom by connecting to support threatened artists, building a global network of organizations assisting artists at risk, and forging ties between arts and human rights organizations. She has nearly two decades of experience in international art programming and network-building, including at the Museum of the City of New York, the Center for Architecture, the National Museum of Ethnology in The Netherlands, and the Musée du quai Branly in Paris. She is co-author of *Freedom of Artistic Expression Through the Lens of the Sustainable Development Goals* (2021) and *A Safety Guide for Artists* (2021), and has led the preparation of numerous reports on the status of artistic freedom and the persecution faced by artists around the world, including in Latin America, Africa, and Asia.
jtrebault@artistsatriskconnection.org

Manojna Yeluri is creative legal consultant, entertainment, and intellectual property rights lawyer. She runs Artistik License—a legal consultancy and platform addressing the needs of artists and creative practitioners. She is also the Asia Regional Representative for the Artists at Risk Connection (ARC), as well as a co-founder of the community project Contracts for Creators. myeluri@artistatriskconnection.org

6. The Disproportionate Effect of COVID-19 on Citizen Participation in Nepal

Vishnu Kumari Tandon

Abstract: This study underlines the challenges to citizen participation in Nepal amid the first wave of COVID-19, where the pandemic affected different groups unevenly. Those worst affected were from marginalised communities. The local planning process, because obligatory, was sustained during the pandemic, yet modifications brought in to cope with COVID-19 disproportionately impacted the marginalised. Firstly, in public forums within settlements, where discussion is held at a grassroots level, marginalised citizens were unable to articulate their self-interests. Secondly, because the policy brought in to facilitate municipalities in the planning process was vague and lacked the capacity to address the needs of marginalised people, its implementation further marginalised them. Thirdly, no digital innovations were available to improve citizen participation on the pretext was that these groups have low digital literacy. This contributed further to the reduction of their participation in local planning during the pandemic.

Keywords: Citizen participation, planning process, COVID-19, digital participation, Nepal

Introduction

This chapter examines the municipal planning process in the Bhuddhabhumi municipality of Kapilvastu District, Nepal during the first wave of COVID-19. The municipal planning process is an annual process with a series of steps organised by the local government to formulate local plans

Gregory Bracken, Paul Rabé, Nurul Azreen Azlan (eds), *Future Practices of Citizenship in Asia and the West: Care of the Self (Volume III)*. Taylor & Francis Group, 2025
DOI: 10.5117/9789048562077_CH06

aimed at building local infrastructure and social development policies based on the proposals of ordinary citizens. This chapter investigates the degree and capacity of ordinary citizens to participate in the planning process and articulate proposals for local projects and policies. This study concedes that the local government faced immense challenges in executing its role to ensure a participatory planning process. Various forms and scales of lockdowns, coupled with new norms of social distancing, limited the involvement of ordinary citizens in the annual participatory planning and budgeting processes in Nepal. Nevertheless, the study also reveals that these restrictions were used as an excuse to prevent participation, with almost no innovations to promote it. This chapter demonstrates the new social realities of participatory practices in Nepal during a health crisis like COVID-19. The first section reviews relevant literature to help understand the scholarly debate around citizen participation. The next section provides a context for understanding the local planning process in Nepal and the possibility of citizen participation in each step of that process. The third section deals with methodology, and the fourth elaborates on and discusses the chapter's findings, outlining three key points: 1) the possibility of citizen participation in the planning process during COVID-19, 2) the impact of COVID-19-related policy on marginalised communities, and 3) the reluctance of the government to encourage digital participation during the pandemic.

Literature review

This section uses existing literature in the field of citizen participation and deliberation in planning to build a framework for the rest of the study. Based on available theories and empirical evidence, I will discuss and test the findings of this research. Many scholars argue that the paradigm of engaging people in planning discussions has been dominating planning theory since the 1980s (Forester 1999; Friedmann 2011; Healey 1997 p.146). This is known as participatory planning (Forester 1999). Participatory planning practices are in accordance with Jürgen Habermas' concept of deliberative democracy (Allmendinger and Tewdwr-Jones 2002 p.10). Deliberative democracy stresses the importance of communication. It is based on the idea that people come together with equal status and mutual respect to discuss the political issues that affect their lives, without the use of any coercive power, and with rationales for a 'common good' to benefit the larger community (Bohman 1997; Della Porta 2013; Elstub 2018; Floridia 2014; Habermas 2007, MacCarthy, and Habermas 2005).

Critics like Iris Marion Young regard the theories of deliberative democracy suggested by Habermas' theory of communicative action as elitist because they promote communicative rationality at the expense of passion and emotion (Young 2003, Habermas 2007). Similarly, James Bohman suggests that a well-functioning democracy should make the public sphere accessible to everyone by providing them with the freedom to join. However, such social freedom is uncertain if a society is unequal. In an unequal society, equality and freedom to choose can be exercised only if governing institutions acknowledge disparities and are committed to making necessary changes to minimise inequality. Simply granting access to participatory space is not enough; not all citizens are able to make use of deliberative opportunities unless they have the freedom and capacity to communicate. Inequality can prohibit citizens from reaching the threshold at which deliberation can occur. Unless this problem is addressed, marginalised citizens cannot break through the 'ceiling' created by their inequality (Bohman 1997). Deliberation occurs among equals (Cohen 1997, Habermas 2007). To ensure a minimum threshold of equality for deliberation, citizens with different needs must be provided with specific opportunities to allow them to develop the necessary capacities. Some scholars have argued that the 'common good' may not be the only goal of deliberative democracy, and that if at all attained, it should be done within the relevant consideration of an unequal society (Abers 2001; Mansbridge 1999). In some situations of inequality in society, self-interest rather than the common good may motivate deliberations. If diversity is not taken into account, the interests of the poor and marginalised can be labelled as illegitimate, based on 'self-interest', and dismissed, based on the legitimate aim of realising the common good (Mansbridge et al. 2010).

Proponents of participatory and deliberative democracy have argued that representative democracy alone cannot ensure the active political engagement of people because, when this type of democracy is engaged in planning or trying to implement policy, it does not seek to create political consensus through dialogue. However, when combined with deliberative and participatory democracy it can ensure that citizens are politically engaged. This notion of deliberative and participatory democracy also contributes to participatory planning (Fung and Wright 2001). Examples of such participatory and deliberative democratic practices are the budgeting policies of Porto Alegre, Brazil, introduced in the 1990s (Baiocchi and Ganuza 2017; Fung and Wright 2001; Heller 2001). These budgets may be the most studied participatory projects in the world. Beginning as a political project to achieve 'radically democratised democracy', they evolved into an instrument for improving governance and advancing the relationship between government and its citizens. After the success of the participatory budgeting of Porto Alegre, local governments of many developing countries adopted these innovative practices in the hope of improving their own governance systems (Baiocchi and Ganuza 2017; Cabannes and Lipietz 2018; Thomas Isaac and Franke 2002).

Nepal also has a number of cases of citizen participation. One important example is a self-managed community-based organisation called the Farmer Managed Irrigation System (FMIS). Studies emphasise that participants in the FMIS share in deliberations to reach decisions (Ostrom et al. 2011; Pradhan 2000). Another well-known example is the Community Forest Management (CFM), where those directly benefitting from the community forest participate in decision-making about which forest products to exploit, and how to sell these products, as well as how to augment forest conservation (Bhattarai 2016). Additionally, some literature also explored government-sponsored participation and participatory planning processes at national and subnational levels. All of these studies elucidated the reasons for the failure or success of these various participatory processes (Pandeya and Shrestha 2016; Bhusal 2018).

During the pandemic, the use of digital tools to enable citizen participation came to the fore. Many countries opted for e-participation in budgeting and planning processes, and participatory procedures were implemented through online platforms in many cities. Examples were the Cluj-Napoca City Hall in Romania and the Citizen Assembly in Turkey, both organised via online platforms (Sahin 2020). Similarly, in Slovakia, some towns conducted participatory processes through digital platforms and through e-mail and Facebook (Bardovič and Gašparík 2021). Moreover, several European countries had been experimenting with e-democracy even before COVID-19 (Mærøe et al. 2021). Nonetheless, studies exploring these participatory practices in Nepal are limited.

This chapter focuses on participatory processes of planning in Nepal during the first wave of the COVID-19 pandemic. Participatory planning requires an informal gathering of people to conduct discussions. However, the restrictions that came with efforts to control COVID-19 curtailed such activities. According to Allegretti and Alves (2020), during the pandemic, only those practices that allowed citizens to play a decisive role survived, whereas other methods whereby citizens played only consultative roles did not survive. This chapter also recognises that a public health crisis like COVID-19 can be a major factor in negatively impacting participatory practices, particularly in an unequal society like Nepal. Although there is little theoretical evidence to explain how pandemics affect participation, many studies do provide empirical evidence to understand these dynamics. This chapter investigates the following research questions: 1) In a country with very diverse ethnicities and stark inequality, do citizens participate for common interest or for self-interest? 2) Do unfavourable situations like the COVID-19 pandemic increase inequality in the name of the common good? 3) Can Nepal adopt digital innovations to enhance its participatory planning processes?

Overview of participatory planning in Nepal

Nepal's experience of participatory planning dates from the 1950s, when diverse participatory programmes were introduced to enable ordinary citizens to have a say. The first attempt to institutionalise participatory planning was made by King Mahendra, who took over as absolute ruler and banned the multi-party system in 1960. To legitimise his regime, the king introduced several initiatives toward administrative decentralisation. For instance, he brought in the Decentralisation Act of 1982, which encouraged people's participation in decentralized planning (Dhungel 2004). However, the act's objectives were not met, mainly because the multi-party system had been banned and elected representatives were strictly monitored. Citizen participation was allowed only as long as it did not disturb the existing power structure (Adhikari 2015; Phadnis 1981).

Only after the restoration of parliamentary democracy in 1990 did ordinary people have a legal right to engage formally in local decision-making, thanks to the Local Self Governance Act (LSGA) of 1999. This period was also marked by the emergence of many politically aware community and ethnic organisations demanding political space and rights (Hachhethu 2008). The LSGA made the participation of these community-based organisations (CBOs) compulsory in the planning process. Several grassroots-level CBOs acted as intermediaries between the government and citizens by participating in the planning process (Acharya and Zafarullah 2017). The LSGA had a provision to allocate at least 20 percent of seats to women in a local election and to nominate people from different ethnic groups for political positions (Dhungel 2011). Post-1990s democracy was progressive thanks to a number of factors, including the reintroduction of the multi-party system, an increased number of NGOs and CBOs, and the transfer of some rights to locally elected representatives. As a result, the introduction of the LSGA was a progressive step toward grassroots participation (Acharya 2016; Dhungel 2011). However, between 2002 and

2016, local democracy was interrupted because local elections did not take place. As a temporary arrangement, local responsibilities were transferred to bureaucrats (Adhikari 2006; Acharya 2016; Pandeya and Shrestha 2016). The absence of elected leaders in decentralised local government was a factor that adversely affected citizen participation (Adhikari 2006), with the result that participatory provisions were never completely implemented during this period.

Moreover, in the post-1990 democratic period, the country was experiencing political instability. In 2015, to address this, Nepal became a constitutional federal state. The motivation behind introducing federalism lay in the desire of the Nepali people and their political parties to end the civil war (1996–2006), and to stop the king from becoming absolute ruler. The people also wanted to provide equal participatory opportunities for the country's one hundred twenty-five castes and ethnicities (Drucza 2017; Lawoti 2012). The first two issues were solved with a peace agreement between the Maoists and the major political parties in 2006 (Comprehensive Peace Accord 2006). The third issue, equal opportunity for participation, was outlined in the Constitution of 2015. At the local level, constitutional commitment to promoting participation was further institutionalised by the Local Government Operation Act (LGOA) of 2017. This act gives citizens the right to participate in decision-making processes related to local policies and programmes. In line with these constitutional and legal arrangements, the seven hundred fifty-three newly formed local government units receive about thirty two percent of the budget (twenty percent from the central government and 12 percent from the provinces) to be utilised through a participatory planning process (Devkota 2020). Nepal's federal constitution allows locally elected representatives to play a vital role in the distribution of local budgets and planning. And the fact that a historic number of women (forty-one percent—including Dalit women (fourteen percent) were elected in the 2017 local election was truly remarkable (Election Commission 2017).

Against the background of the above-mentioned federal setting, this chapter presents a qualitative study of participatory planning in the Buddhabhumi municipality, located in the Kapilvastu District of Lumbini province in southern Nepal. The municipalities have informal planning structures in settlements commonly referred to as *tole,* at the grassroots level, where ordinary citizens can participate and deliberate. Various formal participatory forums also exist at ward and municipal levels, where elected representatives deliberate to filter project proposals. This research examines participation in each of these forums. The participatory planning process has

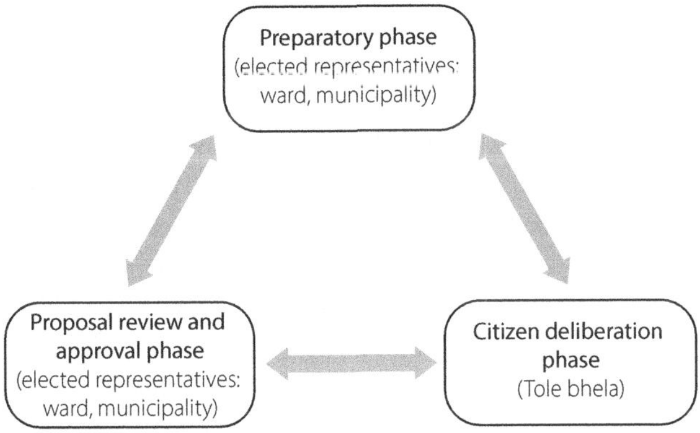

Figure 6.1. Different phases of planning.

aroused an interest among local representatives, who can play an important role in allocating municipal budgets to citizens through planning. For the same reason, it has also raised the expectations of ordinary citizens.

The municipal planning process organised by the new locally elected representatives includes several steps; these include prioritising the project proposal in settlement assemblies, filtering them in ward assemblies, and finalising them in municipal bodies. The planning steps can be broadly categorised into three different phases (see Figure 6.1): 1) the preparation phase, 2) the proposal review, and 3) the approval phase. In the first and third phases, locally elected representatives consult to prepare plans and then filter out the projects proposed by the citizens. This is done by the ward committee, then by the executive committee, and finally by the municipal assembly. Ordinary citizens participate only in the second phase, where they get the opportunity to join the assemblies (*bhela*) in their neighbourhoods or settlements (*tole*). Citizens can elaborate their proposals in these settlement assemblies (*tole bhela*). The Community Based Organisation (CBO) and all households are invited to participate in these deliberations. Thus, the *tole bhela* includes two kinds of citizens: those who are active in CBOs, and those who (while not engaged in CBOs) are available for deliberation (this is covered in the Local Government Operation Act 2017). These three phases are further divided into seven steps in the planning process. This chapter focuses particularly on participation and deliberation in the municipal planning process. The planning process allows local government to make decisions on all expenditure assignments granted by the constitution (twenty-two exclusive and fifteen concurrent matters), and it allows citizens to act as partners in political power distribution.

Methodology

This research examines citizen participation in the planning process in Nepal during the COVID-19 pandemic. Although the planning process is an obligatory responsibility of local government, during COVID-19 each local government responded differently based on their perceptions of their own immediate needs. Data were collected on a field visit to the Buddhabhumi municipality in February 2021. These data consist of interviews with ten ward chairpersons, a mayor, a deputy mayor, and twelve municipal and sub-municipal staff. In addition, a focus group discussion was held, involving fifteen ordinary citizens who participated in the planning process either in 2019 or 2020. These data were analysed, as was the framework issued by central government to address the immediate need for the planning process during the first wave of COVID-19. Secondary information was collected from various sources, including a number of government acts like the Constitution 2015, LGOA 2017, Local Level Planning Formulation Guidelines 2017, as well as other relevant laws, regulations, and directives.

Planning process during COVID-19

This section presents an analysis of the impact of the pandemic at every step of the planning process. Secondly, it examines whether or not a natural disaster like COVID-19 further excludes marginalised communities; it focuses particularly on the impact of the special arrangement introduced by the government to cope with the disease. Thirdly, it investigates whether, in adverse situations, certain innovations could have been introduced to encourage citizen participation.

Every municipality in Nepal is divided into sub-municipal units called wards. Each ward has a ward committee with a total of five elected representatives. Bhuddhabhumi municipality consists of ten wards. Elected representatives from the wards play a major role in the planning process. As mentioned earlier, the seven steps of the planning process can be divided into three phases: 1) preparation, 2) citizen deliberation, and 3) proposal review and approval. Because the planning process is obligatory, it continued even during the pandemic, but with modifications and precautions to minimise the spread of the disease.

Preparation

The first step is preparation. The municipality estimates the internal revenue and the intergovernmental fiscal transfer required for total municipal expenditures. Through the executive committee it submits a report to the federal and provincial governments by 15 January each year. Based on this report, by mid-April the federal and provincial governments prepare a framework for fiscal transfer and provide a municipal budget ceiling. This task was not obstructed by COVID-19 because the first wave of the pandemic did not hit Nepal until late in April 2020.

Thematic sectors

The second step involves determining a budget ceiling for the sub-municipal units known as wards. These have themed sectors, including Economic Development, Infrastructure, Social Development, Forest and Environment, Disaster Management, and Governance and Institutional Development. In 2020, each ward received less than one percent of the total municipal budget. Although the infrastructure budget received a large share, other areas were not prioritised in the same way. However, this step was also not affected by COVID-19.

Citizen deliberation

This is the third step of the planning process, which allows citizens to participate and deliberate. This phase was directly affected by COVID-19 because public meetings and gatherings were banned from mid-April until the end of May 2020. The settlement assemblies (*tole bhela*) could not take place until the beginning of June. In most wards, the settlement assemblies were conducted with minimal participation by citizens (between ten and twelve) to avoid spreading the disease. As a result, the settlement assemblies, which provide a public forum for citizen deliberation, were adversely affected by the pandemic; citizen attendance was greatly reduced. Table 6.1 shows comparative statistics for all ten wards with regard to their status for conducting participatory meetings at the settlement level (*tole*) as well as the budget approvals during fiscal years 2019–2020 and 2020–2021. Whereas about forty to fifty citizens participated in each settlement meeting in the planning for 2019, in 2020 either very few citizens could participate, or the settlement assemblies were cancelled altogether.

Of the ten wards of Bhuddhabhumi municipality, six conducted small gatherings of ten to twelve people and collected their project demands. As the attendance of local citizens in the project selection process was nominal, the discussion did not include as many people as expected. Most participating citizens were from local groups, youth clubs, local social and political networks, or people close to the ward's male elected representatives. Nevertheless, three wards did not conduct any settlement assemblies at

Table 6.1. Attendance of ordinary people in settlement assemblies of Buddhabhumi municipality in the year 2020 v. 2019.

	W1	W2	W3	W4	W5	W6	W7	W8	W9	W10
Number of people in *Tole/ Basti Bhela* 2020 (During the Pandemic)	10-12 People	10-12 People	Assembly was canceled. The projects were taken from last year's list	10-12 People	10-12 People	10-12 People	Assembly was canceled. Ward and local volunteers collected projects.	Assembly was canceled. Ward members and local volunteers collected projects	10-12 People	Assembly was canceled. Ward members and local volunteers collected the project
Number of people in *Tole/ Basti Bhela* 2019	40-50 People	40-50 People	40-50 People	40-50 People	40-50 People	40-50 People	40-50 People	40-50 People	40-50 People	40-50 People

all. Instead, ward members and local volunteers collected information on different projects from the settlements in these wards. In these cases, deliberation could not take place. The remaining wards did not organise any settlement assembly nor collect information about projects through volunteers but did include some projects that had not been discussed in the preceding year's planning.

Although the participation of citizens in the institutional process was adversely affected by COVID-19, none of the ward chairpersons interviewed considered non-participation a challenge. Instead, three participants of the focus group discussion confirmed that, because the elected representatives had not come up with any alternative methods, COVID-19 had been used as an excuse to avoid participation. In fact, the pandemic turned out to be a blessing in disguise for those who had never been interested in organising settlement assemblies because, while it lasted, the role of female and Dalit elected representatives was also greatly reduced.

The projects that people demanded were mostly related to infrastructure issues in their own neighbourhoods, dealing with things like drinking water taps, small tube wells, irrigation canals, irrigation roads, community buildings, etc., things that would be a benefit to their community. Although discussions took place, these largely benefitted the elite. In contrast, projects proposed by people from marginalised communities were mostly ignored by the elite, who were able to manipulate the process to ensure their own interests were met rather than those of the marginalised.

Proposal review and approval

In the fourth step of the planning process, the wards' elected representatives or Ward Committee (consisting of a chairperson, two male members, a female member, and a Dalit female member) filter the proposals collected from the settlement and group them into different thematic categories. Projects considered important by the committees but which cannot be covered by the ward budget are then forwarded to the municipality. In Bhuddhabhumi, during the pandemic, Dalit members did not attend these meetings, whereas they had attended such meetings in previous years.

Proposed plan filtered, integrated by municipality

The fifth step of any plans proposed by the ward committees involved having them filtered by the thematic committee and proposed for integration by the municipality. This stage actually encompasses the fifth, sixth, and seventh steps of the planning process, here bundled together to explain the process more simply. Although discussion occurred to decide which recommended projects to include, some projects were added based on recommendations by the mayor, deputy mayors, or other elected representatives; this was in contravention of the correct procedures for project selection. In the planning process all projects are supposed to be recommended by the people of the settlement assemblies. Once the proposed plans and projects have been filtered by the ward committees, a municipal executive committee then approves them for finalisation. This committee includes ward chairpersons, a mayor, a deputy mayor, and three nominated members from a marginalised community who endorse the selected projects. During the pandemic these meetings took place under the confines of social distancing.

It is noteworthy that the sectorial priorities presented in the municipal assembly in June 2020 were slightly different because the municipality had directed some of its budget to the employment needs of returning migrants (most of them coming back from Gulf countries where they had lost their jobs due to COVID-19 restrictions). These projects were focused mainly on animal husbandry and vegetable farming. However, as the beneficiaries were not included in the discussions, in most cases the budget allocation did not match their needs or interests. For instance, one returnee had an interest in opening a dairy product shop, but as the fund was allocated for other purposes he could not use it and remained unemployed. The grant only benefitted people who owned their own land, not people like this returnee, who did not own anything. As a result, most marginalised people remained marginalised. Nevertheless, the proposal review phase of the planning process was less affected by COVID-19 because by the time it started, in mid-June 2020, some of the restrictions were beginning to be lifted and municipal meetings could be held with appropriate measures taken to counter COVID-19.

Flexible COVID-19 arrangements leading to further exclusions

When COVID-19 hit Nepal, the central government took some immediate action to try and cope with the pandemic while performing municipal tasks as smoothly as possible. One action taken by the government was to issue 'The Framework for Identifying Immediate Needs and COVID-19 Sensitive Planning During the Difficult Circumstances Created by COVID-19' which granted local governments some flexibility by allowing inter-head budget transfer from a previously planned project to new COVID-19 relief projects (Government of Nepal 2020). Such an arrangement was very helpful for municipalities that did not have budgets left over from the previous year's planning cycle to deal with disaster management. It also allowed municipalities to address immediate budget needs for dealing with the pandemic, especially during the period from April to June 2020 (mainly for quarantine and isolation spaces, testing kits, and contact tracing).

Buddhabhumi was one of the municipalities that had dedicated only a negligible amount of its budget to disaster management, and was relieved by the government's flexibility on this issue. An immediate budget was made available by cancelling some of the projects planned for the 2019–2020 cycle. Unfortunately, the projects that were cancelled had been targeted to help women and marginalised communities. Instead, the money was used for COVID-19 relief projects. Out of ten wards, nine projects targeting marginalised communities and women were cancelled. The justification was that these activities required gatherings. None of the ward committees tried to modify the projects to keep them targeted for marginalised communities. Budgets approved in the 2019 planning and supposed to be used in 2020 were now directed toward the creation of quarantine and isolation centres, material relief distribution, etc. As a result, marginalised groups became even more marginalised during the pandemic because their needs were not prioritised; budgets allocated to them had been redirected. Ward representatives claimed that the budget was now being used for the benefit of the whole ward (field observation 2021). This indicates that the political rhetoric of doing things for the common good, for the benefit of the wider community, was undermining the interests of subordinate, marginalised groups.

The planning process in Nepal exemplifies the country's initiative toward deliberative democracy at the local level. Usually, it involves decision-making that benefits the larger community by engaging in a discussion of the common benefits or 'common good'. The government's special arrangement to allow inter-head budget transfers for the sake of this common good during COVID-19 convinced subordinate groups to believe that it was acceptable to use their budgets for the common interests of the wider community. Funding that had been assigned to targeted communities was allotted instead to COVID-19 relief projects. As Mansbridge et al. (2010) stated, a focus on the common good can render illegitimate the self-interest of the poor, thereby increasing inequality. This was underlined when the issues of marginalised communities were side-lined in Nepal during the pandemic; they lost the municipal budget that was supposed to be directed towards them and their needs. The pandemic negatively impacted the institutional participatory process and citizen participation was reduced as a result. The government introduced a policy that looked good on paper, but its vagueness made it 'gender and socially blind'. Had it specified that the budget directed towards marginalised communities and women must be used only by those communities, perhaps the findings of this research would be different.

Innovation with use of digital platforms

With the growing use of the internet in Nepal, the culture of using social networking applications like Facebook has become very common. According to a survey in 2019, Nepal had over ten million Facebook users, which is about thirty-three percent of the country's population. People use social networks to connect with their family and friends and get local information (*Nepali Sansaar* 2019). When COVID-19 hit Nepal many online portals and social media, such as Facebook and YouTube, were used to spread rumours portraying Muslims as carriers and spreaders of the disease (Regmi et al. 2022). Nevertheless, many studies show that despite the danger of misinformation, many countries adapted their participatory practices to include digital platforms (Bardovič and Gašparík 2021; Mærøe et al. 2021; Allegretti and Dias 2020).

In Buddhabhumi no such digital participatory innovation was observed, even though people from the municipalities were well served by broadband, Wi-Fi, and mobile data services provided by mobile phone companies like N-Cell and NTC, which allowed people to use social platforms very easily. Thus, Buddhabumu municipality had easy access to the internet. Moreover, during the first wave of COVID-19 in Nepal, internet connections increased ten times (compared to the non-COVID-19 period (Interview 2021). As a result, more and more people were being informed and entertained by using digital platforms when confined to their houses.

When elected representatives were asked why they did not think of using social media to collect people's opinions, they said that most people were illiterate and did not know how to write their arguments on social media (Interview 2021). However, a study conducted in India, China, and Nepal shows that even non-literate people can have strategies for using mobile phones, by using voice recordings or pictures (Chipchase 2008). This study also shows that people who cannot read or write can easily watch a video or see flyers with images that can be used to communicate the municipality's messages. They can also record their own voices to send messages to the municipality's social media platform. According to the Buddhabhumi municipality's own information, its literacy rate is actually 90 percent (which is high compared to the general literacy rate of Nepal, which is a little over 70%) (Buddhabhumi municipality 2019). In addition to this, the municipality appointed an IT officer with technical knowledge, who could have helped with this outreach. However, his help was not sought in this area. That digital literacy was used as a pretext not to use social networks indicates a lack of political will to facilitate the participatory process.

Conclusion

This chapter shows that institutional participatory practices were adversely affected in Nepal during the COVID-19 pandemic. Public meetings where people could discuss issues relating to their settlements were either poorly attended or cancelled. Although, ideally, these forums promote deliberative democracy at a grassroots level, marginalised citizens were not able to articulate their interests because of the pandemic. Policies brought in to cope with COVID-19 seemed good on paper but failed to meet the needs of this group. In fact, the pandemic became an excuse to further disempower them. Added to this was the fact that these citizens were unaware of what was in their best interest. As a result, elites pushed for their own interests in the name of the common good. During the pandemic, budgets were used for the common benefit of the wider community instead of for the marginalised.

This chapter highlights the new social and political realities of participatory practices that emerged in Nepal during COVID-19. It also questions Nepal's current understanding and definition of 'common good'. It points out that, although a substantial number of people were already using social media (which was unfortunately also used to spread misinformation), the municipality did not consider using it to spread proper information, or to continue with participatory planning projects. No noticeable digital innovation was available to promote or even continue pre-pandemic levels of citizen participation. Political leaders used the pandemic as a pretext to avoid their responsibilities toward these citizens, thereby impairing institutional participatory practices.

In conclusion, we can see that there was a reduction in institutional citizen participation in Nepal during the pandemic, partly because elected representatives were not interested in supporting it and partly because the pandemic became a convenient pretext for avoiding it. This has further accelerated the exclusion of marginalised communities, especially as no apparent effort was made to encourage their participation via digital means. However, although the pandemic negatively impacted participatory practices, some of these practices have resumed since the pandemic ended.

Nevertheless, it must be kept in mind that Nepal's federalism is still in a transitional phase. The LGOA 2017 came into existence in 2017, with newly elected representatives in office that same year. Without prior experience, these newly elected representatives were trying to learn and adapt to their new roles in the federal context when COVID-19 hit. Nepal never had the chance to implement its new participatory provisions. This will be further elaborated on in my Ph.D. dissertation, which focuses on institutional participatory practices in the new federal context of Nepal both before and after the pandemic. It is still too early to assess the long-term impact of COVID-19, as only two planning cycles have occurred since that time. However, one significant impact was the construction of a new hospital. COVID-19 made the municipal government realise the importance of having a medical facility available. Buddhabhumi now has a fifteen-bed hospital with outpatient services that will soon begin to function. When it comes to the issue of health a few lessons have been learned.

Bibliography

Abers, Rebecca. 2001. 'Practicing Radical Democracy: Lessons from Brazil', The Planning Review, 37(147), 32–38. London: Routledge. https://doi.org/10.1080/02513625.2001.10556786

Acharya, Keshav K. 2016. 'Determinants of Community Governance for Effective Basic Service Delivery in Nepal', Dhaulagiri Journal of Sociology and Anthropology, 10 (October), 166–201. https://doi.org/10.3126/dsaj.v10i0.15885

Acharya, Keshav K., and Habib Zafarullah. 2017. 'Service Delivery and Development at the Grassroots: The Evolution and Contribution of Community-Based Organisations in Nepal', Asia Pacific Journal of Public Administration, 39(4), 276–86. London: Taylor & Francis.https://doi.org/10.1080/23276665.2017.140826

Adhikari, Damodar. 2006. Towards Local Democracy in Nepal: Power and Participation in District Development Planning. SPRING Research Series, no. 47. TU Dortmund: SPRING Centre.

Adhikari, Krishna. 2015. 'Rural Development Policies, CBOs and Their Sustainability in Nepal' in Ambika P. Adhikari et al. (eds.), Sustainable Livelihood Systems in Nepal: Principles, Practices and Prospects, 237–62. Kathmandu. IUCN and CFFN.

Allegretti, Giovanni, and Mariana Lopes Alves. 2020. '(In)Stability, a Key Element to Understand Participatory Budgeting: Discussing Portuguese Cases', Journal of Deliberative Democracy, 8(2). https://doi.org/10.16997/jdd.147

Allegretti, Giovanni, and Nelson Dias. 2020. "How to Manage and Reimagine Participatory Budgeting in Covid and Post-Covid Era? Evidences from a Mutual

Learning Space for Portuguese Local Authorities." Paper presented at Participatory Budgeting Workshop 2020, Paris, November 24, 2020.

Allmendinger, Philip, and Mark Tewdwr-Jones. 2002. 'The Communicative Turn in Urban Planning: Unravelling Paradigmatic, Imperialistic and Moralistic Dimensions', Space and Polity, 6(1), 5–24. https://doi.org/10.1080/13562570220137871

Baiocchi, Gianpaolo, and Ernesto Ganuza. 2017. Popular Democracy: The Paradox of Participation. Redwood City: Stanford University Press.

Bardovič, Jakub, and Jozef Gašparík. 2021. 'Enablers of Participatory Budgeting in Slovakia during the COVID-19 Pandemic', Scientific Papers of the University of Pardubice, Series D: Faculty of Economics and Administration, 29(1). https://doi.org/10.46585/sp29011248

Bhattarai, Binod. 2016. 'Community Forest and Forest Management in Nepal', Imperial Journal of Interdisciplinary Research (IJIR), II (11). http://www.onlinejournal.in/IJIRV2I11/078.pdf

Bhusal, Thaneshwar. 2018. 'Examining Citizen Participation in Local Policymaking: An Analysis of Nepal's Participatory Planning Process'. PhD Thesis, University of Canberra, Bruce.

Bohman, James. 1997. 'Deliberative Democracy and Effective Social 321 Freedom: Capabilities, Resources, and Opportunities' in James Bohman and William Rehg (eds.), Deliberative Democracy: Essays on Reason and Politics. Cambridge MA: MIT Press.

Buddhabhumi municipality. 2019. 'Profile of Buddhabhumi Municipality'. Municipal Government, Buddhabhumi, Nepal.

Cabannes, Yves, and Barbara Lipietz. 2018. 'Revisiting the Democratic Promise of Participatory Budgeting in Light of Competing Political, Good Governance and Technocratic Logics', Environment and Urbanization, 30(1), 67–84. https://doi.org/10.1177/0956247817746279

Chipchase, Jan. 2008. 'Reducing Illiteracy as a Barrier to Mobile Communication' in James E. Katz (ed.), Handbook of Mobile Communication Studies. (79–90) Cambridge MA: MIT Press. https://doi.org/10.7551/mitpress/9780262113120.003.0007

Cohen, Joshua. 1997. 'Deliberation and Democratic Legitimacy' in James Bohman and William Rehg (eds.), Deliberative Democracy: Essays on Reason and Politics (67–92). Cambridge MA: MIT Press.

'Comprehensive Peace Accord'. 2006. https://peacemaker.un.org/sites/peacemaker.un.org/files/NP_061122_Comprehensivepercent20Peacepercent20Agreement-percent20betweenpercent20thepercent20Governmentpercent20andpercent-20thepercent20CPNpercent20percent28Maoistpercent29.pdf

Della Porta, Donatella. 2013. Can Democracy Be Saved?: Participation, Deliberation and Social Movements. Cambridge: Polity Press.

Devkota, Khim Lal. 2020. 'Intergovernmental Fiscal Transfers in a Federal Nepal', International Center for Public Policy, Andrew Young School of Policy Studies, Georgia State University, International Center for Public Policy Working Paper Series, at AYSPS, GSU. https://ideas.repec.org/p/ays/ispwps/paper2017.html

Dhungel, Dwarika Nath (ed.). 2004. Nepālamā Vikendrīkaraṇasambandhī Sārvajanika Prayāsaharu. Kathmandu: Institute for Integrated Development Studies.

Dhungel, Dwarika Nath. 2011. Decentralization in Nepal: Laws and Practices. Oslo: Norwegian Institute for Urban and Regional Research.

Drucza, Kristie. 2017. 'Talking About Inclusion: Attitudes and Affirmative Action in Nepal', Development Policy Review, 35(2). https://doi.org/10.1111/dpr.12205

Election Commission. 2017. 'Election Result Book, 1 to 7'. Election Commission, Government of Nepal. https://www.election.gov.np/election/np/election-result-book.html

Elstub, Stephen. 2018. 'Deliberative and Participatory Democracy' in Stephen Elstub et al. (eds.), The Oxford Handbook of Deliberative Democracy (186–202). Oxford University Press. https://doi.org/10.1093/oxfordhb/9780198747369.013.5

Floridia, Antonio. 2014. 'Beyond participatory democracy, towards deliberative democracy: elements of a possible theoretical genealogy', Rivista italiana di scienza politica, 3, 299–326. https://doi.org/10.1426/78850

Forester, John. 1999. The Deliberative Practitioner: Encouraging Participatory Planning Processes. Cambridge MA: MIT Press.

Friedmann, John. 2011. Insurgencies: Essays in Planning Theory. Abingdon: Routledge.

Fung, Archon, and Erik Olin Wright. 2001. 'Deepening Democracy: Innovations in Empowered Participatory Governance', Politics & Society, 29(1), 5–41. https://doi.org/10.1177/0032329201029001002

Government of Nepal. 2020. 'Framework for Identifying Immediate Needs and COVID-19 Sensitive Planning during the Difficult Circumstances Created by the COVID-19'. Ministry of Federal Affairs and General Administration.

Habermas, Jürgen. 2005. 'Lifeworld and System: A Critique of Functionalist Reason' in Jürgen Habermas, The Theory of Communicative Action (trans. Thomas MacCarthy). Boston MA: Beacon.

Healey, Patsy. 1997. Collaborative Planning. Macmillan Education UK. https://doi.org/10.1007/978-1-349-25538-2

Heller, Patrick. 2001. 'Moving the State: The Politics of Democratic Decentralization in Kerala, South Africa, and Porto Alegre', Politics & Society, 29(1), 131–63. https://doi.org/10.1177/0032329201029001006

Isaacs, T.M. Thomas and Richard W. Franke. 2002. Local Democracy and Development: The Kerala People's Campaign for Decentralized Planning. Lanham MD: Rowman & Littlefield.

Lawoti, Mahendra. 2012. 'Ethnic Politics and the Building of an Inclusive State' in Sebastian von Einsiedel et al (eds.), Nepal in Transition (129–52). Cambridge: Cambridge University Press. https://doi.org/10.1017/CBO9781139021869.006 'Local Government Operation Act'. 2017. Government of Nepal.

Mærøe, Anders Røsten, Alexander Norta, Valentyna Tsap, and Ingrid Pappel. 2021. 'Increasing Citizen Participation in E-Participatory Budgeting Processes', Journal of Information Technology & Politics, 18(2), 125–47. https://doi.org/10.1080/19331681.2020.1821421

Mansbridge, Jane. 1999. 'Everyday Talk in the Deliberative System' in Stephen Macedo (ed.), Deliberative Politics Essays on Democracy and Disagreement (211–238). Oxford: Oxford University Press.

Mansbridge, Jane, James Bohman, Simone Chambers, David Estlund, Andreas Follesdal, Archon Fung, Cristina Lafont, Bernard Manin, and Jose Luis Marta. 2010. 'The Place of Self-Interest and the Role of Power in Deliberative Democracy', Journal of Political Philosophy, 18(1), 64–100. https://doi.org/10.1111/j.1467-9760.2009.00344.x

Nepali Sansaar. 2019. 'Facebook – Nepalis Most Loved Social Media App', Nepali Sansaar (15 April). https://www.nepalisansar.com/technology/facebook-nepalis-most-loved-social-media-app/

Ostrom, Elinor, Wai Lam, Prachanda Pradhan, and Ganesh Shivakoti. 2011. Improving Irrigation in Asia. Edward Elgar Publishing. https://doi.org/10.4337/9780857938022

Pandeya, Ganesh Prasad and Shree Krishna Shrestha. 2016. 'Does Citizen Participation Improve Local Planning? An Empirical Analysis of Stakeholders' Perceptions in Nepal', Journal of South Asian Development, 11(3), 276–304. https://doi.org/10.1177/0973174116667097

Phadnis, Urmila. 1981. 'Nepal: The Politics of Referendum', Pacific Affairs, 54(3), 431. https://doi.org/10.2307/2756788

Pradhan, Prachanda. 2000. 'Farmer Managed Irrigation Systems in Nepal at the Crossroads'. https://dlc.dlib.indiana.edu/dlc/bitstream/handle/10535/331/pradhanp041500.pdf?sequence

Regmi, Pramod R., Shovita Dhakal Adhikari, Nirmal Aryal, Sharada P. Wasti, and Edwin van Teijlingen. 2022. 'Fear, Stigma and Othering: The Impact of COVID-19 Rumours on Returnee Migrants and Muslim Populations of Nepal', International Journal of Environmental Research and Public Health, 19(15), 8986. https://doi.org/10.3390/ijerph19158986

Sahin, Savas Zafer. 2020. 'Turkey's COVID-19 Pandemic Response from a Practitioners Perspective' in Paul Joyce et al (eds.), Good Public Governance in a Global Pandemic. (105–108). IIAS Public Governance Series, Vol.1.

Young, Iris Marion. 2003. 'Activist Challenges to Deliberative Democracy' in James S. Fishkin et al (eds.), Debating Deliberative Democracy. Oxford: Blackwell.

About the author

Vishnu Kumari Tandon received her PhD in December 2023 from L'École des Hautes Études en Sciences Sociales (EHESS), Paris; her research focused on federalism and participatory democracy. Currently, she serves as a Social Development and Citizen Engagement Consultant at the World Bank, and she holds the position of Senior Program Officer at the International Commission for Dalit Rights (ICDR) in Washington, D.C. Additionally, she contributes as an Associate Researcher at Centre d'Études Sud-Asiatiques et Himalayennes, Paris. Furthermore, as a co-founder of the Federalism Project in Paris, she is actively engaged in creating a mobile, interdisciplinary platform for researchers from different horizons working on federalism and participation in Asia. She is currently assembling a multidisciplinary volume on Federalism and Participatory practices in Asia. Ms. Tandon also served as a Teaching Fellow at the Institute of Political Studies (Sciences Po) and the Institut National des Langues et Civilisations Orientales (INALCO) in Paris. She has also had several years of professional experience in governance, citizen participation, and gender equality, obtained while working with national and international organizations in Nepal, the Netherlands, the Democratic Republic of the Congo, France, and the United States.
vishnutandan@gmail.com

7. Connecting Government COVID-19 Measures and the Exercise of Citizenship

A Comparative Case Study of the Netherlands and Vietnam

Seohee Kwak

Abstract: The COVID-19 pandemic prompted countries worldwide to implement measures, including restrictions on gatherings and travel. This study examines how governments' responses to citizens exercising their rights varied based on the overall level of freedom in the countries. To compare contrasting cases, the Netherlands (a democratic state) and Vietnam (an authoritarian state) were selected. Analysing incidents from 2020–2021, both governments aimed to control the pandemic yet exhibited distinct approaches. These differences stem from varying norms of citizenship and their expression through formal political institutions. Findings suggest similarities in rationales but notable disparities in tipping points and control intensity.

Keywords: COVID-19, citizenship, protest, online criticism, government response

Introduction

COVID-19 hit virtually every part of the world in 2019. Governments introduced a variety of measures to contain the spread of the virus, handle the infected, and protect their citizens. However, governments were not able to please every citizen, with some of them criticising and opposing the imposed COVID-19 measures. This study starts by raising the question of whether and how government restrictions and responses to citizen action

---

Gregory Bracken, Paul Rabé, Nurul Azreen Azlan (eds), *Future Practices of Citizenship in Asia and the West: Care of the Self (Volume III)*. Taylor & Francis Group, 2025
DOI: 10.5117/9789048562077_CH07

around COVID-19 measures have differed across different political regimes. More specifically, it aims to discover the experiences of people exercising their rights as citizens to take political action and get involved in public affairs during the pandemic period and to relate these to the concepts of citizenship formulated by the existing institutions.

To compare two different countries situated at different ends of the freedom spectrum, this study selected the Netherlands and Vietnam; the former is depicted as a free, democratic state and the latter as an authoritarian state. Among several indices, I refer to the Freedom in the World report which assesses a wide-ranging spectrum of citizen's rights across countries. According to the Freedom in the World, the Netherlands scored 97 out of 100, being labelled a 'free' country with 39 out of 40 on political rights and 58 out of 60 on civil liberties (Freedom House 2024a). In contrast, Vietnam scored 19 out of 100, being labelled as 'not free' with 4 out of 40 on political rights and 15 out of 60 on civil liberties (Freedom House 2024b). According to categorical definitions of authoritarian regimes made by Levitsky and Way (2010), Vietnam, a single-party regime, is a 'full authoritarian regime'.

Both democratic and authoritarian regimes have citizenship norms, yet what matters is the characteristics and manifestations of citizenship, which are shaped differently by their institutional contexts. This study focuses on the nexus between the institutional contexts—laws, rules, policies, and organisations—and the political behaviours of state actors and citizens seeking to understand their interplay in society. By investigating several incidents of political action that occurred in the two countries in the period of 2020-2021, this study identifies similarities and differences in 1) the approaches by which citizens in the Netherlands and in Vietnam took action against government COVID-19 measures and 2) the responses of the governments to citizens who took political action against their COVID-19 policies. In operationalising the research questions, this study focuses on three different, but closely interrelated, dimensions: 1) the forms of political action taken by citizens; 2) the norms of citizenship expected and/or imposed by the formal political institutions; 3) the tipping points and types of control exercised by state actors.

This study is a qualitative analysis of the collected media reports. At the initial stage of data exploration, I searched for data on political action in the respective countries using various keywords: public protest, demonstrations, criticise, social media, etc. I reviewed twenty-five media reports and government press releases covering incidents of political action and state response in the Netherlands and in Vietnam. The protests studied are not exhaustive; several incidents were investigated for which media reports provide sufficient information on the dynamics between citizens and state actors such as local governments and the police. Instead of simply counting the occurrence of political action, I have focused on the characteristics of citizens' political action against the governments' COVID-19 measures and the responses of state actors.

This paper is organised as follows. Section 2 provides the analytical framework that guides the study by combining norms of citizenship with new institutionalist approaches. Sections 3 and 4 are committed to elaborating events of political action that occurred in the Netherlands and Vietnam. A descriptive account of the events is given, backed by the collected qualitative data. Section 5 delineates the findings and insights drawn from the investigation of the two countries, identifying a matrix of similarities and differences, followed by a conclusion in Section 6.

Analytical framework

Due to its multiplicity and complexity, no consensus has been reached on the definition of citizenship. In particular, the theoretical range of citizenship rights is broad, encompassing not only fundamental legal rights but also social compensation or labour market participation rights (Janoski and Gran 2002). Janoski (1998, 9) defined citizenship as 'passive and active membership of individuals in a nation-state with universalistic rights and obligations at a specified level of equality', while Dalton (2008, 78) looked at citizenship norms in a more politically oriented sense, defining them as 'a shared set of expectations about the citizen's role in politics'. Thus, studies on the norms of citizenship have been guided by two different dimensions in elucidating a relationship between a citizen and a state: duty-based citizenship as a legal status conforming to rules and obligations required by the state, and rights-based citizenship focused on engagement, activities and exercising of one's rights (Dalton, 2008; Kymlicka and Norman 1994; van Deth 2007). Furthermore, studies on citizenship have conceptually expanded from citizenship as a legal status with duties and responsibilities to citizenship that encompasses social recognition and identities (Isin and Turner 2002; Raney and Berdahl 2009). As argued by Kymlicka and Norman (1994, 360) on 'a balance of rights and responsibilities' for a more appropriate conception of citizenship, the dynamics between what citizens are entitled to and what they are obliged to do should be identified in empirical case studies.

Citizenship has been examined from diverse perspectives taking it as not being fixed but multi-faceted and socially constructed through the dynamic influence of institutions, policies, and socio-cultural practices (Yarwood 2014). Cross-country analyses have been conducted on the manifestation of citizenship norms across different socio-economic statuses, histories, and democratic levels (Bolzendahl and Coffé 2013; Cenker-Özek et al. 2021; Coffé and van der Lippe 2010; Hooghe and Oser 2015; Hooghe et al. 2016; van Deth et al. 2007). However, less research has articulated the similarities or differences in the interplay of the behaviours of actors and the formal political institutions between two contrasting political regimes: an established democracy and an authoritarian, single-party regime. This study aims to fill this gap by taking a broadly political conception of citizenship, understood as the membership of an individual accompanied by the duties and rights *vis-à-vis* a nation-state.

For the analytic focus of this paper, the rights of citizens are limited to legal and political rights, more specifically, freedom of speech, freedom of assembly or protest, and the right to participate in public affairs: in particular how and to what extent people (can) exercise their rights, as citizens, to engage in the government's COVID-19 measures. With regard to political action, legal rights are represented by casting a vote in elections while political rights include civil society group membership, petition signing, and participating in demonstrations. Although aware that not only citizenship norms but also different social identities generated and perceived by citizens influence political participation (Raney and Berdahl 2009), I set the conceptual focus of this study on the dynamics between the institutional conditions and citizens, as actors situated within the given institutions, at an aggregate level.

According to a definition by one of the institutionalist scholars, North (1990, 3), institutions refer to 'the rules of the game in a society or, more formally, the humanly devised constraints that shape human interaction'. In addition to 'hard' institutions, indicating the formal set of rules and apparatus enforcing the rules, there are 'soft' institutions, involving conventions and practices informally produced and accepted in a given context (Pennington 2009, 14–15). In this study, (formal) institutions refer to the sets of rules and organisations that affect behaviours of societal members. Since new institutionalism emerged in the late 1970s and 1980s to better delineate the interplay between the different components of institutions and the behaviours of individuals, new institutionalist approaches have received constant attention in political studies (Chappell 2006; Hall and Taylor 1996; Lowndes and Roberts 2013; March and Olson 2005; Peters 2012; Schedler 2009). Hall and Taylor (1996) provided an extensive account of the three main schools of thought of new institutionalism: rational choice, and historical and sociological institutionalism. Each variant of the new institutionalist approach has its own strengths and weaknesses in explaining the complexities of the institutions, yet ample room exists for synthesizing these different thoughts in comparative politics (Pennington 2009).

My main concern here does not lie in rigorously testing a single specific thought of new institutionalism. Arguing that institutions serve as decisive factors in shaping the behaviours of state actors and citizens, I take a comprehensive approach when noting the influence of the predetermined set of rules in a society. It is not the first time that new institutionalism has been applied in investigating individual and collective political action in democratic and authoritarian regimes (Schedler 2009). I assume that social appropriateness and legitimacy are generated in different ways across the different societal contexts of the Netherlands and Vietnam. Behaviours of actors are guided by the institutions which frame and (re)produce social norms and conventions, as individuals tend to do what is socially appropriate (Hall and Taylor 1996).

The Netherlands: Protests in public spaces

As the COVID-19 situation rapidly deteriorated, the Dutch government announced multiple measures including a ban on gatherings in an attempt to prevent the spread of the virus. Over the two years of the pandemic, depending on the situation, the Dutch government adopted a cycle of tightening and lifting of restrictions that inevitably brought about inconveniences to people's daily lives. Following growing complaints and frustration with the measures, the pattern of political action noticeable in the Netherlands was public protest, regardless of the government's temporary prohibition of assembly.

In June 2020, around 400 protesters who gathered to oppose the lockdown and social distancing rules were arrested for their refusal to leave a park, the Malieveld in The Hague. According to reports and videos released online, a clash broke out between some protesters and the police, the latter using shields and batons and firing a water cannon. The municipality had banned the assembly, citing the social distancing rules. However, the police tolerated it without applying repressive measures until the estimated number of protesters exceeded a thousand and some extreme football fans from different regions joined the protest. As a result, the city shut down a few areas and requested dispersion (RTL Nieuws 2020).

Another eye-catching event of mass protest broke out in January 2021, marked by its violence. In January 2021, people took to the streets of several cities to oppose the introduction of the 21.00–04.30 curfew announced by the government. Clashes occurred between protesters and the police in at least ten cities as the protests turned violent, with the setting on fire of bikes and cars, the looting of shops, and the throwing of fireworks and stones at police officers. As a consequence of these aggressive behaviours, around 240 people were arrested across the country (Dutch News 2021). In Eindhoven and Amsterdam, the police also deterred protesters by using repressive means such as firing water cannons and tear gas (Dutch News 2021). In addition, hundreds of people marched the streets of The Hague on 25 January 2021 to oppose the government's regulation of the corona pass, making proof of vaccination compulsory to enter cafes, restaurants, and other public spaces (The Guardian 2021). Following the violent actions of some protesters, the police arrested more than a hundred people (The Guardian 2021).

A series of other protests in multiple cities continued throughout the year as the Dutch government maintained or even tightened COVID-19-related regulations. In mid-November 2021, protests broke out for several days across the country. Hundreds of people gathered in Rotterdam on 20 November, setting fire to police vehicles and throwing projectiles at the police. The protesters condemned the government's corona pass plan and the ban on fireworks for New Year's Eve celebrations. As the protest turned violent and injuries occurred, state authorities took repressive responses; the municipality of Rotterdam announced a state of emergency, closing down the train station, and the police fired warning shots, used water cannons, and arrested at least 20 people (BBC 2021). An emergency ordinance was issued in another city, Enschede, and the police used batons to break up protesters; five police officers were injured in The Hague after a severe clash, with protesters throwing stones, and at least sixty-four people were arrested in three provinces (Deutsch 2021).

On 2 January 2022, another mass protest was staged by thousands of people in Amsterdam in opposition to the government's tight coronavirus lockdown measures, including a ban on assembly. People gathered in a public square and marched down the streets holding banners with the words 'Freedom' and 'Less repression'. In response, the Mayor of Amsterdam issued an emergency ordinance authorising the police to disperse the protesters; a large number of riot police were stationed to cordon off protesters and make them leave the area (Euronews 2022). As the protest continued, the police used batons and shields to disperse the crowds. As a result of the clash, at least 30 protesters were detained, and four police officers were injured (Reuters 2022).

Another protest broke out on 16 January 2022 as thousands of citizens took to the streets of Amsterdam to oppose the government's continued lockdown measures that compelled non-essential businesses to shut for weeks right before the year-end holidays and throughout the new year period. Citizens participating in the protest condemned the government for curtailing people's freedoms. The protesters took non-violent approaches by marching, chanting, and holding placards and yellow umbrellas. The police were dispatched, but no heavy-handed control occurred.

Online activism was another common form of political action. For instance, an online petition calling for the abolition of the corona vaccination check rules addressed to the House of Representatives drew more than 874,000 signatures on Petities.nl. However, a thread of the protest events demonstrates that mass protest was not a one-time episodic event, but was repeatedly chosen by like-minded Dutch citizens as a distinctive form of political action to get actively engaged in the government's COVID-19 policies. The major driving factor behind the street protests was some citizens' opposition to the government's lockdown measures. Protesters called for a relaxation of the strict policies that were constraining people's lives, in many cases criticising the government for curtailing individual freedoms. In this process of speaking out, Dutch citizens did not encounter state control with regard to the exercising of their rights to freedom of speech and assembly. When state actors did intervene and practice their authority over citizens, it was usually when political action had turned into riots and aggression, causing harm to other individuals and property.

Vietnam: Limitations in expression

Compared with the Netherlands, even before the COVID-19 pandemic, in Vietnam public protest is a risky form of political action. The right to assembly is stipulated in the Constitution, but there are no specific regulations on demonstrations. A loophole remains by which the state can frame protest as a disturbance of the public order, which will be discussed in greater detail in the next section. During the COVID-19 pandemic period, the Vietnamese government imposed tight restrictions to contain the virus, including an intercity travel ban. From August to October 2021, the government adopted a strict lockdown in Ho Chi Minh City and some other provinces, preventing people from leaving their houses and with troops controlling people's movements and supplying food and aid to residents (Reuters 2021). Due to the combination of existing institutional contexts and the particular situational contexts of the pandemic, protests in public spaces had not been observed in Vietnam as noticeably as in the Netherlands. Unlike in the Netherlands, Vietnamese political action against the government's COVID-19 policies was mostly concentrated in cyberspace.

Individual online activism often resulted in repressive responses by state authorities. Six hundred and fifty-four citizens who posted their critical opinions about COVID-19 issues on platforms such as Facebook and YouTube were forced to attend so-called 'working sessions'. They were ordered to delete their posts in the period of January to March 2020, and some of them were fined or placed in detention (Human Rights Foundation 2020). This control over criticism and demands made online over COVID-19 policies persisted in 2021. In July 2021, the Hanoi Department of Justice issued regulations that established sixteen designated behaviours as offences during the COVID-19 pandemic; one of these was to post false or distorting information about the COVID-19 situation on the Internet, subject to a maximum of seven years imprisonment, a fine of up to đ200 million (approx. €800), or a several year ban from getting certain jobs (Thư Viện Pháp Luật 2021).

In August 2021, Tien Giang province arrested a thirty-year-old man who had posted critical opinions on COVID-19 policies; he had called for the government to provide financial subsidies to citizens for utility bills and to halt the use of a China-developed COVID-19 vaccine (Radio Free Asia 2021b). The charge brought against him was the same as with other cases: spreading false information detrimental to the state. Another citizen, followed by a large number of people online, criticized the government's handling of the pandemic and other political issues; his house was searched and he was arrested in the same period (CIVICUS 2021). In another case, in September 2021, several other citizens were fined, detained, or arrested because of their online criticism of government COVID-19 regulations like Ho Chi Minh City's lockdown and restrictions causing people to struggle to meet basic needs such as food (Radio Free Asia 2021c). The police in another city, Can Tho, arrested a man for the same reason: he had been posting and sharing 'false' information and criticizing the government's COVID-19 responses; these were deemed acts of 'abusing freedom and democracy' (Radio Free Asia 2021a).

The events introduced above exhibit a pattern in which Vietnamese citizens who expressed their views on the government's practices were underpinned by their rights to access information and to criticize in the interest of citizens; contrary to their logic, it is noticeable that state authorities framed citizens' criticism of the COVID-19 measures as a violation of the state's order or interests. The Vietnamese government used judicial institutions to silence and repress citizens who exercised their rights of expression (CIVICUS 2021). Along with the established Penal Code that criminalises 'anti-state propaganda' and 'abusing democratic freedoms', Vietnamese authorities arrested and prosecuted many citizens on the charge of disseminating false information or taking advantage of the pandemic period to spread inappropriate news detrimental to the government. Thus, the cases of citizens' online action and detention or arrest demonstrate that the Vietnamese authorities equated criticism of COVID-19 policies with criticism of the party-state, framing it as spreading of distorted and undesirable information.

Mapping the matrix: Differences in manifestations of citizenship

In both the Netherlands and Vietnam, citizens became involved in public affairs during the COVID-19 pandemic by expressing their critical opinions on the governments' COVID-19 policies. Setting aside the frequency and features of these political actions, citizens' exercising of their rights may appear to be similar in the two countries. However, the characteristics of political action and state behaviours showed a marked difference. Table 7.1 demonstrates the different citizenship norms manifested both in the forms of political action taken in response to the governments' COVID-19 measures and the behaviours of state actors towards citizens.

In the Netherlands, although public assembly was temporarily banned by the Dutch government during the COVID-19 pandemic period in the name of public safety, many Dutch citizens across several cities exercised their rights as citizens to raise their voices on public affairs by participating in protests. They chose to participate in protests by themselves and did not face immediate or unexpected repression because of their political action. Besides, the exercising of their rights was respected to the extent that it did not cause harm to others. Depending on the COVID-19 situation, state authorities tolerated demonstrations that had been reported prior to the occasion by imposing a few conditions (e.g., no illegal violence or fireworks) and designating the routes of the demonstrations to allow for preventive searches of citizens by the police.

As for policing protests, the 2012 Police Act gives the police authority to use force when deemed necessary, following a pre-warning. Firearms and pepper spray are allowed under limited conditions specified by the Act. Further, any citizen perceiving police action as inappropriate or unjust can file a complaint to the National Ombudsman, an independent institution

Table 7.1. Matrix of citizenship norms, political action, and state responses.

	Manifestations of citizenship norms	Common forms of political action taken by citizens	Thresholds of state control
The Netherlands	- Citizens' free choice to use their rights to freedom of speech and assembly - Citizen's exercising of their rights is respected	- Mass protest - Occupying public spaces - Chanting and holding signs - Violence in some cases	- Violence causing injury or damage to property - Physical aggression towards the police - Resistance against the police's orders
Vietnam	- Citizens' limited freedom in choosing the way to exercise their rights - Citizens' duties of conformity to the state outweigh their rights	- Posting critical opinions and sharing information online (e.g., social media)	- Criticism of the government's COVID-19 policies

that is empowered to carry out impartial investigations on the conduct of state actors. For instance, the Public Prosecution Service proceeded with prosecution of two police officers who had been excessively heavy-handed and used physically repressive action towards demonstrators in 2021 (*De Volkskrant* 2021). The tipping point of state control to thwart the protests showed a clear and expectable pattern; the police used physical means of control when protests escalated into violence and threatened injury to persons or damage to property. Repression of the protests in the Dutch cases studied shows little evidence that state actors used illicit measures to quell citizens in order to maintain their hold on power. In the Netherlands, citizens' rights to expression are guaranteed as long as that expression does not harm other people or property. For instance, protesters chanted anti-government slogans during their assemblies even with the police surrounding them, but the police did not crack down on the protesters because of their messages of criticism or opposition per se.

It is noticeable that a large group of Dutch citizens took to the streets and actively, sometimes violently, expressed their dissatisfaction with the government's COVID-19 measures. They took advantage of their opportunities to exercise their citizenship, whereas the Vietnamese citizens mainly submitted to the formal political institutions that criminalise critical action both in public spaces and in cyber space. On the other hand, the Netherlands case can be characterised by relatively bold expressions of anger towards the government, ranging from occupying streets for mass marches to causing damage to individuals and property. Direct, but modest forms of action (e.g., petitions and demonstrations) are usually accompanied by the condition that citizens can 'take advantage of civil rights' like freedoms of speech and assembly (Yarwood 2014, 102). Taking advantage of their given rights, any Dutch citizen, regardless of socio-economic status, could participate in the protests.

As Cenker-Özek et al. (2021) found in established democracies, the protests in the Dutch case are attributable to the full-fledged practice of rights-based citizenship that values an active and self-expressive form of political action in citizens. In the Netherlands, power relationships between citizens and the state are not asymmetrically—albeit not perfectly symmetrically—institutionalised; citizens are able to condemn state actors and hold them to account. Because political rights are explicitly guaranteed in the Netherlands, Dutch citizens were able to gather in public spaces to hold protests *en masse* with a low risk of arbitrary or unpredictable repression. Democratic regimes are generally less likely to exercise repression than authoritarian regimes, but despite this comparatively lower likelihood, they also tend to respond repressively to contentious political actions such as aggressive forms of protest (Carey 2006).

The tipping point of state control in the Netherlands is clear and expected: the use of violence. The police intervened only when the protests turned disruptive, damaging to property, or dangerous to the security of other citizens or the police. In other words, a clearly expectable line was observed between toleration and repression. The Dutch authorities took repressive approaches only in response to violent protesters. State intervention and control is marked by a reactive response to behavioural aggression of citizens, but is far from taking political retaliation for citizens' criticism of the government. The range of citizenship available to Dutch citizens, in terms of both their rights and obligations in taking political action, was not only clearly institutionalised but manifested in practice.

As Schedler (2009, 331) said of authoritarian regimes, 'the *nominally democratic* institutions they set up remain *substantively authoritarian*' (italics in original). The Vietnamese political regime, run under a single-party system, has nominally democratic institutions that stipulate the rights of citizens but that, in reality, prevent Vietnamese citizens from expressing their disagreements or grievances with what the government is doing. The Vietnamese state has been run by a single party, the Communist Party of Vietnam (CPV), since its unification in 1976. The state leadership and bureaucracies at central and local levels are filled by CPV members, and its constitution guarantees the CPV a dominant role, declaring it the leading force in society. Considering that robust state organisations serve a central role in the stability of authoritarian regimes (Levitsky and Way 2010), the Vietnamese single-party regime has achieved status quo in the political system by ensuring the state apparatus is dominated by CPV members and by employing legal instruments that prohibit opposition. Without a formally accepted opposition party in the Vietnamese legislature, even conventional forms of political action such as voting are not a substantive way for citizens to hold the political elite accountable.

Democratic political institutions in authoritarian regimes, those that seemingly guarantee elections and civil liberties, should warrant caution since they, in practice, make the playing field uneven, distinctly skewed in favour of those who hold power (Levitsky and Way 2010). According to the 2013 Law on Reception, Vietnamese citizens are entitled to file complaints to state agencies at national or sub-national levels, yet the scope and topics of complaint are confined to those not perceived to stand against the state. This law seems to be one of the co-optation instruments that mitigates public dissent by channelling it into a formal channel and process. Moreover, the most dominant institutional instrument in the manifestation of citizenship in Vietnam is the Penal Code. The Penal Code demonstrates a very low tipping point for repression towards Vietnamese individuals who exercise their political rights. Under the existing political institutions, 'good', 'law-abiding' citizens are those conforming to the institutionalised channels of political action, such as participating in elections and submitting a formal complaint to competent state agencies that does not go against the public order or the state's interests. Under such conditions, protesters have faced repression ranging from short-term detention to long-term imprisonment regardless of whether they use violent approaches or whether they criticize government COVID-19 measures or raise other pressing issues.

On the one hand, some Vietnamese citizens do criticize the government despite it being a seemingly far from rational choice due to the significant risk of repression. On the other hand, most Vietnamese citizens avoid public protest, situating themselves in the limited repertoire of political action that is consolidated and imposed by formal political institutions. Vietnamese citizens dissatisfied with the government's COVID-19 measures tended to flock to online spaces rather than to easily identifiable offline demonstrations. However, even individual actions of posting or blogging on cyberspace were repressed. The duty of citizens to conform to institutions outweighed their rights to freedom of speech and assembly; some words online even led to citizens being fined or arrested in the name of violating the regulations. In Vietnam, citizens' endeavours to exercise their rights to freedom of speech and assembly are pushed to the margins in the name of public order or the state's interests. Criticisms or complaints about public affairs are often deemed infringements of these interests. Critical posts online were perceived as going 'against the rules' since such activities are often classified as disruptive or even subversive acts. For authoritarian leaders, staying in power is the institutional imperative that drives them to shape rules and organisations so as to manage vertical and horizontal threats to the status quo (Schedler 2009). Thus, criticism of policies is often interpreted as criticism of the party-state. Such interpretation then justifies the approaches of state actors to control the political behaviour of citizens.

Referring to definitions by Honari (2018, 952), there are two dimensions of repression: 'experienced repression' which means the actual experiences of citizens, and 'perceived repression', which is how citizens perceive the constraints and coercive practices they may face as a consequence of political action. The existing Vietnamese political institutions serve to keep both dimensions of repression high for Vietnamese citizens in exercising their rights to freedom of speech and assembly. This institutional context of a heightened risk leads Vietnamese citizens to internalise, either voluntarily or involuntarily, the idea that critical political action is inappropriate for a citizen and goes against the rules laid out by Vietnamese political institutions. State authorities thus selectively apply existing legal instruments to undermine the rights of citizens. Moreover, security officers made use of the COVID-19 situation when approaching perceived offenders, like the husband who posted critical comments on Facebook regarding the human rights abuses of the Vietnamese government.

The two countries, the Netherlands and Vietnam, have different boundaries in how they conceptualise citizenship, and in how conflicts between the duties and rights of citizenship are institutionalised (van Deth 2007). As argued by Bolzendahl and Coffé (2013), the normative construction of 'good' citizenship is associated with the types and degrees of political action accepted and respected by state actors. In Vietnam, being law-abiding outweighs individual liberties at the discretion of state actors rather than being based on a clear set of criteria, prevailing across topics and features of citizens' political action. Such patterns hinder Vietnamese citizens from being actively engaged in public affairs. State authorities can exert control over citizens, pigeon-holing various criticism on policies under one category, 'against the state'. Hence Vietnamese citizens run a high risk of repression for criticism or opposition. The phrase 'the state's interests' enshrined across the legally binding documents in Vietnam leaves much room for the state to apply discretionary interpretation and application in controlling citizens' exercising of their rights while emphasizing their duty to conform to the state.

Conclusion

This paper found that the Dutch and Vietnamese governments' measures to restrict citizens' freedoms had similar rationales based on communal interest and the control of the pandemic. However, in both countries the political affiliations of the protesters remain uncertain, at least on the surface. While specific political groups may have played a more active role or covertly orchestrated protests to introduce an anti-government narrative, the composition of the protesters in both countries did not exhibit a significant inclination towards a particular political orientation. Instead, the motivation and engagement behind these contentious political actions were driven primarily by normative values associated with freedom and rights of citizens. At the constitutional level in both the Netherlands and Vietnam the rights to freedom of speech and peaceful assembly are enshrined.

However, the norms of citizenship play out differently. The threshold and intensity of control that state actors exerted on their citizens varied distinctively. The repertoires of citizenship available to citizens are constructed and applied differently in the two countries, attributable to how formal political institutions construct citizenship norms. For Dutch citizens the available repertoires of political action are broader; their protests were direct, active, and boldly critical of the government's COVID-19 measures. Those available to Vietnamese citizens are concentrated on sporadic online actions, individualised and anonymised. In the Netherlands, the rights and duties of citizens in engagement with public affairs are not only clearly institutionalised but can be realised. In contrast, in Vietnam, exercising of citizenship through such political action is undermined due to normative conflicts with the institutionalised obligations imposed on citizens whereby they may not stand against the state's interests. However, these obligations are so obscure that they seem applicable to any contentious political action at the discretion of state actors.

In the case of Vietnam, a wider discrepancy is observed between the formal political institutions—the laws guaranteeing rights to expression and assembly—and the actual practices of citizens and state actors. The party-state yielded significant institutional power to police and punish citizens who criticised the government's policies. Vietnamese laws thus enable state actors to criminalise citizens' criticism or opposition to the government. Within this institutional context, overall political opportunities and repertoires of dissent for Vietnamese citizens are greatly diminished compared with those of Dutch citizens. Unlike in the Netherlands, the Vietnamese state imposes on citizens responsibilities and obligations for public order at the expense of their rights to freedom of speech and assembly. I conclude that what distinguishes the Dutch and the Vietnamese cases in terms of engagement in public affairs is that the duty-based norm of citizenship and the rights-based norm of citizenship are not necessarily mutually exclusive for Dutch citizens, but they do seem to be comparatively so for Vietnamese citizens. In Vietnam, under an authoritarian political context, the discourse on citizens' rights is overshadowed by the discourse on social order and state interests, which leaves ample room for state authorities to restrict citizens from exercising their rights.

Having said that, I would like to highlight a few limitations that researchers of political action, including myself, may need to consider for future research. Firstly, it is methodologically challenging to measure political action using a precisely determined set of criteria. Moreover, direct observation of multiple events of protest or online postings in real time is difficult. However, there is always another way. First, an examination of qualitative media data, despite possible weaknesses like bias or selective coverage, means that research can be sufficiently viable to provide valuable knowledge on how and why a particular event of political action took place. Secondly, a comparative analysis of democracies and authoritarian regimes often gives rise to a debate over comparability and generalisability. A simple assessment of the dimension and extent to which one country is more democratic than another may miss an opportunity for a contextualised understanding of two different regimes. It is worth reiterating here that the way (democratic) citizenship is framed and interpreted varies across countries that have different historical and social characteristics. I have avoided establishing pre-determined criteria for characterizing political action, but have inductively elucidated similarities, differences, and the logic behind them in the two countries on the basis of the textual data collected.

Citizenship features a set of rights and responsibilities of citizens in a given jurisdiction. These rights and duties are not clearly separable, but they are intimately interrelated in the extent to which citizens conceive and exercise citizenship in society. New institutionalism was a helpful analytical lens in this comparative analysis, allowing for identification of the relationship between political action and behaviours of state actors. It shed light on the importance of institutional arrangements in shaping and even (for authoritarian regimes) manipulating the conception of citizenship. Citizenship norms in both the democratic and authoritarian regimes are institutionalised, but they showed marked differences in the relative prioritisation and applicability of citizens' rights and responsibilities.

Bibliography

BBC. 2021. Rotterdam Police Clash with Rioters as Covid Protest Turns Violent (20 November). https://www.bbc.com/news/world-europe-59355950.

Bolzendahl, Catherine, and Hilde Coffé. 2013. 'Are "Good" Citizens "Good" Participants? Testing Citizenship Norms and Political Participation across 25 Nations', *Political Studies*, 61(1_suppl), 45–65.

Carey, Sanine C. 2006. 'The Dynamic Relationship between Protest and Repression', *Political Research Quarterly*, 59(1), 1–11.

Cenker-Özek, Cerem I., Didem Çakmaklı, and Ekrem Karakoç. 2021. 'Rights and Responsibilities: Citizenship Norms and Protest Activity in a Cross-Country Analysis', *Social Science Quarterly*, 102(4), 1394–1407.

Chappell, Louise. 2006. 'Comparing Political Institutions: Revealing the Gendered "Logic of Appropriateness"', *Politics & Gender*, 2(2), 223–235.

CIVICUS. 2021. Crackdown on Online Critics Persists in Vietnam as News Decree Controlling Livesteaming Proposed (27 September). https://monitor.civicus.org/updates/2021/09/27/crackdown-online-critics-persists-vietnam-new-decree-controlling-livestreaming-proposed/.

Coffé, Hilde, and Tanja van der Lippe. 2010. 'Citizenship Norms in Eastern Europe', *Social Indicators Research*, 96(3), 479–496.

Dalton, Russell J. 2008. 'Citizenship Norms and the Expansion of Political Participation', *Political Studies*, 56(1): 76–98.

De Volkskrant. 2021. OM Vervolgt Twee Agenten voor Geweld tijdens Coronaprotest [The Public Prosecution Service Prosecutes Two Police Officers for Violence during Corona Protest] (17 December). https://www.volkskrant.nl/nieuws-achtergrond/om-vervolgt-twee-agenten-voor-geweld-tijdens-coronaprotest~b30e50b0/?referrer=https%3A%2F%2Fwww.google.com%2F.

Deutsch, Anthony. 2021. Third Night of Rioting Erupts over Dutch COVID-19 Rules (22 November). Reuters. https://www.reuters.com/world/europe/dutch-police-detain-dozens-second-night-covid-19-rioting-2021-11-21/.

Dutch News. 2021. Dutch police Arrest 240 in a Night of Rioting Nationwide (25 January). https://www.dutchnews.nl/news/2021/01/dutch-police-arrest-around-200-in-a-night-of-rioting-nationwide/.

Euronews. 2022. Thousands Gather to Oppose Dutch Virus Measures Despite Ban (2 January). https://www.euronews.com/2022/01/02/thousands-gather-to-oppose-dutch-virus-measures-despite-ban.

Freedom House. 2022a. *Freedom in the World 2024: Netherlands* https://freedomhouse.org/country/netherlands/freedom-world/2024.

Freedom House. 2022b. *Freedom in the World 2024: Vietnam.* https://freedomhouse.org/country/vietnam/freedom-world/2024.

Guardian, The. 2021. Dutch Protesters March through The Hague against 'Corona Pass' (25 September). https://www.theguardian.com/world/2021/sep/25/dutch-protesters-march-through-the-hague-against-corona-pass.

Hall, Peter A., and Rosemary C.R. Taylor.1996. 'Political Science and the Three New Institutionalisms', *Political Studies*, 44(5), 936–957.

Honari, Ali. 2018. 'From "The Effect of Repression" toward "The Response to Repression"', *Current Sociology*, 66(6), 950–973.

Hooghe, Marc, and Jennifer Oser. 2015. 'The Rise of Engaged Citizenship: The Evolution of Citizenship Norms among Adolescents in 21 Countries between 1999 and 2009', *International Journal of Comparative Sociology*, 56(1), 29–52.

Hooghe, Marc, Jennifer Oser, and Sofie Marien. 2016. 'A Comparative Analysis of "Good Citizenship": A Latent Class Analysis of Adolescents' citizenship Norms in 38 Countries', *International Political Science Review*, 37(1), 115–129.

Human Rights Foundation. 2020. Vietnam's COVID Success Belies Escalating Crackdown on Rights (10 August). https://hrf.org/vietnams-covid-success-belies-escalating-crackdown-on-rights/.

Isin, Engin. F., and Bryan S. Turner (eds.). 2002. *Handbook of Citizenship Studies.* Thousand Oaks CA: SAGE.

Janoski, Thomas. 1998. *Citizenship and Civil Society: A Framework of Rights and Obligations in Liberal, Traditional, and Social Democratic Regimes.* Cambridge: Cambridge University Press.

Janoski, Thomas, and Brian Gran. 2002. Political Citizenship: Foundations of Rights, in Engin F. Isin and Bryan S. Turner (eds), *Handbook of Citizenship Studies*,13–52. Thousand Oaks CA: SAGE.

Kymlicka, Will, and Wayne Norman. 1994. 'Return of the Citizen: A Survey of RecentWork on Citizenship Theory', *Ethics*, 104(2). 352–381.

Levitsky, Steven, and Lucan Way. 2010. *Competitive Authoritarianism: Hybrid Regimes After the Cold War.* Cambridge: Cambridge University Press.

Lowndes, Vivien, and Mark Roberts. 2013. *Why Institutions Matter: The New Institutionalism in Political Science.* London: Bloomsbury.

North, Douglass Cecil. 1990. *Institutions, Institutional Change and Economic Performance.* Cambridge: Cambridge University Press.

Pennington, Mark. 2009. 'Theory, Institutions and Comparative Politics' in Judith Bara and Mark Pennington (eds.), *Comparative Politics: Explaining Democratic Systems* (13–40). Thousand Oaks CA: SAGE.

Peters, B. Guy. 2012. *Institutional Theory in Political Science: The New Institutionalism*. London: Bloomsbury.

Radio Free Asia. 2021a. Vietnam Punishes Critics of Government's COVID-19 Response (10 August). https://www.rfa.org/english/news/vietnam/dissent-08102021185946.html.

Radio Free Asia. 2021b. Vietnamese Facebook User Fined for 'Fake News' as CriticismGrows of Government's Handling of Pandemic (3 September). https://www.rfa.org/english/news/vietnam/fine-09032021182640.html.

Radio Free Asia. 2021c. Vietnam Arrests Facebook User for Posts Criticizing COVID-19 Policies (6 October). https://www.rfa.org/english/news/vietnam/posts-10062021173801.html.

Raney, Tracey, and Loleen Berdahl. 2011. 'Shifting sands? Citizens' National Identities and Pride in Social Security in Canada', *American Review of Canadian Studies*, 41(3), 259–273.

Reuters. 2021. Vietnam Deploys Troops to Enforce COVID Lockdown in Largest city (23 August). https://www.reuters.com/world/asia-pacific/vietnam-deploys-troops-enforce-lockdown-largest-city-2021-08-23/.

Reuters. 2022. Dutch Police Disperse Anti-Lockdown Protesters in Amsterdam (2 January). https://www.reuters.com/business/media-telecom/dutch-police-disperse-thousands-protesting-against-lockdown-measures-2022-01-02/.

RTL Nieuws. 2020. Ongeregeldheden Den Haag Stonden Los van Coronaprotest [Disruptions in The Hague independent of Corona Protest] (22 July). https://www.rtlnieuws.nl/nieuws/nederland/artikel/5161028/protest-den-haag-corona maatregelen-demonstranten-malieveld.

Schedler, Andreas. 2009. 'The New Institutionalism in the Study of Authoritarian Regimes', *Totalitarismus und Demokratie*, 6(2), 323–340.

Thư Viện Pháp Luật. 2021. 16 vi phạm về phòng chống COVID-19 sẽ bị phạt tiền, phạt tù [16 Violators of COVID-19 Prevention and Control will be Fined and Imprisoned] (25 July). https://thuvienphapluat.vn/tintuc/vn/thoi-su-phap-luat-binh-luan-gop-y/36712/16-vi-pham-ve-phong-chong-COVID-19-se-bi-phat-tien-phat-tu.

Van Deth, Jan W. 2007. 'Norms of Citizenship' in Russell. J. Dalton and Hans-Dieter Klingemann (eds.), *The Oxford Handbook of Political Behaviour* (402–417). Oxford: Oxford University Press.

Van Deth, Jan W., José Ramon Montero, and Anderes Westholm. 2007. *Citizenship and Involvement in European Democracies: A Comparative Analysis*. Abingdon: Routledge.

Yarwood, Richard. 2014. *Citizenship*. Abingdon: Routledge.

About the author

Dr Seohee Kwak earned her doctoral degree from the International Institute of Social Studies, Erasmus University Rotterdam. Previously, she worked as a gender and development researcher at a government-affiliated institute in Seoul, South Korea. Dr Kwak has published a range of journal articles, book chapters, and online articles on contentious politics in democratic and authoritarian states. Her research focuses specifically on Southeast and Northeast Asia. Her areas of interest include protests, social movements, state repression, democratic governance, and authoritarianism. Currently, Dr Kwak serves as a lecturer at Leiden University, where she teaches a variety of courses.
s.kwak@fsw.leidenuniv.nl

8. Reclaiming Democratic Citizenship while Tackling COVID-19 in South Korea

Suk-Ki Kong and Hyun-Chin Lim

Abstract: Considering the need to reclaim democratic citizenship in Korea, we here revisit and reflect critically on the 'K-quarantine' model of COVID-19 pandemic management employed by the Korean government between 2020 and 2022. Although the K-quarantine model was highly effective in managing the COVID-19 pandemic, it faced limitations of discrimination, exclusion, and inequality in Korean society. We have examined the Korean quarantine model critically by addressing COVID-19's unjust social impacts on Korean society. We also foresee huge barriers ahead, including an infodemic, shrinking NGOs, and reduced advocacy for public health. Arguably, we need to reclaim democratic citizenship and reduce unjust and unequal social impacts. To conclude, we propose that diversity, deliberation, participation, accountability, transparency, and independence are core factors for reclaiming democratic citizenship based on citizen consensus rather than mere compliance.

Keywords: K-quarantine model, democratic citizenship, public health, discrimination, consensus

Introduction

This chapter revisits and reflects critically on the 'K-quarantine' model of COVID-19 pandemic management with reference to cosmopolitan citizenship (Kong 2012). The K-quarantine model focuses on the government's quick response to and effective management of virus spread by mobilising the 'three Ts': testing, tracking, and treatment, maintained through tireless

Gregory Bracken, Paul Rabé, Nurul Azreen Azlan (eds), *Future Practices of Citizenship in Asia and the West: Care of the Self (Volume III)*. Taylor & Francis Group, 2025
DOI: 10.5117/9789048562077_CH08

sacrifice and commitment on the part of medical staff, volunteers, and public servants. Many Korean experts argue that the K-quarantine model was highly effective in managing the COVID-19 pandemic. They highlight three weapons that were key to the model's success: group learning prior to the pandemic, government leadership, and the collaboration of civil society in South Korea. Despite worldwide praise for and envy of the model, however, the model faced the limitations of discrimination, exclusion, and inequality in Korean society. These weak points were revealed amid the continuation of the pandemic from its outbreak in 2020 to 2021 and 2022. Unfortunately, many Korean citizens eventually became exhausted with both the frequent restrictions in daily life and the unequal social impacts. As a result, their pride in and solidarity with the model diminished.

Given this situation, we try not only to examine why the K-quarantine model, in some ways, became unpopular among citizens but also to explore how the model can be revitalised in a way that amends its past weaknesses. To reflect on the model in this way, we focus our research framework on how, during the pandemic era, the Korean people engaged in public education, debates, and participation concerning public health, all of which contributed to promoting democratic citizenship (Scholte 2003). This framework will highlight why the government failed to move beyond citizens' mere compliance to a broader public consensus, in order to maintain support from the public in general (Kong 2017; 2020). This chapter also critically examines the model by addressing the unjust social impacts of COVID-19 in Korean society. We have, for example, witnessed increasing hatred, discrimination, and stigmatisation toward social minorities (Kong 2020). COVID-19 had disproportionate negative impacts on those who were infected, platform workers, the elderly, migrant workers, women, children, people with disabilities, and sexual minorities (Horton 2021). Although the Korean government played a pivotal role in handling the COVID-19 crisis, it also struggled with challenges such as discrimination, exclusions, and distrust among people. Korean citizens were also straddling between public safety and human rights and were reluctant to advocate for social minorities concerning universal access to public health resources like facemasks and vaccinations.

This chapter focuses on how such divisions and distrust increased or decreased among Korean citizens with reference to privacy, hatred, and unequal social impacts, which deepened the marginalisation of social minorities. We have come to realize the urgent need to reclaim democratic citizenship and reduce the unjust and unequal social impacts of the pandemic period. We also foresee huge barriers in case of future crises, including an infodemic (too much information—including false or misleading information—during a disease outbreak), shrinking NGOs, and reduced advocacy for public health while democratic citizenship is being revitalised (Kong 2020; Kim 2013). In conclusion, this chapter proposes that Korean citizens recognise social minorities as people and protect their privacy, as well as respect open spaces where they can participate creatively in rebuilding the trust that was weakened during the pandemic. Diversity, deliberation, participation, accountability, transparency, and independence are core factors for reclaiming democratic citizenship based on public consensus rather than mere compliance.

A glimpse into the Korean government's response to COVID-19

South Korea was praised worldwide for managing the COVID-19 pandemic well. In 2020, the K-quarantine model served as a benchmark for other countries (Fisher and Choe 2020). But, as the pandemic continued longer than we expected, the government struggled with various challenges surrounding privacy, social inequality, and public health. We briefly highlight some of the key features of the government's three years of efforts tackling the COVID-19 pandemic in reference to citizenship and human rights (J. Lee, 2021; Byun et al. 2020). Even though the government demonstrated good leadership through the mobilisation of experts, officials, and volunteers, huge challenges remain to be considered moving forward, the main one being the 'return of the strong state' versus 'shrinking civil society' (Brechenmacher et al. 2020).

The government's COVID-19 response was characterised by a top-down strategy. We will roughly divide the response processes into three categories: Rounds 1, 2, and 3, which correspond to the years 2020, 2021, and 2022. Interestingly, each round evoked its own responses among citizens: respectively, fear and compliance, patience and cooperation, and exhaustion and resistance.

Round 1: The 'three Ts' and citizen compliance (2020)

In 2020, when COVID-19 first occurred, Korean civil society voluntarily followed the government's quarantine policy out of fear. Korea's K-quarantine strategy was to quickly combine the three Ts: to test, track, and treat, responding effectively to the pandemic in a top-down way (H. Lee 2020). How effective was this K-quarantine model? Two significant factors contributed to its effectiveness: the sacrifices of medical staff and public servants, and peoples' voluntary participation in the social distancing measures and the wearing of masks. Without the dedication of the medical staff in the quarantine process, the initial response process would not have been effective (Byun et al. 2020; Suh 2021). However, as the pandemic continued many medical staff became exhausted, and as reasonable compensation for their dedication was delayed, the foundation of the K-quarantine model began to waver. It was undoubtedly important for people in Korea to participate actively in following the two crucial guidelines of social distancing and wearing masks in order to prevent the spread of COVID-19 in the early stages.

Despite the early effectiveness of the K-quarantine model, Korea also witnessed a violation of the human rights of socially marginalised and vulnerable groups. The phenomena of discrimination, hatred, and surveillance were significant limitations of the government's response in Round 1. A number of such episodes took place in 2020. First, early in that year a national online petition to the Blue House requesting that the government ban the entry of Chinese people in relation to COVID-19 collected 7,618,111 signatures. This petition was the third-largest public petition in history (Chung 2022, 217). Far-right groups even staged a protest in front of the Chinese embassy in Seoul, demanding a ban on Chinese nationals entering the country. In early 2020, first, all people of foreign nationality, and then only those who were undocumented, were not allowed to purchase face masks from pharmacies, as sales were restricted only to those with Korean national ID cards.

Then Prime Minister Chung Sye-Kyun formally referred to the latter residents as 'undocumented' (rather than using the term 'illegal') migrant workers for the first time at a Central Disaster and Safety Countermeasures Headquarters meeting on 9 April 2020. However, when the possibility that they could get infected emerged as a serious threat to public health, weeks later, on 20 April 2020, the government allowed them to purchase face masks as well (Woo 2022, 223). Unfortunately, this decision was not based on protecting the human rights of undocumented workers but rather a temporary decision made in order to maintain the effectiveness of the K-quarantine model. The government was only concerned that if undocumented people were trapped in the misconception of 'illegal' residents and then tried to hide, society as a whole would be exposed to a greater risk of infection, as they could trigger the spread of COVID-19. Thus, the government eventually allowed undocumented people to be tested and treated at no cost if suspected to be infected or if tested positive. Additionally, officials of the Ministry of Justice were to be exempt from the obligation to notify the immigration office of these people's undocumented status and personal information. In light of this episode, Korean nationals should ask themselves to what extent they agree with the premise that all members of society are safe only when the most vulnerable—undocumented migrant workers—are safe. About 390,000 undocumented residents live and work in Korean society. Korean citizens still faced major challenges not only to recognise these residents as equals in society but also to ensure that their human rights were legally protected as the pandemic continued (J. Lee 2021; Woo 2022).

These episodes indicate the return of a strong state focused only on ensuring the effectiveness of the K-quarantine model to prevent the spread of COVID-19 while neglecting the rising hatred in Korean society toward migrant workers, students of foreign nationality, and travellers. The government made the mistake of publicly releasing information on the contact routes of confirmed cases, thereby negatively impacting all related shops and restaurants. Further, the social divide between the Korean national majority and the stigmatised minority groups accelerated because of the spread of misinformation and fake news on social media (Hwang 2020). The government even tried to introduce a new policy that those in self-isolation would have to wear so-called safety bracelets. Such a policy could have caused serious human rights violations of individual freedom and privacy. Political conflicts, antagonisms, and social distrust were being stirred up by the spread of distorted information and by policies narrowly focused only on stopping the spread of the virus.

Round 2: Vaccination and citizen cooperation (2021)

In March 2021, the Seoul Metropolitan Government issued an administrative order requiring all workers of foreign nationality in Seoul to be tested for COVID-19. This aroused a lot of criticism, including a Seoul National University statement that the order stigmatised people of foreign nationality as a source of virus infection and incited hatred among people of Korean nationality. The Seoul Metropolitan Government accepted the criticism and changed the administrative order into a recommendation. This incident shows the discriminatory nature of Korean society—and especially the government—towards foreign nationals and particularly migrant workers. In the same vein, vaccine nationalism emerged in Korea as in other countries (Bollyky and Brown 2020a, 2020b). Payments by the government's emergency disaster relief funds were also made on a discriminatory basis. In the case of Gyeonggi Province, with more than 480,000 residents of foreign nationality, these residents were excluded from the first Disaster Basic Income payment of 100,000 won ($80) per person (Lee 2021, 76). A year later, some foreign nationals—but only those married to Korean nationals—were, like Korean nationals, made eligible for the pandemic relief funds. These instances during the pandemic have, sadly, revealed the current attitude of Korean society toward people of foreign nationality.

During Round 2, in addition to discrimination and division, securing vaccines became a key issue in quarantine policy. As vaccine development and dissemination proceeded in a compressed fashion, several Western countries took the lead in the vaccination process. As it was difficult for Korea to obtain vaccines in the early stages, Korea's political circles started competing to secure vaccines. In Seoul, people used various apps to search for 'leftover doses' of vaccines from those in priority groups who had skipped their appointments. Even if any leftover vaccine appeared, it would disappear instantly—faster than a ticket for a BTS concert (Cave 2021). Such high demand for vaccines tempted politicians to attempt to secure vaccines for their own political interests without collaboration with the government. This politicisation of vaccines, related to political interests, occurred during the vaccination process. The K-quarantine model drove some presidential candidates to try to mobilise political support by securing vaccines. In the meantime, the vaccination process also exposed divisions, discrimination, and hatred towards the poor, vulnerable, and minority groups. In one example of political intervention in the vaccination process in 2021, Lee Jae-Myung, then governor of Gyeonggi Province and one of the leading prospective presidential candidates of the then-ruling Democratic Party of Korea, voiced his own ideas on the vaccination process, thereby contributing to public confusion. At a provincial parliamentary session in April 2021, Lee expressed his plan to examine the possibility of independently bringing in vaccines from overseas (Hong 2021). Lee argued that the most important measure for achieving herd immunity was the procurement and rollout of vaccines and that Gyeonggi Province was taking practical steps to introduce vaccines independently of the central government. In response to Lee's claims, the head of Korea's Central Disaster Management Headquarters (CDM) immediately rejected the possibility of provincial governments seeking an alternative path to introduce overseas vaccines. Despite widespread criticism, Lee advanced his independent vaccine procurement project one step further to request an examination to introduce Russia's Sputnik V vaccine. His rationale was that Sputnik V showed a higher efficacy rate and that the government should consider all options, as the COVID-19 pandemic is a security issue affecting the lives of the people.

Despite various political interventions and chaos, as well as delays in the government's securing sufficient vaccines, people in Korea were actively vaccinated. Eventually, they reached high rates of primary and secondary vaccinations more quickly than expected.

Round 3: 'Living with COVID-19' and citizen resistance (2022)

As the number of confirmed COVID-19 infections went up and down in repeated waves due to the introduction of new variants—from Alpha to Delta to Omicron (Borowiece 2021)— Korean citizens were becoming exhausted. In December 2021, low numbers of infections rose rapidly again due to the new variant, Omicron. Rather than trying to lower the number of confirmed cases, the Korean government shifted its policies to focusing on the care of critically ill patients and reducing the number of deaths. The government saw a decline in the voluntary cooperation of citizens in response to its social distancing scheme. One group of relatively underprivileged small business owners began to fear bankruptcy more than the virus spread amid the absence of an adequate social safety net. Given this situation, at the end of 2021, the government introduced its 'living with COVID-19' policy.

In reality, the Korean government continued to struggle with the Omicron variant, only just passing the peak of 626,000 new daily infections by March 2022. By April, the cumulative number of confirmed cases was approximately seventeen million. At the time, the vaccination rates in Korea—87.7 percent had received their first shot, 86.8 percent had received their second, and 64.5 percent had received their first booster shot—were among the highest in the world (NCOV 2022). The government announced its 'With COVID-19' policy and lifted many restrictions, in particular the limits on private gathering sizes and multi-use facility operating hours, on 18 April 2022. The indoor mask mandate was maintained but it was permitted to remove masks when outdoors on 23 May 2022.

Korean civil society began to pay more attention to public health, local communities, solidarity, and citizenship beyond the K-quarantine model in the midst of the ongoing pandemic. Koreans tried to reflect on the public health system, including increasing the number of healthcare facilities and medical staff, which had become a top priority since the outbreak of COVID-19. Civil society also emphasised strong government leadership as well as fulfilling one's civic responsibilities beyond simple sympathy and cooperation. The real purpose of civil society is to improve the democratic capacity of the public, but it needs to reorient itself to be able to guarantee everyone's basic right to survival through securing public healthcare. At the same time, Korea needs some self-reflection as a society on how to protect individual privacy and eliminate the kind of collective discrimination that occurred in the K-quarantine model. In particular, platform workers, temporary contract workers without job security, and workers in specific occupations like care faced discrimination and had to cope by themselves with the intensified social inequality during the pandemic (Kang and Huh 2022).

In short, when reviewing the years 2020, 2021, and 2022, we learned that the Korean government's initial reaction to COVID-19 can be summarised as the return of a strong state. For a little more than two years, the government stuck to following the K-quarantine model by relying on the 3 Ts, medical staff and public officials' sacrifices and commitment, and contact tracing through surveillance. It also faced new challenges, such as the stigmas imposed by Korean society on minorities, fake news regarding COVID-19, the politicisation of the vaccination process, the unequal burden of care falling on women, the neglect of care for social minorities, etc. These issues pointed to a need for the government to shift its COVID-19 policymaking emphasis from enforcing compliance to cultivating consensus among the people. Without society's consensus, the government was more likely to struggle with anger and resistance from the people. The challenges facing the government and civil society changed, becoming greater and more complicated from Round 1 to Round 3. To overcome such limitations in the future, we argue that the reclaiming of democratic citizenship is a core task for both government and civil society in order to overcome unjust social impacts such as those that emerged during the pandemic era as well as to prepare for future pandemics in South Korea.

Framework: Democratic citizenship matters!

This chapter suggests a tripartite relationship model for promoting democratic citizenship in a pandemic era. Based on Jan. A. Scholte's framework, we argue that a trilateral model of public participation, education, and debate can contribute to promoting citizen consensus and engagement during a pandemic (Scholte 2003). In the decision-making process, if citizens are excluded or marginalised from actively responding to the pandemic, their citizenship itself can become distorted or unbalanced. If citizen involvement disappears from the decision-making process, their consensus with government policy will diminish, and civil society itself will shrink (Lim and Kong 2020). In the early stages of the COVID-19 pandemic, government policy focused on public participation simply to get citizens' compliance rather than expanding public education and debate to reach a consensus. The resulting response was praised worldwide by the media as effective, which elicited pride and patience among Koreans. However, the government's response was unable to resolve the crucial issues of Korean nationals' hatred, stigmatisation, and discrimination against socially vulnerable groups; Korean society's serious economic inequalities; or protecting the right to life of social minorities.

Democratic citizenship revitalised

It is essential to evaluate the K-quarantine model with reference to civic engagement—that is, democratic citizenship—by focusing on three key mechanisms: public education, debate, and participation. These key factors can contribute to forms of civic engagement that include citizens in the process of tackling the pandemic, while also improving their cognitive process (learning), deliberation process (debating), and participation process (collaborating) during the pandemic era. Such engagement and exercising of democratic citizenship can facilitate mutual recognition and communication and improve trust and solidarity among citizens (Kong and Lim 2020). While responding to COVID-19, to what extent did Korean civil society become actively engaged in such processes? Citizens were marginalised in terms of their engagement in public health governance, resulting in a democratic deficit and, instead, the return of a strong state (Kim 2013). By emphasising only control of the spread of infection, the government neglected the human rights of minorities, who were left to struggle with discrimination, exclusion, hatred, and stigmatisation. People paid little attention to exclusion, segregation, and selfishness related to class, gender, nationality, age, etc.

Although online activities expanded during the pandemic, many people had difficulty distinguishing factual information from fake news due to the flood of information on social media. Sympathising with self-affirming claims concerning public assistance, emergency disaster relief funds, what constitutes a good landlord during the pandemic-induced economic downturn, the extent of digital surveillance, and gig labourers, many fell into fierce diatribes rather than understanding the issues on the basis of facts and carefully persuading others so as to develop a consensus. In the pandemic era, the government emphasised the K-quarantine model as a master frame, pushing aside other crucial issues like safety, life, individual freedom, privacy, and the welfare of social minorities. Likewise, some local governments heavily biased towards local development also favoured local interest groups and ambitiously tried to control individual freedoms by mobilising digital surveillance systems. Minorities became more vulnerable to panopticon-like digital surveillance initiatives while at the same time excluded from full access to the public health system. We argue that without democratic citizenship, models like the K-quarantine model are not sustainable and will force such compliance of citizens in the direction of increasing resistance. Given these problems, we must revisit and reflect on the K-quarantine model in a critical way with reference to democratic citizenship.

The K-quarantine model: Effective but unsustainable

The notable effectiveness of the K-quarantine model during the early stages of the pandemic was contingent on several significant contextual conditions. Prior to COVID-19, Korean society had undergone a series of learning processes related to public health and democracy. In 2003, the country suffered from the SARS (Severe Acute Respiratory Syndrome) pandemic, and in 2014, Koreans learned the importance of effective national leadership during the national crisis around the sinking of the Sewol Ferry. In 2015, MERS (Middle East Respiratory Syndrome), with its high fatality rate, threatened the entire society and exposed vulnerabilities in the public health system. In 2016, a lawsuit was filed over deaths caused by a humidifier disinfectant. In response to serious fine dust pollution in 2017, many Korean people became accustomed to wearing face masks without much reluctance. In other words, these various threats gave Korean citizens earlier opportunities to learn the importance of both public health and democracy (Kim 2013). With the advent of the COVID-19 pandemic in 2020, Korean citizens cooperated more actively and promptly, faithfully following government guidelines regarding the use of masks and social distancing. As a result of these previous learning experiences, the Korean government benefited from a level of citizen compliance and cooperation envied by many Western governments.

These past experiences enabled the Korean government to succeed in implementing an agile and effective quarantine response strategy. It tried to respect expert opinions and collaborate closely with public health experts. In particular, it provided a system capable of handling large-scale testing in order to trace and prevent the spread of infections. At the same time, it made the daily number of positive tests public, encouraging the public to participate voluntarily in preventing the spread of infections. Moreover, the public mask distribution system was very effective as an initial response measure, as it ensured that a basic quantity of masks was available. The government kept encouraging people's cooperation by saying, 'The best vaccine is correctly wearing your mask and social distancing'. Medical staff and public officials, with the overall compliance and cooperation of ordinary people, worked hard and shared creative ideas that contributed to preventing the spread of COVID-19 infections. For example, Korea was the first to introduce drive-thru testing, which was then expanded worldwide. The Korean government secured personal information to track the movements of confirmed COVID-19 patients in quarantine through a mobile app. Of course, this measure also sparked debate about the invasion of privacy and restrictions on individuals' freedom of movement (K.S. Lee 2020; Byun et al. 2020; Kim et al. 2020).

In spite of active social compliance with quarantine guidelines for wearing masks and maintaining social distancing, cluster infections often occurred at religious gatherings or entertainment venues during periods in which social distancing was relaxed. More and more human rights violations occurred and the socially vulnerable and minorities were blamed for cluster infections. Further, some people tried to stigmatise individuals from these populations as 'super-spreaders', ignoring the fact that anyone could become a super-spreader. There is an urgent need to protect the socially disadvantaged, who are more likely to be exposed to cluster infections particularly due to their working, living, and social conditions. While insisting on the K-quarantine model in the pandemic's early phases, the government seemed to disregard the increasing discrimination against, as well as hatred and stigmatisation of, individuals labelled super-spreaders through fake news, as well as unauthorised disclosures of their identities via social media (Lee 2021).

'With COVID-19' policy based on civic engagement

As the ups and downs of COVID-19 continued for a little over two years, the fatigue of the people had almost reached its peak by the time the government eased the limits on private gathering sizes and multi-use facility operating hours on 18 April 2022. By then, the economic damage sustained by small businesses and the psychological stress of having to comply with limitations on private gatherings had become too much for many to remain patient any longer, and the possibility existed that continuance of those specific measures could lead to resistance against the government. After this time, the policy direction shifted to treatment and care focused on seriously ill patients. It was also difficult to demand the same level of devotion of medical staff and public officials because many had become burnt out (Suh 2021; Kim 2021; Lee 2021; Byun et al. 2020). Now was the time to reorganise the healthcare system, enabling it to deal with infections sustainably while paying attention to the adverse socioeconomic impacts of the pandemic—that is, increased social inequality. The collapse of many small- and medium-sized businesses could not be overlooked amid both the pandemic and the social distancing measures (Chun 2021; Kang and Huh 2021). The debate about whether to focus on controlling the virus spread through stronger quarantine measures or on easing restrictions on the movement of people with the aim of stimulating the economy continued. From Round 1 to Rounds 2 and 3, the government changed its policy orientation from prioritising quarantine to pushing for universal vaccination, and 'With COVID-19' still relied on certain key aspects of the initial K-quarantine model like rapid testing, quarantining if confirmed positive, frequent hand washing, and required mask wearing indoors.

In short, the Korean government put emphasis on controlling the number of confirmed infections in Round 1, expecting that the pandemic would end quickly. Meanwhile, in Round 2, the people became exhausted from the stricter measures, and the socially vulnerable and minorities were marginalised in the policy-making process, even facing human rights violations like required discriminatory testing based on nationality or hatred against members of certain groups. Furthermore, the social impacts of COVID-19 were further accelerating socioeconomic polarisation. Unjust social impacts increased, marginalising the socially vulnerable and minorities and delaying transparent and open discussions about the public health system. Whereas in some ways, civil society seemed to have shrunk during the pandemic, in other ways, the power of the state had been strengthened. While paying attention to the social injustices that intensified during the pandemic, one must closely examine the obstacles blocking the exercising of democratic citizenship as a key mechanism.

COVID-19's unequal social impacts

Disasters produce unequal effects. In Round 1, the impact of the unprecedented disaster called the COVID-19 pandemic was concentrated on the socially disadvantaged, such as irregular workers, people with disabilities, migrant workers, and sexual minorities (Lee 2021). While most Korean nationals rushed to buy masks to comply with the government's quarantine measures, migrant workers without health insurance and even residents of foreign nationality with Korean health insurance were not allowed to purchase masks at pharmacies. Whereas most services, classes, and work arrangements went online or contactless due to concerns of infection and the social distancing measures, people with disabilities, many of whom desperately needed care, became isolated and uncared for. Koreans entered an 'untact' world, where all products could be ordered and delivered through online platforms. Delivery workers, receiving skyrocketing order volumes, delivered hundreds of items until dawn regardless of the heat or cold weather, and some even ended up dying due to overwork (Chun 2021; Kang and Huh 2021).

The master frame, the K-quarantine model, made people overlook these darker issues. Both the elderly who absolutely needed care, and Korea's care workers, many of whom were also seniors, became increasingly exposed to a high risk of infection. As the pandemic and social distancing measures continued, the untact system rapidly changed social relations based on the platform economy (K.S. Lee 2020). But many people with disabilities simply could not follow social distancing measures. In addition, many migrant workers were excluded from accessing government information because the government provided limited translations in only a few languages. Many small businesses run by the self-employed could no longer be sustained and collapsed due to a lack of customers. Women were some of the first and hardest hit by unemployment and the decreasing number of available job opportunities, particularly during the early phase of the pandemic. Even worse, the burdens of childcare, children's education, and care for the elderly were concentrated intensively on women. In other words, women were more likely to face a double or triple burden amid the pandemic.

The country also witnessed increasing hatred and discrimination against those who were deemed super-spreaders, as well as against those from specific countries or even regions in the country where cluster infections had originated. Such victims argued that these social stigmas were much scarier than the virus itself (Chung 2022). Major conservative news media used the phrase, the 'Wuhan virus', to highlight the origin of the virus rather than using its official name, particularly during the first year of the pandemic. Some conservative commentators even argued that Chinese tourists as well as students should be banned from entering Korea as potential spreaders. As of 2019, students of Chinese nationality accounted for 44.4 percent (71,067) of the foreign students in Korea (160,165). Meanwhile, the number of confirmed cases from China accounted for less than 1 percent of the total number of cases from overseas (Lee 2021; Chung 2022). These prejudices and hateful reactions can be seen as attempts to shame and blame particular groups for the pandemic. They reveal widespread ignorance of pandemics as well as a lack of human rights awareness. In many cases, even Korean Chinese who had never visited China before the outbreak of COVID-19 faced criticism as potential spreaders. Such hatred and stigmas further reinforced ethnocentrism among Korean citizens. Although the K-quarantine model was effective in many ways in controlling the virus spread in the early phases of the pandemic, social discrimination had the adverse effect of dividing Korean society internally and increasing injustice and inequality.

As mentioned above, self-employed entrepreneurs running small- and medium-sized enterprises suffered the most severe damage from COVID-19. Countless jobs and employment opportunities related to tourism, the airline industry, restaurants, and hotels, were suspended. Although the government's emergency disaster support funding helped to a certain extent, it was difficult for many of the self-employed or those working in these industries to survive on their own, so they jumped into the platform economy (Chun 2021; K.S. Lee 2020). The platform economy, especially the delivery industry, does not discriminate in employment based on education, age, or gender, unlike other industries, and so absorbed a large number of workers. However, as labour and social protections for platform workers were sparse, many platform workers died from overwork or accidents. In 2020, while more than 2,000 people lost their lives due to COVID-19, 2,062 workers died from industrial accidents (Lee 2021). In other words, during the pandemic era workers were more likely to lose their lives every day at work from overwork or accidents.

Likewise, many migrant workers also lost their jobs and faced double or triple difficulties during the pandemic. They struggled with hardships like job losses, layoffs, wage discrimination, reduced social relationships, reduced services, and weakened access to medical institutions. Shockingly, they were excluded from the emergency disaster support funding scheme even though they paid for Korea's national health insurance service, local taxes, and resident taxes (Lee 2021; Woo 2022); this amounted to a clear human rights violation. Even though they had to pay health insurance premiums, they were not allowed access to proper medical treatment. Migrant workers' right to health in Korea should have been guaranteed by lowering their burden and increasing their access to medical services.

While critically reviewing the effective aspects of the Korean government's response in Round 1, it was also easy to identify the dark sides. The K-quarantine model infringed on people's individual freedoms and right to privacy, while overlooking hatred and discrimination against the socially disadvantaged and minorities. Moreover, a romantic notion remained that the pandemic could be completely controlled through digital monitoring—that is, via surveillance systems and digital technology (K.S. Lee 2020). We, therefore, need to look beyond the short-term effectiveness of the K-quarantine model, which encountered major challenges in the mid- to long-term. To reduce unequal socio-economic impacts, public support should be provided first and foremost for the elderly, children, people with disabilities, migrants, women, and platform workers.

We realise that it is of utmost importance to encourage people to participate voluntarily, rather than monitoring and controlling them from above, in order to tackle a pandemic in the longer term. Korean citizens actively participated in three rounds of COVID-19 vaccinations in accordance with the government's vaccination policy in 2021. With the major surges of infections caused by the Delta and Omicron variants in 2021 and early 2022, dedicated medical staff and civil servants became burnt out and exhausted. Their dedication and commitment could no longer be taken for granted (Suh 2021; Lee 2021; Byun et al. 2020). Many nurses quit their jobs during the pandemic. In early 2022, the government could no longer stick to the existing K-quarantine model because anger and resistance among the people had intensified as a result of the absence of a deliberative and participatory process involving the people from the bottom up. In other words, the K-quarantine model should be enriched by prioritising citizens' voluntary participation through learning, debate, and consensus decision-making (Kong 2020). Without the deliberation process of civil society, possibilities for the sustainability and ongoing applicability of the K-quarantine model will inevitably become very slim.

At the same time, the K-quarantine model still faces many obstacles to being fully accomplished. Such obstacles have been reinforced by a communication crisis. The lack of communication makes it difficult to build trust based on social consensus among people. Misinformation or disinformation, such as fake news on social media, blocks the ears and eyes of the people and leads people to search only for information that fits their own thoughts and claims. Many public servants continue to spend a lot of energy fighting against this problem. Some have frankly said that they find it more difficult to fight against the infodemic (a term referring to too much information, including false or misleading information, during a disease outbreak) rather than the real virus. An infodemic can spread incorrect information about the causes of and prescriptions for diseases among the public. For instance, at a large-scale conservative rally held at Gwanghwamun in Seoul on 15 August 2020, many participants who did not believe in the government's quarantine measures deliberately turned off their cell phones and used cash instead of credit cards so that their whereabouts could not be traced later by epidemiological investigators (J. Lee 2021). Even if such rally attendees opposed the government for political reasons, such attempts to thwart government measures could harm public health because blindly based on false or misleading social media information as well as by refusing to communicate with the government. As a result, democratic citizenship based on an open and deliberative process faces various threats.

What could end up happening is a vicious cycle of what is called the 'self-confirmation effect', which reinforces hostile, confrontational relations among political interests and logics rather than discussion and deliberation based on respect for diverse opinions (Hwang 2020). It is important for citizens to persuade the other party and to understand each other to reach an agreement, but social media and fake news bypass this deliberation process. As a result, the socially vulnerable and minorities are excluded and marginalised from the public sphere, and democratic citizenship suffers. Citizenship should be guaranteed regardless of nationality, race, religion, region, gender, educational background, or socio-economic background. The government cannot impose on citizens perpetual commitment to a particular policy. At the same time, citizens, need to make every effort to overcome passive attitudes and to participate actively in debates over government policy.

This section has highlighted COVID-19's unequal social impacts within Korean society and emphasised democratic citizenship as an approach to overcoming them. We learned that the proliferation of fake news about the pandemic on social media caused a communication crisis and became an obstacle to actualising democratic citizenship. At a certain point, the public's patience and cooperation reached a peak. We also learned that vaccination and rapid treatment were able to mitigate but not overcome the effects of the pandemic. New variants continued to emerge, revealing a need for a more viable solution: democratic citizenship as the social and political vaccine and treatment for the pandemic. Korean society needed to take note of the challenges ahead and move toward reviving democratic citizenship.

Challenges ahead for democratic citizenship

When no formal barrier to voting or participating in politics exists, we can all be said to be equal. Living as a citizen means caring for other citizens. Citizenship implies that citizens must carefully consider their responsibilities not only to themselves but also to other citizens. Citizens must take this seriously (Tronto 2021). During the pandemic, the socially underprivileged and minorities were excluded from social care and experienced limitations in accessing resources to care for themselves. They were unable to participate actively in major regional and national agendas, decision-making, or public interest activities. As a result, their citizenship was further weakened and vulnerable.

I suggest focusing on three challenges ahead for promoting democratic citizenship. During the COVID-19 pandemic, civil society—especially civil movement organisations (hereafter CMOs) and NGOs—was rapidly shrinking. Local CMOs reduced by COVID-19 could not afford to properly maintain traditional activities like advocacy and social services. CMOs are supposed to help provide social services, listen to and represent minor voices, collect opinions, and connect them to policies. Such missions were not easy to maintain amid the continued 'untact' reality. During the three years from 2020 to 2022, Korean CMOs did not pay much attention to realigning and changing their goals to match the concerns of the pandemic era. As a result, members of minority groups had difficulty exercising their citizenship on their own and gradually became passive beneficiaries in the public sphere, policy-making, and implementation processes. CMOs should first focus more on their role as mediators of communication and cooperation. Advocacy for socially disadvantaged and minorities is still important.

Second, as the COVID-19 pandemic continued, Korean society focused more on advocating for the right to health. In reality, the right to health does not apply equally to all people. People who get exposed to cluster infections and the areas in which they live are often subjected to hatred and stigma. Even after they recover from the virus, the wounds of discrimination and stigma against the infected and their family members, and even the areas where they live, remain much longer than one would expect. Many are more afraid of stigma than of getting infected with the virus. Just as there should be no discrimination against recipients or providers of care, a fair compensation system should be guaranteed for care providers. At the time of this study, the future of the COVID-19 pandemic was still uncertain, but the subsiding of the pandemic was expected to end the use of the K-quarantine model. Whatever 'new normal' now ensues may pose an even greater threat to people's right to health. The dedication of medical staff should be recognised, and care work should no longer be entrusted only to specific groups. Democratic citizenship can be implemented if everyone enjoys the right to health.

Third, during the pandemic era, there were intense value conflicts among a variety of stakeholders. The Korean government tried to brand its COVID-19 response strategy in terms of the K-quarantine model, utilising it as a diplomatic tool to enhance the nation's status. In reflecting on the Korean developmental state model, we need to evaluate the K-quarantine model in relation to value conflicts and competition regarding public healthcare, health rights, and democratic citizenship. The K-quarantine model was based on state leadership, development, economic growth, productivity, competition, and individualism rather than on safety, the environment, equality, diversity, public health, and support for the community. The strong leadership, with discipline and control, modelled in K-quarantine required 'compliant citizenship'. The Korean society will face urgent challenges of how it not only minimises social inequality but also enhances democratic citizenship. Korean society must aim for social cohesion in diversity rather than segregation, exclusion, and discrimination. Such value conflicts become even more serious when expanded globally. We may inevitably expect more conflicts of values.

Conclusion

Following the COVID-19 outbreak in mid-January 2020, Korean society was at first very effective and active in responding to the key issues they faced. This effectiveness, however, depended on citizens' compliant cooperation, perseverance, dedication, and commitment. Despite the high vaccination rate during Round 2, the end was nowhere in sight and many citizens were becoming exhausted. Some complained that they could no longer bear the social and economic damage brought on both by the pandemic and the government's restrictions on movements and gatherings to control virus spread. Despite the relaxing of many social distancing measures in Round 3, new variants continued to emerge and waves of infections continued.

The continued pandemic situation made it necessary to reflect on the K-quarantine model, which was based on strong state controls and surveillance from above. It is now clear that a more sustainable response strategy is needed should new pandemics emerge. The response process must be based on citizen consensus, which will contribute to restoring democratic citizenship. In other words, what should be valued most is not citizens' compliance but consensus to nourish key features of democratic citizenship such as diversity, deliberation, participation, accountability, transparency, and independence. In a context in which Korean society has become increasingly polarised and individualised, the task amounts to nothing less than restoring democratic citizenship to prevent the socially vulnerable and minorities from being marginalised in the public deliberation process.

Going beyond the K-quarantine model involves a collective awareness that a sustainable strategy for the next pandemic should be based on citizen consensus. For such a strategy, the government should be responsible for providing not only more accurate and transparent information but also a more transparent and open public sphere, allowing people to discuss with each other freely to decide how to respond to a pandemic in the future. Our study made clear that the government's response to a pandemic through a system of control and monitoring from above had only limited results. Moreover, citizens themselves should take a more responsible approach toward public health in a pandemic situation to ensure that no one is excluded or alienated from the right to health. People should continue to learn and discuss with each other, actively participating in the implementation process, to ensure that everyone is guaranteed the right to health. They need to become more aware of who their neighbours and communities are. Many are temporary contract workers, platform workers, the elderly in need of care, children, women, migrant workers, and people with disabilities—none of whom must be marginalised. So far, we have reflected only on a small portion of the unequal and unjust social impacts of the pandemic and the K-quarantine model. People's psychological stress and mental health have become a profound challenge that must be dealt with, also in the future (Kim 2021, 218–221). It is neither justified nor valid to make separate individuals responsible for restoring normal life. Ultimately, we must strive to restore local and democratic communities of care. This challenge faces not only Korean society but also civil society worldwide.

Bibliography

Bollyky, Thomas J., and Chad P. Brown. 2020a. 'The Tragedy of Vaccine Nationalism', *Foreign Affairs* (27 July). https://www.foreignaffairs.com/articles/united-states/2020-07-27/vaccine-nationalism-pandemic

Bollyky, Thomas J., and Chad P. Brown. 2020b. 'Vaccine Nationalism will Prolong the Pandemic: A Global Problem Calls For Collective Action', *Foreign Affairs* (29 December). https://www.foreignaffairs.com/articles/world/2020-12-29/vaccine-nationalism-will-prolong-pandemic

Borowiece, Steven. 2021. Once a COVID success story, South Korea sweats through summer of Delta surge, *The Guardian* (29 July). https://www.theguardian.com/world/2021/jul/29/once-a-covid-success-story-south-korea-sweats-through-summer-of-delta-surge

Brechenmacher, Saskia, Thomas Carothers, and Richard Youngs. 2020. 'Civil Society and the Corona Virus: Dynamism Despite Disruption', *Carnegie Endowment for International Peace*. https://carnegieendowment.org/2020/04/21/civil-society-and-coronavirus-dynamism-despite-disruption-pub-81592

Byun, Jin-Kyung, M.N. Kim, and S.W. Lim. 2020. *Long Thin and Fondly: How to Survive the Pandemic Era*. SISAIN (in Korean).

Cave, Damien. 2021. Why Asia, the Pandemic Champion, remains miles away from the finish line, *The New York Times* (15 June). https://www.nytimes.com/2021/06/15/world/asia/asia-coronavirus.html#:~:text=While%20the%20languishing%20varies%20from,from%20a%20shortfall%20in%20vaccines.&text=In%20some%20places%2C%20like%20Vietnam,vaccination%20campaigns%20are%20barely%20underway

Chun, Hye-Won. 2021. *Things Not Mentioned About Work: From Dependent Entrepreneur to Platform Workers* (in Korean). Seoul: BokSea.

Chung, Hoe-Ok. 2022. *Why I am Asian: The Politics of Hate and Discrimination* (in Korean). Seoul: Humanitas.

Fisher, Max and Sang-Hun Choe. 2020. How South Korea Flattened the Curve, *The New York Times* (23 March). https://www.nytimes.com/2020/03/23/world/asia/coronavirus-south-korea-flatten-curve.html#:~:text=By%20identifying%20and%20treating%20infections,the%20lowest%20in%20the%20world

Hong, Yong-Deog. 2021. *The Hankyoreh Shimun* (15 April) (in Korean). https://www.hani.co.kr/arti/area/capital/991213.html

Horton, Richard. 2021. *The COVID Catastrophe: What's Gone Wrong and How to Stop It Happening Again*. Bristol: Polity Press.

Hwang, Chi-Sung. 2020. *The Rhetoric and Forensic Of COVID-19 Disinformation* (in Korean). Seoul: Humanitas.

Kang, Hye-In and Hwan-Joo Huh. 2021. *The Rider is On the Way* (in Korean). Seoul: Humanitas.

Kim, Chang-Yeop. 2013. *Right to Health: Health Justice and Democracy* (in Korean). Seoul: Humanitas.

Kim, Dongtaek, Suk-ki Kong, Angelmo Lee, Seonhwa Jang, and Kyungshin Lee. 2020. *Characteristics of Korea's COVID Response from the Standpoint of Democratic Governance*. KOICA. https://www.dbpia.co.kr/journal/articleDetail?nodeId=NODE10494763

Kim, Hyun-Soo. 2021. *What Children Have Lost During COVID-19* (in Korean). Seoul: Denstory.

Kong, Suk-Ki. 2012. 'Politics of Cosmopolitan Citizenship: The Korean Engagement in the Global Justice Movements', *Citizenship Studies*, 16(1).

Kong, Suk-Ki. 2017. *Divided Gap between Neighborhood and Citizenship* (in Korean). Seoul: Zininzin.

Kong, Suk-Ki. 2020. 'The Korean Public's Response to COVID' in Kim et al. (eds.), *Characteristics of Korea's COVID Response from the Standpoint of Democratic Governance*. KOICA.

Kong, Suk-Ki, and Hyun-Chin Lim. 2020. *Local Community Has Solution for Future: Revitalizing Locality in Korean Society* (in Korean). Seoul: Zininzin.

Lee, Heesu. 2020. "Elite South Korean Contact Tracers Show the World How to Beat COVID," *Time* (27 July 27).

Lee, Jae-Ho. 2021. *When You Get Sick, We Get Sick Too* (in Korean). Seoul: Idea.

Lee, Kwang-Suk. 2020. *Against Techno-Fetishism: Platform Capitalism and Technology Temptation* (in Korean). Seoul: Inmul & Sasang.

Lim, Hyun-Chin, and Suk-Ki Kong. 2020. 'Civic Engagement in the Energy Transition Since Fukushima and Its Impact on Renewable Energy Policy Competition in South Korea', *Korea Observer*, 51(3), 463–483.

NCOV. 2022 (April 21). http://ncov.mohw.go.kr/

Scholte, Jan Aart. 2003. *Democratizing the Global Economy: The Role of Civil Society.* Coventry, UK: Centre for the Study of Globalization and Regionalization.

Suh, Joo-Hyun. 2021. *Is It Really Okay to Get Corona Virus?* (in Korean). Seoul: Beomun Education.

Tronto, Joan C. 2013. *Caring Democracy: Markets, Equity, and Justice.* New York: NYU Press.

Woo, Choon-Hee. 2022. *Struggles with Perilla Leaves: 1,500 Days with Cambodian Migrant Workers in Korea* (in Korean). Seoul: Gyoyangin.

About the authors

Suk-Ki Kong is Research Professor of the Asia Centre of Seoul National University. He studied sociology and received his B.A. and M.A. from the Department of Sociology at SNU and his Ph.D. from the Department of Sociology at Harvard University. He is also an Adjunct Professor at the Graduate School of Public Policy and Civic Engagement at Kyung Hee University. His major fields of research are social movements, human rights, civil society, and social economy. His publications and research articles focus on social movements, civil society, democracy and citizenship, local community and resilience, and social economy in East Asia as a comparative context.
skong@snu.ac.kr

Hyun-Chin Lim is Professor Emeritus of Sociology at Seoul National University and a Member of the National Academy of Sciences, Republic of Korea. He is also an Adjunct Professor of Asian-Pacific Studies Institute at Duke University. He received his B.A. and M.A. in Sociology from Seoul National University, and his Ph.D. in Sociology from Harvard University. He has presented papers at many professional conferences and has given public lectures on crucial development issues. His publications include more than 55 books and over 250 scholarly articles on dependency, development, democracy, and civil society in East Asia and Latin America.
hclim@snu.ac.kr

Part III.

Future Challenges

9. Cambodia's New 'Ecological Citizens'

Looking at Environmental Activism in the Kingdom Today

Stephanie Benzaquen-Gautier

Abstract: Founded in 2012, the environmental activist group Mother Nature Cambodia has become one of the Hun Sen government's main targets of repression. This chapter will attempt to analyse why the group's activities pose such a challenge for the ruling Cambodian People's Party, which often paints its members as 'enemies' of the nation. It contrasts Mother Nature Cambodia's campaigns with the government's 'green' politics, reframed as a kind of spectacular 'environmentality' that covers up the plundering of resources by circles of officials and businesspeople. Using a selected set of videos, the chapter discusses Mother Nature Cambodia's use of images to enact a type of ecological citizenship that has the potential to open the way for radically new forms of activism, especially for younger generations.

Keywords: Cambodia, environmental activism, ecological citizenship, environmentality, Mother Nature Cambodia, tactical media

Introduction

'Please help conserve the biodiversity, the seabed, islands, beaches, waterfalls, mangroves, etc.', Cambodia's Ministry of Tourism enjoins the population in a recent promotional video[1]. This plea may certainly make some ecological activists happy, but chances are that most will greet it with scepticism, to say the least. In the wake of civil society, environmental activism has greatly advanced in Cambodia during the past twenty years. Ranging from government-compatible managerial approaches to confrontational advocacy, it involves numerous actors, including state officials, conservation organisations,

1 'Recent developments in Preah Sihanouk province', posted on YouTube, March 2022.

Gregory Bracken, Paul Rabé, Nurul Azreen Azlan (eds), *Future Practices of Citizenship in Asia and the West: Care of the Self (Volume III)*. Taylor & Francis Group, 2025
DOI: 10.5117/9789048562077_CH09

international and local NGOs, villagers, politicians, journalists, and academics. In the late 1990s, geographers Philip Hirsch and Carol Warren argued that environmentalism functioned as a legitimising discourse for opposition forces in Southeast Asia because it created an alternative, possibly less dangerous, site for expressing dissent. Nevertheless, with Cambodia now reverting to full authoritarianism and cracking down on any form of opposition (Loughlin and Norén-Nilsson 2021; Sutton 2018; Un 2019), environmental activists have become a target. Many are currently sitting in jail, awaiting trial. Hirsch and Warren also argued that environmental activism could potentially generate radically new politics for the twenty-first century (Hirsch and Warren 1998, 2, 21). It is a claim that environment scholars Sarah Milne and Sango Mahanty have explored further by showing how new identities, agencies, and spaces of contestation emerge from the frictions between the different environmental actors (2015). In this line of thought, the chapter assesses the transformative dimension of ecological activism in Cambodia today. It focuses on the organisation Mother Nature Cambodia (Meada Tomechiet, thereafter MNC). Within a few years, the organisation has attracted a strong following at home and abroad thanks to its bold campaigns and visuals. Of course, MNC is not the only environmental organisation in the country to employ powerful imagery and the internet[2]. However, its masterly use of 'tactical media' (videos, social media platforms) sets it apart. This chapter first contrasts the Cambodian government's 'green politics' with the re-articulation of citizenship proposed by MNC. The question of how new political ideas and practices take root and spread is more important than ever in the digital age. The chapter goes on to discuss MNC's visual production, reflecting on the methodologies that may help register the emergence of radical activism. It suggests that visuality not only offers a potential epistemology for approaching novel conceptions of citizenship but also plays a role in their advent. Through the analysis in this chapter I aim to contribute to the understanding of the transformation of the space of politics in present-day Cambodia.[3]

Hun Sen's ecological show

'I use the word "crackdown" not "educate". We don't have time for education anymore', declared prime minister Hun Sen in November 2021 (Kimmarita

2 The Prey Lang Community Network (PLCN) is another example; see Parnell 2021.

3 This chapter was written before prime minister Hun Sen's transfer of power to his eldest son Hun Manet, officially prime minister since August 2023.

and Orm 2021). This statement was the government's reaction to the alarming report of Royal Academy president Sok Touch on the situation in the Tonle Sap Lake wetlands (Mao 2021). The police were instructed to arrest any official involved in deforestation crimes in the region, and the Anti-Corruption Unit was ordered to build cases and prosecute the culprits. Has environment protection become the new mission of Cambodia's strongman? This sounds ironic considering that government members (including the prime minister himself) have been endlessly plundering the country's natural resources for their own profit. Indeed, the irony was not lost on Hun Sen's main political opponent (in exile), Sam Rainsy, who branded the ruling Cambodian People's Party's (CPP) iron-fisted environmental policies as mere 'green-washing' (Rainsy 2021). Cambodia ranks high on the list of countries vulnerable to climate change—a state of affairs resulting from its developmental model (foreign direct investments, deregulation) and the persistence of 'Cold War capitalist culture' (i.e., the deeply entrenched forms of elite capture that have emerged with the Cold War and prospered thanks to neoliberalism)[4]. The organised pillage of the country's natural resources by the CPP elite and affiliated tycoons (or *oknha*)[5] has been consistently documented over the years (Beban 2021; Biddulph 2014; Frewer and Chan 2014; Le Billon 2010; Scheidel and Work 2018). Lately, with Cambodia's regional integration through infrastructure corridors (Belt and Road Initiative, Great Mekong Subregion), the government has learned to improve its manner of engaging with ecological discourse in order to pass for a serious political and economic partner. In fact, while Hun Sen complained about corrupt officials, his Environment Minister Say Samal attended Cop26 in Glasgow and reiterated Cambodia's commitment to reducing greenhouse gas emissions before 2030 (Haffner 2021). Australia-educated Say Samal, appointed minister in 2013, purportedly to reform Cambodia's environmental laws, is the respectable façade of the CPP's green politics. He is the one who conveys the message that 'Cambodia feels the [climate change] crises directly and takes them seriously' (Sun 2021). The coexistence of these domestic and international discourses, the punitive one for the Cambodian population and the one tailored for international ears, perfectly encapsulates the CPP's type of environmental governance or 'environmentality'[6].

4 The term was coined by scholar Wasana Wongsurawat. Nordic Asia podcast 'Popular protests in the age of #MilkTeaAlliance', NIAS, 25 June 2021.

5 *Oknha* is a honorific title ('nobleman' or 'lord') bestowed by royal decree to civilians, mostly business people, who have contributed more than US$500,000 to the government.

6 Alternatively called eco-, green, and environmental governmentality.

The latter concept builds on Michel Foucault's 'governmentality' (lectures at the Collège de France, 1978). It describes the 'complex interplays of power in the environmental governance of human-environment interactions' (Barnhart 2016). The term is used in a range of disciplines, such as governance theory, eco-politics, and environmental studies. Some scholars (particularly in forestry studies) see it as a means to engage critically with continuities in the colonial and postcolonial administration of natural resources. Others associate it with eco-management, in tandem with 'resilience' (Berkes and Folke 2011). This second interpretation explains why some theorists perceive the 'will to improve'—as anthropologist Tania Murray Li calls the nexus of governmentality, development, and environment—mostly through its 'inequitable and/or exploitative effects'. These scholars reject the reductive view of humans and nonhumans as a field of intervention for scientists, engineers, and technocrats (Luke 2011b, 97, 102, 104, 107). For them, environmentality is a global ideology that must be resisted in all possible ways, from participatory knowledge to concrete political actions, and even civil disobedience (Escobar 2008; Fischer 2000). What all these perspectives have in common, though, is the issue of power/knowledge and the social practices that enact it. Culturally oriented interpretations of environmentality, such as that of political scientist Arun Agrawal, focus on the 'mediating organisational forms' and representational regimes through which the state tries to transform people's imagination and behaviours *vis-à-vis* environment. Agrawal offers a nuanced view of 'the relationship between government and subject formation', which he sees as 'one of mutuality and dependency, rather than agonism and autonomy' (Agrawal 2005, 13, 30, 170, 198). Similarly, anthropologist Robert Fletcher proposes an alternative model of environmentality, in which different forms of governmentality can overlap and combine. He suggests a four-part typology including a disciplinary form, a sovereign form, a neoliberal form, and what he calls, with Foucault, a form 'according to truth' (based on revelation and traditional knowledge) (Fletcher 2017; 2010). These relationships explain how environmentality has become one more field of activity to which Hun Sen applies what is now officially called his 'win-win' policy. Originally a strategy to end the civil war in the 1990s, 'win-win' has been turned in recent years into a 'philosophy' that works in every realm of life, as long as it is associated with 'peace', 'stability', and 'development', the three pillars of current state rhetoric. With 'win-win', you can simultaneously be the severe headmaster, ready to chastise uncooperative citizens, and also the champion of sustainability, open to innovation—and both make a good show.

The government's action in the Tonle Sap wetlands was immediately made visible to the public. The military police posted on its Facebook page pictures of rifle-armed uniformed units prepared for action. The government-aligned media reported the arrests and trials of the 'bad apples', mainly lower functionaries from the provincial administration and police. Unsurprisingly, this staging of punishment and environmental concern masks the kleptocracy, extraction, plundering, and violence against activists that goes on behind the scenes. It is the smoke screen of 'Hunsenomics', a term coined by journalist Sebastian Strangio to describe the 'blend of old-style patronage, elite charity, and predatory market economics' that took off in the 1980s, as Cambodia transitioned to a free market (Strangio 2014, 135, 138). Hun Sen's ecological show stands between the observer and the CPP's shadow economy.

Over the years, the government has learned how to orchestrate a performance of compliance with international (Western) desiderata through empty gestures and 'holographic management schemes that never seem to emigrate from PowerPoint presentation to reality' (Strangio 2014, 179). For example, the Environmental and Natural Resources Code (ENR) Say Samal began drafting in 2015 in collaboration with legal experts, NGOs, and UN agencies, has been abandoned and the consultants cut off from the process (Nachemson 2020). This spectacle of proactive reformism using all the correct terminology (sustainability, smart technologies, e-participation, 'incentivising technological innovation') not only hides reality, but with its bureaucratic maze of reports, plans, commissions, and acronyms, it generates even more opacity.

Behind this technocratic cover, the government is able to carry out the major reconfigurations it needs to ensure its grasp on the country's resources. The granting of Economic Land Concessions (ELC) and Special Economic Zones (SEZ), for example, remains extremely opaque. Another tool at the government's disposal is the legal apparatus, adjusted to maintain the CPP system. The Sub-Decree 30 signed by Hun Sen in March 2021, for instance, has put environmentalists on alert. On paper, it sounds good. It confirms the transfer of protected land in the Koh Kong province (southwest Cambodia) to Cambodians who lost their lands when these became a conservation area. Yet, the fact that few families have received lands so far and that most of the lands listed in the sub-decree overlap with or sit adjacent to ELC conceded to tycoons worries activists. They suspect a new modality of land grabbing for logging operations and private development (Orm 2020; Flynn et al. 2021). The 'official agenda [is] to keep development safely quarantined from politics', says Strangio (2014, 231). In contrast, MNC's agenda is to bring 'development' back into the public debate, by countering Hun Sen's spectacular environmentality with a totally different kind of imagery.

The first campaigns of MNC

If there is an organisation that does not believe in the CPP's 'green' politics, it is, without a doubt, MNC. Founded in 2012 by monks Sok Chantra, Prum Thomacheat, and Spanish national Alejandro Gonzalez-Davidson, MNC has rapidly become a key player in the field. Its first campaign in 2013–2014 was against the construction of a hydropower dam in the Areng Valley, a site located in the Central Cardamoms Protected Forests (CCPF) in the Koh Kong province. Gonzalez-Davidson had been living in Cambodia since 2002, working first as an English teacher and then, as his level of Khmer improved, as an interpreter for organisations and as a human rights monitor in prisons (Gonzalez-Davidson 2015). At that time, he grew increasingly interested in the connections between human rights violations and the 'state-sponsored pillage of the country's natural resources' (Radio Free Asia 2021). Since 2009, Gonzalez-Davidson has made numerous trips to the CCPF and the Areng Valley and sometimes spent several weeks there[7]. With its wetland forest, the Areng Valley is a biodiversity hotspot that hosts over thirty endangered wildlife species, such as the Siamese crocodile, the pleated gibbon, and the Asian 'dragonfish'. Moreover, it is home to a Chong ethnic community of 1,500 people, who have resided in the area for several centuries. The dam project had been in the pipeline since 2006. Environmental groups, suspecting that it was just an excuse to open up the area to timber logging and wildlife poaching, expressed their concerns. The first companies involved in the dam project, China Southern Power Grid and China Guodian Corporation, pulled out because the project was not deemed economically viable (International Rivers). The dam would produce only 108 Megawatt for a cost of US$327 million. The project was shelved, but rumours about it began to resurface in 2010. In 2012, the Chinese company Sinohydro decided to back the project. The Environmental Impact Assessment (EIA), which had been commissioned and approved by the government in 2011, has never been made public. Yet, it was clear that the flooding of up to 20,000 hectares for the reservoir was an ecological disaster in the making, and a social one as well, since the villagers would hardly be compensated for the loss of their livelihood and ancestral lands.

The Areng Valley was isolated (no phone signal, no electricity), and therefore MNC organised the campaign at two levels. On-site, the group's members went from house to house to explain to villagers the extent of the dam's impact and inform them about their legal rights. They simultaneously

7 See Luke Duggleby's beautiful photo-reportage 'The Fight for the Areng Valley'.

launched a social media campaign to raise public awareness. The video of Gonzalez-Davidson swimming down a river despite the presence of crocodiles, joking about the leeches on his legs, and praising (in Khmer) the place's natural beauty went viral. The campaign gathered momentum. In November 2013, on MNC's invitation, forty monks from the Independent Monk Network for Social Justice Group travelled from Phnom Penh—by bus, car, motorbike, and on foot—to the Areng Valley to perform a symbolic ordination of trees[8]. Their wrapping of a two-hundred-meter-long piece of saffron cloth around a hundred trees was a visually powerful action—closely monitored by AK-47s-armed police (Phak 2013). In May 2014, MNC, locals, and activists from around the country set up a blockade camp with banners and tents to prevent Sinohydro surveyors from accessing the site. The roadblock was maintained until September, when several community members and activists (including Gonzalez-Davidson) were arrested. The campaign continued unabated, with petitions to the government, motorcade marches to provincial government offices, and a strong online presence. In early 2015, Hun Sen announced that the plan would be suspended until 2018. In February 2017, the project was put on hold indefinitely[9]. The Areng Valley campaign had shown the potential of bringing under the same flag locals, dissident monks, grassroots activists, media-savvy youth, and transnational organisations[10]. For environmentalist Marcus Hardtke, the Areng Valley protest was the 'first home-grown environmental movement in Cambodia [...] built on a broad coalition [...] and strong roots in the urban Khmer youth'[11]. The next years would confirm the innovative dimension of MNC's activism, and its political possibilities.

In 2015, MNC began investigating large-scale sand mining in Koh Kong estuaries. The sand was exported to Singapore for land reclamation projects. Dredging operations had started in 2008 after Indonesia, so far Singapore's main supplier, had finally imposed a blanket ban on sand mining and export due to environmental damage (2007). In 2009, the international

8 Founded by monk But Buntenh (who went into hiding in 2016), the network became active in August 2013 and took part in campaigns for workers' rights and land claims.

9 The project remains a part of Cambodia's Department of Energy Master Plan, with the idea to build a power line through the Cardamoms Protected Forest (EarthRights International).

10 As Milne underlines, life in the valley was 'far from being [the] socially homogenous rural idyll' depicted in MNC's campaign. Not all villagers opposed the dam. Obviously, the CPP exploited the divisions, painting MNC as an affiliate of the political opposition and warning of the consequences of associating with them (2017, 32-33).

11 In addition to MNC, the coalition included Samreth Law Group, Independent Monk Network for Social Justice, Khmer Youth Empire, and groups such as Wildlife Alliance, International Rivers, and Conservation International.

NGO Global Witness produced the first report on the subject ('Country for sale'), followed by journalists Sebastian Strangio and Vong Sokheng's investigation for The Phnom Penh Post. They revealed a complex system with multiple sand suppliers and buyers, in which tycoon Ly Yat Phong's LYP Group played a central role as a broker for international companies. The Koh Kong Department of Industry, Mines and Energy confirmed that local companies had been granted concessions over a small area. However, it was obvious that they were mining outside the designated areas and deeper than permitted by their licenses, with a disastrous impact on the ecosystem.

It was partly at the local communities' request that the MNC decided to intervene. The group documented the traffic of unmarked vessels, barges, and Panama-registered ships. It also helped the locals file petitions and organise protests. In April 2015, fishing families tied their motorboats to barges for several days until the crews drove away (Hul 2015). A couple of months later, emboldened by their first success, they boarded and tried to tow barges away. They were acting as dutiful citizens who try to enforce the law, said Gonzalez-Davidson (in Aun 2015). Given the reaction of the authorities, though, MNC shifted the campaign online. In April 2016, the group released a video in which member Thun Ratha, buried neck-deep in the sand, revealed that Cambodia had exported seventy-three million tons of sand, bringing Cambodia US$700 million (instead of the 2.6 million tons and US$5.5 million recorded on official documents). 'Where has all this sand gone?' asked Thun Ratha, requesting from the Ministry of Mines a public explanation (that never came). The exposure was possibly too much for Singapore, especially as Gonzalez-Davidson announced that MNC was considering a civil class lawsuit in the city-state itself as its next move (Au-Yong 2017; Radio Free Asia 2017). In November 2016, Cambodia imposed a temporary ban on dredging and export of sand for land reclamation in coastal Koh Kong. This became official in June 2017. The campaign was a success.

Towards a new form of environmental/political activism

Victory, however, came at a price. In 2015, Prum Thomacheat, Sok Chantra, and three other MNC members were arrested and sent to jail on the charge of 'threats to destroy' property[12]. That same year, Gonzalez-Davidson was

12 Sim Samnang, Tri Sovichea, and Sun Mala remained in pre-detention for almost a year; see Khy 2016.

deported and banned from Cambodia[13]. In 2017, after a long sequence of harassment, MNC requested its removal from the Interior Ministry registry of NGOs and declared that it would now function as a 'movement of concerned citizens' (Mech and Ananth 2017; Thompson 2017). In recent years, the government has leveraged the COVID-19 crisis to further silence its 'enemies'. In September 2020, MNC activists Thun Ratha, Long Kunthea, and Phuon Keoreaksmey were arrested for causing 'social chaos' (an offense punishable by up to twenty months in prison). Kunthea had been planning a one-woman march in Phnom Penh, wearing white like a nun, to approach Prime Minister Hun Sen's residence to raise awareness about the infilling of the Boeung Tamok Lake. Keoreaksmey was to record and live-stream the event, while Ratha would comment on social media. During the trial in May 2021, Gonzalez-Davidson was convicted as an 'accomplice' and sentenced in absentia. He called the verdict a 'travesty of justice' based on 'utterly bogus charges' (Surrusco 2021). In June 2021, it was the turn of Sun Ratha, Yim Leanghy, and Ly Chandaravuth to be arrested while they were documenting the dumping of raw sewage into the Tonle Sap River. The three activists were charged with insulting King Sihamoni and Hun Sen and plotting to overthrow the government (a crime punishable by up to ten years in jail). The alleged proof was the video of a Zoom meeting with Gonzalez-Davidson in which the MNC members had allegedly referred in a disrespectful way to the king and the prime minister. The arrest triggered a wave of protests from Cambodians as well as human rights organisations worldwide (Mong 2021; Hunt 2021). Foreign government representatives in Cambodia publicly expressed their concern. With the coming Asia-Europe Meeting (ASEM) and chairmanship of ASEAN (2022), this was bad publicity for the government. In November 2021, the Appeal Court suspended parts of the sentences. The six activists were released on bail, but not acquitted[14]. The government's pattern of harassment (especially through the legal frame) raises the question of why MNC seems to be such a challenge to the CPP. To answer this, I propose to look at the group's activism through the lens of 'ecological citizenship'.

The latter notion appeared in the late 1980s as the impact of globalisation on the formation of political communities led to a broad reconsideration of citizenship across political science. To those wondering whether citizenship could be extended beyond the nation-state, ecology presented paths worth

13 In December 2014, he was informed that his visa would not be renewed. He decided to overstay and was arrested and deported in February 2015.

14 They remain under strict judicial supervision (three-year probation) and cannot leave the country; see FIDH 2021; Cowan 2021.

exploring, particularly the supra-national forms of governance needed to address global-scale environmental crises. While some theorists regarded 'ecological citizenship' as simply a subset of existing categories, others tried to define it as a new type, *sui generis*, of citizenship. As the conversation progressed throughout the 1990s and early 2000s, the 'conceptual diversity' of the notion expanded (Melo 2008, 114). A first set of differences emerged around the definition of responsibilities and duties (moral nature versus pragmatic approach, asymmetry versus reciprocity). The second contentious point was inclusiveness. For Andrew Dobson, a major figure in this debate, ecological citizenship is 'fundamentally anthropocentric' since it is produced by the material activities of humans as they go about their daily lives. It is thus both intra- and inter-generational since a person's 'ecological footprint' will affect people who live far away as well as people who do not yet exist (Dobson 2003, 105-106, 111)[15]. Some theorists suggested that it should go further and also entail nonhumans (Curtin 2002; Smith 1998; van Steenbergen 1994). Authors generally agree that ecological citizenship is distinct from other forms of global citizenship.[16]Some even prefer to speak of 'earth citizens' (van Steenbergen 1994) or 'planetary citizens' (Steward 1991). More recently, the discussion has moved towards including the possible contribution of ecological citizenship to the construction of a different democratic model, mostly through transformed modalities of participation and representation (Kenis 2016; Sáiz 2005). Key topics in this discussion are the emphasis on the economic and socio-political dimensions of environmental crises (Barry 2006) and the importance of the shift from individual to collective action (Latta 2007). If, as Dobson argues, ecological citizenship participates in the emergence of a new political space, then it must be approached as a practice rather than a status since it is deployed in a not-yet-existing institutional environment (Luque 2005). This view resonates with Elizabeth Jelin's conception of citizenship as 'always in the process of construction and transformation' (Jelin 2000, 53), and Liette Gilbert and Catherine Phillips's performative citizenship as a 'continual process of creation and transformation of both nature and society (Gilbert and Phillips 2003, 317).

Although MNC claims that it is not a political party, its discourse is political[17]. From the start, the group has highlighted the structural dimension of

15 The United Nations report 'Our Common Future' (Brundtland Report), published in 1987, was the first to announce the 'rights of as yet unborn human beings'.

16 Van Steenbergen posits the 'ecological' or 'earth citizen' contra the 'global capitalist', 'world citizen', and 'environmental manager'. Unlike the others, the 'ecological citizen' has a sense of and attachment to locality and relates to Earth as a life form and habitat (1994, 149-151).

17 'We're not a political party. We don't even engage in large-scale protests', Gonzalez-Davidson on Radio Free Asia (2021).

environmental degradation and the role of the government and its associates. The MNC website could not be clearer: 'development' and 'poverty reduction' are being used 'as a pretext by a small elite of well-connected individuals and corrupt, ruthless government officials to amass vast fortunes, causing widespread destruction of the nation's natural resources and gross human rights violations'. In contrast to the opaque technicality of governmental decision-making, MNC uses a language everyone can understand. By creating conditions for the environment to become (again) the object of public debate, the activists re-politicise the ecological struggle and articulate it in relation to the issue of justice, in terms of distribution, common/public goods, and asymmetries in citizens' abilities to exercise their rights. MNC has always linked the question of participation to the engendering of knowledge: '[People's] opinions, rights, and well-being are completely ignored, and they are denied participation in even the most basic democratic processes' (MNC website). The group is not only concerned with improving people's access to reliable media sources and information. It also tries to show that anyone can acquire knowledge through direct experience, thus becoming part of the public debate on environment and governance. In this respect, the group's ecological citizenship operates as an inclusion mechanism (all the more so as it takes the question of indigenous under-representation very seriously). Through its actions and videos, it provides a social learning track for what it means to become a citizen. Therefore, if MNC is not, properly speaking, a political party, it nevertheless remains a political movement in the sense it proposes an alternative model of political praxis, citizen subjectivity, and state/society relationships. This model is not a part of Cambodian political culture. However, thanks to social media, it has been gaining currency, especially in the younger generation, a key demographic class for the government since people under 30 make up 65 percent of the population. As one MNC activist aptly puts it: 'If more of us join these kinds of campaigns, then there wouldn't be any kind of clampdown because when people stand up together, the government must rethink about its activities' (Rainforest Rescue 2021).

Reframing MNC activism as ecological citizenship, thus, helps understand better the government's reaction and increasingly aggressive rhetoric about the group. A few years ago, Hun Sen declared, 'This NGO caused all kinds of trouble'[18], and lately, the accusation that MNC uses environmental activism as a cover for subversive political action has become a recurrent theme

18 Ironically, he said this during the inauguration of the Lower Sesan II hydropower dam in Stung Treng province (northeast Cambodia); see Ven 2017.

in official public addresses. In June 2021, after the arrest of Sun Ratha, Leanghy, and Chandaravuth, an Interior Ministry spokesman said that the '[MNC] objective is to rebel against the government, using means that are not through elections' (Johnson 2021). A Justice Ministry spokesman underscored the point, claiming that 'their environmental work [is] just an excuse, but behind it, they [engage] in criminal activities' (Khy 2021). A government spokesman even called MNC a terrorist group (Ouch and Surrusco 2021). Pro-state social media have been equally virulent. During the May 2021 trial, the government-aligned website Fresh News referred to an anonymous Facebook 'Get Rid of Traitors' that accused MNC of being linked to the then-dissolved opposition Cambodia National Rescue Party (CNRP)[19], and of working in the pay of the Americans. The 'proof' was a document that showed an alleged donation of a few hundred dollars from the US-based MacArthur Foundation. 'Get Rid of Traitors' sounded like a discourse of the past: '[MNC's] actions are totally ill-intended under the pretence that their group loves the national territory, loves the environment and forests, but in fact they are an inciting group to pollute society' (Surrusco 2021). Fresh News described the activists as people 'full of evil intentions' whose activities are 'sponsored by terrorist financing' (Fresh News 2021). The fact that MNC has been in the public eye for several years, monitored by human rights organisations, embassies, and international media (Le Monde; The Guardian), is possibly the reason why its members have been spared the fate of activists such as Chut Wutty or Taing Try, both killed while they were investigating illegal logging (in 2012 and 2014 respectively). Yet, the government has gone out of its way to frame MNC as an enemy of the nation and delegitimise the group's actions. When Thun Ratha took the stand during his trial, he vehemently countered that view, reminding the court that MNC's only enemy is environmental destruction (Mech 2021).

MNC's 'citizenly visual acts'

The main vehicle of MNC's ecological citizenship is its videos (in Khmer with English subtitles). The group first turned to video making because they needed to produce their own material, since no media were covering the

19 The CNRP leader Kem Sokha was arrested in September 2017 on the charge of treason and accused of collaborating with the United States to overthrow the government. In November 2017, the Supreme Court dissolved the CNRP and banned 118 of its senior officials from having any political activity in Cambodia for five years.

issues they were working on. As the government's harassment forced MNC activists to shift their interventions from physical to online space, the videos took centre stage and became one of MNC's 'most successful strategies'. The videos are two to three minutes long and shot on location. They mix 'thorough investigation and easy-to-digest messages', generally delivered as a kind of performance. They are posted on MNC website, YouTube channel, and Facebook (with about 443,000 viewers). The punchy delivery, the clarity of the information presented, and the direct address to authorities have gained MNC a growing circle of supporters. The videos often go viral and are 'talked about in homes and workplaces throughout the country' (Gonzalez-Davidson to Civicus 2021). In the past couple of years, the group has adapted its style because of the state's increased repression. In the works produced between 2018 and 2021, activists altered their voices and hid their faces, using hoodies, masks, sunglasses, and scarves. At some point, they even used a puppet (Amaro 2018). However, they were worried that delivery by disguised speakers would be less effective (Ouch and Surrusco 2021). Therefore, since the six were released in November 2021 they have reappeared in person, more upbeat, defiant, and determined than ever. These videos are not only a creative dramatisation of environmental issues, but by documenting the dark side of Hunsenomics[20], they have an evidentiary function and produce a much-needed counter-visuality to the CPP's ecological spectacle. Drawing on sociologist Emilio Luque's notion of 'citizenly speech act' (Luque 2005, 213), I would even suggest that MNC's videos are 'citizenly visual acts' that intervene in concrete social contexts. They form an illustrated manual of critical citizenship that shows people 'how to exercise their rights and to have the freedom to work' (Keoreaksmey, quoted by Flynn and Vantha 2021). In the next sections, I propose to look more closely at a selected set of videos to see how they convey MNC's 'ecological citizenship'.

The 'sand videos'

There are three 'sand videos'. In the first one (April 2016, 300k shares), Thun Ratha, up to the neck in the sand, describes the sand traffic in Singapore. This is illustrated with pictures of sand-dredging operations and screenshots of the investigation conducted by MNC in the official data provided by a UN website. As highlighted earlier, the video had a strong impact. It even triggered a parliamentary opposition-led anti-corruption commission to

20 Scott opposes the 'open interaction between subordinates and those who dominate' and the 'discourse that takes place "offstage," beyond direct observation by powerholders' (1990: 2, 4).

question government officials (Lay and Willemyns 2016). In the second video (May 2016, 1.5 million views), Thun Ratha, once more buried in sand, thanks people for their support and keeps asking the relevant ministries the same questions: what happened to the sand? And where is the money generated by the traffic? A small Cambodian flag is planted close to him. It sends a clear signal. Ratha acts as a patriot by exercising his citizen rights to inquire and inform others about a topic of interest to the nation. In the third video (August 2017, 4.5 million views, 150k shares), Keoreaksmey, Ratha, and a third activist, again up to their necks in sand, denounce the extraction of silica sand in Sihanoukville and Koh Kong provinces. Each is wearing a head wrap with a different flag: Taiwan for Keoreaksmey, Singapore for Ratha, and India for the third member (three countries involved in importing sand from Cambodia). This time, the activists ask the Minister of Mines and Energy to take responsibility and resign. Obviously, what makes the videos so powerful is the performance itself. The burial of the body in the sand suggests the regaining of sensorial experience as a basis for political action – an idea that some theorists place at the core of ecological citizenship (Reid and Taylor 2000, 440, 446-447). Physically touching the issue (and not simply touching upon it) becomes thus MNC's modus operandi to make people care. It transforms 'purported facts and objects into matters of concern of care by thinking with and for neglected labours and marginalised experiences [as] a way to remain in touch with problems erased or silenced by thriving techno-scientific mobilisations' (Puig de la Bellacasa 2017, 108). MNC's embodied activism stands in stark contrast to the ecological 'optics' of the state. Ratha and the others are figuratively and literally in touch with the issue, whereas the authorities, with their 'spectacular' environmentality, are completely 'out of touch'. The three activists demonstrate a lived, 'authentic' connection to the reality of environmental degradation, a 'kinship between the being of the earth and the being of bodies' (Reid and Taylor 2000, 441-442). The videos show people how to think differently about the agency involved in knowing and, from there, about their own engagement in the public debate. Thus, they suggest a practical entryway into the performative dimension of (ecological) citizenship. Not only do they present 'good citizens' in action, but they also point to a different 'political imagination of the possible' (Puig de la Bellacasa 2017, 110).

The 'corruption videos'

One strength of the MNC videos is that the group members are not afraid of naming and shaming bad environmental actors, including 'the army, the police, politicians at all levels, and local authorities' (Gonzalez-Davidson to Civicus 2021). The exposure of cronyism and corruption is a theme that runs through all the videos, as the group seeks to demonstrate the CPP's opaque system of extraction and profit: who gets what, when, why, how, and how much. There are two sets of books in Cambodia, says Strangio: the 'public statements of Cambodian ministers who present their mirage of "good governance"', and the 'submerged economy' (of lucrative activities) that remains off the books (Strangio 2014, 138-139). In other words, to draw on anthropologist James Scott's well-known observations, there are the public and hidden transcripts of Hunsenomics. MNC activists have no access to the government's hidden transcripts. However, through the juxtaposition of official records (often from Customs and Excise) and documents obtained through investigation, they are able to reveal the disparities between the public book and the shadow economy. They can be big, national cases (like the sand-mining operations) or individual ones, pointing to discrepancies between a person's official wages and lifestyle. In the video 'An act of magic or outright corruption?' (April 2019, 1.65 million views), Kunthea and Keoreaksmey, wearing tops made of fake banknotes, propose to help the Anti-Corruption Unit. So far, the latter has prosecuted only minor cases (mainly involving provincial administration and police officers). These are 'small fish in a sea [...] full of sharks and whales', say the two activists, while on-screen, a photo montage of the faces of several tycoons appears. They then suggest that the Unit investigate Phara Mongkol, a cabinet chief at the Ministry of Land Management (and also the minister's son), who managed to buy a sumptuous US$8 million house in Sydney with his US$500 civil-servant salary. MNC's request for transparency and accountability is deeply linked to the issue of distributional justice. In the 'Iron Man video' (February 2021), for example, two activists in bright yellow hoodies, gloves, and masks discuss the import of over 400 tons of gold (worth US$16 billion) that have not been taxed. They compare this lack of taxation of a product involving only a minority to the taxation of imported goods widely used by Cambodians such as medicine and motorbikes. Imagine if this gold had been taxed, says one of the activists, holding a large calculator in her hand, even ten percent would have sufficed to buy COVID-19 vaccines for everyone and support all those who lost their jobs during the pandemic. This denunciation of corrupt practices segues into the re-moralisation of the sphere of politics. It repositions the moral argument—governing as doing right by the people—into political praxis itself, and as the basis of governmental legitimacy.

The 'Koh Kong Krao [island] videos'

In July 2019, MNC launched a new campaign, this time for preserving Koh Kong Island. The site itself is still untouched, barely inhabited, but for the small fishing village of Ao Latan. However, danger is looming with the pending construction of a road along the entire length of the island's coast. This road would pave the way for logging, wildlife poaching, and casinos and resort buildings. The involvement of the LYP Group (which received the concession of the Koh Kong SEZ in 2019) and China's investment company Union Development Group is, of course, alarming. In the video that kick-started the campaign, Thun Ratha stands on one of the island's pristine beaches, describing the beauty of the natural environment. In the following sequence, he sits in a kayak not far from the shore and explains the impact of 'development' on Koh Kong Krao's ecosystem. Photos of wildlife, plants, waterfalls, and mangroves appear on screen, soon followed by pictures of piles of trunks, slain animals, high-rises under construction, and sewage leakages in Sihanoukville. The contrast between the site's beauty and the horror of destruction is powerful. Interestingly, what makes it even more compelling is the end of the video, an aerial view of the island, and a soundtrack of a song by Sin Sisamouth. The drone footage can be interpreted as a parody of the corporate imagery of development, which often resorts to aerial views with lyrical background music. Here, however, the association with the most popular male singer in Cambodia in the 1960s (killed by the Khmer Rouge) cannot but trigger the connection between Koh Kong Island and Cambodia's 'Golden Age', as people often think, in hindsight, of the post-independence period (1955–1970). This repositions Koh Kong Krao within the realm of heritage. Protecting the island thus means protecting the nation's identity. In August 2022, MNC released two new videos, resuming their campaign after the disruption of the arrests and trial. In the first video, Keoreaksmey, upbeat and dressed in white, stands on the pier of Ao Lantan. She first says how happy she is to be 'with you all after being away for such a long time'. As the frame gets larger, we discover the landscape around the village. Keoreaksmay is then filmed at different spots (waterfall, trees), while she explains that three years since the concession was granted one can still see 'no sign of development' other than destroyed forest patches. Google Earth images show the zones in question framed by red-lined rectangles. Keoreaksmey refers to Article 62 of the 2001 Land Law (the document appears on screen), according to which an ELC that has not been exploited for more than twelve months without proper justification shall be cancelled. Therefore, she kindly asks the government to revoke the ELC and give the island back its status as public land so that it can be designated as a national park. The second video is a follow-up, but even more. It was shot during a three-day visit to the island by MNC activists and youth from the region. Images of the beautiful landscape alternate with footage of young activists submitting to the Environment Ministry a petition to classify Koh Kong Krao as a protected area. Keoreaksmey urges the ministry to react to the petition, and her request is then picked up by some twenty young people who repeat, one after another, 'Please respond'. The end of the video (always including Sin Sisamouth's song) shows the group relaxing and drinking coconut water on the beach near a thatched hut, before boarding a small boat. This uplifting video is probably what the CPP government fears the most—activists not cowed by months in jail and fully supported by young people who do not hesitate to show their faces. Not only are MNC's videos going viral; it is now MNC's activism itself that has become viral—a sign that politics can be joyous and that change may finally be on the way.

Conclusion

Using MNC as a case study, this chapter has examined the potential of environmental activism to generate radically new politics, as suggested twenty-five years ago by Hirsch and Warren with regard to Southeast Asia. To do so, it has built on 'ecological citizenship', a notion that is diversely interpreted but that, by and large, emphasises the inclusive and processual dimensions of citizenship. More specifically, the chapter has discussed MNC's use of 'tactical media' through the prism of visuality. It has shown how, within a few years, the group's videos evolved from being informative and performative to enacting and even enabling a form of viral activism, as a growing number of young people now claim agency in the public debate on ecological matters.

Expectedly, this type of critical and participatory citizenship is at odds with the government's treatment of 'environmental subjects' (in the sense of both the Cambodian people and the environmental issues at stake). In the current context of repression, it is difficult to say what the future of such activism will be. MNC seems to have returned to physical peaceful protest activities, with a march to commemorate the death of Kem Ley (July 2022). The symbolism is strong: the murder of this popular political commentator in 2016 shook Cambodia to the core. The reference to him also supports the reframing of the six activists as warriors ready for sacrifice. The government may well maintain that MNC activists are 'traitors' and 'enemies,' but MNC now has its own version of patriotism to oppose the official rhetoric. 'Our guys don't breathe air. They breath hope', said Gonzalez-Davidson after the trial (Flynn and Phoung 2021). Let us hope that they will succeed in breathing life into a new sustainable, just, and democratic society.[21]

Bibliography

Agrawal, Arun. 2005. *Environmentality: Technologies of Government and the Making of Subjects*. Durham NC: Duke University Press.

Amaro, Yesenia. 2018. 'Mother Nature turns to puppets to protect its activists'. *The Phnom Penh Post* (12 March).

Aun Pheap. 2015. 'Activists board dredging barges in Koh Kong'. *The Cambodia Daily* (28 July).

Au-Yong, Rachel. 2017. 'Strict rules for import of sand'. *The Strait Times* (January 23).

Barnhart, Shaunna. 2016. 'Environmentality', *Discard Studies* (27 July). https://discardstudies.com/2016/07/27/environmentality/

Barry, John. 1999. *Rethinking Green Politics: Nature, Virtue, and Progress*. Sage Publications.

Beban, Alice. 2021. *Unwritten Rules: State-Making through Land Reform in Cambodia*. Ithaca: Cornell University Press.

Berkes, Fikret, and Carl Folke (eds.). 2000. *Linking Social and Ecological Systems: Management Practices and Social Mechanisms for Building Resilience*. Cambridge: Cambridge University Press.

Biddulph, Ralph. 2014. 'Can Elite Corruption Be a Legitimate Machiavellian Tool in an Unruly World? The Case of Post-Conflict Cambodia', *Third World Quarterly*, 35(5), 872–887.

Blomberg, Matt. 2021. 'Why Cambodia's environmentalists fear new internet firewall', *Thomson Reuters Foundation News* (6 April).

CIVICUS. 2021. 'Cambodia: "This is a textbook case of organised crime with links to the state"' (11 November).

Cowan, Carolyn. 2021. 'Newly released Cambodian activists honoured among Front Line Defenders awardees', *Mongabay* (29 November).

Curtin, Deane. 2002. 'Ecological Citizenship' in Engin F. Isin and Bryan S. Turner (eds.), *The Handbook of Citizenship Studies* (293–304). Sage Publications.

Dobson, Andrew. 2003. *Citizenship and the Environment*. Oxford: Oxford University Press.

21 In July 2024, Ly Chandaravuth, Thun Ratha, Long Kunthea, Phuong Keoreaksmey, Binh Piseth, Rai Raksa, and Pork Khoeuy were sentenced to six years in prison, and Gonzalez-Davidson, Sun Ratha, and Yim Leanghy to eight years in prison for 'anti-state plot'.

Duggleby, Luke. n.d. 'The fight for the Areng Valley'. https://maptia.com/lukeduggleby/stories/the-fight-for-the-areng-valley

Escobar, Arturo. 2008. *Territories of Difference: Place, Movements, Life*. Durham NC: Duke University Press.

FIDH (International Federation for Human Rights). 2021. 'Cambodia: ongoing arbitrary detention of three Mother Nature Cambodia activists' (9 November). https://www.fidh.org/en/issues/human-rights-defenders/cambodia-ongoing-arbitrary-detention-of-three-mother-nature-cambodia

Fischer, Frank. 2000. *Citizens, Experts, and the Environment: The Politics of Local Knowledge*. Durham NC: Duke University Press.

Fletcher, Robert. 2010. 'Neoliberal Environmentality: Towards a Poststructuralist Political Ecology of the Conservation Debate', *Conservation & Society*, 8(3), 171–181.

Fletcher, Robert. 2017. 'Environmentality Unbound: Multiple Governmentalities in Environmental Politics', *Geoforum*, 85, 311–315.

Flynn, Gerald, Andrew Ball, and Phoung Vantha. 2021. 'Carving up the Cardamoms: conservationists fear massive land grab in Cambodia', *Mongabay* (1 July).

Flynn, Gerald, and Phoung Vantha. 2021. '"They breathe hope" Mother Nature on prison, freedom and the future', *Cambodianess* (29 November).

Fresh News. 2021a. 'Three Mother Nature Cambodia activists arrested' (June 18).

Fresh News. 2021b. 'Three Mother Nature Cambodia activists confess their crimes' (23 June).

Frewer, Tim, and Sopheak Chan. 2014. 'GIS and the "Usual Suspects"—[Mis] understanding Land Use Change in Cambodia', *Human Ecology*, 42(2), 267–281.

Gilbert, Liette, and Catherine Phillips. 2003. 'Practices of Urban Environmental Citizenship, Rights to the City and Rights to Nature in Toronto', *Citizenship Studies*, 7(3), 313–330.

Global Witness. 2009. 'Country For Sale: How Cambodia's elite has captured the country's extractive industries' (February).

Gonzalez-Davidson, Alejandro. 2015. 'Cambodia: peaceful direct action has saved one of our most beautiful forests'. *The Guardian* (27 October).

Haffner, Andrew. 2021. 'Cambodia skirts net-zero pledge at COP26, rehashes old target', VOD (20 November).

Hirsch, Philipp, and Carol Warren. 1998. 'Through the Environmental Looking Glass: The Politics of Resistance and Resources in Southeast Asia' in Philipp Hirsch et al. (eds.), *The Politics of Environment in Southeast Asia: Resources and Resistance* (1–28). Abingdon: Routledge.

Hul, Reaksmey. 2015. 'Fishermen claim victory against sand dredgers'. *The Cambodia Daily* (13 April).

Hunt, Luke. 2021. 'Cambodian environmental group suspends operations amid court cases', *The Diplomat* (30 December).

Jelin, Elizabeth. 2000. 'Towards a Global Environmental Citizenship', *Citizenship Studies*, 4(1), 47–63.

Johnson, Kay. 2021. 'Cambodia activists say conservation group a frequent government target', *Reuters* (30 June).

Kenis, Anneleen. 2016. 'Ecological Citizenship and Democracy: Communitarian against Agonistic Perspectives', *Environmental Politics*, 25(6), 949–970.

Khy, Sovuthy. 2016. 'Mother Nature activists found guilty, freed', *The Cambodia Daily* (2 July).

Khy, Sovuthy. 2021. 'Alleged Mother Nature Zoom meeting posted as "evidence" of royal insult', *CambojaNews* (22 June).

Latta, Alex. 2007. 'Locating Democratic Politics in Ecological Citizenship'. *Environmental Politics*, 16(3), 377–393.

Lay, Samean, and Alex Willemyns. 2016. 'Minister faces music on sand', *The Phnom Penh Post* (16 December).

Le Billon, Philippe. 2002. 'Logging in Muddy waters: The Politics of Forest Exploitation in Cambodia', *Critical Asian Studies*, 34(4), 563–586.

Li, Tania Murray. 2007. *The Will to Improve: Governmentality, Development, and the Practices of Politics*. Durham NC: Duke University Press.

Long, Kimmarita, and Buntthoeurn Orm. 2021. 'Do not defile Tonle Sap forest or else', *The Phnom Penh Post* (28 November).

Loughlin, Neil, and Astrid Norén-Nilsson. 2021. 'The Cambodia's People Party's Turn to Hegemonic Authoritarianism: Strategies and Envisaged Futures', *Contemporary Southeast Asia*, 43(2).

Luke, Timothy W. 2011. 'Environmentality' in John S. Dryzek, Richard B. Norgaard, and David Schlosberg (eds.), *The Oxford Handbook of Climate Change and Society* (96–110). Oxford: Oxford University Press.

Luque, Emilio. 2005. 'Researching Environmental Citizenship and its Publics', *Environmental Politics*, 14(2), 212–225.

Mao, Sreypich. 2021. 'Tonle Sap forests, life on the line in campaign: Sok Touch', VOD (30 November).

Mech, Dara. 2021. 'We are the enemies of environmental destruction', VOD (19 October).

Mech, Dara and Ananth Baliga. 2017. 'Environmental NGO Mother Nature dissolved', *The Phnom Penh Post* (18 September).

Melo, Carme. 2008. 'Promoting Ecological Citizenship: Rights, Duties, and Political Agency', ACME, 7(2), 113–134.

Milne, Sarah. 2017. 'On the Perils of Resistance: Local Politics and Environmental Struggle in Cambodia', *IIAS Newsletter*, 78, 32–33.

Milne, Sarah and Sango Mahanty (eds.). 2015. *Conservation and Development in Cambodia: Exploring Frontiers of Change in Nature, State and Society*. Routledge.

Mother Nature Cambodia. https://mothernaturecambodia.org/home.html

Nachemson, Andrew. 2020. 'In Cambodia, a sweeping new environment code languishes in legal limbo', *Mongabay* (26 August).

Orm, Bunthoeurn. 2020. '30K Koh Kong families set to receive land titles', *The Phnom Penh Post* (10 February).

Ouch, Sony and Matt Surrusco. 2021. 'We have to hide our face: Cambodia's eco-activists go undercover', *New Naratif* (18 January).

Palatino, Mong. 2021. 'Environmental activists convicted in Cambodia for planning "one-woman walk"', *GlobalVoices* (16 May).

Parnell, Terry. 2015. 'Story-Telling and Social Change: A Case Study of the Prey Lang Community Network', in Sarah Milne and Sango Mahanty (eds.), *Conservation and Development in Cambodia: Exploring Frontiers of Change in Nature, State and Society* (258–278). Abingdon: Routledge.

Peet, Richard, and Michael Watts (eds.). 1996. *Liberation Ecologies: Environment, Development, Social Movements*. Routledge.

Phak, Seangly. 2013. 'Monks enter forest fray', *The Phnom Penh Post* (8 November).

Puig de la Bellacasa, María. 2017. *Matters of Care: Speculative Ethics in More-Than-Human Worlds*. Minneapolis: University of Minnesota Press.

Radio Free Asia. 2017. 'Cambodian sand could build a foundation for legal action in Singapore' (1 May).

Radio Free Asia. 2021. 'Interview: "Young people will be so scandalized by it that they will become activists"' (7 May).

Rainsy, Sam. 2021. 'Being green is enough to get you jailed in Hun Sen's Cambodia', *The Geopolitics* (23 June).

Reid, Herbert, and Betsy Taylor. 2000. 'Embodying Ecological Citizenship: Rethinking the Politics of Grassroots Globalization in the United States', *Alternatives: Global, Local, Political*, 25(4), 439–466.

Rainforest Rescue. 2021. 'Mother Nature activists released on bail' (1 December).

Rubin, C.M. 2022. 'The global search for education: filmmaker Kalyanee Mam on connecting to the land, the forests, and the oceans around us' (5 February). https://www.cmrubinworld.com/the-global-search-for-education-filmmaker-kalyanee-mam-on-connecting-to-the-land-the-forests-and-the-oceans-around-us/

Sáiz, Angel Valencia. 2005. 'Globalisation, Cosmopolitanism and Citizenship', *Environmental Politics*, 14(2), 163–178.

Scheidel, Amin, and Courtney Work. 2018. 'Forest Plantations and Climate Change Discourses: New "Green" Grabbing in Cambodia', *Land Use Policy*, 77, 9–18.

Scott, James C. 1990. *Domination and the Arts of Resistance: Hidden Transcripts*. New Haven CT: Yale University Press.

Smith, Mark J. 1998. *Ecologism: Towards Ecological Citizenship*. Minneapolis: University of Minnesota Press.

Steward, Fred. 1991. 'Citizens of the Planet Earth' in Geoff Andrews (ed.) *Citizenship* (65–75). London: Lawrence and Wishart.

Strangio, Sebastian. 2014. *Hun Sen's Cambodia*. Chiang Mai: Silkworm Books.

Strangio, Sebastian, and Sokheng Vong. 2009. 'Sand mining spikes in Koh Kong estuaries', *The Phnom Penh Post* (10 March).

Sun, Narin. 2021. 'As Gov't talks climate resilience, Sihanoukville heads in a different direction', VOA (16 November).

Surrusco, Matt. 2021. 'Embassies, rights advocates decry Mother Nature verdict', VOD (7 May).

Sutton, Jonathan. 2018. 'Hun Sen's Consolidation of Personal Rule and the Closure of Political Space in Cambodia', *Contemporary Southeast Asia*, 40(2), 173–195.

Thompson, Nate. 2017. 'In Cambodia, activists risk prison to expose ecological scars of sand mining', UNDARK (25 October).

Un, Kheang. 2019. *Cambodia: Return to Authoritarianism*. Cambridge: Cambridge University Press.

Van Steenbergen, Bart. 1994. *The Condition of Citizenship*. Thousand Oaks CA: SAGE.

Ven, Rathavong. 2017. 'Mother Nature NGO is trouble, says Hun Sen', *Khmer Times* (26 September).

Voun, Dara. 2022. 'Royal Academy president Sok Touch on his Tonle Sap wetlands investigation', *The Phnom Penh Post* (17 March).

Yeophantong, Pichamon. 2014. 'Cambodia's environment: good news in Areng Valley?', *The Diplomat* (3 November).

Young, Sokphea. 2021. Citizens of Photography: Visual Activism, Social Media, and Rhetoric of Collective Action in Cambodia', *South East Asia Research*, 29(1), 53–71.

About the author

Stéphanie Benzaquen-Gautier is a cultural theorist and research associate at the School of Humanities, University of Nottingham. She has conducted research as a Postdoctoral Fellow in the ERC project 'Cultures of Occupation in Twentieth-Century Asia' (COTCA) at the University of Nottingham (2019–2021) and in the Art Histories program at the Forum Transregionale Studien and ICI-Institute of Cultural Inquiry in Berlin (2018–2019). She has contributed to essay collections, exhibition catalogues, and journals such as *South East Asia Research, International Criminal Law Review, Journal of Asian Studies, Mémoires en Jeu,* and *Media, Culture & Society*. She is currently working on her first monograph *'Beyond Skulls: Western Visual Culture and the Cambodian Genocide'*.
SD.BenzaquenGautier@gmail.com

10. Establishing Green Habits

The Role of NGOs in Depoliticising Environmental Governance in Urban China

Virginie Arantes

Abstract: This chapter explores the role of environmental NGOs in cultivating green habits among Chinese citizens. It analyses the emergence of green citizenship in urban areas, considering the concepts of environmental authoritarianism and post-politics. Two trends are discussed: grassroots organizations promoting moral and civic duty, and the subsequent depoliticization of environmental issues. Studying local-level NGO activities reveals the diverse relationships involved in environmental governance within an authoritarian context. It highlights that NGOs are constrained by the post-political reality of the eco-city, reducing their actions to promoting and cultivating a green community consciousness among Chinese people. Overall, this chapter contributes to understanding the non-confrontational everyday strategies the state uses to exercise power in environmental matters.

Keywords: Green citizenship, depoliticisation, NGO, environmental governance, post-politics, urbanism, Shanghai, environmental authoritarianism

Introduction

In the past fifteen years, the concept of ecological civilisation (*shengtai wenming*) has become an important step in building 'Xi Jinping Thought on Socialism with Chinese Characteristics for a New Era' (*Xi Jinping xin shidai zhongguo tese shehui zhuyi sixiang*). The values and development concepts of ecological civilisation were first proposed in 2007 by President Hu Jintao, leader of the Chinese Communist Party (CCP) from 2003 to 2013;

Gregory Bracken, Paul Rabé, Nurul Azreen Azlan (eds), *Future Practices of Citizenship in Asia and the West: Care of the Self (Volume III)*. Taylor & Francis Group, 2025
DOI: 10.5117/9789048562077_CH10

these concepts were enshrined in the constitution in 2018 by his successor, President Xi. Under 'Xi Jinping's Thought', the concept was developed as the basis for the country's overall national development strategy. As of 2021, it became one of the five strands of the CCP's approach to government: economic, political, cultural, social, and environmental development. The promotion of ecological civilisation under the rule of Xi Jinping is now a certainty. As green ideas have become a consensus among the Chinese, environmental challenges, values, and narratives are now embedded in the country's broader strategy (Arantes 2022).

Within the framework of this 'green' ideology, Chinese leaders are committed to cultivating ecological ethics and morality among the populace. Citizen engagement and contribution are seen as key to achieving eco-environmental progress (Gao and Xu 2018), as demonstrated by the 'Beautiful China, I am an Actor' Action Plan, which aims to raise citizen awareness of an ecological civilisation (2021-2025)[1]. While there has been a notable recent increase in articles discussing citizenship (Distelhorst and Fu 2019; C. Hsu et al. 2020; C. L. Hsu 2017), few examine the relationship between environmental politics and citizenship issues. In line with current academic debates on the CCP's 'fluid' and 'in the making' repertoire of governance practices (Shue and Thornton 2017) and a post-political critique of current depoliticised accounts of environmentalism (Hammond 2017; Swyngedouw 2010; 2011), this chapter examines the conditions necessary for the emergence of new forms of 'green' citizenship in China's urban areas, a topic that has received limited attention in existing scholarly literature. By focusing on two trends—the role of grassroots environmental organisations in promoting the individual's moral and civic duty (Hammond 2017) and the subsequent depoliticisation of environmental issues—this chapter presents the argument that the regime has succeeded in thwarting the thriving 'third realm', analysed in the early 2010s as a potential threat (Thornton 2013a; 2013b), while seizing the opportunity to strengthen the party's hand at the grassroots level.

The literature has made significant strides in measuring the extent to which environmental governance processes in China have become

1 This action plan was been compiled by the Ministry of Ecology and Environment, the Central Propaganda Department, the Central Guidance Commission on Building Spiritual Civilization, the Ministry of Education, Communist Youth League, and the All-China Women's Federation. Along with extending the promotion of Xi's ecological civilisation, the Action Plan aimed to cultivate ecological morality and mobilise society. See '*Shengtai huanjing bu youguan fuze ren jiu 'meili zhongguo, wo shi xingdong zhe' tisheng gongmin shengtai wenming yishi xingdong jihua* (*2021-2025 nian*)', Ministry of Ecology and Environment, available at http://www.gov.cn/zhengce/2021-03/01/content_5589520.htm (last accessed 28 August 2022).

authoritarian. Referred to as 'authoritarian environmentalism' in the literature (Gilley 2012a; Eaton and Kostka 2014; Moore 2014, 20; Chen and Lees 2018; Ahlers and Shen 2018; Shen and Jiang 2021), these studies gauge the CCP's efforts to assert control over all environmental policy decisions, using top-down and non-participatory mechanisms. A (re)centralisation of state power and a reduction in local autonomy characterises government's state-led, top-down enforcement tools, techniques, and technologies (Chen and Lees 2018; Eaton and Kostka 2014). However, limited attention has been given to the assessment of emerging approaches to environmental governance that increasingly rely on 'soft' and subtle participatory mechanisms at the local level. In this chapter, I draw on Mark Beeson's concept of 'environmental authoritarianism' (2010a, 2016, 2010c) to assess the CCP's ability to instrumentalise the environment to gain political capital and the contribution of environmental organisations toward achieving this goal. After explaining the argument for using 'environmental authoritarianism' as a framework to explore the CCP's dual use of coercive and participatory approaches in local environmental politics, I show how environmental organisations have become key players in bringing new meaning to what it means to be a 'good' environmental citizen. I then explain how these processes depoliticise the use of environmental issues for authoritarian ends. Lastly, I explore potential avenues for resistance.

The data in this work were collected from ethnographic fieldwork conducted in Shanghai from September 2016 to June 2017 as part of my doctoral dissertation focusing on environmental governance issues. The fieldwork involved immersive and prolonged periods of personal observation, including twenty semi-structured interviews. Detailed field notes were taken, and informal on-site interviews were conducted with residents, workers from environmental organisations, local leaders, activists, and volunteers. In addition to the data collected in a real environment, digital ethnography techniques were employed. I have also used secondary data from various paper and live-based texts, posters, and videos, especially from academic journals, speeches, and political discourses by President Xi, social media, and field research materials.

It is worth noting that the number and scope of non-profit, non-governmental, and other social organizations in China have experienced rapid growth over the past three decades, as have their partnerships with the government and private sector. In China, these organizations are collectively referred to as social organisations (*shehui zuzhi*). They are categorised into three main types: foundations (*jijinhui*), social groups (*shehui tuanti*), and private non-enterprise units (*minban fei qiye danwei*). For the purpose of this analysis, I will focus primarily on the third category, which may also encompass trade and professional associations or state-organised organizations (Corsetti 2019). However, the organisations that serve as the foundation for this chapter are primarily bottom-up organisations that, in a Western democratic-liberal context, would typically be referred to as NGOs (non-profit organisations). These NGOs are legally registered and self-governing, and have varying degrees of connection with the state. They are non-profit, socially oriented, and aimed primarily at promoting social and/or environmental goals. Throughout the remainder of this chapter, I will therefore utilise the term 'NGO'.

Environmental authoritarianism

The wake-up call

It is widely recognised that China's remarkable economic boom, while improving living standards, has had detrimental effects on the environment. The massive industrialisation process has resulted in biodiversity loss and an evident ecological crisis across the country. Since the mid-2000s, China's growing environmental catastrophe has thus become one of the top concerns of the population (Wike and Parker 2015). Widespread water and air pollution have become commonplace, particularly in developed coastal areas, leading to nationwide environmental protests (Steinhardt and Wu 2016; J. Jing 2000; Johnson, Lora-Wainwright, and Lu 2018; Johnson 2013). From the mid-2010s, unrest and discontentment intensified. Chai Jing's documentary *Under the Dome* (2015) played a role in this rise as it unveiled the contradictory roots of environmental protection and economic growth. During this period, as pollution increasingly affected public health and well-being, various groups within Chinese civil society, including environmental organizations, environmental journalists, investigative reporters, and activists, grew more confident in expressing their concerns (Shapiro 2013). This marked a turning point in the history of Chinese civil society, leading to a pluralisation of voices and an emerging environmental consciousness among the Chinese population. Some scholars saw this as evidence of a new chapter beginning for China's civil society (Lu 2007; J. Chen 2010; Kassiola and Guo 2010; Geall 2013; J. Y. J. Hsu 2014), notably the growth of environmental organisations led by Friends of Nature, China's first environmental NGO, founded in 1993.

Nevertheless, despite all the adversities, no steps towards democracy have been taken. The Party-state has not only learned to change, modernise, and adapt to the new economic and social reality (Cabestan 2014), but it has also tightened its control and regulation over dissenting voices. This has been achieved through various centralisation efforts, including the implementation of laws, regulations and policies that shape the role of non-state actors (Xu and Byrne 2021). A substantial body of literature, particularly since Xi Jinping took power, has focused on analysing the coercive mechanisms employed to regulate environmental practices. As mentioned earlier, the concept of 'authoritarian environmentalism' has been applied by many scholars examining the measures taken by those in power to (re)centralise decision-making and fortify central control through vertical layers of governance and institutional reforms. Such measures include performance evaluations, monitoring, and legal frameworks (Eaton and Kostka 2014; Shen and Jiang 2021; Mertha 2009; Ahlers and Shen 2018). While I acknowledge that President Xi Jinping's approach to environmental governance has been shaped by the increased use of 'sticks', it is essential to recognise the existence of 'carrots' and horizontal mechanisms that operate within the consensus-based framework of ecological civilisation to promote new forms of 'green' citizenship and power.

Consensual politics in the Anthropocene

In recent decades, environmental problems have emerged as one of the most significant and pressing crises in China. In the early 2010s, air pollution-related deaths reached alarming levels, with approximately four thousand people dying every day (Rohde and Muller 2015). This dire situation sparked a political consensus on the need to respond to an ever-deeper ecological crisis. Under this condition and in response to the potential threat of social unrest (Steinhardt and Wu 2016), my analysis supports the hypothesis that the CCP has recognised the imperative of tackling environmental issues and is utilising them to uphold the party's hegemonic ideology and maintain the status quo. In essence, the adoption of green narratives by political elites, aligning with the global scientific and societal consensus on climate change, illustrates how the environmental crisis is being leveraged as an opportunity to expand authoritarian reach and power.

Undoubtedly, China has made serious efforts to address environmental problems over the past twenty years. However, as Naomi Klein (2007) argues, we should not underestimate how different forms of shocks can be seized as opportunities by those in power to advance their political, economic and social agendas. While it has become very difficult to argue against the CCP's green ambitions, we cannot separate these motivations from the Chinese state's pursuit of performance legitimacy (Teng and Wang 2021). Chinese leaders envision ecological civilisation as being attainable by the people, but under the leadership of the party. Similar to Klein's concept of 'disaster capitalism', which posits that neoliberal capitalism both contributes to disasters and exploits them to expand its influence, the findings presented in this chapter support the assertion that the Party-state, through a political instrumentalisation of environmental narratives, has redefined China's environmental challenges on its own terms. As Teng and Wang (2021) contend, the CCP's policy responses to climate issues have prioritised top-down regulatory power on the part of the central state. Within the framework of political consensus, China's top-down governance structure and vertical accountability system have been strengthened.

Against this backdrop, this chapter shifts its focus away from the central top-down processes and towards analysing the 'discreet' changes taking place at the local level. Its objective is to examine the interplay between authoritarian positions on the environment and the restructuring of Chinese civil society's role in governance. More specifically, it aims to identify signs of the post-political condition, characterised by the emergence of a politics of consensus, within Chinese urban environmental policy. Through a detailed analysis delving deep into a specific location (Shanghai) and a particular type of actor (NGO), this article seeks to provide profound insights into the construction of environmental subjects by mobilising 'techno-managerial *dispositives*' (Swyngedouw 2019, xv) within an idealised vision of environmentalism.

Prompting participation and foreclosing spaces for contention

Previous observations indicate that authoritarian models of environmental governance undermine local communities and civil society by means of oppressive measures and suppression of dissent (Shen and Jiang 2021; Eaton and Kostka 2014b; Economy 2010; Mertha 2009). These policy processes, characterised by command-and-control mechanisms and an autonomous state (Lo 2015), stand in stark contrast to more democratic and participatory forms of environmentalism (Chen and Lees 2018). Unlike in liberal political systems, the participation of non-state actors serves the state and does not animate environmental politics (Beeson 2010b; Gilley 2012b). While the government has established new openings to get individuals or organisations, such as judges, prosecutors, environmental NGOs, and Chinese citizens, involved in governance processes (Van Rooij et al. 2016), the growing presence of actors, particularly NGOs' at the local level does not signal a shift towards civil society's emancipation (Howell, Martinez, and Qu 2021). This outcome arises not only from coercion and control but also from the suppression and diffusion of the political potential inherent in environmental concerns. Alongside the centralisation efforts discussed earlier, a consensual and expert-led approach to policymaking has replaced the spaces of environmental contention that had expanded during Hu Jintao's tenure (Fu and Distelhorst 2018). Even when non-state actors assume new roles, the hegemonic struggle within which these processes unfold diminishes the space for dissent and counter-hegemonic discourses to emerge.

As will be explored in more detail below, the CCP's discourse on ecological civilisation, its strong commitment to climate strategies, and its pursuit of green objectives restrict the ability of NGOs to challenge the dominant narrative set by the Party-state regarding sustainability. This leads to the depoliticisation of environmental movements, as the 'green' consensus strategically confines the scope of action and debate to avoid disrupting the hegemonic discourse. In this context, the mobilisation potential of NGOs is not only limited by restrictive measures such as registration obstacles and limited funding but also by a form of ecological commitment aimed at supplementing the overarching goals of the state. Furthermore, NGO 'participation' in governance processes results in a dispersion of responsibility, where knowledge of environmental issues is employed, on the one hand, to strengthen and cultivate individuals' moral and civic duties. On the other hand, various planning practices and assertive forms of command-and-control governance (e.g., mandatory classification) are camouflaged and even legitimised.

NGOs' role in shaping habits: A post-political critique

Since Xi Jinping assumed leadership of the party and state, he has employed both institutional mechanisms (e.g., strengthening the party's authority over the state) and informal measures (e.g., implementing laws and regulations to limit local government power) while exerting tight control and regulation over social forces (e.g., media or NGOs) to establish a segmented space. For instance, under the government's procurement of NGO services, although NGOs have taken on new roles in governance, policymakers ensure that they adhere to their prescribed plans. Some scholars refer to this combination of expanding the role of NGOs while maintaining control over them as 'technologies of statecraft' (Howell, Martinez, and Qu 2021). Although initially, NGOs had some flexibility due to a lack of robust legal foundations[2],

2 Many organisations developed in a grey zone, either registering with the Ministry of Industry and Commerce as for-profit companies or not registering at all. During 2014–2016 period, President

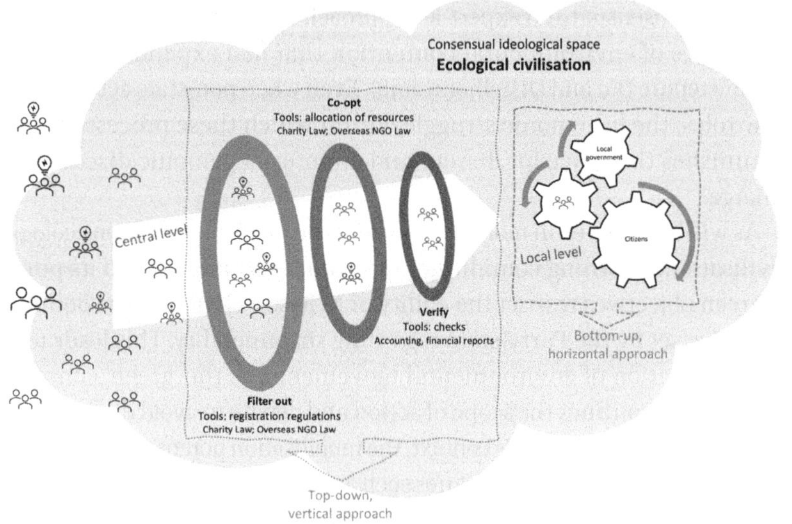

Figure 10.1. NGOs' role in environmental authoritarianism (source: author drawing).

the introduction of the Charity Law and the Overseas NGO Management Law in 2016 put an end to leniency. Alongside severe restrictions on funding and registration processes, local officials have been tasked with creating 'blacklists' of groups deemed suspicious by the government (Shieh 2018; Teets and Hsu 2016; Han 2018a).

Sorted out, graded, or dismissed (see Figure 10.1), NGOs play an important role in environmental authoritarianism (Fulda 2017; Han 2018b). On one hand, they serve to ensure that local authorities adhere to the central government's agenda. On the other, they assist local governments in enforcing environmental compliance and promoting citizen engagement. These strategies are particularly evident in policies in favour of sustainable development, such as selective waste sorting, sustainable mobility, combatting food waste, and, more generally, processes of individualisation aimed at developing 'rational' and consensual views on environmental protection. Within this constellation of power and disempowerment, and politicisation and depoliticisation, environmental issues become 'empty signifiers',

Xi passed several security-oriented laws: the National Security Law, the Cybersecurity Law, so as the Charity and Overseas NGO Law. See Shawn Shiew (2017) 'The Origins of China's New Law on Foreign NGOs', *ChinaFile*, available at https://www.chinafile.com/reporting-opinion/viewpoint/origins-of-chinas-new-law-foreign-ngos (last accessed 10 August 2022).

as they ultimately foster the integration of diverse goals while reducing differences and opportunities for contestation (Brown 2016; Ernstson and Swyngedouw 2019). This is characteristic of what some scholars refer to as post-politicisation.

Although debate is ongoing regarding the precise definition of a state of post-politics (Wilson and Swyngedouw 2015, 7), proponents of the post-political critique, such as Chantal Mouffe, Jacques Rancière, and Slavoj Žižek, concur that the concept provides a framework for examining how those in power undermine our capacity to perceive opportunities for change by enforcing hegemonic assumptions. While post-political tendencies are seemingly pervasive in society at large, they appear particularly persistent in eco-political discourses, as highlighted by Kenis and Lievens (2014, 537). Environmental politics, particularly in relation to climate issues, serve as a striking example of post-politics due to their emphasis on seeking consensus, promoting cooperation, understanding the psychology of change, and avoiding conflict (Kenis and Lievens 2014).

Such processes and patterns have been particularly observed and analysed in contexts driven by a neoliberal agenda. In his book, *Promises of the Political* (2019), Swyngedouw provides a detailed analysis of how environmental concerns, among other factors, tend to adopt consensual and depoliticising forms, ultimately shaping new forms of what he refers to as 'governance-beyond-the-state'. In this type of governance, increased involvement of civil society in self-managing and governing does not imply democratisation per se. Swyngedouw emphasises that these seemingly horizontally organised and polycentric '*ensembles*' actually signify a form of 'greater autocratic governmentality' (2019, 4–5). Although civil society actors, often NGOs, may be empowered within this mode of governance, it is important to recognise its 'Janus-faced' nature and its inherent drawbacks. The relation between the state and civil society is (re)articulated through the delegation of state functions to responsible yet 'unauthorised actors' who lack democratic or other forms of legitimacy (Beck 1999, 41, cited in Swyngedouw 2019, 15). As a result, the democratic character of the political sphere is undermined, allowing the ruling elite, which determines 'the rules of the game' (Swyngedouw here referring to market forces), to diffuse responsibilities and emphasise that individuals must take responsibility (Swyngedouw 2005).

Inderif Straume highlights the systematic tendency to frame societal structural issues as matters of individual concern, a process referred to as 'structural individualisation' (2005). Rather than addressing and politicising socio-environmental problems, policymakers redirect political energies towards technical and managerial approaches that invite public participation but within a post-political framework. The environmental authoritarian style of governance discussed here unfolds in such a manner. Under the banner of ecological civilisation, ethical and moral values are established as key components to support socialist modernisation and the pursuit of a green techno-managerial economic development system (Westman and Huang 2022). Corresponding to Swyngedouw's critiques of European liberal democratic contexts, China's model exhibits a strong bias towards maintaining capitalist rationalities (Hansen, Li, and Svarverud 2018; Westman and Huang 2022). To achieve this objective, Chinese leaders are restructuring governance strategies to position individual actors as responsible for their own actions. NGOs play a prominent role in this reconfiguration of practices associated with 'governance-beyond-the-state'.

A cooperative way of governing-beyond-the-state

As discussed above, environmental authoritarianism in China involves the state employing a dual use of coercive mechanisms and engaging new actors to achieve its goals. As Lynette Ong's book, *Outsourcing Repression* (2022), illustrates, the state engages a range of non-state actors, or what she refers to as 'brokers', to impose its will on society, thereby avoiding backlash and resistance, particularly in urban areas where violent repression is less tolerated. Ong categorises these brokers into political, social, or economic types, 'allow[ing] the state to govern, implement challenging policies, and resolv[e] conflict via proxy' (2022, 127)[3]. The interactions and influences of the Chinese state on the development of NGOs, which fall into Ong's category of social brokers, have been extensively examined, namely the emergence of government purchasing of social services. The research project, *The Politics of Services Subcontracting to NGOs in China*, led by Jude Howell, provides valuable insights in this regard[4]. In Shanghai, significant emphasis has been placed on the government's procurement of NGO services (Thornton 2013a; Jia and Su 2009; Carrillo, Hood, and Kadetz 2017; Yu and Guo 2019),

3 According to Lynette Ong, political brokers derive their power from the state (e.g., residents, village committees), and social brokers rely mainly on their social capital (e.g., volunteers). In contrast, economic brokers use their close relationship with both the state and society to facilitate deal-making between the two.

4 See ESRC Project titled 'The politics of services subcontracting to NGOs in China', available at https://gtr.ukri.org/projects?ref=ES%2FP001726%2F1#/tabOverview (last accessed 22 August 2022).

with particular attention given to the work of Hsu and Hasmath (2014, 2013). Operating under what they call a 'local corporatist model', various mechanisms, including cooperative governance arrangements with NGOs, are developed to mobilise social actors while keeping them under the strict guidance of the authorities. This aligns with the intensive Party-building efforts described by Thornton, which began in the late 1990s (Thornton 2013a).

In an article that reviewed academic research on service procurement in China, Martinez, Qu, and Howell (2021, 15) highlighted an ongoing controversy regarding the effects of contracting on state-society relations. While various narratives analyse the pros and cons of procurement in terms of efficiency, capacity, and quality of services, the impact on state-society dynamics remains a subject of debate:

> some scholars argue that contracting develops the sector of service-delivery social organisations, to the point of even building state-nonprofit relationships towards collaborative governance (Jing and Hu, 2017); while others argue it extends the mechanisms of state control over social organisations in a strategy of 'welfarist incorporation' (Howell 2015; 2019).

Ong's conclusions align with my analysis in Shanghai, as I have argued in previous work (Arantes 2022). It is important to note, for instance, that labelling such relations as 'collaborative governance' (Y. Jing and Hu 2017; Y. Jing 2015; Ansell and Gash 2008) can be misleading. While I acknowledge the increasing exchange between local governments and NGOs, I disagree with Jing's characterisation of collaborative governance as a power-sharing process. Instead, what we observe is a delegation of power from the government to certain types of NGOs. Therefore, the term 'cooperative' better captures the current power dynamics between state and non-state actors. I agree with a group of scholars who claim that contracting has tightened government control over NGOs. No genuine power-sharing exists; rather, NGOs are selectively chosen based on their utility to the regime, and their activities are quickly absorbed and institutionalised to best suit government priorities.

Within this context of 'hybrid socialism-neoliberalism', as described by Howell et al. (2021) involving a combination of socialist rationalities with competitive market rationalities, these processes can be seen as a form of governmentality aligned with broader goals of economic efficiency and environmental objectives, as demonstrated in my PhD dissertation (2020) on 'discreet' modes of governance (Arantes 2022). These processes are directly influenced by the 'Guiding Opinions on the Government Purchasing of Services from Social Forces' introduced by the Chinese government in 2013, with further development at the municipality level. Shanghai, as a pioneer in service procurement, has been particularly active in establishing multi-channel participation programmes and opening spaces for NGOs to engage in community governance and citizen-centred processes and services (Y. Jing and Gong 2012; Y. Jing and Hu 2017). Operating within this 'system of governance at a distance', which involves deepening governance through welfare, social work, and social organisations (Howell, Martinez, and Qu 2021), NGOs function as branding tools to advance China's 'green' ambitions (De Jong et al. 2016), such as promoting waste recycling or greening communities. Similar to Swyngedouw's analysis of 'governing-beyond-the-state' in Western contexts, 'governing at a distance' requires active participation by citizens at both individual and collective levels (Bray 2006; Leung and Xu 2015 cited in Howell, Martinez, and Qu 2021).

The Party-state utilises a combination of strong leadership and environmentalism to justify assertive forms of governance. According to Slavoj Žižek, this type of governance reflects a process of post-politicisation, where politics or dispute are increasingly replaced by hard and soft technologies of surveillance (management) of environmental or other domains (Žižek quoted in Swyngedouw 2019, 27). Those who are perceived as irresponsible or non-consensual, either for challenging the CCP's hegemony or opposing development thinking, are excluded. At the same time, those who align with top-down managerial and technocratic practices are co-opted by the regime. Within this framework, NGOs are constrained from acting against the discursive imaginaries of ecological civilisation, and their actions end up trapped in roles that perpetuate the state's vision of an ecological civilisation. Harvey Neo, in his analysis of Singapore, views such governance practices as a means to an end (Jobin, Ho, and Hsiao 2021, 120), ultimately strengthening political stability through non-confrontational means.

In the following section, I draw upon my previous work, which explores waste as a lens to examine the evolving dynamics of moral responsibility among individuals in post-reform urban China (Arantes 2023). By doing so, I aim to illuminate the intricate micropolitics surrounding NGOs at the local level and show how the growing engagement of civil society in governance does not necessarily indicate a fundamental shift towards liberal democracy or the requirement for strict and forceful policies. Instead, it signifies a purposeful blending of coercive mechanisms and participatory processes to promote novel notions of citizenship and, ultimately, centralised control.

Waste sorting is the new fashion (*xin shiwang*)

Too often, analysis of authoritarian contexts like China focuses on coercive processes and outcomes, overlooking the significance of everyday politics. By examining the activities of NGOs in their daily operations, I have witnessed how this 'governance-beyond-the-state' is increasingly shaped by the power of individuals and their role in creating a beautiful and green China. In previous research, I highlighted the significance of waste management as an important arena for evaluating innovative governance practices (Arantes, Zou, and Che 2020; Arantes 2023). For a more comprehensive understanding, I recommend referring to the features, strengths, and limitations of the green account system (Xiao et al. 2020; Zhou et al. 2019). However, this article shifts focus to a less explored aspect: the depoliticisation of environmental issues through cooperative approaches that stimulate new forms of public advocacy, civic participation, and local-level citizenship.

To provide context, since 2019 the Shanghai Municipality has enforced mandatory waste sorting for its citizens, implementing state bureaucratic measures within neighbourhood communities (*shequ*)[5]. The new system requires Shanghai residents to sort their waste into four categories: recyclables, hazardous materials, and so-called wet and dry waste. Failure to comply with the regulations will result in penalties. However, implementation of this system did not take place out of thin air. Shanghai's recycling system is the result of years of local experimentation involving various stakeholders. For instance, to encourage the public to get involved in waste sorting at source, the government has created multiple solutions to encourage public participation in source waste sorting. One notable initiative is the 'green account (*lüse zhanghu*)' incentive scheme introduced in 2013, which rewards individuals with points for proper waste sorting and disposal; these points are redeemable for gifts. Within this system, individuals are monitored daily by a multitude of actors—community leaders, volunteers, NGOs, or waste pickers—to ensure compliance. These cooperative mechanisms within communities establish new arenas where the implicit and explicit state-building efforts of the state are implemented and new meaning is given to the behaviour of the individual as a citizen.

Achieving the city's green ambitions requires everyone to be on board. According to several NGO workers I interviewed, this can be challenging. They,

5 In the Memorandum on Promoting Urban Shequ Construction, *shequ* is defined as 'a social collective formed by those residing within a defined geographic boundary', and the territory of a *shequ* is 'the area under the jurisdiction of the enlarged residents' committee' (Tang and Sun 2017).

along with retirees I encountered in Shanghai communities, emphasised the difficulty of altering people's ingrained habits. One NGO leader argued that persuasion must be carried out with meticulous care and attention to detail. President Xi himself recognises this challenge. As he stated, 'strengthen[ing] guidance, adapt[ing] measures to local conditions, continu[ing] to advance and persevere by doing the work meticulously and solidly' are indispensable for the development of an effective waste classification system[6].

In this model of cooperative governance, the role of NGOs as intermediaries (Latour 2005) is significant in shaping the behaviour of green citizens[7]. Through their work, they establish and normalise standards of acceptable behaviour, relying on their 'expert' knowledge. Liulin (pseudonym), a Shanghainese woman working at one of the environmental NGOs involved in the programme, conveys on her WeChat: 'To become a good citizen, recycling is an obligation'[8]. As rightly argued by Ong, 'Persuasion is the least costly of all the tools in material terms and in backlash minimisation. Carrots draw directly on material resources, and as citizens' income levels rise, the threshold for material inducements also increases' (2022, 9).

To implement the programme, environmental organisations closely cooperate with residential committees at the lowest level of China's urban administrative hierarchy. They actively recruit and train volunteers, predominantly comprised of retirees, many of whom are party members. Within this framework, as discussed earlier, NGOs play a crucial role as indispensable actors in the horizontally organised governance structures of cooperative governance. In addition to educating local stakeholders about the programme, NGOs closely monitor volunteer groups that supervise residents on-site. In this configuration, I contend that NGOs serve as indirect instruments for convergence and control at the grassroots level, representing a powerful arm in the state's horizontal governmental technologies for implementing official directives.

In line with *shequ* institutions, which are considered the fundamental units of social, political, and administrative organisations in urban areas (Zhang, Yung, and Chan 2018; Rowe, Forsyth, and Kan 2016), the activities of NGOs contribute to the promotion of active and responsible citizens. As Wan

6 Source: Xinhua News Agency, published in the electronic communication platform of the State Council of the PRC, http://www.gov.cn/xinwen/2019-06/04/content_5397457.htm (last accessed 26 August 2022).

7 Here I refer to Latour's concept of intermediary. According to the French sociologist, an intermediary 'transports meaning or force without transformation' (Latour 2005, 39).

8 Translated by the author. Original passage in Chinese: '*zuowei yi ming hao gongmin, laji fenlei shi ying jin de yiwu*'.

(2015, 15) argues, 'To mobilise them (elderly volunteers), the *Shequ* institutions embrace a hybrid of Maoist and Confucian discourses to strengthen their values as senior citizens'. To encourage residents to live in disciplined ways, the discourse emphasises individual 'activeness' or 'progressiveness'. By utilizing volunteers who possess deep social connections within the neighbourhood community, *shequ* institutions aim to maintain social order. The role of NGOs aligns with the description provided by Wan (2015), as they employ individual rhetoric to encourage citizens to adopt specific behaviours.

Their actions aim to foster self-reflection and individual responsibility for waste management. The activities primarily revolve around education regarding 'green' responsibility, which seeks to enhance individuals' awareness of their roles through educational approaches emphasising behavioural practices and cultivating green identities. As highlighted by one NGO leader I interviewed, environmental NGOs play a crucial role in 'nurturing future green citizens' (*peiyu weilai de lüse gongmin*). They have emerged as vital players in accomplishing a key objective of the party: to strengthen the construction of citizens' ecological morality, as outlined in the 'Outline for the Implementation of the Morality Construction of Citizens in the New Era' (*Xin shidai gongmin daode jianshe shishi gangyao*).

During my fieldwork, I witnessed the increasing transfer of the climate 'burden' onto citizens' shoulders through the presence of NGOs at the community level. The Party-state simultaneously leverages strong leadership and environmental protection to justify assertive forms of governance. This is achieved by bridging the gap between stricter regulations and individual behaviour. Therefore, I argue that NGOs play a major role in developing individual environmental sentiments as a collective endeavour. They not only transform a social problem into an individual issue but also contribute to three key objectives outlined in the aforementioned 'Action Plan': the promotion of ecological culture, the cultivation of ecological morality, and the broad mobilisation of society to realise ecological civilisation. Consequently, topics related to counter-hegemonic goals, such as degrowth or environmental justice in waste management, are marginalised and overlooked in the public sphere.

I contend that two main factors contribute to this phenomenon. Firstly, NGOs tend to focus on professionalising their work in specific areas, such as waste management, marine plastic, urban gardens, or education. As Barker (2010, 10) puts it, they evolve into specialised knowledge professions. By leveraging their expertise, NGOs collaborate with citizens and gather their input and feedback, thereby enhancing governance efficiency. However, their expertise can easily be co-opted by the state machinery, as the more specialised their knowledge becomes, the more depoliticised it tends to be. Secondly, I contend that the growing role of environmental NGOs in governance, through their grassroots leadership and expert positions, perpetuates the consensual ideological construction of ecological civilisation by normalising the role of individuals in achieving environmental goals. I perceive this as a process of post-politicisation, which contributes to the de-politicisation of environmental issues and the reduction of spaces for dissent.

'Tactics' of resistance

As discussed earlier, the combination of environmental authoritarianism and the post-political condition imposes constraints on NGOs, limiting their ability to challenge the prevailing status quo and present alternative environmental visions. Trapped within this post-political context, the increasing specialization of their expertise unintentionally reinforces established hierarchies of authority. However, it is crucial to question whether their agency is entirely eliminated. Are there possibilities for spaces of resistance to emerge? In this final section, I will delve into a more detailed exploration of the irreversibility of the post-political condition by focusing on de Certeau's concept of 'tactics' (2011).

According to de Certeau, societies operate within a dual structure: the dominant system (such as China's authoritarian regime) and the users, who are often considered passive within this system (e.g., NGOs and citizens) (Demirpolat 2021). To maintain their overarching framework those in power develop 'strategies', which are then appropriated and used by individuals or groups. In contrast to the pessimistic views of Foucault or Lefebvre regarding individual agency, de Certeau (2011) argues that within spaces of power, those characterised as weak or passive can engage in 'tactics' that can be seen as an 'art of the weak'.

While I have observed how the post-political condition impacts the agency of NGOs, it remains crucial not to underestimate the potential for 'tactics' to emerge within the complexity of today's global cities, despite the regime's efforts to reinforce discipline through various practices, whether authoritarian or more cooperative. Here, de Certeau's conceptualization of resistance becomes promising, as it acknowledges the pervasive power of the state while highlighting the possibility of everyday activities as 'tactical' responses to specific strategies of urban planning. According to the French scholar, 'tactics' are adaptations to the environment created by the strategies of the powerful. Contrary to 'strategies', which are undermined by unpredictability (such as COVID-19), tactics are actions in a constant state of reassessment and correction. As one leader of an NGO stressed during a weekend spent picking waste outdoors in the mountains in Hangzhou, 'We are in a time when many windows were closed, but we should strive and continue as they could open when you least expect it'. Even though the case study in the following chapter strongly indicates that NGOs are becoming 'arms of the state', one should not disregard their capacity for adaptability. Despite the restrictions faced by NGOs, they are constantly developing spaces to increase their agency.

During my observations with several NGOs, for instance, they actively criticised the state's inaction during discussions with local leaders and among themselves. They also promote narratives of degrowth and waste reduction that challenge the state's sustainable development narrative. I also witnessed numerous instances of such 'tactics' among the general population, such as people undermining recycling facilities, refusing to comply with metro scanner machines, driving cars without license plates, or tagging propaganda posters and walls. These 'pedestrian-level' tactics resist the disciplinary control of space (Beaumont 2020). By simply opening one's eyes to the Metropole's history of dissent, resistance, and everyday actions, it becomes apparent that the city is not solely a site for those in power to assert their disciplinary authority. Therefore, I believe that in the years to come, scholars should focus on street-level resistance as a significant area of study. Additionally, as Chu indicated in Chapter 3, recovering lost or forgotten struggles could be a way of assessing 'tactics' of adaptation, such as 'strategies of invisibilisation', for instance, by paying attention to how NGOs redefine or reframe certain issues or terms in a way that downplays their significance or diverts away from critical aspects, as well as how they purposefully feed on and reconstruct the state's ambitions to continue developing their goals. Related to this, it is important to consider how NGOs invisibilise certain activities. As I have personally witnessed, they discreetly organise screenings of censored documentaries or collaborate with other NGOs working in the same field, thus maintaining a level of secrecy in their resistance efforts.

Conclusion

Focusing on the local level, I argue that China's eco-authoritarian model of governance unfolds through everyday micropolitics. Contrary to the perception that environmental authoritarianism relies solely on coercive measures, I posit that it involves a combination of top-down enforcement and bottom-up participatory mechanisms driven by non-state actors.

This chapter presents three interconnected conclusions. Firstly, I contend that environmental governance in Chinese cities has expanded to emphasise the environmental responsibility of the individual as an important element in building an ecological civilisation. The institutional narrative highlights individual behaviours as key to addressing environmental issues and seeks to align them with the consensus model promoted by the party and state. In this context, I employ the concept of environmental authoritarianism to examine the fusion of coercive and participatory mechanisms in achieving authoritarian objectives. Secondly, I demonstrate how NGOs, through their localised actions and 'the dissemination of their 'expertise', play a significant role in governance and the shaping of novel forms of citizenship. Various localised governance and educational tools encourage individuals to behave as 'green' citizens, aligning with top-down, 'rational', and consensual perspectives of environmentalism. Thirdly, I argue that these processes exhibit strong parallels with the notion of post-political urban management, as they standardise individualisation and state-led consensus narratives, thereby depoliticising contemporary understandings of environmental issues and their treatment. This chapter thus illustrates how civic engagement becomes a tool, rather than a threat, for authoritarianism to empower itself.

Overall, the government's approach involves incorporating all NGOs it deems useful and non-threatening into an increasingly institutionalised system of social governance. Simultaneously, it opposes and suppresses NGOs that are seen as challenging the party's authority. By focusing on the actions of these non-state actors at the local level, we gain insights into the diverse relationships through which environmental authoritarianism is mobilised and enacted. This analysis reveals that NGOs are subject to the post-political reality of Shanghai, whereby their actions are constrained to choreographed efforts aimed at promoting and cultivating a green community consciousness among the Chinese people. Such arrangements are particularly evident in specific subdistrict-level spaces (Chung 2018), such as neighbourhood communities, where NGOs serve as tools in the state's community-building strategy (*shequ jianshe*) (Bray 2006). However, as the last section asserts, more empirical studies should assess the emergence of 'tactics' of resistance at the local level. Indeed, in increasingly global and complex cities where various interests collide, a multitude of competing strategies representing different interests can reshape each other, opening spaces for the 'weak' to develop new 'tactics' and increase their agency.

Bibliography

Ahlers, Anna L., and Yongdong Shen. 2018. 'Breathe Easy? Local Nuances of Authoritarian Environmentalism in China's Battle against Air Pollution', *China Quarterly*, 234, 299–319. https://doi.org/10.1017/S0305741017001370

Andres, Lauren, Phil Jones, Stuart Paul Denoon-Stevens, and Lorena Melgaço. 2020. 'Negotiating polyvocal strategies: Re-reading de Certeau through the lens of urban planning in South Africa', *Urban Studies*, 57(12), 2440–2455. https://doi.org/10.1177/0042098019875423

Ansell, Chris, and Alison Gash. 2008. 'Collaborative Governance in Theory and Practice', *Journal of Public Administration Research and Theory*, 18(4), 543–71. https://doi.org/10.1093/jopart/mum032

Arantes, Virginie. 2020. *From the Avoidable to the Desirable: The Chinese Communist Party 'Green' Authoritarian Strategy. Shanghai as Case Study*. Brussels: Université Libre de Bruxelles.

Arantes, Virginie. 2022. *China's Green Consensus: Participation, Co-Optation, and Legitimation*. Abingdon: Routledge.

Arantes, Virginie. 2023. 'What Type of Trash Are You? Steering "Green" Citizenship and Self-Responsibility in Urban China' in Viktor Pál and Iris Borowy (eds.), *Waste and Discards in the Asia Pacific Region: Social and Cultural Perspectives*. Abingdon: Routledge. https://doi.org/10.4324/9781003332916

Barker, Derek W.M. 2010. 'The Colonization of Civil Society', *Kettering Review*, 28(1), 8–18.

Beaumont, Matthew. 2020. *The Walker: On Finding and Losing Yourself in the Modern City*. Brooklyn: Verso Books.

Beeson, Mark. 2010a. 'The Coming of Environmental Authoritarianism', *Environmental Politics*, 19(2), 276–94.

Beeson, Mark. 2010b. 'The Politics of East Asia's Environmental Crisis: The Coming of Environmental Authoritarianism?', In Marquina, A. (eds) *Global Warming and Climate Change. Energy, Climate and the Environment Series*. Palgrave Macmillan, London, p. 465–80. https://doi.org/10.1057/9780230281257_27

Beeson, Mark. 2016. 'Environmental Authoritarianism and China', In Teena Gabrielson et al. (eds), *The Oxford Handbook of Environmental Political* Theory, online edn. https://doi.org/10.1093/oxfordhb/9780199685271.013.14

Bray, David. 2006. 'Building "Community": New Strategies of Governance in Urban China', *Economy and Society*, 35(4), 530–49.

Carrillo, Beatriz, Johanna Hood, and Paul I. Kadetz. 2017. *Handbook of Welfare in China*. Cheltenham: Edward Elgar. https://doi.org/10.4337/9781783472741

Chen, Geoffrey C., and Charles Lees. 2018. 'The New, Green, Urbanization in China: Between Authoritarian Environmentalism and Decentralization', *Chinese Political Science Review*, 3(2), 212–31.

Chung, Yousun. 2018. 'Continuity and Change in Chinese Grassroots Governance: Shanghai's Local Administrative System', *Issues and Studies*, 54(4). https://doi.org/10.1142/S1013251118400106

Corsetti, Gabriel. 2019. 'How Many NGOs Are There Really in China?' *China Development Brief.* https://chinadevelopmentbrief.org/reports/how-many-ngos-are-there-really-in-china/

De Certeau, Michel. 2011 [1980]. *The Practice of Everyday Life* (trans. Steven Rendall). Oakland: University of California Press.

De Jong, Martin, Chang Yu, Simon Joss, Ronald Wennersten, Li Yu, Xiaoling Zhang, and Xin Ma. 2016. 'Eco City Development in China: Addressing the Policy Implementation Challenge', *Journal of Cleaner Production*, 134, 31–41.

Demirpolat, Aznavur. 2021. 'Understanding De Certeau's Concepts of Strategy and Tactics in Relation to the Educational Policy Analysis', *Educational Policy Analysis and Strategic Research*, 16(3), 350–362.

Distelhorst, Greg and Diana Fu. 2019. 'Performing Authoritarian Citizenship: Public Transcripts in China', *Perspectives on Politics*, 17(1), 106–21.

Eaton, Sarah, and Genia Kostka. 2014. 'Authoritarian Environmentalism Undermined? Local Leaders' Time Horizons and Environmental Policy Implementation in China', *China Quarterly*, 218(1), 359–80.

Fu, Diana and Greg Distelhorst. 2018. 'Grassroots Participation and Repression under Hu Jintao and Xi Jinping', *The China Journal*, 79(1), 100–122.

Fulda, Andreas. 2017. 'The Contested Role of Foreign and Domestic Foundations in the PRC: Policies, Positions, Paradigms, Power', *Journal of the British Association for Chinese Studies*, 7.

Gao, Jian and Weiyue Xu. 2018. 'Study on the Way to Cultivate the Eco-Citizen, Facing Difficulties and How to Break Through' in *3rd International Conference on Contemporary Education, Social Sciences and Humanities* (*ICCESSH 2018*) (1094–1098). Dordrecht: Atlantis Press.

Gilley, Bruce. 2012. 'Authoritarian Environmentalism and China's Response to Climate Change', *Environmental Politics*, 21(2), 287–307. https://doi.org/10.1080/09644016.2012.651904

Hammond, Philip. 2017. *Climate Change and Post-Political Communication: Media, Emotion and Environmental Advocacy.* Abingdon: Routledge.

Han, Heejin. 2018. 'Legal Governance of NGOs in China under Xi Jinping: Reinforcing Divide and Rule', *Asian Journal of Political Science*, 26(3), 390–409. https://doi.org/10.1080/02185377.2018.1506994

Hansen, Mette Halskov, Hongtao Li, and Rune Svarverud. 2018. 'Ecological Civilization: Interpreting the Chinese Past, Projecting the Global Future', *Global Environmental Change*, 53, 195–203. https://doi.org/10.1016/j.gloenvcha.2018.09.014

Howell, Jude. 2004. *New Directions in Civil Society: Organizing around Marginalized Interests. Governance in China.* https://www.researchgate.net/publication/30528345_New_directions_in_civil_society_organising_around_marginalised_interests

Howell, Jude, Regina Enjuto Martinez, and Yuanyuan Qu. 2021. 'Technologies of Authoritarian Statecraft in Welfare Provision: Contracting Services to Social Organisations', *Development and Change*, 52(3). https://www.researchgate.net/publication/353744773_Technologies_of_Authoritarian_Statecraft_in_Welfare_Provision_Contracting_Services_to_Social_Organizations

Hsu, Carolyn L. 2017. *Social Entrepreneurship and Citizenship in China: The Rise of NGOs in the PRC.* https://doi.org/10.4324/9781315543598

Hsu, Carolyn, Jessica Teets, Reza Hasmath, Jennifer Y.J. Hsu, and Timothy Hildebrandt. 2020. 'The Construction and Performance of Citizenship in Contemporary China' in *American Sociological Association Annual Meeting* (*San Francisco, USA*).

Hsu, Jennifer Y.J., and Reza Hasmath. 2013. 'The Rise and Impact of the Local State on the NGO Sector' in Jennifer Y.J. Hsu and Reza Hasmath (eds.), *The Chinese Corporatist State: Adaptation, Survival and Resistance* (120–135). Abingdon: Routledge. https://doi.org/10.4324/9780203080139

Hsu, Jennifer Y.J., and Reza Hasmath. 2014. 'The Local Corporatist State and NGO Relations in China', *Journal of Contemporary China*, 23(87), 516–34. https://doi.org/10.1080/10670564.2013.843929

Jia, Xijiin, and Ming Su. 2009. 'Final Report on Government Procurement of Public Services People's Republic of China'. Asian Development Bank.

Jing, Jun. 2000. 'Environmental Protests in Rural China', in Elizabeth J. Perry, Mark Selden (eds.), *Chinese Society: Change, Conflict and Resistance* (143–60). Routledge.

Jing, Yijia. 2015. *The Road to Collaborative Governance in China.* https://doi.org/10.1057/9781137542182.

Jing, Yijia, and Ting Gong. 2012. 'Managed Social Innovation: The Case of Government-Sponsored Venture Philanthropy in Shanghai', *Australian Journal of Public Administration*, 71(2): 233–45. https://doi.org/10.1111/j.1467-8500.2012.00767.x

Jing, Yijia, and Yefei Hu. 2017. 'From Service Contracting To Collaborative Governance: Evolution of Government-Nonprofit Relations', *Public Administration and Development*, 37(3), 191–202. https://doi.org/10.1002/pad.1797

Jobin, Paul, Ming-Sho Ho, and Michael Hsin-huang Hsiao. 2021. *Environmental Movements of the Anthropocene in East and Southeast Asia.* Singapore: ISEAS Publishing.

Johnson, Thomas. 2013. 'The Health Factor in Anti-Waste Incinerator Campaigns in Beijing and Guangzhou', *China Q*, 356.

Johnson, Thomas, Anna Lora-Wainwright, and Jixia Lu. 2018. 'The Quest for Environmental Justice in China: Citizen Participation and the Rural–Urban Network against Panguanying's Waste Incinerator', *Sustainability Science*, 13(3), 733–46.

Kenis, Anneleen, and Matthias Lievens. 2014. 'Searching for "the Political" in Environmental Politics', *Environmental Politics*, 23(4): 531–48. https://doi.org/10.1080/09644016.2013.870067

Klein, Naomi. 2007. *The Shock Doctrine: The Rise of Disaster Capitalism*. Macmillan.

Latour, Bruno. 2005. *Reassembling the Social: An Introduction to Actor-Network-Theory*. Oxford: Oxford University Press.

Leung, Joe C.B., and Yuebin Xu. 2015. *China's Social Welfare: The Third Turning Point*. Hoboken: John Wiley & Sons.

Lo, Kevin. 2015. 'How Authoritarian Is the Environmental Governance of China?' *Environmental Science and Policy*, 54, 152–59. https://doi.org/10.1016/j.envsci.2015.06.001

Martinez, Regina, Yuanyuan Qu, and Jude Howell. 2021. 'Government Contracting Services to Social Organisations in China: A Review of Research for Future Enquiry', *Social Policy and Society*, November, 1–21. https://doi.org/10.1017/S1474746421000622

Mertha, Andrew. 2009. '"Fragmented Authoritarianism 2.0": Political Pluralization in the Chinese Policy Process', *China Quarterly*, 200, 995–1012. https://doi.org/10.1017/S0305741009990592

Middeldorp, Nick, and Philippe le Billon. 2019. 'Deadly Environmental Governance: Authoritarianism, Eco-Populism, and the Repression of Environmental and Land Defenders', *Annals of the American Association of Geographers*, 109(2), 324–37. https://doi.org/10.1080/24694452.2018.1530586

Moore, Scott M. 2014. 'Modernisation, Authoritarianism, and the Environment: The Politics of China's South-North Water Transfer Project', *Environmental Politics*, 23(6), 947–64.

Ong, Lynette H. 2022. *Outsourcing Repression: Everyday State Power in Contemporary China*. Oxford: Oxford University Press.

Rohde, Robert A., and Richard A. Muller. 2015. 'Air Pollution in China: Mapping of Concentrations and Sources', *PloS One*, 10(8): e0135749.

Rowe, Peter G, Ann Forsyth, and Ye Kan Har. 2016. *China's Urban Communities: Concepts, Contexts, and Well-Being*. Birkhäuser. https://issuu.com/birkhauser.ch/docs/china_s_urban_communities

Shapiro, Judith. 2013. 'The Evolving Tactics of China's Green Movement', *Current History*, 112(755), 224.

Shen, Wei and Dong Jiang. 2021. 'Making Authoritarian Environmentalism Accountable? Understanding China's New Reforms on Environmental Governance', *The Journal of Environment & Development*, 30(1), 41–67.

Shieh, Shawn. 2018. 'The Chinese State and Overseas NGOs: From Regulatory Ambiguity to the Overseas NGO Law' in *Nonprofit Policy Forum*, Vol. 9. De Gruyter.

Shue, Vivienne, and Patricia M. Thornton. 2017. *To Govern China: Evolving Practices of Power.* Cambridge: Cambridge University Press.

Steinhardt, H. Christoph, and Fengshi Wu. 2016. 'In the Name of the Public: Environmental Protest and the Changing Landscape of Popular Contention in China', *China Journal*, 75(1), 61–82. https://doi.org/10.1086/684010

Straume, Ingerid S. 2005. '11. Depoliticizing Environmental Politics: Sustainable Development in Norway' in Robert Paehlke and Douglas Torgerson (eds.), *Managing Leviathan* (191–208). University of Toronto Press. https://doi.org/10.3138/9781442602281-015

Swyngedouw, Erik. 2005. 'Governance Innovation and the Citizen: The Janus Face of Governance-beyond-the-State', *Urban Studies*, 42(11), 1991–2006. https://doi.org/10.1080/00420980500279869

Swyngedouw, Erik. 2010. 'Apocalypse Forever? Post-Political Populism and the Spectre of Climate Change', *Theory, Culture and Society*, 27(2), 213–32. https://doi.org/10.1177/0263276409358728.

Swyngedouw, Erik. 2011. 'Depoliticized Environments: The End of Nature, Climate Change and the Post-Political Condition', *Royal Institute of Philosophy Supplements*, 69, 253–74.

Swyngedouw, Erik. 2019. *Promises of the Political: Insurgent Cities in a Post-Political Environment.* Cambridge MA: MIT Press.

Tang, Ning and Sun, Fei. 2017. 'Shequ Construction and Service Development in Urban China: An Examination of the Shenzhen Model', *Community Development Journal*, 52(1), 10–20. https://doi.org/10.1093/cdj/bsw055

Teets, Jessica, and Carolyn Hsu. 2016. 'Is China's New Overseas NGO Management Law Sounding the Death Knell for Civil Society? Maybe Not', *The Asia-Pacific Journal*, 14(4).

Teng, Fei, and Pu Wang. 2021. 'The Evolution of Climate Governance in China: Drivers, Features, and Effectiveness', *Environmental Politics*, 30(sup1), 141–61. https://doi.org/10.1080/09644016.2021.1985221

Thornton, Patricia. 2013a. '"Civil Society" or "People's Society": Where's the Party?' *China Development Brief*, 27.

Thornton, Patricia. 2013b. 'The Advance of the Party: Transformation or Takeover of Urban Grassroots Society?', *The China Quarterly*, 213 (March). https://doi.org/10.1017/S0305741013000039

Wan, Xiaoyuan. 2015. 'Governmentalities in Everyday Practices: The Dynamic of Urban Neighbourhood Governance in China', *Urban Studies*, 53(11), 2330–2346.

Westman, Linda, and Ping Huang. 2022. 'Ecological Civilisation: A Historical Perspective on Environmental Policy Narratives in China', *International Quarterly for Asian Studies*, 53(2), 181–206.

Wike, Richard, and Bridget Parker. 2015. *Corruption, Pollution, Inequality Are Top Concerns in China: Many Worry about Threats to Traditions and Culture*. Pew Research Center.

Xiao, Shijiang, Huijuan Dong, Yong Geng, Francisco Medel-Jimenez, Hengyu Pan, and Fei Wu. 2020. 'An Overview of the Municipal Solid Waste Management Modes and Innovations in Shanghai, China', *Environmental Science and Pollution Research*, 27(24), 29943–29953.

Xu, Jing, and John Byrne. 2021. 'Explaining the Evolution of China's Government–Environmental NGO Relations since the 1990s: A Conceptual Framework and Case Study', *Asian Studies Review*, 45(4), 615–34. https://doi.org/10.1080/10357823.2020.1828824

Yu, Jianxing, and Sujian Guo. 2019. *The Palgrave Handbook of Local Governance in Contemporary China*. Palgrave Macmillan. https://doi.org/10.1007/978-981-13-2799-5

Zhang, Qi, Esther Hiu Kwan Yung, and Edwin Hon Wan Chan. 2018. 'Towards Sustainable Neighborhoods: Challenges and Opportunities for Neighborhood Planning in Transitional Urban China', *Sustainability* (*Switzerland*), 10(2). https://doi.org/10.3390/su10020406

Zhou, Ming-Hui, Shui-Long Shen, Ye-Shuang Xu, and An-Nan Zhou. 2019. 'New Policy and Implementation of Municipal Solid Waste Classification in Shanghai, China', *International Journal of Environmental Research and Public Health*, 16(17), 3099.

About the author

Virginie Arantes, a political scientist with a Ph.D. from the Université libre de Bruxelles (ULB), currently serves as a postdoctoral researcher supported by the National Fund for Scientific Research (F.R.S.-FNRS). Her previous research centered on China's environmental governance, resulting in the publication of her book, "China's Green Consensus" (2022), which offers insights into authoritarian environmentalism and civil society dynamics. With a holistic approach that integrates insights from political science, environmental studies, and area studies, Virginie explores the intricate interactions between state actors, civil society, and environmental movements. Through her analysis, she uncovers the complexities inherent in shaping policies and practices related to environmental conservation and sustainability within the broader context of geopolitics, nationalism, and cultural dynamics in Asia and beyond.
virginie.arantes@ulb.be

11. Reclaiming the Streets from the Apps?

Rethinking Future Practices of Urban Citizenship in the Digital Age: Perspectives from Vietnam

Marie Gibert-Flutre, Guillaume Trần Huu, and Quê Trần Dinh

Abstract: We focus here on the production of 'platform-mediated public spaces' in contemporary Vietnam with the growing uses of digital applications. We address how platformisation challenges the practices of citizenship. We especially question the possibility of setting up collective organisations in the 'platform-mediated city' and consider access to public spaces. We develop our argument by investigating the reorganisation of the motorbike taxi sector with the arrival of Grab. We offer a grounded perspective to show how precarious drivers use the app to organise themselves in unprecedented ways and recast their performance of citizenship in the face of two forms of power: the authoritarian Vietnamese state and the private (international) platform. Our research contributes to theoretical debates about citizenship and political subjectivities in the digital age.

Keywords: Platform economy, urban citizenship, public space, informal sector, Vietnam

Introduction

In December 2020, the Vietnamese press largely echoed a memorable event in one of the last claimed 'socialist countries' in the world, where any form of social contest is highly controlled and severely condemned. Hundreds of moto-taxi drivers of Grab, the ride-hailing Singaporean company, went on strike and demonstrated in the streets of Hanoi and Ho Chi Minh City (HCMC) (Danh Trọng 2020). This social movement was initiated to protest the unilateral increase in Grab's percentage of ride remuneration, justified by increased governmental taxes. The procession of motorbike drivers was

Gregory Bracken, Paul Rabé, Nurul Azreen Azlan (eds), *Future Practices of Citizenship in Asia and the West: Care of the Self (Volume III)*. Taylor & Francis Group, 2025
DOI: 10.5117/9789048562077_CH11

visually compelling thanks to their assorted green vests and helmets. This unprecedented— though quite ephemeral and mobile—occupation of urban public space was relayed and pursued online through the editing and sharing of thousands of Facebook posts and Zalo messages (a Vietnamese app where private or public groups can be created) from Grab drivers. They shared videos of the demonstrations and compelling messages encouraging the majority of Grab drivers to disconnect their application accounts in protest. Some opinions, however, broke the unanimity of the drivers and prompted lively wider discussions about the assigned place of platform drivers in the urban economy. Prior to December 2020 in Vietnam, strikes were restricted to factory workers. These wildcat demonstrations were significant since they were the first ones affecting the service sector (Buckley 2022a, 72).

The platform economy has become a global phenomenon in the past decade, but it remains deeply rooted in local circumstances and performs in variegated ways in different places. It contributes to the transformation of cities, in particular—materially, socially, economically, and in their ideals—to reach the point that we can identify them as 'co-generative dynamics of platforms and cities' (Rodgers and Moore 2018). Sarah Barns coined the terms 'platform-mediated city' and 'platform urbanism' (2014). She underlines the essence of a technologised urbanity and a relational process that implies 'negotiating new tactics, new players, new governance models and new data-driven business strategies, and new interfaces for everyday interaction' (Barns 2020, 29).

In this chapter, we focus more specifically on the production of 'platform-mediated public spaces' in the specific context of contemporary Vietnam. Beyond the now well-studied economic and labour aspects of this platform urbanism (Abdelnour and Méda 2019; Chan et al. 2021), we address how platformisation challenges the practices of citizenship and citizens' territorial engagement. If access to land remains a crucial issue for most citizens, online access to digital networks has also become decisive in the capacity of dwellers to forge and affirm their 'right to the city' (Lefebvre 1968; Shaw and Graham 2017; Morange and Spire 2020). By turning the digital city (often wrongly regarded as a 'smart city') upside down, in a city-dweller-oriented approach, our chapter focuses on possible forms of 'digital citizenship' in Asia, with much attention to the interrelations between the online and offline worlds. Theoretically, we draw on Henri Lefebvre's conception of space as an active political production (1974). We do not envision urban or digital space as passive backdrops but as active political constructions. In doing so, we join Benvegnù et al., who invite us to address platform urbanism as a 'battlefield' (2021, 694). We argue that digital applications contribute to a recomposition of urban inequalities, with (sometimes unexpected) winners and losers. We especially question the possibility of setting up collective organisations in the 'platform-mediated city' and also consider access to public spaces.

In our work, we understand 'urban citizenship' as the capacity of urban citizens to alter the built, social, and economic environment to meet their needs in a highly performative way (Isin 2017, 501), highlighting the dialectical relation between individual and collective engagements, politics, and urban space. We are particularly attentive to the process of engagement in public spaces—understood both as the urban physical space of citizenship performance and as a more figurative understanding of the term, as a place for expressions of the collective realm. As stated by Doreen Lee, in the current context of transformation and the digitalisation of urban production, 'we must account for how urban development recasts urban citizenship and belonging along biopolitical and temporal lines' (2018, 5). Moreover, contextualising citizenship in the age of platform-mediated public spaces demands no less than 'understanding the relation between the futurity of the ideal citizen and the life trajectories eliminated by such visions' (Lee 2018, 5). Despite their precarious economic and political conditions, we argue that the working life trajectories of Grab motorbike taxi drivers recast the performance of citizenship in urban Vietnam.

We develop our argument by investigating the complete reorganisation of the motorbike taxi sector in Vietnam with the stunning arrival of the GrabBike app on the local market in November 2014. Focusing on small auto-entrepreneurs joining the platform to perform their taxi or delivery services, we propose a grounded perspective from Vietnam, where vulnerable drivers use the platform to organise themselves in unprecedented ways. In doing so, we answer this simple question: where can urban citizenship exist in the platform's economic and managerial model? We hypothesise that various modes of collective organisation and resistance on the part of the Grab drivers (both individually and as part of a group) emerge in the face of two forms of power: the authoritarian Vietnamese state and the private (international) platform. Though perhaps first seen by the drivers as a springboard to employment and a source of income, the platform also turns out to be—under specific circumstances, as our chapter will explain—a springboard to the construction and performance of unprecedented political subjectivities in the urban Vietnamese context. As such, our research seeks to contribute to larger theoretical debates about citizenship and political subjectivities in the digital age in a global context.

Our methodology relies on a three-pronged approach: 1) in-depth interviews with Grab drivers (forty-five interviews—ten in 2019 and thirty-five in 2022) and Grab team leaders (three interviewees with repeated meetings and exchanges in 2022) in Ho Chi Minh City; 2) participatory observations of Grab drivers' communities; and 3) an exploratory 'digital ethnography' of Facebook pages of various Grab driver groups since 2018. The long span of our research, which initially started in 2018, allowed us to grasp some major improvements in the sophistication of the app, its transformations, and its algorithm between 2018 and 2022, as well as the responsive evolution of the drivers' tactics and collective strategies. Temporalities are indeed a key element at stake in understanding urban citizenship in digital times.

In the following section, we posit that the emergence of the platform economy generated what we call a 'three-body problem' in the Vietnamese urban power relationship game: by entering the game, international private apps disrupted the historical bilateral relationship between the Vietnamese state and its informal small entrepreneurs. It paradoxically created unforeseen interstices of negotiation. Section 2 focuses on the variegated modes of the collective organisation of Grab drivers in HCMC that led to the creation of group subjectivity and to possible political subjectivities. Finally, section 3 opens with the theoretical implications of this research and draws attention to the temporalities at stake when it comes to understanding citizenship in the platform age.

The platform economy in Vietnam or the birth of a 'three-body problem'

Informal conflictual sharing of public space as metropolitan background

With more than ten million inhabitants, HCMC is an emerging and rapidly changing metropolis of Southeast Asia marked by a contemporary increase in land pressure and prices. Since the economic reforms of the Renewal (*Đổi Mới*) initiated in 1986, Vietnam has gradually become a market economy and embarked on a process of globalisation. This generates new social inequalities in access to employment and secure spaces for economic activity. Annette Kim estimates that over thirty percent of HCMC's inhabitants depend directly, though most often informally, on public spaces for their economic activities and subsistence (2015, 17). Vietnamese cities are well known for their heavily occupied sidewalks where every footpath intersection is a possible site for street trade. In this urban economic landscape, informal moto-taxi drivers (*xe ôm*) are among the most familiar and visible figures. Spending most of their time waiting for clients, they occupy sidewalks and street intersections, sitting or sleeping on their motorbikes. The success of their business mostly depends on their capacity to secure and occupy the best-located public spaces.

Despite the September 2019 publication of an updated framework by the Vietnam General Statistics Office (Công văn số 1127/TCTK-TKQG), the so-called 'informal sector' (*khu vực phi chính thức*) in Vietnam remains vast and ill-defined. Formal/informal categories are indeed porous and interdependent. Interestingly, street workers do not recognise themselves as 'informal workers' but rather designate themselves as 'freelance workers' or 'independent workers' (*lao động tự do*), meaning workers without any contract. More importantly, they represent a highly fragmented social group, with strong internal hierarchies, where strategies of survival and development at stake are mostly individual or based on interpersonal relations in a highly competitive context (Agergaard and Thao 2011, 411; Kim 2015, 105; Turner et al. 2021, 4; Gibert-Flutre 2022, 282; Zuberec and Turner 2022, 15). Therefore, although they represent a significant portion of urban workers, there is no evidence that they have collective organisation, let alone opportunity for trade union development.

Moreover, the social pact of relative *laissez-faire* in the informal economic sector that has prevailed since the opening of the market economy in the late 1980s is increasingly being challenged by urban authorities. The combination of circulatory and street-trading functions in public spaces has become problematic, giving rise to daily frictions and confrontations that authorities aim to stop (Gibert-Flutre 2020, 48). Official programs to eliminate informal uses of public space have multiplied in the past years. However, beyond laws and newly advertised rules, the Vietnamese state is often more accommodating and flexible than might be expected, especially at the local level, through individual negotiation channels (Gibert and Segard 2015, 15; Vasavakul 2019, 7). As Nguyen Tu Phuong puts it, 'despite a rather comprehensive legal reform developed since the 1990s, interactions between state and society are still heavily shaped by customary norms, precepts, and informal practices: from patron-client networks between business and the state to local government's policy implementation and the courts' handling of disputes' (2019, 187). Individual negotiation with local representatives of the state encourages neither collective engagements in public spaces nor claims to collective rights and shared access to public space on the part of social movements.

Fast digitalisation of the informal sector

The penetration rate of smartphones in the Vietnamese adult population in 2020 was 93 percent, one of the highest rates in Southeast Asia (Nguyen Thi 2020, 52). Smartphones are indeed the most potent instruments of the current super-fast digitalisation of the economy in Vietnam. The extensive use of a growing array of digital applications widely impacts urban practices, such as everyday shopping, access to credit, and urban transportation, transforming the daily interactions between urban dwellers and their cities. Grab, the app originating in Singapore, is Vietnam's most famous embodiment of urban platformisation. In HCMC, where public transport provides less than five percent of daily commutes, Grab's entry into the Vietnamese market in November 2014 with its moto-taxi app, GrabBike, was not surprising. The platform developed so quickly that it now advertises itself as the 'Everyday Everything App' and operates in multiple economic sectors.

Grab remains very secretive about its number of drivers, but we estimate that there were around 200,000 in Vietnam in 2019 (before the Covid-19 pandemic). In the app these drivers are called 'driver partners' (*đối tác*), underlining that they are by no means employees of the Grab society, but only freelance drivers—as in the global platform economy model. They join the platform after registering their IDs and driving licences at the platform's local office and signing a formal commitment document. By signing, they commit not to work for other platforms. Nevertheless, they must buy and maintain their own professional tools, starting with their motorbikes, gas, and outfits. As mere 'partners', they have no insurance, pension, or social security benefits.

The striking arrival of GrabBike in the local game of urban transportation in Vietnam completely disrupted the organisation of informal motorbike drivers (*xe ôm*) (Turner and Hanh 2019, 12; Turner 2020, 5). In the previous economic model, securing a living as a taxi driver depended significantly on the capacity to ensure access to strategic public spaces. This benefitted long-time and locally well-known drivers, who managed to secure an informal piece of public space thanks to local relationships and arrangements. The algorithm at the heart of the GrabBike application completely disrupted this organisation. The platform is now exclusively responsible for allocating rides to drivers and fixing its prices without any possibility of negotiation for the client. Its rates are dramatically lower than those proposed by the historical *xe ôm* drivers, which contributed to the undeniable success of the app with customers. To make these low per-ride payments acceptable, the application has set up a system of rewards and bonuses for drivers, offering them more substantial bonuses when they manage to complete more than fifteen or twenty rides per day. Thus, Grab drivers are pushed to work longer hours—mostly ten to twelve hours a day—and are strongly discouraged from refusing rides. Refusing rides results in a downgrade in the Grab algorithmic system of ride distributions.

This algorithmic management of the workforce led to increased competition and sometimes violent conflicts among moto-taxi drivers, depending on their status (Khanh et al. 2017). While *xe ôm* drivers are thought to be old-fashioned and 'uncivilised' (*không văn minh*), informal entrepreneurs, Grab drivers, who identified themselves during our interviews as 'technological drivers' (*lái xe công nghệ*), benefit from a modern and fairly positive image in Vietnamese society. Wearing the Grab jacket presents an image of modernity. Hence, it is not uncommon to see *xe ôm* drivers wearing the jacket even though they are not working for the app. Our fieldwork study also revealed that Grab drivers are a more diverse group than *xe ôm* drivers. Because the application prohibits drivers over the age of fifty-five from applying, Grab drivers tend to be younger and they come from more diverse backgrounds. This suggests a significant shift from the homogenous group of *xe ôm* drivers consisting of poor older men riding old-fashioned motorbikes and being hard to negotiate with. Despite a loss of autonomy in their working organisation, we hypothesise that the positive representation of technological tools in a quickly digitalising economy helped forge a sense of collective belonging among Grab drivers. This belonging is reinforced—and displayed in the city streets—by their wearing of the same uniform. This proved to be a key element in the construction of unprecedented political subjectivities and collective movements in the urban Vietnamese context.

Managing small entrepreneurship in the platform economy time: Towards a 'three- body problem'

Not only did the Grab app completely disrupt the previous labour organisation of informal motorbike drivers in Vietnam, but it also challenged the governance of the informal sector by the state. By entering the game, Grab —an international private company— disrupted the historical bilateral relationship between the Vietnamese state and small, informal entrepreneurs. It also paradoxically created unforeseen interstices of negotiation for them. We refer to this unprecedented triangle of actors—namely the state, the private companies, and the small freelance entrepreneurs—as the emergence of a 'three-body problem' in the Vietnamese urban power relationship game. This expression initially comes from physics and classical mechanics. It refers to the problem of taking the initial positions and velocities of three-point masses and solving for their subsequent motion, according to Newton's laws of motion and universal gravitation. Unlike two-body problems, no general closed-form solution exists: the resulting dynamical system is chaotic. While the evolving relationships between the state and informal small entrepreneurs in Vietnam, ranging from a negotiated tolerance to a strict opposition (Endres 2014, 613; Turner 2018, 82), are well studied and known, the arrival of the private platform opened up an era of unforeseen negotiations and arrangements among the three sets of actors. This new configuration encouraged some 'driver partners' to organise themselves (individually and, more interestingly, collectively) in unprecedented ways to claim their rights, both regarding specific labour issues and more broadly about their 'right to the city' (Lefebvre 1968).

In contrast with *xe ôm* drivers, towards which the authorities often opposed a need for 'clean public spaces', the Vietnamese state shows a benevolent attitude towards Grab drivers. The state indeed directly benefits from the unprecedented support of a private foreign corporation to address two major urban issues, namely informal labour and a public transport deficiency, even though most drivers continue to occupy sidewalks informally while waiting for clients, as did *xe ôm* drivers. By joining the app as partners, even though not official employees, Grab drivers appear to be formal elements of a highly regarded digital economy. The perception of these small entrepreneurs has shifted as they pay taxes through the intermediation of the private platform. The taxation system lies at the heart of primary litigations and negotiations among the three types of actors. It was precisely a unilateral increase of the app's percentage of ride remuneration (which now reaches a twenty-seven percent commission on each ride), justified by increased governmental taxes, that led to strikes and street demonstrations by Grab drivers at the end of 2020.

At the heart of this 'three-body problem' also lie the labour statutes in times of digital platforms. Although this question goes beyond the mere Vietnamese context, the latter is enlightening as the state sees the 'technological drivers' as formal workers. In contrast, most literature on the platformisation of the economy points to the rapid trend of informalising labour—with a deregulation of the employment relationship, a fragmentation of working-class politics, the exclusion of fundamental welfare rights, the emerging notion of 'partner' as a substitute for 'employee', and an algorithmic-controlled labour process (Chan et al. 2021, 4). Ugo Rossi and June Wang envision the new wave of technology-based urban entrepreneurialism as a peculiar process of 'becoming south of the urban world' (2020) to paraphrase Achille Mbembe's metaphor of 'becoming black of the world' (Mbembe 2017). Specifically, they point to its 'ability to propel the rise of an informal, improvised entrepreneurship' (2020, 484). In his longitudinal study of the Bangkok motorbike taxi business, Claudio Sopranzetti reconstructs the shifting uses of local concepts of 'informality' in Thailand over the past thirty-five years (2021). He interestingly points out that since the launching of the platform of moto-taxi services in 2016,

> conflicts over whether the business should be understood as informal, who gets to control its operations, define its rules and costs, and obtain access to its profit, remain rampant, with frequent outbursts of violence, both between drivers and among drivers, businesspeople, users, and state forces [...] Older drivers defended their rights to expel GrabBike drivers from their area by calling them 'outside the system' and asking the government to enforce the ban on ride-hailing apps that was theoretically introduced in May of 2016 but was never really implemented by officials or taken seriously by passengers (2021, 2).

Our study in Vietnam shows a different interpretation of this type of labour, which is locally envisioned as a formalisation of small entrepreneurship, thanks to the entrance of a private international company into the governance game. Beyond the sole formal/informal issue and labour aspects of platform urbanism, we draw on the 'three-body problem' metaphor to explore how, with the opening of a new triangle of negotiations, platformisation challenges the performative practices of citizenship and citizens' territorial engagement in Vietnam today.

Beyond labour atomisation: Creating collective political subjectivities

Navigating between coffee shops and Facebook groups: Re-engaging with public space as a collective resource

Contrary to much of the research on application workers in the West that highlights an enhanced individualisation and atomisation of work (Webster 2016, 58; Abdelnour and Méda 2019, 40), Grab drivers in Vietnam developed a strong sense of belonging to the same community, creating a group awareness with their own ways of socialising. Despite a distribution of work assignments entirely managed online by the app, drivers connect with each other in urban public spaces, such as in well-equipped parks (for instance, those with shade and available public toilets), on strategic sidewalks (in central areas of the city, around shopping malls, or bus stations), and at coffee shops, which, in Vietnam, are usually wide open to the street and often overflow onto the sidewalk. Coffee shops are particularly important as they are strategic places to begin a day of work where drivers can share useful information, such as security issues, advice about work, and updated information about the functioning of the app, and where they experience the feeling of belonging to a collective of workers. The vast majority of the thirty-five Grab drivers we interviewed in April 2022 invariably began their day of work at local coffee shops where they met other drivers and formed informal help and support groups outside the scope of the app's control.

The Grab drivers first gathered spontaneously to face the violence from the *xe ôm* drivers who accused them of stealing their jobs. In their interviews, they discussed the inherent difficulties of the job, its hazards, and potential dangers, including frequent road accidents and altercations with dishonest customers, which are not addressed nor solved by the app. Despite the digital allocation of rides, city-based strategies, rooted in the sharing of public space, continue to be important for drivers. In addition, besides being a means of promotion for the company, the obligation to wear the Grab 'uniform' is also an easy means of recognition between drivers, facilitating informal meetings and exchanges in public spaces. Thus, wearing this distinctive garment has served as an opportunity for large-scale rallying, which was not possible in the previous locally-based and more individual organisation of *xe ôm* drivers. Our interviewees confirmed that it was very rare to find an isolated driver: almost all are in contact with other drivers in one way or another. This enhances their feeling of safety in an uncertain job because they never know nor get to choose the kind of customer they will have to deal with during the day. However, it also contributes to building a community of not-so-independent workers who engage in claiming new labour rights and, more broadly, a voice in the city.

Apart from casual meetings in the streets or in coffee shops, the Grab drivers share a considerable exchange on social media, such as Facebook or Zalo, which function as a continuation of the public urban spaces. Almost all drivers whom we interviewed regularly use these media to get information, even though they never post anything. In a quickly digitalising economy, Grab drivers' Facebook pages and Zalo public groups soon became central elements in the formation and visibility of drivers as part of a group, both internally and within Vietnamese society at large. In our research, having been granted access to two private Grab drivers' Facebook groups, we performed an exploratory 'digital ethnography'. The Community of Grab 2 Wheels HCMC Partners (*Cộng đồng Đối tác Grab 2 bánh HCM*), which was created in January 2017, had 106,400 members. The Grab Bike Community/

Screenshot of the post on Facebook	**Translation in English**
	Date: 20/01/2022 **Post from Facebook:** 'Be, Grab, Go all use the word 'partner' to circumvent the law. Their motorcycles, their lives, and their efforts that determine the game is the company, the company wants to calculate how the driver must support what is called a partner. Ridiculous.' **Comment 1:** 'Only idiots who defend them. You're right, they call for 'partners' to cooperate and share, but do they allow us to contribute our voice? I spent all my capital on driving, and only them decided how to distribute the amount of money.' **Comment 2:** 'We're just money-making tools for them guys? So, if you want to drive must accept, otherwise, you stop? For them, you are only number 0? You are nothing. Their policy is (no man is indispensable) without you, nothing will be lost? So now you should live on your own. Just drive and find a side job, okay? Do not put heavy the amount of money every day to drive is how much? When you are working as driver, who richer than who? Who suffers more than whom? So now if I can, I will drive for money every day, drive five or ten rides... if they gave me a ride, I will drive if they don't I don't need it. You can create and find social connections around for driving outside the app?? Prioritize your customers anyways...'. **Reply to comment 2:** 'The same for me.. the money from the application is not much but it's ok if the evening your pocket is full. As to the above, I speak only as I think. But it's not a complain... I just feel like I don't have a voice.' **Comment 3:** 'If you can still drive, just drive, my friend, no one is forcing you. They made an application, they have their own rules. If you don't feel like it, just quit. And if you see that you can still make money, ignore it.' **Reply to comment 3:** 'No one can touch them, but don't we even have the right to speak up?' **Reply by the account of comment 3:** 'Does speaking up make you better? Or does it make you more upset? I say that, understand it or not is up to you.' **Reply to comment 3:** 'We don't have the same opinion, so it's not good if we talk more. That's so.'

Figure 11.1. Screenshot of the post on Facebook

Grab 2 Wheel Driver Partners of Ho Chi Minh City (*Cộng Đồng Grab Bike/Đối Tác Tài Xế Grab 2 Bánh TP HCM*), created in July 2019, had 32,650 members. This access enabled us to scrutinise all topics of conversation and associated comments. We focused primarily on analysing three key periods: the Grab drivers' strike of December 2020, the COVID-19 lockdown during the summer and fall of 2021, and the first six months of 2022. Beyond the analysis of discourse and narratives formulated by the drivers themselves, this digital study also served as a basis for engaging with specific drivers during the interview phase.

As observed in the coffee shops, the online discussions of drivers involve sharing of updated practical advice (how to recognise and avoid dishonest customers, where to find good spots to wait for clients, which places provide free parking when picking up a Grab-food delivery order, etc.). However, they also deal with more general issues related to the condition of being a 'technological driver'. For instance, drivers share their often highly critical views on the notion of 'driver partners' (*đối tác*) and evaluate together, through their posts and by following comments, what they consider unfair working conditions, considering the company's economic and symbolic gains. They deliberate about their claims for a revised status, with more protections and social benefits, and strategise ways to have their voices heard. Their posts on social media are diverse and their debates are often animated. That the drivers have varied views is indicated in this extract about their designation and status (see Figure 11.1).

These extensive online debates (often with hundreds of posts on the same topic) contribute in an unprecedented way to shaping a strong group awareness and awaken many drivers to political issues beyond mere exchanges of practical advice. Moreover, the continuity of group gatherings in public spaces provides vulnerable economic actors with the possibility of renewed citizenship. Social media platforms are not passive backdrops; rather, they support active political constructions that allow for progressive engagement and deep interactions of citizens with urban physical space. Grab drivers find themselves on these networks more easily; they are a recognised group in the eyes of the urban population and the authorities but also have a sense of their own identity, which was previously not the case for atomised workers in the vast informal sector. The digital medium has, paradoxically, contributed to the emergence of a collective consciousness among workers.

The ambiguous status of Grab's team leaders in collective action

Spontaneous self-help groups of Grab drivers, both in urban public spaces and online, appeared when Grab started in HCMC, soon informally gathering hundreds of drivers under recognised 'leaders'. The designation of such leaders remains opaque but relies mostly on charisma and insider knowledge. Their availability and the efficiency of their collective engagement are also factors. Our research revealed that HCMC team leaders have strong ties to the underground and mafia world; the latter are respected by other drivers who see the ambiguous position of leaders—and name—them as 'big brothers' (*đại ca*). These spontaneous leaders initially intervened to confront the violence caused by *xe ôm* drivers and soon began collecting the complaints and grievances of Grab drivers on an everyday basis.

When the Grab company discovered the informal existence of these 'leaders' in 2016, they had no other choice but to acknowledge their social utility, as the company refused to take part in any security and social actions on behalf of its 'partners'. At that time, the company was facing fierce competition from other apps to retain its drivers and ensure the shortest wait time for its customers. Team leaders then obtained an official endorsement from the company, and several 'Grab teams' were formalised in the city. Before the COVID-19 crisis, there were 10 Grab teams in HCMC, according to Phạm My Sên, a team leader heading a group of more than 400 drivers in HCMC. We had the opportunity to interview him multiple times and, using a participant observation approach, we followed his collective tasks and activities. These teams of drivers are divided into subgroups, with a total of more than 1000 members. These subgroups serve as a relay between the app and the drivers, as well as a safe space for mutual support among drivers. Phạm My Sên explained that Grab had no choice but to accept these historical leaders because of their influence on drivers. However, the role and image of the team leaders remain ambiguous; certain drivers, who prefer to stay outside such collective organisations, regard them as a way for the company to monitor the drivers and prevent unpredictable and defiant actions. Nevertheless, by observing several of their gatherings, we concluded that they work as informal—but quite efficient—unions in a country where unionising remains highly controlled by the state and is non-existent in the service sector (Buckley 2022b).

The Grab teams directly challenge the labour atomisation often associated with platformed labour. Phạm My Sên's team is called *Liên đội Đoàn Kết* (United Team) or 'Biker United' and produced its own logo to be put on the drivers' motorbikes or clothes to help them identify each other. Grab teams go much further than only regulating relationships between drivers and the platform or answering practical needs. They organise multiple collective actions, thereby participating directly in the emerging capacity of the drivers to organise themselves outside the tight scope of the app's control. They played an especially crucial role during the pandemic crisis and strict lockdown in HCMC in the summer of 2021. Grab teams proved an efficient solidarity network, distributing and sharing food supplies and organising charity actions to help affected drivers' families at a time when state initiatives were scarce and insufficient. The pandemic period can be identified as a key moment in the reinforcement of the Grab drivers' identity and their enhanced pride in being part of it. A year later some drivers appeared to be nostalgic regarding this period of solidarity among drivers, when Grab drivers were viewed positively by the city for their role under lockdown.

During our fieldwork, we also had the opportunity to participate in a highly revealing collective event organised by the 'Biker United' team: a festive picnic organised for all drivers of the team and, more importantly, their families. One participant explained to us what it meant to him to be able to offer such a leisure outing to his wife when he had previously been ashamed to be a motorbike taxi driver. The gathering was scheduled on Sunday, June 19, 2022, at a recreational spot called 'Dragon Farm' rented for the day in the periurban area of HCMC. Team leader Phạm My Sên underlined how the booking was made exclusively thanks to the financial participation of each driver. The drivers made it clear that they did not want to rely on any sponsors.

The event gathered approximately 100 participants, consisting of the team drivers and their families (including 22 toddlers and children). Phạm My Sên and his co-leaders left nothing to chance and carefully organised the day's overall proceedings and each individual activity. Even the arrival was carefully planned, staged, and recorded by a special communications team: drivers from each city district, wearing their Grab shirts despite it being forbidden when off duty, were invited to gather at specific points on the road. A final meeting point was then designated for all groups to meet to travel the final section of the road together. This collective performance displayed the drivers' pride in gathering as a recognisable group. Everyone was given matching clothes to change into upon arrival. Drivers participated in games organised to strengthen group cohesion, and they shared a relaxing day far from their daily concerns. The afternoon started with a distribution of gifts for each member, mostly clothes and accessories like aprons, scarves, bracelets, and badges with the 'Biker United' logo, presented as amulets that embodied the drivers' solidarity.

Later, more official speeches were given. Team leaders referred to the pandemic period as a remarkable time of solidarity among Grab drivers, who demonstrated their capacity as an organisation to serve the urban population during difficult times. A tribute was also paid to four drivers of the team who had died during the pandemic. The speeches were followed by announcements about other communities of team drivers in the neighbouring provinces of the Mekong Delta and in the Central Highlands, around Buôn Ma Thuột. Phạm My Sên encouraged more direct connections with them to establish a strong national network of supportive drivers. He also reminded everyone of how, during the lockdown, a Grab driver from Buôn Ma Thuột had managed to send a truck carrying four tons of food and vegetables to Saigon to be distributed among Grab drivers' families who were facing difficulties. In memory of this surge of solidarity, Phạm My

Sên presented a plan for an upcoming collective motorbike trip to provide donations collected by Saigonese drivers for children of a poor ethnic minority in Đắk Lắk province. Team drivers were invited to participate in the operation in two ways: by collecting school supplies to be distributed to children or by riding as a group to the mountainous area around Buôn Ma Thuột to deliver the goods. This collective trip took place on 1 July 2022 and was heavily posted on the team's social media, such as the 'Biker United' Facebook page and Zalo groups. Videos of drivers wearing green shirts driving together and offering their collected donations were widely shared online and strengthened their collective pride. These videos have been highly effective in producing group cohesion through direct empowerment: they show vulnerable workers reinventing themselves as being capable of direct beneficial actions towards impoverished others.

In a country where the right of association is jeopardised by the official channels of the Vietnam Fatherland Front (*Mặt Trận Tổ Quốc Việt Nam*), Grab drivers create alternative spaces of discussion, mutual assistance, and the construction of social capital, outside the ancient framework of the socialist system (Gibert and Segard 2015, 20). Since political opposition parties are also entirely prohibited in Vietnam, these non-political groups serve as outlets for casual political discussion, with little risk of being accused of breaking the law. Drivers address political issues by targeting the Grab company organisation. In that sense, they take full advantage of the opportunity opened by the three-body problem identified above.

Striking, occupying public space, and reclaiming citizenship: Care of the self 2.0

Beyond collective and empowering actions, Grab drivers also challenge the Vietnamese state and/or the Grab company more directly in unforeseen organisational ways. The climax was reached in December 2020 with the national strikes and street demonstrations by Grab drivers in Hanoi and HCMC, widely relayed in the national and local press and online. These strikes came after a series of smaller ones regularly organised since 2017. The social movement was initiated in protest against the unilateral increase in the app percentage of ride remuneration (now reaching more than twenty-seven per cent), itself justified by the company by increased governmental taxes.

This unprecedented—though ephemeral and mobile—occupation of urban public space was organised and coordinated directly online, through the sharing of posts on Facebook and Zalo by the drivers themselves, without any outside help. Compelling messages and visual memes circulated widely to convince as many Grab drivers as possible to disconnect their accounts on the app. Many drivers took pictures of their disconnected application as a sign of online protest. Grab drivers finally obtained an official meeting between a small group of representatives and the head of Grab HCMC. None of those actions had an immediate positive outcome for the drivers, unlike the 2018 strikes, which temporarily blocked the company's increase in commission on each journey; however, the widescale wildcat strikes in 2020 displayed an advanced degree of self-organisation and directly contributed to reinforcing group subjectivity. By publicly striking, both on the streets and online, Grab drivers in Vietnam demonstrated their citizenship in unprecedented ways.

These strikes were also an important opportunity to engage in vibrant and wider discussions about the assigned place of platform workers in the urban economy and the different ways of fighting for a decent way of life and better labour conditions. Demonstrations and strikes provoked tensions and passionate debates between striking and non-striking drivers. Not all drivers agreed with this action. Phạm My Sên, the team leader of the 'Biker United' team group, refused to call for strikes at the risk of losing his capacity to negotiate daily with the head of Grab in HCMC. Phạm My Sên explained that he had taken on the 'mission' (*sứ mệnh*) of gaining a better recognition of technological drivers' status and a more transparent, fairer regulation of the tax collection by the company. He compared his fight to the Three Kingdoms' war: a contemporary war between Grab, the State, and the drivers. He even regularly uses the nickname Zhao Yun, from a character in the *Three Kingdoms* novel. As a team leader, Phạm My Sên is, however, very careful when criticising the company, and he always balances his criticisms strategically between Grab and the Vietnamese state. His most prominent action was his trip to Hanoi in late 2019 to submit a petition directly to the Ministry of Finance. Unfortunately, the COVID-19 crisis emerged a few weeks later and he never received a reply; however, he did not give up his fight and planned to reiterate his position later in 2022. Despite his lack of success, even being able to submit a petition to the Ministry is a form of formalisation and legitimation for Grab drivers, something *xe ôm* drivers could never have achieved. His strategy once again reflects how he can benefit from the three-body problem situation. As a Grab team leader, he prefers to confront the state rather than the app, and his status as a Grab driver paradoxically gives him the needed legitimacy to do so. His bet is that the state may decrease taxes on platform work, whereby the app would decrease the percentage collected from each driver's ride.

Temporalities at stake or citizenship as a performative work in progress?

Close attention to the variegated modes of organisation in the Grab drivers' collective in HCMC also invites us to rethink citizenship in the platform age through the lens of temporalities. For the actors in our three-body problem, the relationship to time is not neutral but reveals constantly renegotiated power relations. Here we can draw on the distinction between 'tactics' and 'strategy' proposed by Michel de Certeau (1988, 63). The notion of tactics embraces all small day-to-day actions and negotiations undertaken by Grab drivers to deal with the conditions imposed upon them. While merely reactive, tactics reveal a true capacity to adapt to an environment shaped by the strategies of the powerful. In contrast, 'strategy' presumes control and power.

For Grab, the real power of the strategic app is its exclusive control over the timing and pace of updates to the rules of the game. The app is indeed free at any time to update its terms and conditions to its clients and, more importantly, to its so-called 'driver partners', without notice or negotiation. The app uses such unpredictable changes to constantly adapt the profile of its drivers to its commercial needs. At first, Grab advertised that it offered its drivers flexibility of work and allowed drivers to connect or disconnect at any time. Driving for Grab was presented as a modern way to earn an income and attracted many students and part-time workers in its first years of operation. However, after having attracted a wide base of drivers, the app changed the rules of the game to favour regular and full-time connected drivers. The remuneration for each ride was very low, but a reward system promised substantial bonuses if a driver reached fifteen or twenty rides a day. In response to these new regulations, drivers organised their tactics both individually and collectively. On an individual level, for instance, they tended to decline long rides in favour of more frequent short rides in the city centre in the hopes of reaching the bonus threshold of fifteen or twenty rides. On a collective level, some drivers began to share an account to access bonuses more easily. This tactic was efficient for a while, but the app adapted its strategy again. It soon became absolutely forbidden—and duly monitored with facial recognition—to share an account. In addition, Grab drivers were forbidden to download the app of another ride-hailing company.

In the face of these new regulations, drivers began to organise themselves more actively, forming informal teams. Because these teams illustrated the drivers' strong loyalty to the specific app, Grab couldn't suppress them and decided to endorse them. As the algorithmic management of the app reinforced the control of labour over the years, the drivers struck back and fine-tuned their organisation. This constantly evolving working context led to an undeniable change in the drivers' profiles: after years of arm wrestling with the app and the state, current Grab drivers tend to become closer to *xe ôm* drivers socially. Most drivers who did not directly depend on this type of job to earn a living either quit or invested in other services of the app, such as food delivery, which requires a start-up fund to advance the price of customer orders to the restaurant. Drivers who stayed with Grab were the most economically vulnerable and continued their fight to reduce the taxes levied by the state and the app.

The citizenship of app drivers cannot be understood as an outcome of the organisation, but rather as a progressive, performative, and constantly reactivated means of organising. To assess only the rights that drivers achieved from the app or the state through their collective actions, such as strikes and petitions, is to envision their citizenship in a reductive way. Over time, each initiative achieved very practical results in the production of both drivers' citizenship and ordinary public spaces (physically and online). Thus, adding a temporal dimension to the understanding of citizenship opens up a promising research agenda, inviting comparisons of time-management action across metropolitan contexts.

Conclusion: At the crossroads of streets and the digital: Performative practices of citizenship

The new 'co-generative dynamics of platforms and cities' (Rodgers and Moore 2018) forces us to revisit the concept of citizenship and its associated practices as it has become impossible to untangle the process of platform urbanisation and urban politics. This renewed context invites us to broaden our perspective on conventional views of citizenship, by recognising its performative force, given that vulnerable workers are often presented as victims of the platformisation of labour. On the contrary, the progressive formalisation of self-managed drivers' teams and their participation in wildcat strikes demonstrated an advanced degree of self-organisation; each of these actions directly reinforced the group's subjectivity. By entering the Vietnamese economy, as well as the socio-political game, Grab—an international private company—disrupted the historical bilateral relationship between the state and informal small entrepreneurs. We have shown how, for the latter, it paradoxically created new interstices of negotiation. We have referred to this unprecedented triangle of actors as the emergence of a 'three-body problem' in the Vietnamese urban power relationship game. While small entrepreneurs use their new status as formal Grab partners to claim rights to the state in unforeseen open ways, such as street strikes and formal petition initiatives, the state now delegates to a private international company some of its core missions, such as transportation politics and the management and formal taxation of small, formerly informal, businesses. Regarding the app, its effective functioning and development rely on its capacity to attract and maintain an adequate number of loyal drivers in order to claim short waiting times for clients. This necessity implies concessions to drivers despite overarching management. These concessions are primarily visible in the formalisation of unprecedented grab teams in Ho Chi Minh City. As such, platformisation challenges the performative practices of citizenship, statecraft, and digital entrepreneurship in Vietnam today.

By addressing the possible forms of 'digital citizenship' of moto-taxi drivers in a platform economy that mediates the public space context, we showed how citizenship is itself mediated between collective experiences in urban public spaces and digital public space. Performing citizenship is not just a question of participating in pre-defined realms; it entails creating new types of communities and transforming participation in urban politics (online and offline), enacting political scopes, and repositioning representative processes in the city. To reach a more institutionalised form, citizenship in the digital age must also include wider participation in decisions regarding how to harvest, store, and share data and its benefits, including decision-making processes on an institutional level.

Bibliography

Abdelnour, Sarah, and Dominique Méda (eds.). 2019. *Les nouveaux travailleurs des applis*. Paris: Presses Universitaires de France.

Agergaard, Jytte, and Vu Thi Thao. 2011. 'Mobile, Flexible, and Adaptable: Female Migrants in Hanoi's Informal Sector', *Population, Space and Place*, 17(5), 407–420.

Barns, Sarah. 2014. 'Platform urbanism: The emergent politics of open data for urban management', *Conference: American Association of Geographers Annual Meeting,* Tampa, Florida.

Barns, Sarah. 2020. *Platform Urbanism: Negotiating Platform Ecosystems in Connected Cities*. London: Palgrave Macmillan.

Benvegnù, Carlotta, Niccolò Cuppini, Mattia Frapporti, Floriano Milesi, and Maurilio Pirone. 2021. 'Platform Battlefield: Digital Infrastructures in Capitalism 4.0', *South Atlantic Quarterly*, 120(4), 689–702.

Buckley, Joe. 2022a. *Vietnamese Labour Militancy: Capital-Labour Antagonisms and Self-Organised Struggles*. Abingdon: Routledge.

Buckley, Joe. 2022b. 'The Dual Structure of Vietnam's Labour Relations' in Hyun Bang Shin, Murray Mckenzie, and Do Young Oh (eds.), *COVID-19 in Southeast Asia, Insights for a Post-pandemic World* (108–117). London: LSE Press.

Chan, Chris King-chi, Éric Florence, and Jack Linchuan Qiu. 2021. 'Precarity, Platforms, and Agency: The Multiplication of Chinese Labour', *China Perspectives*, 2021(1), 3–7.

Danh Trong. 2020. 'Hàng trăm tài xế tắt app, tập trung trước trụ sở Grab phản đối việc tăng giá cước', *Tuổi Trẻ Online* (7 December). https://tuoitre.vn/hang-tram-tai-xe-tat-app-tap-trung-truoc-tru-so-grab-phan-doi-viec-tang-gia-cuoc-20201207141304728.htm

Endres, Kirsten W. 2014. 'Making Law: Small-Scale Trade and Corrupt Exceptions at the Vietnam–China Border', *American Anthropologist*, 116(3), 611–625.

Gibert, Marie, and Juliette Segard. 2015. 'Urban Planning in Vietnam: a Vector for a Negotiated Authoritarianism?' *Justice spatiale/Spatial Justice*, 8.

Gibert-Flutre, Marie. 2020. 'Between "Network" and "Territory": Ho Chi Minh City's Alleyways as Challenged Liminal Spaces' in Marie Gibert-Flutre and Heide Imai (eds.), *Asian Alleyways: An urban vernacular in times of globalisation* (33–56). Amsterdam: Amsterdam University Press.

Gibert-Flutre, Marie. 2022. 'Rhythmanalysis: Rethinking the Politics of Everyday Negotiations in Ordinary Public Spaces', *Environment and Planning C: Politics and Space*, 40(1), 279–297.

Isin, Engin F. 2017. 'Performative Citizenship' in Ayelet Shachar, Rainer Bauboeck, Irene Bloemraad, and Maarten Vink (eds.), *The Oxford Handbook of Citizenship* (500–523). Oxford: Oxford University Press.

Khánh, Trung, Tiêu Thoả, and Trân Ngọc. 2017. 'Bạo lực, đổ máu trong cuộc cạnh tranh GrabBike – xe ôm truyền thống', *ZingNews.vn* (21 June). https://zingnews.vn/zingnews-post756235.html.

Kim, Annette M. 2015. *Sidewalk City, Remapping Public Space in Ho Chi Minh City*. Chicago: University of Chicago Press.

Lee, Doreen. 2018. 'How Ojek Became Go-Jek: Disruptive Technologies and the Infrastructure of Urban Citizenship in Indonesia: Spotlight On Disruptive Urban Technologies', *International Journal of Urban and Regional Research*. https://www.ijurr.org/spotlight-on/disruptive-urban-technologies/how-ojek-became-go-jek-disruptive-technologies-and-the-infrastructure-of-urban-citizenship-in-indonesia/

Lefebvre, Henri, 1968. *The Right to the City* [*Le droit à la ville*]. Baden-Baden: Anthropos.

Lefebvre, Henri. 1974. *The Production of Space* [*La production de l'espace*]. Baden-Baden: Anthropos.

Mbembe, Achille. 2017. *Critique of Black Reason*. Durham NC: Duke University Press.

Morange, Marianne, and Amandine Spire. 2020. *Vivre et construire le droit à la ville : expériences au Sud. La dimension politique des pratiques citadines*. Paris: Presses universitaires de Paris Ouest.

Nguyen Thi Nguyen Thi Vu. 2020. 'The Development of the Digital Economy in Vietnam', *VNU Journal of Science: Economics and Business*, 36(5), 50–59.

Nguyen Tu Phuong. 2019. *Workplace Justice: Rights and Labour Resistance in Vietnam*. London: Palgrave Macmillan.

Rodgers, Scott, and Susan Moore. 2018. 'Platform Urbanism: An Introduction', *Mediapolis*, 23(4). https://www.mediapolisjournal.com/2018/10/platform-urbanism-an-introduction/

Rossi, Ugo, and June Wang. 2020. 'Urban Entrepreneurialism 2.0 or the Becoming South of the Urban World', *Environment and Planning A: Economy and Space*, 52(3), 483–489.

Shaw, Joe, and Mark Graham. 2017. 'An Informational Right to the City? Code, Content, Control, and the Urbanization of Information', *Antipode*, 49(4), 907–927.

Sopranzetti, Claudio. 2021. 'Shifting Informalities: Motorcycle Taxis, Ride-hailing apps, and Urban Mobility in Bangkok', *Geoforum*. https://www.sciencedirect.com/science/article/pii/S0016718521001068

Turner, Sarah. 2018. 'Run and Hide When You See the Police: Livelihood Diversification and the Politics of the Street Economy in Vietnam's Northern Vietnam' in Kirsten W. Endres and Ann Marie Leshkowich (eds.), *Traders in Motion: Identities and Contestations in the Vietnamese Marketplace* (41–53). Honolulu: University of Hawai'i Press.

Turner, Sarah, Celia Zuberec, and Thi-Thanh-Hiên Pham. 2021. 'Visualizing Frictional Encounters: Analyzing and Representing Street Vendor Strategies in Vietnam through Narrative Mapping', *Applied Geography*, 131(10).

Vasavakul, Thaveeporn. 2019. *Vietnam: A Pathway from State Socialism*. Cambridge: Cambridge University Press.

Webster, Juliet. 2016. 'Microworkers of the Gig Economy: Separate and Precarious', *New Labor Forum*, 25(3), 56–64.

About the authors

Marie Gibert-Flutre is Associate Professor of Geography in the Department of East Asia Studies (LCAO) at the University Paris Cité. Her research deals with the dynamics of public and private spaces in the production and appropriation of urban space in Asia. By critically exploring 'global Asia' from ordinary public spaces and neighborhoods, she turns, in particular,

the traditional approach to 'global cities' upside down and contributes to a renewed conception of metropolisation as a highly situated process, where forces at play locally are both intertwined and labile. As Principal Investigator, she manages the Vietnam case study of the Southeast Asia Neighborhoods Network research programme: SEANNET 2.0: Communities of Learning, Research and Teaching Collaborative. She is also the PI of the DiverCities Project funded by the Global Research Institute of Paris (GRIP). She has recently published *Asian Alleyways: An Urban Vernacular in Times of Globalization* (Amsterdam University Press, 2020), co-edited with Heide Imai.
marie.gibert@u-paris.fr

Guillaume Trân Huu graduated in Vietnamese studies from the University Paris Cité in July 2022. He was part of the DiverCities project funded by the Global Research Institute of Paris (GRIP) in 2021–2022. His Master's thesis is entitled 'The Platformisation of the motorbike taxi market in Vietnam and the Construction of a collective consciousness of Grab Drivers'.
guillaumetranhuu@gmail.com

Quê Trân Dinh is a doctoral student in Geography in a joint programme at the University of Pau and Pays de l'Adour in France (UPPA) and the University Paris Cité. She is also a fellow of the doctoral 'bourse excellence' from the French embassy in Vietnam (2023–2026). Her work focuses on the renewal of urban citizenship in contemporary Ho Chi Minh City with the growing uses of various digital tools. She focuses primarily on the new forms of interactions between city dwellers and metropolitan authorities in the course of urban renewal projects. She was also part of the DiverCities project funded by the Global Research Institute of Paris (GRIP) in 2021–2022.
jaimetrandinh@gmail.com

Acknowledgement

This publication benefited from funding by the Global Research Institute of Paris (GRIP) for the DiverCities project (2021–2022).

12. Care of the Self as a Spatial Practice

The Digital Tools Supporting Physical Activities of Migrant Domestic Workers

Caterina Villani, Barui Kurniawan Waruwu, and Kin Wai Michael Siu

Abstract: This paper explores the collective mediated fitness practices of low-income migrant women in Hong Kong as practices of the Care of the Self. Little is known of how the widespread availability of smartphones and social media has changed the ways MDWs organise their social gatherings across time and diverse urban spaces. To explore the impacts of smartphone technologies on the spatiotemporal structuring of these care practices, we focus on three highly visible fitness groups: Zumba dance, yoga, and martial arts. Through semi-structured interviews and content analysis of MDWs' social media activities, we analyse how digital tools support the operation of collective care practices, their presence in the urban space, and the relations between these activities and citizenship.

Keywords: Care of the self, digital tools, spatial practices, physical activities, migrants, domestic workers

Prologue

During a warm Sunday, with the humid subtropical weather that characterises Hong Kong in July, some cheerful music could be heard in the otherwise empty central business district of the city. With social distancing measures in place, the weekly gathering of migrant domestic workers that typically takes place on Chater Road was somewhat scaled down. A group of twenty women with bright orange uniforms was in the middle of the street, setting up phone stands for live streaming. Some women were chatting, while others were just taking a break after a long work week. Some were coordinating the

Gregory Bracken, Paul Rabé, Nurul Azreen Azlan (eds), *Future Practices of Citizenship in Asia and the West: Care of the Self (Volume III)*. Taylor & Francis Group, 2025
DOI: 10.5117/9789048562077_CH12

group, while others were choosing the next soundtrack with their phones for their Zumba practice. I asked one participant for a short interview on the ongoing dancing activity, and after a few questions, she suggested: 'Why don't you ask the admins? [indicating two fellow women] I will add you to our Facebook group; they are organising all'.

Introduction

A recent branch of scholarship in urban studies is increasingly focusing on amateur fitness practices, such as dancing, running, skating, fighting, and yoga practice, performed in urban spaces of several cities around the world (Latham and Layton 2019; 2020). These activities are commonly observed in urban environments and are known to potentially facilitate social connections, establish social networks, and enable communities to flourish (Simone and Pieterse 2017). Research on fitness activities in urban environments is informed by scholarship on the Care of the Self and performativity. Broadly, these studies investigate how identities are (re)produced through a wide array of practices and performances. Multiple accounts of Foucault's seminal work elaborate on how self-care can become a way to experience somatic pleasure (Foucault 1984). Besides, the *self* is always intertwined with everyday life interactions, formed and altered by societal and bodily practices (Debord 2012). The act of self-care can become a collective practice when different bodies—in particular, bodies of disenfranchised groups who are less visible in cities—come together in streets or squares to dance or perform.

Seeing groups performing collective dances, tai chi, or yoga is an increasingly common experience in urban parks, streets, and street corners of cities around the world (Chen 2018; Loukaitou-Sideris et al. 2016). While research has previously concentrated on professional, extreme, and niche sports activities (for example, mega-events, marathon running, parkour, or skateboarding) and the urban environments that support or hinder them (O'Connor 2018), more mundane fitness activities, which are part of daily life in many cities, are relatively less documented. Concurrently, there is limited research on the plurality of active bodies. Research has focused mainly on youth and on extreme, thrill-seeking groups with their respective urban sub-cultures. Meanwhile, 'other bodies', such as vulnerable groups with precarious working and living conditions, are often less well documented. For example, groups of migrant workers, particularly women, may engage in different fitness and training activities, such as Zumba or martial arts, thus surmounting their daily labour, care duties, and localities.

Collective fitness activities typically rely on the social infrastructure present in cities, the everyday infrastructure that accommodates exercise and sports, such as fitness courts, gyms, and dance studios, or urban public spaces, such as public parks, squares, or streets (Latham and Layton 2019). The social infrastructure provides essential spaces to enable or facilitate collective activities. However, distribution of these supportive environments is often unequal, as wealthier neighbourhoods tend to host more of such activities than peripheral or deprived areas. In addition, race, gender, class, sexuality, and disability also condition people's access to and use of urban facilities for fitness and performance. Understanding how these environments cater to sport and collective fitness activities, and how these practices can be facilitated for ordinary residents is a crucial topic for reimagining a collective urban future (Simone and Pieterse 2017) as well as for a more just city (Low and Iveson 2016).

In Hong Kong, the ethnographic site of our investigation, deep-seated socioeconomic divisions typical of Asian global cities are manifested through the allocation of urban public space. Such space is limited in quality and quantity and is highly contested. Nevertheless, in Hong Kong, spaces for coming together and *counterspaces*, which allow for some degree of inclusivity, are present within the highly unequal urban environment (Villani and Talamini 2023). One such example is visible on Sundays in central areas of the city, with the large-scale gathering of (mainly) women migrant domestic workers (MDW). For workers otherwise relegated to their employer's home, this meeting epitomises the possibility of their claiming part of the city as their own, at least one day per week. The Sunday gatherings show how the powerless use 'underutilised or abandoned space that lies forgotten' (Sassen 2013, 217) in global cities, manifested at an even greater scale in Hong Kong. One way in which this group makes its presence visible is through collective performances in streets and parks during the weekend, when these central areas are empty of office workers (Lai 2010).

While such collective practices of reclaiming public spaces have been present in several Asian cities for decades, more recent disruptions have come about through the widespread use of digital tools and online platforms, which have impacted collective activities. As will be elaborated later in this chapter, smartphones, social media, and messaging platforms such as Facebook, Instagram, TikTok, Messenger, and WhatsApp offer digital affordances for collective activities. Several studies highlight the importance of cyberspace in supporting the logistical, informational, and relational dimensions of collective social movements (Padawangi et al. 2014). With the rising importance of new communication platforms in the urban public sphere, cyberspace offers digital settings for networking and recurrent everyday communications that can create and facilitate collective activities, sharing online and in physical space, and self-promotion (Costa 2018; Trepte 2015).

Cities in Asia are especially relevant locations for investigating cyber-urban relations in social movements. Here, the increasing accessibility of digital online platforms is being studied as a potential door to new participatory collective platforms: 'An online space beyond the geographical' (Padawangi et al. 2014, 8). For example, insurgent social movements have relied on smartphones for the coordination of on-site activities. Our study indicates that the online—new media and communications—and urban space are sometimes strongly linked. However, while social media seem to facilitate networking, they can also have some access restrictions (e.g., technical literacy). Moreover, online platforms may also be subjected to control, regulation, and specific rules. Previous studies also suggest the interdependent dimension of digital media and physical urban spaces for sustaining specific collective activities and larger social movements like protests. In particular, this interconnection could provide 'spaces' for people to interact, allowing for the agency and expansion of social networks of movements (Lim 2014).

By investigating the collective fitness activities of low-income migrant women in Hong Kong, we contribute to an understanding of the relationship between digital and urban spaces in the production of collective everyday fitness activities. These activities are an expression of more ordinary manifestations of this online-physical interdependence (compared to mass protests) and shed light on the diversity among some migrant women's groups that are currently underrepresented in research (e.g., Indonesian women or older women). By analysing MDWs' physical activities as networks engaging physical and online media spaces, this study examines the relationship between spatial practices, digital support, and care. In the remainder of this chapter, we investigate both how digital platforms and social media support fitness practices and how urban areas cater to and support these physical activities.

New directions in the study of leisure activities of migrant domestic workers

Currently, more than 330,000 MDWs are employed in Hong Kong. These full-time live-in caregivers for children, the elderly, or animal companions account for approximately one-tenth of Hong Kong's total working population.

About one-third of Hong Kong households with children rely on MDWs for childcare (thirty-two and a half percent) (HKSAR Census and Statistics Department 2021). MDWs are mainly women who migrate from Southeast Asian countries, primarily the Philippines (fifty-seven percent), Indonesia (forty-one percent), and other countries such as Thailand and Cambodia (two percent). A basic two-year employment contract stipulates that they must live in their employer's residence, and grants them twenty-four hours off weekly. It also includes some other basic labour protection measures, including the ability to participate in labour organisations. Restrictive migration policies make MDWs subject to heavy control and precarious contracts and ensure that they are denied pathways to citizenship or long-term residency status. This group is also highly subject to regulation and discipline by employers, which (as highlighted by our respondents) may include control of mobile phone use or even denial of access to specific spaces in the house or city.

Although MDWs are subject to strict labour conditions and may seem to be a disempowered group, multiple accounts in relevant literature reveal their agency and the urban tactics they use to subvert existing hierarchies of power. We see this in the ways they use to reproduce and express their identity during leisure time, which is mainly on Sundays (Constable 1997; 2009; Law 2001). Their mass presence, and the ordinary use they make of public space can be studied as a manifestation of resistance and resourcefulness (Kwok 2019). For example, specific activities like beauty styling and beauty pageants can be a means to connect personal appearance with civic engagement (Chu and Catalan 2020). Larger collective activities involving dancing and singing are studied as outlets for greater labour demands and collective longings (Lai 2010). In summary, the cosmopolitan landscape (Law 2002) created by these social Sunday activities creates a safe space for this group to use their limited leisure time and increase their agency.

In recent years, multiple groups of MDWs practising fitness activities have made their presence felt in gathering spaces. Although dance and cultural performances in public spaces have previously been linked with labour struggles and political rallies, more ordinary fitness practices have also occurred. Activities such as group dancing, yoga, and martial arts are typically visible in places like Chater Road and Victoria Park. However, the mechanism behind the organisation of these activities has been less studied. In addition, MDWs—often considered a homogeneous community—show distinctive differences along ethnic, cultural, and religious lines and in their spatial occupation practices.

Furthermore, digital tools have become essential in the daily life of migrant domestic workers for the organisation of their leisure activities. While some workers are forbidden to use their phones during the working day, especially if their employer is present, most of them can use them after completing their duties or when their employer leaves the house. Research has concentrated on the impact of smartphone use on the personal relationships of MDWs, on their intrafamilial parenting practices (Waruwu 2021), or as a means of collective empowerment (Wisnu Wijaya et al. 2022). Yet, the impact of increasingly popular online platforms (e.g., Facebook, Instagram, WhatsApp) on the organisation of MDWs' collective activities remains unclear.

Studying MDWs' fitness activities

Our investigation focuses on three fitness groups, all highly visible in recognised MDW gathering spaces. These groups comprise mainly MDWs who perform Zumba group dance on Chater Road, yoga at Central Ferry Pier and Shau Kei Wan, and *pencak silat*, a martial art native to Indonesia, in Victoria Park (see Figure 12.1). This study employs qualitative methods, including participant observation in Hong Kong's public spaces, semi-structured direct interviews, and data collection from Facebook and WhatsApp groups of the relevant fitness groups. To examine transcribed and documentary material we used content analysis. On-site observation of the fitness activities took place from September to December 2021, before the stringent anti-pandemic restrictions implemented in Hong Kong led to heavy patrolling of public spaces by authorities.

Through on-site participant observations of MDWs' leisure practices, we were able to identify the organisers and participants of the three fitness groups. Figure 12.1 shows the main gathering locations. While Zumba and martial arts are organised by and consist mainly of MDWs, yoga practice (in Pier 9) is organised by one migrant woman. However, this activity is open to (and targets) a wider audience. We collected nine semi-structured interviews and ten informal interviews with participants and selected the organisers and the participants of the fitness groups using a purposive and snowball sampling procedure.

Direct semi-structured phone interviews with these organisers and participants were collected between December 2021 and July 2022. Surinem is a self-taught yoga instructor from Indonesia and one of the leaders of a migrant organisation in Hong Kong (Interview #1). Indy is a yoga practitioner from Indonesia (Interview #2), and Asty is a former leader of the martial arts group (Interview #3). Rina, Asty's protégé, is also a member of the martial arts group (Interview #4). Carmel (Interview #5), Liliana (Interview

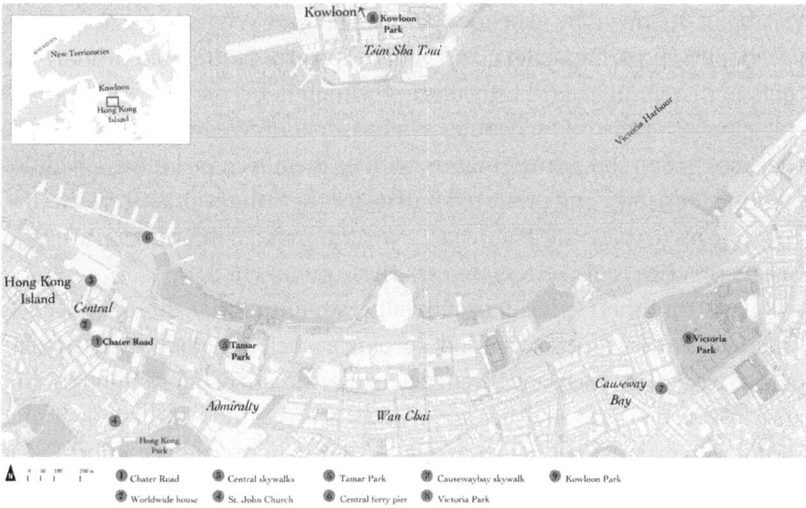

Figure 12.1. Migrant domestic workers' typical gathering places on Sundays.

#6), and Regina (Interview #7) from the Philippines are organisers of the largest Zumba group training in Chater Road and *admins* of its Facebook group. Cilo (Interview #8) and Angie (Interview #9) from the Philippines frequently join the Zumba classes. (All names of interviewees have been altered to maintain anonymity.)

Most of the MDWs we interviewed began to be actively involved in fitness activities only after they moved to Hong Kong and familiarised themselves with the city, its public space, and its social infrastructure. The Zumba group was founded by its main instructor in 2018 as a spin-off group of friends from a different Zumba practice who gathered at Central Ferry Pier. These women later created the Zumba Facebook group, now having more than one thousand online members, with about forty of them dancing each Sunday. Zumba participants usually give a minimum voluntary contribution (about HK$20) to join a two-hour class on Sunday afternoons in Chater Road. The yoga and martial arts groups are free of charge. Surinem's yoga participants usually consist of about fifteen members. Indy's group has twelve members, and the martial arts group has up to thirty members.

Digital tools supporting physical activities

Respondents reported using various communication platforms to facilitate their physical activities. The most common media for organizing events was

Facebook, followed by Facebook Messenger and WhatsApp group chats. Facebook groups, Messenger, and WhatsApp groups are used primarily as tools to distribute useful information, which helps members coordinate collective priorities and schedules. For example, on Wednesdays the Zumba Facebook group shares information with its members, including schedules, meeting locations, and preferred outfits for the Sunday practice, as well as any changes to these (see Figure 12.2). Weather-related information affecting fitness practice is also circulated via these group chats.

Apart from their informational value, we found that these media also function as tools of social cohesion, keeping participants connected throughout the week. This was done through a regular stream of information to build anticipation for the event. Yoga and martial arts practitioners have dedicated WhatsApp groups. These group chats enable them to share information about the events throughout the week. Members shared pictures of their new workout gear and links to tutorial videos on YouTube. The respondents said that the constant flow of messages throughout the week reminds them of their ties to other members, thereby reducing the sense of isolation they often experience living in employers' homes. This social function of the group chats solidifies the importance of membership in these fitness-based groups, as it allows individual members of a marginalised group to find their place in a society where they are largely (and in some cases) systemically overlooked (Oktavianus and Lin 2021).

Compared to Facebook groups, dedicated WhatsApp and Facebook Messenger group chats are preferred as participatory decision-making platforms. These are spaces where members discuss, make decisions, and exchange suggestions or comments on the fitness practice. The Zumba group chat is essential for discussions regarding location, time, soundtracks, and outfit changes and for giving feedback to the admins who organise the activity. Our respondents expressed the importance of the participatory character of these groups. As Carmel, the admin of the Zumba Facebook group noted, 'Admins should be friendly and not too bossy [...] I can tell that we [Zumba group] are very close because we treat each other equally and listen to preferences' (Interview #5). Digital platforms also support the organising of bigger events, such as competitions, anniversaries, parties, and seasonal celebrations that can take up to a month to be set up. For the Zumba group, these events typically involve several steps to engage participants and online cooperation between different dancing groups, instructors, charities, and other organisations. The involvement of wide networks of actors for these events is made possible primarily through participation in online groups and chats throughout the week. This reinforces the importance of the online platform for scaling up the organisation of MDWs' activities when fitness is a means to reach broader aims like fundraising for humanitarian causes.

Access to these online platforms differs across groups. Existing members can add new members to the group chat for yoga groups. Although the Zumba Facebook group is private, it is open to new members and frequently accepts them. As such, the entry barriers to the yoga and Zumba groups are low. However, for the martial arts group, only those officially inducted into the group are eligible to join the chat and only group leaders may add new members. This procedure was a social ritual in its own right; people not only welcome new inductees into the group, they congratulate them for succeeding in joining. Asty, former leader of the martial arts group, revealed that there is currently a waiting list for new joiners. For Surinem, the closed system of the WhatsApp group makes it suitable to share pictures of individual members as they hold a yoga pose (see Figure 12.2). They share the images among themselves to see and correct any wrong postures. Surinem noted that members always look forward to seeing these pictures after the exercise.

Nevertheless, specific rules govern the online spaces, and the admins of each group often enforce them. As unwritten rules, the yoga and martial arts group chats promote positive attitudes and supportive language. Carmel (Interview #5), Liliana (Interview #6), and Regina (Interview #7) clarify that when accepting new members in the online Zumba group, they ask them to share content related to the fitness activity and 'avoid any negativity', which is seen as unsocial behaviour. Similarly, using foul language or body shaming can lead to a member's ban from the Zumba group.

During the weekly practice, some groups allow their members to stream the fitness activity on the group's or the members' individual profiles. Sharing (live) videos appears to be an important activity for Zumba participants. Respondents find it a good way to connect with fellow Zumba *aficionados*, friends, and families in their home countries. Video livestreaming appears to be a way to promote a different (health-minded) identity. As Cilo notes, 'I want my family to see that I am not *just* sitting on the streets, I am doing something, I am burning [calories]' (Interview #8). Similar videos are, at the same time, tools for member recruitment through word of mouth. Interestingly, for privacy reasons both yoga and martial arts groups do not allow members to livestream their practice. Sharing videos requires the consent of all members. The formation of social media rules observed among MDWs can be understood as part of the ritual mechanism of group membership and group boundaries that are crucial in collective self-care practices. For a social group to thrive, clear boundaries must exist between

Figure 12.2. a) Members' feedback on the yoga WhatsApp group, b) Schedule and outfit shared on the Zumba Facebook group, c) Lifestyle and rules of the Zumba group.

the in- and out-groups, and certain thresholds must be met by potential new members (Collins 2004). Whether regarding the rules about who can join the group chats or how to handle online privacy issues, we found MDWs increasingly confident in activating their agency while also thoughtful in their adherence to their collective norms and rules.

From online coordination to presence in city spaces

All the fitness groups gathered regularly in public spaces for their practice. The choice of a specific location is based on its targeted audience. Zumba and martial arts groups have established meeting locations for MDWs, where they can be visible to potential new members and newcomers to the city. The yoga group near Central Pier aims to involve a wider audience and targets a location far from these other gathering spaces. Although none of these spaces requires bookings, appointing a person to arrive an hour early to 'hold the place' is a recurrent spatial occupation practice for smaller fitness groups such as yoga and martial arts. For larger groups, speakers and higher sound levels are essential in establishing their use of space in competition with other groups on the same street.

Locational aspects appear to be very important in choosing a gathering space. Every MDW newcomer to the city will likely visit Chater Road and the nearby Worldwide House to connect to the Filipino community. In contrast, the Indonesian community usually gathers in Victoria Park and Causeway Bay. Surinem holds her yoga sessions at a shaded part of a public seating area in Sau Kei Wan every Sunday from three to five pm. This allows her to appeal to a broader array of participants, including local Hong Kong youth and foreign professionals from other countries.

Indy organised her yoga in an open area near Central Ferry Pier 9. She said that this location is suitable for her and other participants because it is accessible and spacious. Interestingly, while Surinem selected her venue based on her intention to recruit domestic helpers who gather around the vicinity, Indy picked her spot because it is not a popular location for domestic helpers.

When asked about the space where the fitness practice occurs, respondents usually mention that there are few available outdoor spaces for their large groups and location considerations are important in deciding where to gather. Among the four spaces observed, Surinem's yoga and the martial arts gathering spaces consist of urban parks where members practice on a grass surface. In contrast, the Chater Road space and Indy's yoga location at the ferry pier consist of a large asphalt and pavement surface (see Figure 12.3). None of these locations are shaded, weather-protected, or equipped for fitness practice, nor do they include urban furniture to accommodate these social activities. As a result, both Surinem's and Indy's yoga activities are contingent upon the weather because neither space is roofed. When it rains, the event is cancelled. Similarly, Zumba organisers and participants explain that in case of inclement weather, they 'pray it will stop before four pm [when Zumba starts]' (Interview #6).

The martial arts group has been training in the same spot in Victoria Park for the last twelve years, and members are not concerned about the weather. They brave heat and rain as part of their endurance exercise. Asty, the group's former leader, explained that although the grass field where they work out is packed with Indonesian workers every Sunday, they have never encountered any problem or competition for the space because the regular park users know their schedule. More competition for space occurs on Chater Road, where the Zumba members with powerful speakers weekly assert and re-negotiate the space as their own.

Similarly to the online platforms, these weekly fitness practices in public spaces have clear rules. Usually, the organisers of the Zumba Facebook groups continue to refer to themselves as 'admins' during these weekly gatherings. They are the ones enforcing the regulations. With numerous phone stands live streaming the dance activities, Zumba participants are given a clear layout of where the phone stands are permitted (in the front) and where they obstruct free movements and dances (between dancers). Similarly, in line with the healthy lifestyle Zumba admins promote, certain objects, such as beer cans, are not allowed to be used as phone stands. Participants who appear intoxicated are also excluded from the practice.

Figure 12.3. Fitness activities in space.

Physical activities and collective citizenship practices

Each group showed a particular connection between fitness practice and their understanding of citizenship practices. Asty explained that, for her, the martial arts group is an ambassador of Indonesian culture (Interview #3). Performing this activity enables her to take pride in her nationality and ethnicity. She fondly recalls how the Hong Kong police department invited her group to perform at a cultural event in 2017. She was proud to perform in front of locals and other foreigners in Hong Kong. According to Asty, this is one of the ways in which she shows her patriotism and love for her home country. At the same time, she uses the activity as a platform to advocate for her compatriots and, more broadly, for the empowerment of migrant workers. Echoing a similar sentiment, the organisers of the Zumba practice are highly motivated by showing MDWs' agency and visibility in the city and by providing them with alternative leisure options. Numerous compatriots who are newcomers to the city will visit Chater Road during their first day off. Newcomers and long-term workers interested in picking up a new hobby will likely see this Zumba group as soon as they exit the subway station. For the organisers, providing and promoting health-and-care-related leisure options to their peers is crucial. Regina said, 'We just encourage them [MDWs] to join us for stress relief. Some people don't really find a group of friends that really treat them as family. We are here, so far from our family and we can have many different problems' (Interview #7). Carmel adds, 'You exercise your body, and then it makes you laugh. So, it's not only your body that becomes happy. It's your soul' (Interview #5).

Participation in collective physical activities may also overlap with the civic and organisational duties of MDWs. For Surinem, yoga is also a means of recruiting people to join organisations dedicated to fighting overcharging among migrant helpers in Hong Kong. She acknowledges the reluctance of fellow helpers to join social organisations for fear of their employers' disapproval. By approaching them through physical activity, such as yoga, Surinem claims that her fellow helpers are more willing to join (Interview #1). As such, this physical activity is a supplementary practice that helps them establish a more robust community; this, in turn, strengthens their collective presence in Hong Kong. Another respondent, Indy, explained that her weekly yoga sessions helped her cope with the discrimination she faced when she first moved to Hong Kong (Interview #2). She recalled her experience when a taxi driver did not understand the directions she was giving him in English, and he yelled, 'Go back to your country!' Her yoga sessions allowed her to meet local residents of Hong Kong, who have taught her Cantonese. In the group, she also meets other expatriates who help her feel more confident.

Discussion and Conclusion

While seemingly unrelated, the three constructs examined in this study—physical activities, urban landscape, and identity performance—are increasingly intertwined in city life around the world. This study investigated the interrelatedness of these three constructs in the context of self-care among a marginalised migrant population, namely migrant domestic workers (MDWs) in Hong Kong. Given the technological saturation in Hong Kong, we also looked at the critical role played by the pervasiveness of digital media in materialising the civic and cohesive potentials of these activities.

We found that various fitness practices, particularly yoga, Zumba, and martial arts, emerged as tools to enhance MDWs' collective empowerment, self-care, engagement, and advocacy. To varying degrees, fitness activities are a means for MDWs to exercise agency in the city. The MDWs' agency coexists with their living with precarity, residing in the city on short-term working permits, and not having access to long-term residence or citizenship. Beyond the formal meanings of citizenship in a global city, MDWs establish new spatial practices that reinterpret their civic role as part of the city and of communities. While most MDWs' routines and mobilities during the week are highly controlled and confined to domestic spaces and their role as home carers, their personal interests and identities emerge during the weekend. Indeed, we found that Zumba, yoga, and martial arts activities offer MDWs not only physical benefits but also a symbolic context within which they hone their leadership skills and self-care practices. In particular, yoga serves as a secondary function in recruiting people to join an organization dedicated to labor protection in Hong Kong. Zumba enables organisers to engage proactively with and deliver care to newly arrived MDWs and offer alternative leisure activities while redefining the use of a sought-after street in the financial district. Finally, martial arts groups offer opportunities for members to exercise self-discipline and national pride during their time abroad.

Physical activity (enabled primarily by online platforms) is a supplementary practice that occurs in ordinary urban spaces and helps MDWs establish a more robust community. This sense of community, in turn, strengthens their collective presence in Hong Kong. Fitness practice contributes significantly to group identity formation both online and in urban spaces. Different participants can freely join Zumba and yoga practice. For example, Zumba participants are distinguished by bright-coloured uniforms and adherence to health-related behaviours (e.g., no smoking or drinking). For the martial arts group, a clear boundary existed between members. Marking the in-group versus the out-group gives the MDWs a sense of visibility as participants.

Digital media, particularly Facebook and WhatsApp, enable an efficient weekly appropriation of urban space by MDWs, similar to what is observed in larger social movements (Padawangi et al. 2014). Social media platforms emerged as virtual spaces in which collective activities can be organised and social identities validated. At the same time, different digital media inevitably introduced some restrictions to members who were not allowed (or lack the means to) to access them. The interdependent dimension between online and physical space becomes evident during the weekly Zumba practice. Livestreaming allows MDWs to be present in both dimensions and connect to fellow dancers, families, and friends in the digital space.

In Hong Kong these mundane and everyday practices do not rely on established fitness infrastructure or training spaces as in other cities (Latham and Layton 2020). They appear to create shared space and social cohesion and should thus be recognised at a policy level as an integral part of the public city. However, looking at the fitness practices of three groups of low-income migrant women also sheds light on the precariousness and fragile nature of their lives in the city, from many parts of which they are often excluded. Although not officially considered part of the city's place-making activities, MDWs' fitness practices contribute to their quality of life and awareness of their rights as well as a better understanding of a just city (Mitchell 2003). These collective practices also give an alternative meaning to the role of citizenship for those who lack formal pathways to it. Alternative citizenship practices are entwined with matters of care for the body and well-being, as well as care for each other, and are a way of keeping their own cultural practices alive. The streets and parks where these collective care practices occur support new meanings and understandings of citizenship. To echo the words of Suzanne Hall (2021,155):

> In writing [of] the street as world I am compelled to explore the alternative resumptions to belonging that can only be formed at the edge, since they emerge through the realities of exclusion. A citizenship of the edge gives us an edge grammar that rearticulates citizenship as an adaptive and audacious constitution.

Bibliography

Chen, Caroline. 2018. 'Designing the Danceable City', *Journal of the American Planning Association,* 84(3–4), 237–249. doi: 10.1080/01944363.2018.1526645

Chu, Cecilia and Marta Catalán Eraso. 2020. 'Beyond the Sunday Spectacle: Foreign Domestic Workers and Emergent Civic Urbanisms in Hong Kong' in Im Sik

Cho et al. (eds.), *Emerging Civic Urbanisms in East Asia*. 245–266. Amsterdam: Amsterdam University Press.

Collins, Randall. 2004. *Interaction Ritual Chains*. Princeton: Princeton University Press.

Constable, Nicole. 1997. *Maid to Order in Hong Kong: Stories of Migrant Workers*. Ithaca: Cornell University Press.

Constable, Nicole. 2009. 'Migrant Workers and the Many States of Protest in Hong Kong', *Critical Asian Studies*, 41(1), 143–164. doi: 10.1080/14672710802631202

Costa, Elisabetta. 2018. 'Affordances-in-practice: An Ethnographic Critique of Social Media Logic and Context Collapse', *New Media & Society*, 20(10), 3641–3656. doi: 10.1177/1461444818756290

Hall, Suzanne. 2021. *The Migrant's Paradox: Street Livelihoods and Marginal Citizenship in Britain*. Minneapolis: University of Minnesota Press.

HKSAR Census and Statistics Department. 2021. Thematic Household Survey Report No. 72: Employment of domestic helpers.

Kwok, Evelyn. 2019. 'Little Manila: An Unlikely Crowd of Resistance in Hong Kong', *Architectural Theory Review*, 23(2), 287–314. doi: 10.1080/13264826.2019.1656264

Lai, Ming-yan. 2010. 'Dancing to Different Tunes: Performance and Activism among Migrant Domestic Workers in Hong Kong', *Women's Studies International Forum*, 33(5), 501–511. doi: 10.1016/j.wsif.2010.07.003

Latham, Alan. and Jack Layton. 2019. 'Social Infrastructure and the Public Life of Cities: Studying Urban Sociality and Public Spaces,' *Geography Compass* 13(7), 12444. doi: 10.1111/gec3.12444

Latham, Alan. and Jack Layton. 2020. 'Kinaesthetic cities: Studying the Worlds of Amateur Sports and Fitness in Contemporary Urban Environments', *Progress in Human Geography*, 44(5), 852–876. doi: 10.1177/0309132519859442

Law, Lisa. 2001. 'Home Cooking: Filipino Women and Geographies of the Senses in Hong Kong', *Ecumene*, 8, 264–283.

Law, Lisa. 2002. 'Defying Disappearance: Cosmopolitan Public Spaces in Hong Kong', *Urban Studies*, 39(9), 1625–1645. doi: 10.1080/00420980220151691

Lim, Merlyna. 2014. 'Seeing Spatially: People, Networks and Movements in Digital and Urban Spaces', *International Development Planning Review*, 36(1), 51–72. doi: 10.3828/idpr.2014.4

Loukaitou-Sideris, Anastasia, Lene Levy-Storms, Lin Chen, et al. 2016. 'Parks for an Aging Population: Needs and Preferences of Low-Income Seniors in Los Angeles. http://dx.doi.org/10.1080/01944363.2016.1163238 82(3)

Low, Setha, and Kurt Iveson. 2016. 'Propositions for More Just Urban Public Spaces', *City* 20(1), 10–31. doi: 10.1080/13604813.2015.1128679

Mitchell, Don. 2003. *The Right to the City: Social Justice and the Fight for Public Space*. New York: Guilford Press.

O'Connor, Paul. 2018. 'Hong Kong Skateboarding and Network Capital' *Journal of Sport and Social Issues*, 42(6), 419–436. doi: 10.1177/0193723518797040

Oktavianus, Jeffry, and Wan-Ying Lin. 2021. 'Soliciting Social Support from Migrant Domestic Workers' Connections to Storytelling Networks during a Public Health Crisis', *Health Communication*, 38(6), 1179-1188. https://doi.org/10.1080/10410236.2021.1996675

Padawangi, Rita, Peter Marolt, and Mike Douglass. 2014. 'Introduction to the Special Issue: Insurgencies, Social Media and the Public City in Asia', *International Development Planning Review*, 36(1), 3–13. doi: 10.3828/idpr.2014.1

Sassen, Saskia. 2013. 'Does the City Have Speech?', *Public Culture*, 25(270), 209–221. https://doi.org/10.1215/08992363-2020557

Simone, AbduMaliq, and Edgar Pieterse. 2017. *New Urban Worlds: Inhabiting Dissonant Times*. Cambridge: Polity Press.

Siu, Kin Wai Michael. 2010. 'Open for All: Open Spaces and New Urban Lifestyles', *The International Journal of the Humanities*, 7(12), 25–38.

Siu, Kin Wai Michael, and Yihua Huang. 2015. 'Everyday Life under Modernist Planning: A Study of an Ever-transforming Urban Area in Hong Kong,' *Urban Design International*, 20(4), 293–309. https://doi.org/10.1057/udi.2015.16

Trepte, Sabine. 2015. 'Social Media, Privacy, and Self-Disclosure: The Turbulence Caused by Social Media's Affordances', *Social Media + Society*, 1(1). doi: 10.1177/2056305115578681

Villani, Caterina, and Gianni Talamini. 2023. 'Making Vulnerability Invisible: The Impact of COVID-19 on the Use of Public Space in Hong Kong', *Journal of Planning Education and Research*, 00(0). https://doi.org/10.1177/0739456X231205795

Waruwu, Barui Kurniawan. 2021. 'Smartphone Mothering and Mediated Family Display: Transnational Family Practices in a Polymedia environment among Indonesian Mothers in Hong Kong', *Mobile Media and Communication*, 10(1), 97–114. https://doi.org/10.1177/2050157921998408

Wisnu, Wijaya Sevanus, Janson Watson, and Christine Bruce. 2022. 'A Virtual Ethnography Study of Indonesian Migrant Domestic Workers' Empowerment in Online Communities,' *Behaviour & Information Technology*, 42(7), 921–939. doi: 10.1080/0144929X.2022.2052184

About the authors

Caterina Villani (PhD) is Assistant Professor in Urban and Regional Planning in the School of Architecture, Planning and Environmental Policy at University College Dublin. Her research investigates three main areas: urban design, transport policy, and critical urban theory. She holds a PhD in Architecture and Civil Engineering from the City University of Hong Kong, funded by the Hong Kong PhD Fellowship (2017–2020). Previously, Caterina

was a PolyU Distinguished Postdoctoral Fellowship (2021–2023) recipient at the School of Design at The Hong Kong Polytechnic University. Her work interlays the areas of social sustainability, policy research, spatial planning, and sharing practices, aiming to combine multi-disciplinary approaches to envision more inclusive urban forms and processes.
caterina.villani@ucd.ie

Barui K. Waruwu (PhD, City University of Hong Kong) is an Assistant Professor at the Department of Humanities and Creative Writing at Hong Kong Baptist University. His work examines the sociocultural implications of smartphones and social media on transnational family relationships, migrants' community building, as well as relational stress and communal resilience. His first- and solo-authored research papers have been published in international peer-reviewed journals, including New Media & Society, Mobile Media & Communication, and Media, Culture & Society.
louis_waruwu@hkbu.edu.hk

Kin Wai Michael Siu is Associate Dean (Research), Eric C. Yim Professor in Inclusive Design and Chair Professor of Public Design, School of Design, PolyU. He is Founder and Leader of Public Design Lab. He is Fellow of numerous professional engineering and design organisations. He has been invited by a number of universities as visiting professor and scholar, including the University of Cambridge, Massachusetts Institute of Technology (Fulbright Scholar), National University of Singapore (ASIA Fellow), UC Berkeley, Tsinghua University, CAFA, and Wuhan University of Technology. His research areas are in public design, policy and management of public design, user reception, inclusive design, and FlexiDesign. He solely owns over 50 US and international patents and design registrations, and over 50 international invention and design grand awards. He has published over 500 research papers in top-tier academic journals.
m.siu@polyu.edu.hk

Acknowledgements

We would like to acknowledge the research support of Eric C. Yim Endowed Professorship (8.73.09.847K) and the PolyU Distinguished Postdoctoral Fellowship Scheme (DPFS) (1-YWBV). The first author would like to acknowledge the research support of the APEP China Seed Fund (2024/2025). The authors wish to thank the participants and organisers of the fitness groups and the other interviewees who participated in the research.

Epilogue

Citizenship in the Digital Age

Gregory Bracken, Paul Rabé, Nurul Azreen Azlan

Citizens' rights are under threat in the twenty-first century because of an increasingly polarised and authoritarian world. This can be seen in a number of the chapters in this book, particularly in Parts Two and Three where we see human agency diminished by authoritarian regimes. This epilogue explores how citizens' rights are being eroded because of the fact that decisions affecting lives and well-being are increasingly abdicated to algorithms in the interest of efficiency. We begin with a brief overview of some recent literature on social media and the role played by algorithms. Here, we also look at the challenges and opportunities of Artificial Intelligence (AI). We argue that the erosion of human agency that has resulted from the rise of the internet actually began in the second half of the twentieth century when, in the United States, television began to lower the level of political discourse, turning it into something more akin to entertainment than a meaningful exchange of views. We also examine the role of the internet's business model, which focuses on profit over public service. This focus is compounded by a lack of effective regulatory oversight and is all part of the ethos of surveillance capitalism, which we will examine in the last section. The epilogue ends with a note of hope, however, because we believe that it will *always* be possible to have agency as citizens as long as people use that agency, not allowing the precious rights that previous generations have fought for to disappear simply for the sake of entertainment.

Social media

It is becoming more difficult (for some) to distinguish fact from fiction. An example is when someone does an online search for something like: 'climate change is …'. People get different results depending on who and where they

Gregory Bracken, Paul Rabé, Nurul Azreen Azlan (eds), *Future Practices of Citizenship in Asia and the West: Care of the Self (Volume III)*. Taylor & Francis Group, 2025
DOI: 10.5117/9789048562077_EPIL

are. This is because the responses are carefully curated by algorithms that enable social media companies to keep people engaged for longer on their platforms. This ensures more screen time for the companies to show more advertisements, all specifically tailored to the user—because this is their only source of income.

This stratagem to keep people engaged results in what is known as a 'filter bubble'. Jaron Lanier outlines how the algorithms used by social media companies tend to 'gravitate toward corralling people into bubbles, because to engage a group is more effective and economical' (Lanier 2019, 75–76)—by so doing, they can present people with more accurately targeted advertising. The problem with this is, as Lanier points out, that it results in tunnel vision, whereby people's own views are soothingly reinforced and alternative views can be regarded as unacceptable. This leads to a world in which people are presented with 'alternative facts', often believing them to be true, no matter how unlikely they may be: myths like the world is flat, or that COVID-19 vaccines are harmful, or that climate change is not happening. These are all absorbed and passionately believed in. Truth in the twenty-first century is apparently not just relative; it is up for grabs, and strength of conviction (often referred to by the tautology 'lived experience') counts more than an objective assessment of reality.

This has had a rather unfortunate effect on social media's tone, which has soured and polarised public debate, making it shrill, partisan, and Manichean. We will examine how this came about in a moment, but let us first observe the damage that this passive 'corralling' is doing to human agency and citizenship.

Jaron Lanier asks the question 'How can you remain autonomous in a world where you are under constant surveillance and are constantly prodded by algorithms run by some of the richest corporations in history?' (Lanier 2019, 2). He points out that these companies 'have no way of making money except by being paid to manipulate your behavior' (2), i.e., to keep people longer engaged with their screens. He also points out that this is 'unethical, cruel, dangerous, and inhumane' (7). 'If only', he muses, 'we could just get rid of the deleterious business model, then the underlying technology might not be so bad' (27).

Cathy O'Neil says that mathematical models (like algorithms) should be 'our tools, not our masters' (O'Neil 2017, 207). She warns that if we 'treat mathematical models as a neutral and inevitable force, like the weather or the tides, we abdicate our responsibility' (218). Where this abdication could lead is outlined in Dave Eggers' dystopian satire of the near future: *The Every: Or at Last a Sense of Order, or the Final Days of Free Will, Or Limitless Choice is Killing the World*. In this book, he says that '[t]he world is undergoing a movement toward authoritarianism [...] People think the world is out of control. They want someone to stop the changes. This aligns perfectly with what the Every [a sort of amalgamation of Google, Facebook, Amazon, etc.] is doing: feeding the urge to control, to reduce nuance, to categorize, and to assign numbers to anything inherently complex. To simplify. To tell us how it will be. An authoritarian promises these things, too' (Eggers 2021, 297–298).

Artificial Intelligence (AI)

Another development of concern to some people is Artificial Intelligence (AI). AI is commonly understood as something that should make our lives easier by freeing up time for more meaningful pursuits. Yet current trends seem to indicate the opposite. In cases where people are doing menial tasks their work is made harder by surveillance technology that enables them to be monitored more effectively (for example, through registering keystrokes on computer keyboards or using cameras to observe workers in Amazon warehouses). Another concern has been raised by Geoffrey Hinton, former vice president and engineering fellow at Google, who quit his job in May 2023; he says that he regrets his work in developing AI because it will soon be more intelligent than we are (*New York Times* 2023; Heaven 2023). Hinton is known as the 'godfather' of AI because of his pioneering work in deep learning (which enables systems to learn from experience to improve efficacy—in turn implementing some of the most important techniques that operate modern AI). AI is different from human intelligence, not only in its sheer speed and order of magnitude but also because it is divorced from any basic human concerns. AI enables computers to think more quickly than humans, and it even enables them to act more like humans. They do this via Hinton's deep learning, which enables them to figure out what to do without specific instructions.

AI has begun to replace some jobs and will continue to have a great effect on what people do and how they do it. Some jobs will indeed be replaced by AI, but those that require human qualities like empathy (nurses, doctors, councillors, teachers, etc.) will not be so easily replaced. Nor will jobs that require mobility, dexterity, and problem-solving in unpredictable environments, like those of plumbers or electricians. Mundane work, or work that relies mainly on calculation, will most likely be replaced by AI (and will be done more efficiently and accurately). Some workers will definitely have to upskill or even do entirely different work in order not to be made redundant.

Even some creative jobs may not be safe: art, music, writing, etc., can all be produced by AI programmes. Nevertheless, creativity in coming up with new political or business strategies will still require human intuition and ingenuity.

AI can be used to great effect if used wisely and ethically. It can help knowledge workers analyse and expand their work by brainstorming new ideas; it can also be useful for picking up typographical errors or doing slow, mundane work like checking codes. It can even be used to identify biases people may not realise they have in their work. The key is to not be afraid of it. AI is a tool, one that can be used to work more efficiently, but it is not going to supplant humans as a species. Many people will indeed have to evolve their skills if they want to stay relevant, but that could also be an advantage.

One major concern, however, is the people who are developing AI. The question is, are they doing it ethically? Government control has been weak in regulating social media (as we will see below when we look at the origins of the digital turn). Geoffrey Hinton himself warns that investment is needed if AI is to be safely controlled; protection is needed from what he calls 'bad actors' (*New York Times* 2023). Much better oversight is needed in the future development of AI to avoid repeating the mistakes made with social media.

The need for human agency

Dave Eggers argues that 'people prefer the reliable nature of morality-through-surveillance over the ephemeral promises of the gods/Gods of the past' (Eggers 2021, 475) because '[p]rayers to God were rarely answered, while shouts into cyberspace always receive a response, even if misspelled and hateful. Everything God offered—answers, clarity, miracles, baby names—the internet does better' (475–476). And he notes that '[i]t came from both sides [...] The motivations of the companies, yes, to consolidate and measure and profit from the data [...] But the everyday human side, no. Our overwhelming preference to cede all decisions to machines, to replace nuance with numbers... It surpassed all my nightmares. Every day, we make another machine that removes more human agency' (545).

Shoshana Zuboff warns that machine processes are replacing 'human relationships so that certainty can replace trust' (Zuboff 2019, 351). But the problem with allowing computers to do the thinking people should be doing is that, as Cathy O'Neil points out, 'for all of their advances in language and logic [they] still struggle mightily with concepts' (O'Neil 2017, 95). 'They "understand" beauty only as a word associated with the Grand Canyon, ocean sunsets, and grooming tips in Vogue magazine. They try in vain to measure "friendship" by counting likes and connections on Facebook. And the concept of fairness utterly escapes them. Programmers don't know how to code for it, and few of their bosses ask them to' (O'Neil 2017, 95).

As Jon Alexander and Ariane Conrad stress, citizenship 'is not about the passport we hold, and it goes far beyond the duty to vote in elections. It's a state of engagement, more verb than noun. We look around, identify the domains where we have some influence, and we roll up our sleeves and make things happen' (Alexander and Conrad 2022, 7).

This resonates with Gregory Bracken's concept of citizenship in Chapter One of the first volume in this trilogy, *Ancient and Modern Practices of Citizenship in Asia and the West*, 'Citizenship and the Good Life' (2019). There he shows how citizenship, as it developed in ancient Greece and Rome, as well as in China at the same time, was above all *active*. Alexander and Conrad say that to survive and thrive, people must step into what they call the Citizen Story. 'We must see ourselves as Citizens—people who *actively* shape the world around us, who cultivate meaningful connections to their community and institutions, who can imagine a different and better life, who care and take responsibility, and who create opportunities for others to do the same' (Alexander and Conrad 2022, 11; italics added). These authors see society as currently inhabiting a Consumer Story, where people are 'entitled and passive' (12). This story has come to feel inevitable, unbreakable (13), like O'Neil's mathematical models. It is also 'morally justified by a vague theory that every one of us pursuing our own self-interest will add up to collective interest' (16) (this is something that we will return to later when discussing Shoshana's Zuboff's concept of surveillance capitalism). Alexander and Conrad argue that '[o]nce we see ourselves as Citizens, we [will] demand that our organisations and institutions treat us as such' (37). According to them, to be a Citizen is 'to care, to take responsibility, to acknowledge one's inherent power [...] to cultivate meaningful connection to a web of relationships and institutions' (95). Being a Citizen 'implies engagement, contribution, and action rather than a passive state of being or receiving'. It is 'a *practice*' (95; italics added).

Thinking that social media provides some form of twenty-first-century town square where humans can interact as if it were the *agora* of ancient Athens is misguided. As Jaron Lanier points out, '[i]f you share a space with people who aren't looking at their smartphones, you are all in that space together' (Lanier 2019, 75). 'You have a common base of experience [and it] can be an amazing feeling, it's a big reason why people go to clubs, sports events, and houses of worship'. But, he says, 'when everyone is on their phone, you have less of a feeling for what's going on with them. Their experiences are curated by faraway algorithms. You and they can't build unmolested commonality unless the phones are put away' (75).

Shoshana Zuboff, in her magisterial *The Age of Surveillance Capitalism*, shows how the idea that networked form has some kind of indigenous moral content is an illusion, that 'being "connected" is somehow intrinsically pro-social, innately inclusive, or naturally tending toward the democratisation of knowledge'. She sees surveillance capitalism as 'parasitic and self-referential. It revives Karl Marx's old image of capitalism as a vampire that feeds on labour'. But instead of labour, it is feeding 'on every aspect of every human's experience' (Zuboff 2019, 9).

The origins of the digital turn

How did this situation come about? The internet developed mainly in the United States. According to Rikke Frank Jørgensen, it existed for decades within defence and academic circles, with the government providing resources for its development. There was no revenue model as such and, in fact, commercial activity was actually prohibited. Then came privatisation, which affected everything, 'from the physical backbones of the network to end users' activities' (Jørgensen 2019, 124). The United States, as Jørgensen ruefully points out, is 'a country with a weak culture of communication media as public service' (Jørgensen 2019, 125).

During the Cold War, the media were used differently by different political systems: Communist countries used them to educate their populations; they were a form of propaganda but also contained a lot of culture and entertainment (but no advertisements). The United States had a very different model: entertainment to make money (we will come presently to the regrettable effect this has had on public discourse). Revenue came from advertising. Often, television programmes were simply a sort of padding between the advertisements (literally known as 'commercial breaks'), which led to the birth of programmes like the soap opera: a popular form of entertainment featuring good-looking actors in often outlandish plots sponsored (initially) by soap companies, whence the name (see also Jørgensen 2019, 130–131). Western Europe sat somewhere between the two. The British Broadcasting Corporation (BBC), for example, saw itself as a public service. According to its royal charter, it acts in the public interest, serving its audiences through impartial, high-quality, and distinctive output and services that inform, educate, and entertain. To this day, the BBC has no commercial advertising.

When the internet was privatised, companies like Google and Facebook needed to find a way to make money; they could not make it simply by providing a service. They soon realised that all the information they were amassing from users' behaviour (which had been used to provide better service and was known initially as 'data exhaust') could be employed instead to target advertising more accurately by exploiting users' known preferences. In their desire to maximise profits, these companies realised they could make more money from advertisers by better targeting their advertising. This was the birth of data mining, where every action online (and off, thanks to GIS tracking on mobile phones, what Jørgensen calls 'a new axis for control' [129]) can be monitored to make the advertisements shown more likely to hit home.

This has led to a problem because, as Jørgensen says, social media companies want 'to keep users on the platform for as long as possible in order to increase advertising profits through monetizing data [...] and one way to do this is to display content that users agree with' (74). This content need not be true, but only consistent with users' known views. We saw earlier Cathy O'Neil's highlighting of algorithms' difficulty with concepts like beauty or justice; the problem is that they also cannot differentiate between truth and fiction. Mark Zuckerberg, CEO of Facebook (now Meta) said 'I just believe strongly that Facebook shouldn't be the arbiter of truth of everything that people say online' (*The Guardian* 2020): all that these companies seem to be doing is providing more and more of the same content, regardless of how false or dangerous it may be.

This is how people fall into what are known as 'rabbit holes'—an idea taken from Lewis Carroll's *Alice in Wonderland* (1865)—where they end up believing that the world is flat, or something equally false, despite concrete evidence to the contrary. They believe whatever is reinforced by what they see online. Falling into a rabbit hole (or being kept in one due to circumstances) is nothing new; in the fourth century BCE Zhuangzi said '[y]ou can't discuss the ocean with a well frog—he's limited by the space he lives in' (Zhuangzi 1996, 97). Whether in a well or a rabbit hole, the internet should be able to dispel ignorance. The internet provides access to the sum total of human knowledge; it also, unfortunately, provides a lot of content that is simply not true. People need the skill to differentiate fact from fiction. The internet, so wonderful at delivering access to knowledge is also, sadly, undermining that access by corralling users into filter bubbles, sometimes containing false information.

Television's influence on the development of social media

The difficulty of distinguishing fact from fiction is one issue. Another, and potentially even more dangerous issue for society, began when companies started showing different advertisements to different people—even when they were looking at the same content. As Jørgensen says, once individual users could be individually targeted the idea of the audience as a collective disappeared (Jørgensen 2019, 127). The 'online unbundling of content from audience introduces a sophistication, an individualization, and adaptability that calls into question the very idea of the public sphere' (131). As Jon Alexander and Ariane Conrad put it: 'We give our data away for free in return for treats [...] Meanwhile, nefarious actors use that data to shape our societies' (Alexander and Conrad 2022, 108).

The problem of distinguishing fact from fiction on the internet must be dealt with somehow in the twenty-first century if society is to have any hope of establishing and maintaining objective truths. Yet this difficulty goes back decades. Neil Postman already identified a dramatic and irreversible shift in the content and meaning of public discourse in the 1980s, an era he saw as 'the decline of the Age of Typography and the ascendancy of the Age of Television'. He noticed that the influence of print was waning and 'the content of politics, religion, education, and anything else that comprises public business must change and be recast in terms that are most suitable to television' (Postman 1987, 9). He showed how, 'under the governance of the printing press, discourse in America was different from what it is now [1987], generally coherent, serious and rational; and then how, under the governance of television, it has become shrivelled and absurd' (18). One of his most compelling points is that 'definitions of truth are derived, at least in part, from the character of the media of communication through which information is conveyed' (19) and that 'the concept of truth is intimately linked to the biases of forms of expression' (26). Basically, the premise of his visionary book is that 'the form in which ideas are expressed affects what those ideas will be' (36), with the result that the internet has delivered what could be termed a 'post-truth' world.

Postman gave the example of how the telegraph in the nineteenth century wrapped the 'continent in an information grid [and] created the possibility of a unified American discourse'. But in so doing, it 'destroyed the prevailing definition of information [and] gave a new meaning to public discourse' (75). Telegraphy gave 'legitimacy to the idea of context-free information; that is, to the idea that the value of information need not be tied to any function it might serve in social and political decision-making and action, but may attach merely to its novelty, interest, and curiosity'. In other words, the 'telegraph made information into a commodity, a "thing" that could be bought and sold irrespective of its uses or meaning' (76). It would seem, then, that the 'death of context' is nothing new.

Television in the twentieth century 'achieved the status of meta-medium—an instrument that directs not only our knowledge of the world, but our knowledge of *ways of knowing* as well' (91; italics in original). Postman's argument was that 'television's conversations promote incoherence and triviality; that the phrase "serious television" is a contradiction in terms; and that television speaks in only one persistent voice—the voice of entertainment' (92–93).

Postman also makes an interesting distinction between a technology and a medium by saying that 'a technology is to a medium as the brain is to the mind'. Technology is 'merely a machine [whereas a medium is] the social and intellectual environment a machine creates' (98). He warns that only those who 'know nothing of the history of technology believe that a technology is entirely neutral [because each] technology has an agenda of its own' (99).

What differentiates television from social media is that with television 'you never know who is watching, so it is best not to be wildly offensive'. Television 'is not congenial to messages of naked hate' because, as Postman points out, 'haters with reddened faces and demonic gestures merely look foolish' (134). Social media, on the other hand, seem to encourage hate, with anonymous trolls saying the most outrageous things to complete strangers; things they probably would not dream of saying in person or in a physical social context.

However, both television and social media agree that '[y]ou can get your share of the audience only by offering people something they want' (140).

Neil Postman regards the television age as a dystopia, not as in George Orwell's *1984*, where books are banned, but more like Aldous Huxley's *Brave New World*, where 'there would be no reason to ban a book, for there would be no one who wanted to read one'. 'Orwell feared those who would deprive us of information. Huxley feared those who would give us so much that we would be reduced to passivity and egoism' (1987, vii). As Huxley saw it, 'people will come to love their oppression, to adore the technologies that undo their capacities to think'. 'Orwell feared that the truth would be concealed from us. Huxley feared the truth would be drowned in a sea of irrelevance' (vii-viii). In *1984*, 'people are controlled by inflicting pain. In *Brave New World*, they are controlled by inflicting pleasure' (viii). One of Postman's most chilling points is that '[a]n Orwellian world is much easier to recognize, and to oppose, than a Huxleyan' (181). Yet, he does offer some hope because, as he points out, 'no medium is excessively dangerous if its users understand what its dangers are' (186).

Surveillance capitalism

Michel Foucault questioned the more 'humane' forms of punishment that came with the Enlightenment when prison sentences replaced torture and public execution. He asked whether these changes were the advance they seemed. This question has profound implications for the understanding of society. New disciplines of punishment and control took hold when there was no longer a need to make an example of criminals to keep the rest of the population in order, as had been the case in the Middle Ages. And with that change came new mechanisms of power that could recruit subjects more effectively than older ones, with their more overt displays of sovereign power. The Age of Enlightenment discovered the body as the object and target of power, and it used new disciplines to tame it: compulsory education, army conscription, as well as increased standardisation across professional disciplines like medicine and law.

The role that physical space can play in facilitating power relations and the ways in which humans interact with each other is neatly summed up in Foucault's famous phrase '[s]tones can make people docile and knowable' (Foucault 1995, 172). He gives a number of examples to show how space can influence human behaviour. The school is 'a machine for learning, in which each pupil, each level and each moment, if correctly combined, were permanently utilized in the general process of teaching' (165). Discipline, according to Foucault, produces a 'docile' body, making it easier to be subjected, used, transformed, and improved. Discipline increases a body's economic utility and diminishes its political agency (through obedience). Discipline is 'the specific technique of a power that regards individuals both as objects and as instruments of its exercise' (170). It does this through observation and surveillance. 'By means of surveillance, disciplinary power becomes an "integrated" system' (176). 'The power in the hierarchized surveillance of the disciplines is not possessed as a thing, or transferred as a property; it functions like a piece of machinery. And, although it is true that its pyramidal organization gives it a "head", it is the apparatus as a whole that produces "power" and distributes individuals in this permanent and continuous field' (177).

Once bodies are inserted into this apparatus they produce 'bio-power', which Foucault sees as being 'an indispensable element in the development of capitalism; the latter would not have been possible without the controlled insertion of bodies into the machinery of production and the adjustment of the phenomena of population to economic processes' (Foucault 1990, 140–141). 'But this was not all it required; it also needed the growth of both these factors, their reinforcement as well as their availability and docility;

it had to have methods of power capable of optimizing forces, aptitudes, and life in general without at the same time making them more difficult to govern' (141). In other words, adjusting populations to economic processes requires them to be docile.

This resonates with Shoshana Zuboff's comment about surveillance capitalism mentioned above, where she referenced Karl Marx's image of capitalism as a vampire feeding on labour, with 'labour' now being every aspect of the human experience. Internet users willingly insert themselves into this apparatus every time they go online and render up every aspect of their lives so that others can profit from them. Zuboff tells us that '[s]urveillance capitalism operates through unprecedented asymmetries in knowledge and the power that accrues to knowledge. Surveillance capitalists know everything *about us*, whereas their operations are designed to be unknowable *to us*. They accumulate vast domains of new knowledge *from us*, but not *for us*. They predict our futures for the sake of others' gain, not ours' (Zuboff 2019, 11; italics in original). She stresses that it is 'not an accident of overzealous technologists, but rather a rogue capitalism that learned to cunningly exploit its historical conditions to ensure and defend its success' (17). She points out (quoting Mark Weiser) that the 'most profound technologies are those that disappear, that weave themselves into the fabric of everyday life until they are indistinguishable from it' (200). By accepting 'the idea that technology must not be impeded if society is to prosper [...] we surrender to technological determinism' (225). 'Inevitabilism precludes choice or voluntary participation. It leaves no room for human agency' (226). According to Zuboff, 'industrial civilization flourished at the expense of nature and now threatens to cost us the Earth, an information civilization shaped by surveillance capitalism and its new instrumentarian power will thrive at the expense of human nature and will threaten to cost us our humanity' (11–12).

Society needs to rethink this model because, as Jaron Lanier (already quoted above) pointed out, '[i]f only we could just get rid of the deleterious business model, then the underlying technology might not be so bad' (Lanier 2019, 27).

Conclusion

Citizens' rights are under threat in an increasingly digitised world. This is because of an over-reliance on the algorithms that are driving surveillance capitalism, with the result that society is abdicating its responsibilities (and even its abilities) for decision-making. Social media companies should be made to change their business model. If that does not work, then people can simply turn them off (something that could not be done with the telescreens in *1984*). If that is too much to ask, then people could at least limit their use of social media—have fewer apps, turn off notifications from time to time, and have tech-free hours or days. Advertisements are unlikely to be missed and quality of life may increase.

Currently, there is a lack of robust regulatory oversight into how social media companies use data. Because these companies have one aim, profit, governments should do more to force them to change their business model. If surveillance capitalism is allowed to continue subsuming society to the lowest common denominator of market-driven profit-taking, it will not be good either for society or for the individuals who form it.

Social media could, perhaps, be likened to alcohol. A little is enjoyable, even good, but too much can lead to problems. Abuse and addiction can lead to serious problems. Social media, just like alcohol, can alter behaviour (i.e., keep people online more than is good for them; it can even turn some into trolls). By wise use of social media (and other digital developments like AI) lives can be enriched. The key is to see technological advances as tools, something to be used to improve life, not dominate it. People must be able to make intelligent use of these tools and not allow themselves to be used by them.

In the recent past, society has successfully adapted itself to digital tools like pocket calculators, personal computers, mobile phones, and even dating apps. Although all of these things have improved lives, people must still exercise human agency when using them. Otherwise, they may end up losing precious rights that previous generations have fought for.

Citizenship needs to be understood as *active* (as highlighted earlier). In order to think of it as active, Emmanuel Kant's plea to *Sapere aude!* can help. This quote (originally from Horace) can be translated as 'dare to know!'—although a better translation might be 'dare to think!' Humans will have agency only as long as they make use of it, and they need to ensure that they do so. Citizens must be *active* if they are to thrive in this Digital Age.

The chapters in this trilogy explore what it means to live in the built environment in Asia and the West. We can see how some ideas have come down to us through the ages only to reassert themselves in new, sometimes surprising, but still vital ways. All of the investigations across the three volumes help us to reflect on real-world issues, especially the challenges faced by both individuals and society as a whole. These studies also allow people to plan better for the future because they suggest new ways of dealing with these problems. We stress again that in order for individuals to be able to do this (at all, let alone properly) they need to be *engaged*. Citizens need to understand how to take care of themselves and, by so doing, be better able to care for those around them. Engagement is necessary for society to function. This takes us right back to Chapter One of Volume One, where we saw Cicero's fundamental tenets not to harm a fellow human being nor to profit at another's expense because both of these actions undermine the bonds that hold society together. Without a healthy society, people will not be able to lead fulfilled and flourishing lives. Without a healthy society, people will lose the very foundation on which their rights as individuals depend.

One final note: Aristotle said that for life to be worth living it *must* be for something that is an end in itself. He narrowed this down to three possibilities: pleasure, virtuous action, and wisdom. Everyone needs to see that their own happiness and the ability to flourish in life in order to *be* happy are linked to these three things. They provide not only the key to understanding Aristotle's philosophy, so carefully elucidated in the *Eudemian Ethics*, but are also simply good rules to live by. If people aim to live in a way that allows for, and actually provides, pleasure, virtue, *and* wisdom then they will be able to live their best possible lives and be good, caring citizens.

Bibliography

Alexander, Jon, and Ariane Conrad. 2022. *Citizens*. Kingston upon Thames: Canbury Press.

Aristotle. 2011. *The Eudemian Ethics* (trans. Anthony Kenny). Oxford: Oxford University Press.

Bracken, Gregory. 2019. 'Citizenship and the Good Life' in Gregory Bracken (ed.) *Ancient and Modern Practices of Citizenship in Asia and the West: Care of the Self Volume I* (21–46). Amsterdam: Amsterdam University Press.

Carroll, Lewis. 2003 [1865]. *Alice in Wonderland*. London: Penguin Classics.

Eggers, Dave. 2021. *The Every: Or At Last a Sense of Order, Or The Final Days of Free Will, Or Limitless Choice Is Killing the World*. New York: Vintage.

Foucault, Michel. 1990 [1976]. *The History of Sexuality Volume I: An Introduction* (trans. Robert Hurley). New York: Vintage.

Foucault, Michel. 1995 [1975]. *Discipline and Punish: The Birth of the Prison* (trans. Alan Sheridan). New York: Vintage.

Heaven, Will Douglas. 2023. 'Deep Learning Pioneer Geoffrey Hinton Has Quit Google', MIT Technology Review (1 May). https://www.technologyreview.com/2023/05/01/1072478/deep-learning-pioneer-geoffrey-hinton-quits-google/

Huxley, Aldous. 2004 [1932]. *Brave New World.* New York: Vintage.
Jørgensen, Rikke Frank (ed.). 2019. *Human Rights in the Age of Platforms.* Cambridge MA: MIT Press.
Lanier, Jaron. 2019. *Ten Arguments for Deleting Your Social Media Accounts Right Now.* New York: Vintage.
New York Times. 2023. '"The Godfather of A.I." Leaves Google and Warns of Danger Ahead' (1 May). https://www.nytimes.com/2023/05/01/technology/ai-google-chatbot-engineer-quits-hinton.html
O'Neil, Cathy. 2017. *Weapons of Math Destruction: How Big Data Increases Inequality and Threatens Democracy.* London: Penguin.
Orwell, George. 1984 [1949]. *1984.* London: Penguin.
Postman, Neil. 1987. *Amusing Ourselves to Death: Public Discourse in the Age of Show Business.* London: Methuen.
Weiser, Mark. 1991. 'The Computer for the 21st Century', *Scientific American* (special issue on Communications, Computers and Networks) (September).
Zhuangzi. 1996. *Chuang Tzu: Basic Writings* (trans. Burton Watson). New York: Columbia University Press.
Zuboff, Shoshana. 2019. *The Age of Surveillance Capitalism: The Fight for a Human Future at the New Frontier of Power.* London: Profile Books.
Zuckerberg, Mark. 2020. *The Guardian* (28 May). https://www.theguardian.com/technology/2020/may/28/zuckerberg-facebook-police-online-speech-trump

About the authors

Gregory Bracken is Assistant Professor of Spatial Planning and Strategy at TU Delft and one of the co-founders of *Footprint*, the journal dedicated to architecture theory. From 2009 to 2015 he was a Research Fellow at the International Institute for Asian Studies (IIAS) Leiden where he co-founded the Urban Knowledge Network Asia (UKNA). His publications include *The Shanghai Alleyway House: A Vanishing Urban Vernacular* (2013), *Asian Cities: Colonial to Global* (2015), *Contemporary Practices of Citizenship in Asia and the West* (2020), and *Ancient and Modern Practices of Citizenship in Asia and the West* (2019).
G.Bracken@tudelft.nl

Paul Rabé is Academic Coordinator of the Cities Cluster at the International Institute for Asian Studies (IIAS), Leiden, as well as overall coordinator of the Urban Knowledge Network Asia (UKNA) and the River Cities Network: Engaging with Waterways in the Anthropocene (RCN). Paul is also series

editor of Amsterdam University Press's Asian Cities Book Series and is Lead Specialist in Urban Land Governance at the Institute for Housing and Urban Development Studies (IHS), Erasmus University Rotterdam, where he is also joint coordinator of the Urban Environment, Sustainability, and Climate Change academic track. A political scientist by training, with a doctoral degree (2009) in policy, planning, and development from the University of Southern California's Sol Price School of Public Policy, Paul has over twenty-five years of experience in advisory work, capacity development, research, and teaching on urban policy topics, focused on urban land governance and the intersection of land (use) and the management of water and water bodies in urban and peri-urban areas.
p.e.rabe@iias.nl

Nurul Azreen Azlan is Lecturer in Architecture and Urbanism at Manchester School of Architecture (MSA). After graduating as a Part II architect from Universiti Teknologi Malaysia and spending some time in practice, she pursued a master's in urban design at the Bartlett, UCL. She completed her PhD at the TU Delft, where she wrote a dissertation on the spaces of protest in post-colonial Kuala Lumpur (2018). Post-PhD, she taught and researched architecture and urban design at Universiti Teknologi Malaysia (2018-2022). Prior to joining MSA, she was an NUS Fellow at the Asia Research Institute (ARI), National University of Singapore, under the NUS Southeast Asia Fellows Programme.
n.azlan@mmu.ac.uk

List of Figures and Tables

Index

For Product Safety Concerns and Information please contact our EU representative GPSR@taylorandfrancis.com Taylor & Francis Verlag GmbH, Kaufingerstraße 24, 80331 München, Germany

Printed and bound by CPI Group (UK) Ltd, Croydon, CR0 4YY
14/09/2026
02216260-0007